Theonomy

Theonomy

A Reformed Critique

William S. Barker & W. Robert Godfrey
Editors

Academie Books Grand Rapids, Michigan
Zondervan Publishing House

THEONOMY: A REFORMED CRITIQUE
Copyright © 1990 by William S. Barker and W. Robert Godfrey

ACADEMIE BOOKS is an imprint of Zondervan Publishing House,
1415 Lake Drive, S.E., Grand Rapids, Michigan 49506.

Library of Congress Cataloging in Publication Data

Theonomy : a Reformed critique / general editors, William S. Barker,
  W. Robert Godfrey.
     p.   cm.
    Includes bibliographical references.
    ISBN 0-310-52171-8
    1. Dominion theology–Controversial literature.   2. Reformed
Church–Doctrines.   3. Law (Theology)   I. Barker, William S.
II. Godfrey, W. Robert.
BT82.25.T44   1990
230'.046–dc20   90-34845
                                           CIP

Edited by Gerard Terpstra

Printed in the United States of America

90 91 92 93 94 95 96 / AF / 10 9 8 7 6 5 4 3 2 1

Contents

Preface

A school of thought bearing the label "Christian Reconstruction" and characteristically using the term *theonomy* (literally, the law of God) has been making an impact on American religious and political life in recent years. Since the publication of Rousas John Rushdoony's *Institutes of Biblical Law* (Nutley, N.J.: Craig, 1973, 890 pages) and of Greg L. Bahnsen's *Theonomy in Christian Ethics* (Nutley, N.J.: Craig, 1977, 619 pages) this school of thought has produced a vast amount of literature, influenced the Christian-school movement, affected many churches, and stimulated some previously quietistic evangelicals to political activity.

Having begun in Reformed or Calvinistic circles, theonomy has in the last decade proved attractive to a wider group of American evangelicals and fundamentalists, including some charismatics. At the same time several of the earlier spokesmen for theonomy have fallen out into different camps, with the result that it is difficult to describe theonomy or Christian reconstruction as a single movement. Although realignments and a general state of flux in what originally appeared to be a unified school of thought prevent it from being termed a movement, it is not so nebulous that certain leading characteristics cannot be identified. This is especially true in the writings of Rushdoony, Bahnsen, and, to a lesser extent for the purposes of this volume, Gary North, David Chilton, and Ray Sutton.

Chief among these leading characteristics are an emphasis on the Old Testament law; stress on the continued normativity not only of the moral law but also of the judicial law of Old Testament Israel, including its penal sanctions; and belief that the Old Testament judicial law applies not only to Israel, but also to Gentile nations, including modern

America, so that it is the duty of the civil government to enforce that law and execute its penalties. Christian reconstruction hence has the appeal of claiming to apply biblical principles to contemporary society in a way that will express the dominion of Christ. Usually, Christian reconstruction is characterized by a postmillennial eschatology.

Various efforts have been made in recent years to provide a response to theonomy or Christian reconstruction. Several of these have come from dispensational sources. The purpose of this volume is to offer a reply from within the Reformed camp, from which theonomy has sprung. As members of the faculties of Westminster Theological Seminary (Philadelphia) and Westminster Theological Seminary in California, the authors of this book share with theonomy many basic theological commitments, such as the full authority and inerrancy of the Scriptures as the written Word of God, a defense of the faith opposed to the autonomy of human reason, the sovereignty of God not only in salvation that is wholly by grace through faith in Jesus Christ but also in every sphere of life and thought, the kingship of our Lord Jesus Christ, and the ongoing authority of God's law. We agree also with theonomy's opposition to prevalent antinomianism. The point at issue, however, is one of fundamental hermeneutical perspective: How is the Israelite theocracy under the Mosaic law to be understood and its typological significance related to the proper role of the church and of the state today? The Westminster Confession of Faith states that to Israel, "as a body politic, He gave sundry judicial laws, which expired together with the State of that people; not obliging any other now, further than the general equity thereof may require" (XIX, 4). What is the force of that "expiration" and how are questions of "general equity" to be determined? Our concern is for the effect of theonomy on churches and Christian people. Some might consider it inevitable that teaching that stresses the authority of God's law and its application to contemporary society should be broadcast in dogmatic tones. In a culture lacking objective standards it is not surprising that disciples of theonomy or Christian reconstruction should be characterized by zeal. But as seminary teachers we have had former students, now pastors, come to us for guidance because of the disruption of their churches over a sincere layperson's zeal for theonomy as the one true understanding of the Scripture's teaching.

Our desire is to offer a constructive critique. We approach the subject from our Reformed and Presbyterian commitments to the Westminster Confessional Standards and our Calvinistic heritage as the soundest and most comprehensive understanding of biblical faith and practice. As we see it, theonomy in various ways represents a distorted view of that tradition. Particularly, we believe it overemphasizes the continuities and neglects many of the discontinuities between the Old Testament and our time.

Not every contributor to this volume necessarily agrees with every point made by the other contributors. In fact, the reader will discover differences on secondary points. The Westminster Seminary tradition is one of academic freedom within a framework of firm commitment to the authority of the Bible and to our doctrinal standards as a faithful expression of that truth. We hope that our reply to theonomy will stimulate dialogue and encourage us all to further understanding of God's Word.

The chapters in this volume can be read in any order. Each one is independent and can stand on its own as a critique of a certain aspect of theonomy. Yet there is a flow that can be appreciated by reading them in the order in which they appear.

Brief comments by the editors introduce each of five sections and a final conclusion. Part I seeks to provide basic orientations to the matter of application of biblical law. Part II contrasts theonomy with other systematic approaches to biblical theology. Part III deals with New Testament teaching concerning the nature of the continuity of Old Testament law. Part IV addresses what we perceive as triumphalist dangers in theonomy. Part V is concerned with the historical question of theonomy's relation to the heritage of John Calvin and the Puritans. The Conclusion seeks to end the volume with a constructive challenge to theonomy.

We trust that the reader will peruse these chapters with Bible open and ready at hand. We encourage you to be like the Bereans of Acts 17, who examined the Scriptures every day to see if what they had been taught was true. The main result of this book, we pray, will be rich Bible study, with the discovery of helpful principles of interpretation and stimulus to obedient application of God's revealed will.

William S. Barker
W. Robert Godfrey

PART ONE

THEONOMY AND BIBLICAL LAW: BASIC ORIENTATIONS

At the core of the Christian reconstruction movement is its emphasis on the continuing authority of the Old Testament law, including its penal sanctions. An age-old problem for the church and for Christian theology has been the relation of the law and the gospel. New Testament Christianity, because of the Judaic emphasis on the Mosaic Law, had to wrestle with this question. The Protestant Reformation again had to come to grips with the same question. In their proclamation of the gospel of grace, of justification by faith alone, neither the apostles nor the sixteenth-century Reformers eliminated the law. The Jewish ceremonies were fulfilled in the sacrifice of Christ, but the moral law continued to function as an expression of God's will and his holy character.

Robert Knudsen describes the New Testament fulfillment of the Old Testament law. The legal cast of the Old possessed within it the promise, but with the coming of Christ there is a shift. The age of the Spirit does not have a legal cast; the legal arrangements are no longer "up front." There is continuity in that the law still expresses the will of God, but the Old Testament is to be understood in terms of the New rather than vice versa.

Tremper Longman addresses the most controversial of the continuities that theonomy finds between Old Testament law and modern society, that of the Mosaic punishments. He points out the cultural differences between Israel and

America and also their different places in redemptive history. He also shows the subjectivity and flexibility inherent in the Old Testament itself with regard to penal sanctions of the law.

Chapter One

May We Use the Term Theonomy...?

Robert D. Knudsen

Robert D. Knudsen

Robert D. Knudsen (Ph.D., Free University of Amsterdam) is Professor of Apologetics at Westminster Theological Seminary (Philadelphia). With other degrees from the University of California (Berkeley), Westminster Theological Seminary, and Union Theological Seminary (New York), he has taught at Westminster since 1955. He is the author of *The Idea of Transcendence in the Philosophy of Carl Jaspers* and *The Encounter of Christianity with Secular Science: History; Psychology; Sociology.*

Chapter One

May We Use the Term Theonomy...?

"For the law was given through Moses; grace and truth came through Jesus Christ" (Jn 1:17). It was with this bold contrast that the writer of the fourth gospel announced the coming of the new age. The age introduced by the giving of the law at Sinai was coming to an end; a new age was at hand.

The life and message of John the Baptist also expressed this contrast. They reflected his own position in the history of redemption. Standing on the threshold of the new age, John looked back on what had gone before and anticipated what was to come. When he was asked who he was, he "confessed freely, 'I am not the Christ'" (Jn 1:20). He said, "Among you stands one you do not know. He is the one who comes after me, the thongs of whose sandals I am not worthy to untie" (vv. 26–27). John's message was couched in terms of this sharp contrast. He himself stood at the end of an age that was passing away; he announced an age that was coming. This new age began with the appearance of the Messiah, Jesus Christ. When John saw Jesus, he said, "Look, the Lamb of God, who takes away the sin of the world! This is the one I meant when I said, 'A man who comes after me has surpassed me because he was before me'" (vv. 29–30).

The New Testament clearly sets the new over against the old, and it presents the new as superior in every respect. If God spoke before through the prophets, "in these last days he has spoken to us by his Son" (Heb 1:2). The priesthood in the old order was temporal, but the priesthood of Christ is eternal. This is not a priesthood of mortal men; it is a priesthood founded "on the basis of the power of an indestructible life" (7:16). Perfection could not be attained through the Levitical priesthood, on the basis of which the law was given; it came through Christ, who is "a priest forever, in the order of Melchizedek" (v. 17). Christ is not a priest of the first covenant, with which there was something wrong (Heb 8:7), but of the new covenant, which is "founded on better promises" (v. 6). According to this New Testament teaching, the law was "imperfect," the gospel is "perfect"; the law was "shadow," the gospel is "reality"; the law was "old," the gospel is "new." "By calling this covenant 'new,' he has made the first one obsolete; and what is obsolete and aging will soon disappear" (v. 13).

Anyone who wants to be true to the biblical message of salvation must give full weight to this sharp distinction. It was in terms of this dichotomy that the apostle John characterized the difference between the old and the new dispensations. This theme recurs again and again in the New Testament. The law had to give way to the gospel.

It would be a great mistake, however, to interpret this distinction, important and even indispensable as it is, apart from its full context. It is indeed a recurrent theme in Scripture: there is a marked contrast between the law and the gospel. Nevertheless, the New Testament and the Old Testament are closely tied together. In relation to the new age the old is expectation. It is on the order of the chrysalis of a butterfly, which must be cast aside when the butterfly emerges; nevertheless, like a chrysalis, the old bears the new. It is also true that the new relates to the old. The New Testament message of salvation stands in unbreakable connection with what has gone before and is even founded on it.

In view of the teaching of the Scriptures themselves, it is clear that the contrast between the law and the gospel cannot be understood out of context. The Scriptures will not allow for the idea that the gospel appeared only after the law had been removed. There is a broad stream of gospel truth that courses through the entire Old Testament. Neither will the Scriptures allow for the idea that the entrance of the gospel meant the abolition of law in every respect. Christ said, "I tell you the truth, until heaven and earth disappear, not the smallest letter, not the least stroke of a pen, will by any means disappear from the Law until everything is accomplished" (Mt 5:18; cf. Lk 16:17). The Scriptures indeed teach that Christ is the "end" of the law, but this does not mean only the termination of the law; Christ is also the "end" of the law in the sense of being the completion, the fulfillment, of the law. He is not only *finis* but also *telos*. He said that he had not come to destroy the law or the prophets: "I have not come to abolish them but to fulfill them" (Mt 5:17). With the Advent an era, the dispensation of "the law," came to an end; but in Christ the law came to its fulfillment. "Christ is the end of the law so that there may be righteousness for everyone who believes" (Ro 10:4).

The relation of law and grace, of sin and salvation, is seen more clearly if we view it in the light of the teaching of the apostle Paul in his letter to the Galatians. There he writes that the promise of grace was given already to Abraham (Gal 3:8b). It was properly established by God himself (v. 17). The promise, Paul continues, antedated the law; therefore, the law did not and could not annul the promise, which was given through faith: "The law, introduced 430 years later, does not set aside the covenant previously established by God and thus do away with the promise" (v. 17). The promise continued on, anticipating the preaching in the New Testament of God's gracious salvation. It served as a foundation for this preaching and even for the dispensation of the law itself.

From this passage we learn that "the law," in the sense I have been speaking of it above, was superimposed on the line of promise. As it were, the law encapsulated the promise; but it by no means annulled it. In fact, it depended on it. It could not be understood apart from it.

If then "the law" stood in this relationship to the line of promise, which was finally the promise of the free grace that appeared in Christ Jesus, how can the New Testament so often speak of the law and the gospel antithetically? Does not Paul himself say that "the law" is not "opposed to the promises of God" (Gal 3:21)? We can answer this question if we arrive at a more precise understanding of what is meant here by "the law."

In the above passages, as well as many others in Scripture, "the law" refers to a particular arrangement or dispensation. It refers to the Mosaic economy, considered as a whole. God gave the law to Moses, to whom he spoke in the cloud and in the fire (Dt 5:22). Various observances and ceremonies were typical of this economy. The New Testament very often sets this old dispensation in sharp contrast to the new one, which appeared with the coming of Christ.

In view of Paul's teaching, we can understand that "the law" was a temporary arrangement of a unique kind. It was superimposed on the line of promise, in the interests of this promise itself, which was given to Abraham and fulfilled in Jesus Christ. Seen from the standpoint of the new covenant, this law was "shadow" in contrast to "reality"; but it also had a function. As Paul says, "The law was put in charge to lead us to Christ" (Gal 3:24). We might think of it as corralling people, so that they could be moved in the right direction. The law had the purpose of showing people their sin and of leading them to Christ (vv. 19, 23). The law also prefigured the salvation that was to come in Christ. Given through Moses, the law was a temporary arrangement; it had a divinely given purpose, but when this purpose had been accomplished, it was set aside. Again, as Paul says, "Now that faith has come, we are no longer under the supervision of the law" (v. 25).

To understand what was set aside when grace and truth came in Jesus Christ, one must see how the dispensation of the law was characterized. What was unique about it?

Taken as a whole, the old covenant, "the law," had a legal cachet. This covenant was entered through circumcision, the cutting off of the foreskin of the Israelite males, an act by which the people of God were sanctified, i.e., set apart to God (Ge 17:10–13; Dt 10:15–16). The meaning of circumcision ran deeper than this physical cutting; but it was clear legally that any male who was to belong to the covenant community had to be circumcised and that any male who was not circumcised could not, for this very reason, belong to this community (Ge 17:14; Ex 4:24–26). The law made it clear what was required of the people. Simply speaking, they were to obey Moses (Nu 12). They were to observe certain practices, and they were to avoid others. Some transgressions led directly to expulsion from the community of God's people. Others indeed were punished by death. One who despised Moses' law died (Heb 10:28). If one was delinquent in obeying the ordinances, he became ceremonially unclean.

He then had to become ceremonially clean if he was to remain among the covenant people. The people were required to bring their sacrifices to the priests at appointed times and according to strictly delineated rules. The Israelite belonged to the community of God's people, which was required to conform to the Mosaic ordinances. These were spelled out for him in great detail. Having complied with these commandments, one remained part of the covenant community. One remained within the camp.

That the old covenant, considered as a whole, had a legal cachet does not mean, however, that everything that was taken up in it was legally qualified. To see this, one need only look at the context within which it was given.

In the preamble to the law God announced himself as the one who had brought the children of Israel out of Egypt. He is the covenant God, who has been faithful to his promises. He has called forth his people from the house of bondage. His covenant promises are not expressed in legal terms; it is only the outworking of God's covenant purpose that is expressed in this way. Further, on the heels of God's statement of his covenant faithfulness there is the proclamation of the "first and great commandment," the commandment of love: "Hear, O Israel: The Lord our God, the Lord is one. Love the Lord your God with all your heart and with all your soul and with all your strength" (Dt 6:4–5). This great commandment flows directly from God's declaration of his oneness and his covenant faithfulness. It is not couched in legal terms. One may also refer to the Ten Commandments. These are indeed commandments, but they are not formulated in legal terms. It is not stipulated exactly what would constitute keeping them or transgressing them, or exactly what the rewards and punishments might be.

In the very giving of the law to the people there was a witness to the limitations of its legal form. It is clear that the meaning of the covenant was that God would be a God to them and that they would be his people. Further, it was always possible to conform to the legal expression of the law and yet not answer to its deeper meaning.

The restrictedness of the legal form of the old covenant is observed in the sacrificial system itself. After God gave the Ten Commandments and certain specific laws, he instructed Israel how he had provided for the atonement of their sins.

He presented an entire sacrificial system. This was indeed set forth in detail and legal form—one knew exactly what he was to bring to the priest in order to atone for his sins and exactly what the consequences would be of any failure to obey—but this sacrificial system revealed in its very form the limitations of keeping the law. No matter how punctual one was in observing the commandments, the fact that he had to bring his sacrifices instructed him that his obedience was imperfect. His sins had to be atoned for. The limitations are very clear as one looks at the provision for taking the sins of the people and placing them outside the camp. At an appointed time the hands of the priest were laid on the head of a goat, symbolically transferring to it the sin and the guilt of the people. Then the goat was banished. It was driven into the wilderness (Lev 16:20–22). This act signified that the sins of the people had no place within the camp. They had to be removed if the people were to enjoy the presence of God, which had been promised to them through Abraham. Their sins were thereby also removed from before the Lord, who would not tolerate them in his presence. This provision of sacrifices showed that the obedience to the law that was required if the people were to remain within the camp fell short. The deeper reason that the people could remain inside was not that they themselves had fulfilled the law but that their sins had been removed vicariously and placed outside.

The New Testament tells us clearly that the old covenant, "the law," was imperfect. I have said that this imperfection did not arise simply from the fact that in the old covenant the law had received a legal expression; nevertheless, the fact that it as a whole had a legal tone made it possible for one to keep its provisions in a manner characteristic of it and yet offend its deeper meaning. One could observe merely the "letter" of the law, failing to express its "spirit," and yet remain within the covenant community. The old covenant indeed foreshadowed the new, but it fell short of the new. It was shadow, in contrast to the reality that was to come.

Thus "the law," which was legally qualified and which encapsulated everything within its legal chrysalis, always witnessed to its own inadequacy. It was superimposed on the line of promise, but it never abolished it; it gave the commandments a particular form, but it could never exhaust their deeper meaning; loving God meant observing the legally qualified prescriptions that he himself had established, but these were nothing apart from the love that was the proper response to the one God who has revealed himself in his covenant faithfulness.

In view of the above characterization of "the law," we can understand that it could not be conceived properly as resting in itself. Even though it had a legal quality, the law constantly acted so as to break through its own constraints. Within the old dispensation there were strands that were not legally qualified, and these acted so as to break through the legal form. Throughout, the old covenant offered glimpses of what lay beyond it and on what it depended.

I have implied that "the law" was a legal expression of law in a deeper sense. To be sure, there is a difference between law and any legal expression of law. It must be said here that there is a difference between God's law and any legal expression of it such as that which characterized the old dispensation. The latter depended on the former: "the law" depended on the commandments, which, in turn, depended on the great commandment.

The people of Israel should have discerned what lay beyond the legal form of the law. They should have seen that satisfying the conditions for remaining among the covenant people did not itself mean that they were responding properly to the covenant God. They should have been able to look past the legal form of the law, but in this they often failed. Many times they "obeyed" but not from the heart. As the law was misunderstood in this way, it was externalized. This externalization did not arise, however, simply because the law had been given a legal cast. It arose because of an ignoring of the deeper meaning of the law and a misunderstanding of its intent.

Thus the prophets had to call Israel again and again to "true obedience." As Samuel said to Saul as he was returning from the conquest of the kings: "Does the Lord delight in burnt offerings and sacrifices as much as in obeying the voice of the Lord? To obey is better than sacrifice, and to heed is better than the fat of rams" (1Sa 15:22). Christ condemned the teachers of the law and the Pharisees for their external obedience to the law: "You give a tenth of your spices—mint, dill and cummin. But you have neglected the more important matters of the law" (Mt 23:23). Christ also spoke of the "inner meaning" of the law: "You have heard that it was said, 'Do not commit adultery.' But I tell you that anyone who looks at a woman lustfully has already committed adultery with her in his heart" (Mt 5:27–28). The ministry of John the Baptist began with a call to repentance: "The ax is already at the root of the trees, and every tree that does not produce good fruit will be cut down and thrown into the fire" (Mt 3:10; cf. Lk 3:9). John proclaimed a new age. The people had to understand that what was needed in their lives was not surface change, but a new life. Pushed to the extreme, the prophetic utterances could draw a sharp line between the legal provisions of the law and the matters of the heart: " 'The multitude of your sacrifices—what are they to me?' says the LORD. I have more than enough of burnt offerings, of rams and the fat of fattened animals. I have no pleasure in the blood of bulls and lambs and goats" (Isa. 1:11).

Such hypocrisy, of course, was not limited to ancient Israel. It is often present in the New Testament period as well. But external obedience was more typical of the Old Testament. Formal obedience was all that was necessary to remain within the camp.

If one "did the works of the law" in this external sense, then, was he truly doing the works of the law? The answer must be no. The answer is clear from the prophetic rejection of such external obedience. Christ objected strenuously to the practices of the Pharisees, who fulfilled all the demands of "the law" outwardly but inwardly were like foul-smelling tombs. External obedience to "the law" was no true obedience at all. "The law" was an expression of something deeper, apart from which it could not be understood.

This depth is seen in Christ's interpretation, his "spiritual" interpretation, of the commandments. Now, was this spiritual interpretation rigorous? Did he take the commandments and, as it were, stretch them out to their limit? If so, many would ask whether this was warranted. Should not one content himself with a normal, a moderate, interpretation of the law? If it was interpreted in such a rigorous fashion, how could anyone keep it? When Jesus told the young man who said that he had kept the commandments that he must sell all his possessions and give to the poor, even the disciples were astonished and asked, "Who then can be saved?" (Mt 19:25).

Christ did not overextend the meaning of the commandments when he gave them their spiritual interpretation. He was simply expressing their inner, that is, their true meaning. This meaning should have been clear to the Israelites in view of their own history.

That they understood the law as a system through which to attain righteousness meant that they had misunderstood it. They transformed this arrangement, which God himself had established for a special purpose, into something God had not intended at all, a system of works-righteousness. This was, on the one hand, to overestimate the place of the law. They could do this only because they had wrenched the law out of context. It was, on the other hand, to overestimate what they themselves could accomplish. They thought that by keeping the "letter" [KJV] of the law, the "written code" [NIV], they could satisfy the righteous demands of God, whereas, in fact, they could not even obey the written code fully. Scripture tells us clearly that this distortion issues from the "fleshly mind" [KJV], "the sinful nature" [NIV], which attempts to establish its own righteousness instead of accepting the righteousness offered by God himself (Ro 10:3; 1Co 2:14).

That people understood the law to be a way of attaining righteousness before God means, I repeat, that they had misunderstood it. Indeed, God had intended the law, as the expression of his will, to be a way of life (Ro 7:10), and insofar as people obey God's will they are blessed (Ps 119; Jas 1:25); but because of sin the law became an instrument of death (Ro 7:10, 11, 13). Therefore, the apostle Paul could write, "If a law had been given that could impart life, then righteousness would certainly have come by the law" (Gal 3:21). But, given the presence of sin, there was no such law! The dispensation of the law, then, was given for a specific purpose. It was not opposed to the promise, Paul said, because it was intended to corral people and lead them to Christ, in whom the promise is fulfilled; however, having been misunderstood and having been taken as a system of works-righteousness, the law stood diametrically opposed to the gospel of free grace in Christ Jesus.

At this point we can appreciate the full force of the

statement of the apostle John that the law was given through Moses but grace and truth came through Jesus Christ. We see "the law" as a legally qualified system that had been externalized and that furthermore had become a system of works-righteousness. This is what had come to stand diametrically opposed to the promise. When the apostle Paul contrasted the free grace that is in Christ with the law, he was setting grace up in antithesis to a monolith, an entire, externalized system by which it was thought that one could attain righteousness before God. This accounts for the sharpness of the contrast.

When, therefore, the Scriptures contrast law and grace, as Paul does consistently in Galatians, this goes deeper than simply relating one dispensation, considered as a divine arrangement, to another. Dispensations are related thus, e.g., when the dispensation of the law is regarded as a possible way of salvation (by way of obedience to the law) in contrast to salvation by grace. Some classical dispensationalists spoke as if the "dispensation of the law" was established to test whether Israel could attain righteousness by satisfying the demands of the law. But such a possibility had already been cut off because of sin. Thus, the relation must be viewed otherwise. The old dispensation indeed had a specific purpose, but not to ascertain whether one could attain salvation by his works. It was intended to hold us prisonere, "locked up" until the coming of Christ, and to presage that coming (Gal. 3:22–25). It was the fleshly mind that transformed this arrangement into a system of works righteousness. It was this system that stood diametrically opposed to the promise. The law had to give way to the gospel!

One can see that throughout Israel's history the Old Testament dispensation, which was imperfect, was indeed like a chrysalis that was showing signs of bursting and of disclosing the new, which it contained in itself. Provision was made in the old covenant for the people through the daily sacrifices. But all this was consummated in the great Passover, the commemoration of the Exodus, when the people had been covered by the blood sprinkled on the lintels and doorposts of their houses and had thus been protected against the visitation of the angel of death, who took all of the firstborn sons of Egypt. This salvation was much more than a legal satisfaction for the individual sins of the people; it was the great redemption, the paradigm of the final redemption that was to be realized in Jesus Christ. As the people were leaving Egypt, they were baptized into Moses in the cloud and in the sea (1Co 10:2). This baptism spoke of a death and a resurrection, of a total commitment. It foreshadowed the New Testament believer's dying and rising with Christ. Within the old covenant itself there was ample testimony to the fact that what is required by God is not external obedience, a formal, legalistic observance of the law, but a heart commitment, a commitment of the entire person to the covenant God, who is faithful to his promise. That the old dispensation was "shadow" made one look forward to the reality of salvation in Christ.

Now, what changes took place when the new arrived, when "the law" gave way to "grace and truth" in Jesus Christ? Against the above background, the picture can be brought into focus. The chrysalis, the expression of the law in legal form that characterized the dispensation of the law, fell away, allowing what was inside to come to free expression.

If the old age, taken as a whole, was the age of the law, the new age is the age of the Spirit. Now the line of promise, which was present before but was encapsulated in the dispensation of the law, has been set free. Abraham had been promised a seed; his descendants would be more than one could number. The Scriptures tell us that this "seed" was Christ . Further, the words of God that are called the Ten Commandments were also set free. Now their "deeper" meaning, i.e., their true meaning, stands at the forefront. Further still, the shadows have given way to reality. The ancient sacrificial system has been dismantled. Now Christ has been offered once and for all for the sins of his people. He himself bore our sins on the cross, himself having been set outside the city gate (Heb 13:12).

The new age, the age of the Spirit, is set sharply over against the dispensation of the law. The apostle Paul writes, ". . . circumcision is circumcision of the heart, by the Spirit, not by the written code" (Ro 2:29). Again, Paul writes, "We have been released from the law so that we serve in the new way of the Spirit, and not in the old way of the written code"

(Ro 7:6). Another reference is especially telling: "He has made us competent as ministers of a new covenant—not of the letter but of the Spirit; for the letter kills, but the Spirit gives life" (2Co 3:6). In this dichotomy, the "letter" is identified with the old covenant, the "Spirit" with the new. The old is bondage; the new is freedom in Christ.

This dichotomy runs through the teaching of the New Testament. Paul likens the old dispensation to Hagar, who was the bondwoman, and the New Testament dispensation to Sarah, who was the freewoman (Gal 4:22–23). In this allegory, the apostle Paul expresses the difference between the two covenants. The one is a covenant of bondage, the other is a covenant of freedom. When the apostles and elders were faced with the question whether believers had to be circumcised and obey the law of Moses in order to be saved, Peter said, "Why do you try to test God by putting on the necks of the disciples a yoke that neither we nor our fathers have been able to bear?" (Ac 15:10). After Paul explained the allegory of Hagar and Sarah, he wrote, "It is for freedom that Christ has set us free. Stand firm, then, and do not let yourselves be burdened again by a yoke of slavery" (Gal 5:1).

But if the age of the law encapsulated things that did not have a legal cachet, the age of the Spirit is not opposed to law in any and every sense. The Old Testament prophets do not characterize the age of the Spirit as one of lawlessness. Some, like the so-called "enthusiasts," have misunderstood at this point and have fallen into antinomianism. To the contrary, the prophets characterize the age of the Spirit as a time when the law of God will be written on people's hearts, when the true meaning of the law and of obedience to the law will come to expression.

In this regard, the teaching of the Scriptures differs sharply from that of modern humanism. According to the latter, law has its source, its ultimate origin, in autonomous human personality. According to the Bible, on the contrary, the human personality is subject to God's will, which is expressed in his law. The issue, then, is whether the law has been "internalized," in the sense that obedience to it is a matter of the heart and its inclinations. If the law is fully "internalized," obedience to it is as natural as breathing the air. Here the law is not "external," in the sense of impinging from outside on the "thoughts and intents of the heart"; it

comes spontaneously to expression, because the "thoughts
and intents of the heart" are in harmony with it.

If one speaks of internalization here, however, he must
take care. The prevailing view is that law is per se external,
or even foreign, to human life and that it must be "internalized" if it is to square with autonomous human personality.
According to the Scriptures, God's law as such is not
external. In its original intent, it is not foreign to man and to
his life. The Scriptures teach that love, as the service of God
with one's whole heart, is what characterized man in his
original, sinless estate. It was internal; it was man's natural
attitude.

Looking ahead, as they were faced with the outright
sinfulness or external obedience of the people, the prophets
discerned a time when the people of God would no longer be
disobedient and when their obedience would be more than
outward conformity to the requirements of the law. As
Jeremiah writes, "No longer will a man teach his neighbor,
or a man his brother, saying, 'Know the Lord,' because they
will all know me, from the least of them to the greatest" (Jer
31:34). This passage is reflected in the Book of Hebrews,
where the writer says that God declared that he would
establish a new covenant with the house of Israel: "I will put
my laws in their minds and write them on their hearts. I will
be their God, and they will be my people" (Heb 8:10). This is
the way in which freedom is understood in the new
covenant. In the new covenant arrangement, it is characteristic that obedience comes from the heart. Obedience is of the
Spirit, and not of "the written code."

The biblical idea of freedom is clearly expressed in the
illustration of the servant and the son (Gal 4:1–7). The
servant or slave stood at the periphery of the family. He was
dependent for his actions on what others said. He took
orders as to what he was supposed to do and not to do. In
contrast, the son stood at the center of the family. He had
free access to its affairs; he stood in a relation of intimacy to
its head, the father. Significantly, he did not take orders from
someone else; he himself was the guide of his own actions.
In this sense, he was autonomous. But this illustration
cannot be used to support a humanistic view of freedom, as
if the human spirit were the source, the origin, of law. It can
only mean that one who is a son guides his own life,

according to the law, which is not external but is written on his heart.

The New Testament teaches that Christian believers are sons and not servants (Gal 4:6–7; cf. Heb 3:5–6). They have the law written on their hearts, not just on tables of stone. They do of themselves, of their own inclination, what is required by the law. And the love of the heart is not contrary to law. Christ himself said, "If you love me, you will obey what I command" (Jn 14:15).

To obtain a further appreciation of this biblical teaching, let us again look at the meaning of the law. In the discussion, I have used the term in various ways, according to the teaching of Scripture. I have spoken of the dispensation of "the law," which was a special arrangement introduced by God with a pedagogical purpose. I have also spoken of the Ten Commandments, of which I have said that they themselves are not expressed in legal terms; they were encapsulated in the dispensation of the law, which was not entirely legal but which had a legal cast. Finally, I have spoken of "the first and great commandment," the commandment of love, which followed upon God's announcing himself as the one God, the faithful covenant God, who had brought the children of Israel out of Egypt. He said through Moses, his servant: "Hear, O Israel: The LORD our God, the LORD is one. Love the LORD your God with all your heart and with all your soul and with all your strength" (Dt 6:4–5). This "summary" of the commandments, which is better thought of as their heart and soul, was reiterated by Jesus Christ, who called it "the first and greatest commandment" (Mt 22:38). One may also use the term to refer to the order that God has placed in the cosmos, through which he speaks in his general revelation. It is through this general revelation that we can understand that there is a distinction between the law and the legal.

We often speak of the "law of love" as the "summary" of the Ten Commandments. This is acceptable. This commandment, as we find it in Deuteronomy and as it was quoted by Jesus Christ, indeed summarizes what is contained in these commandments. We might interpret the word *summary* in such a way, however, as to obscure the relationship that the "law of love" has to the Ten Commandments. The latter should not be thought of as a set of individual statements or rules, each standing by itself, which were then given general expression in the law of love (a typical nominalist error); instead, one should think of the law of love as the heart and soul of the commandments. If one truly loves, in the biblical meaning of the word *love*, he has kept all the commandments. If, on the contrary, he has "kept" all the commandments without love, he has kept them only externally. In a sense, as we have seen, he has not kept them at all. The commandments are of a piece. They hang together. In fact, in their deeper meaning, they are one. They are all expressions of love for God and for one's neighbor. Looking at them from another direction, we see that they come to a focus in this love and do not have their meaning apart from it. Thus the apostle Paul could show the Corinthian Christians "the most excellent way": "And now these three remain: faith, hope and love. But the greatest of these is love" (1Co 13:13).

In the light of what has been said above, one can understand the oft-criticized statement of the church father Augustine, "Love God and do what you will." Many people object to this statement. The Ten Commandments, they argue, are the content of the law of love; therefore, how can one know what love is apart from the commandments? To say "Love God and do what you will" is inadequate. There is some truth to this criticism. In our age, as in many others, the word *love* has been so emptied of its meaning that it is difficult to understand what is intended by a statement such as that of Augustine.

If one understands love in its full scriptural connotation, however, one can make much more sense of the Augustinian saying. In this light, love must be understood in terms of the total response of the whole person to God, as he has been revealed in Christ. This is the God who brought his people Israel, body and soul, out of Egypt. Were not the people of God baptized into Moses by their passage through the Red Sea (1Co 10:2)? Are not all believers baptized into Christ, dying with him and being raised with him into a new life? We are to love God in Christ wholly. As the Scriptures say, "We were. . .buried with him through baptism into death in order that, just as Christ was raised from the dead through the glory of the Father, we too may live a new life" (Ro 6:4). If we look at the catalog of virtues that spring from love (1Co

13:4–7), we can understand more fully how one can say, "Love God and do what you will."

It is easy to show that love for God and for one's neighbor issues in the commandments. No one who loves God will want to serve any other god. No one who loves God will set anything within the creation in his place. No one who loves God will desire to empty his name of meaning by using it carelessly or inappropriately. No one who loves God will deprive him of the worship that is rightly his. Furthermore, no one who loves God will despise his fellow man, taking his life unlawfully from him, or desiring to take his possessions. He will not lose himself in a misplaced desire, a jealousy, for what his neighbor possesses. As the apostle Paul says, "He who loves his fellow man has fulfilled the law" (Ro 13:8; cf. Gal 5:14). The commandments flow from love in its full scriptural sense, and they depend on it.

In the age of the Spirit, the commandments are still in force. In fact, it is commanded that one love God and his neighbor. A true love will not ignore these commandments. Further, in the age of the Spirit, there are legal arrangements. But the focus has shifted. The age of the Spirit does not have a legal cast; the legal arrangements are no longer "up front." Instead, the New Testament believer, as a son or daughter and not a servant, will serve God in Christ as one who has died and is risen with Christ, so that he or she may live a new life. In the age of the Spirit, the focus is on serving God freely, from the heart.

In various connections, we observe how we are to serve God—in obedience to his will as expressed in his law but not in a way that is legally qualified. I will refer here to the family, to marriage, and to the church.

The well-regulated family will establish firm rules, some of them with a legal cast. Children need such rules. Rules provide a structure within which children can grow. In the loving environment of the home, on a simple scale, the child must know exactly what is required of him and what the consequences will be if he breaks the rules. As a child matures, however, he will need fewer and fewer rules of a legal kind. Maturity will not bring with it an abandonment of the principles that make a good home; but, as the child matures, he will follow them by reason of personal understanding and conviction. Thus there is an analogy also within the modern family to the passage from the Old Testament to the New Testament economy. The Old Testament believer was like a child, who needed to be under the guidance of tutors and governors; but when children are older, they should have the maturity and understanding to do what is right of their own volition. In the grown family, there is indeed some place for legally qualified rules; but these will have a place only because they are useful: when they are no longer useful, they will be put aside.

A marriage relationship should be nurtured according to sound biblical principles. These will not have a legal cast, however. Of course, there is always a legal side to the relationship of husband and wife—think, for example, of the legal consequences of their marriage vows—but in a healthy marriage relationship the legal will not be "up front." Any marriage in which the legal is "up front" is already in serious trouble.

In the church, the elders must give careful attention to what makes the church the church: the sound preaching of the Word, the proper administration of the sacraments, and the faithful exercise of discipline. But none of these is legally qualified, not even church discipline. Discipline in the church is, first of all, a matter of applying sound biblical principles. Good discipline manifests itself in how well the commands of Christ are presented and followed, in the power of the Holy Spirit. At times, e.g., when there is controversy or when discipline cases cannot be resolved by simple admonition, the legal is very much in evidence; but such times are difficult for the church, no matter how necessary it is to go through them, and it is good when they are left behind and the church can return to its normal life.

In the New Testament age the legal is still present. As some have argued, there is a legal side to all human relationships. There is a legal side to the family, to marriage, and to the church. But in the New Testament period the legal is not "up front"; rather, it comes to the fore only when that is needful.

It is interesting that the exemplary case of discipline in the New Testament, the judging and punishing of Ananias and Sapphira, did not take place within a legally qualified situation, such as we find in the Old Testament dispensation. When the disciples brought their possessions to the common treasury, there was no stipulation as to how much they should bring. Ananias and Sapphira were judged, not because they did not bring a set amount, but because they purposefully misrepresented what they had done. They were judged for hypocrisy. Having sold their land, they were completely free to decide how large a gift they would bring; but they agreed between themselves that they would pretend that their sacrifice was greater than it actually was. Faced with this dissimulation, Peter said, "Ananias, how is it that Satan has so filled your heart that you have lied to the Holy Spirit and have kept for yourself some of the money you received for the land? Didn't it belong to you before it was sold? And after it was sold, wasn't the money at your disposal? What made you think of doing such a thing? You have not lied to men but to God" (Ac 5:3–4). It is also interesting that the punishment of Ananias and Sapphira, though a just retribution, was not part of a legally established scheme. This judgment was intended to serve as a warning to the church, not to set a pattern for church discipline.

In all their relationships New Testament believers do not have less responsibility than their Old Testament counterparts for obeying God's will as expressed in his law; in fact, they have greater personal responsibility, because it is not legally stipulated exactly what they should and should not do. The New Testament constantly assumes that believers are not servants but sons and daughters, with both the privileges and the responsibilities of those who are children in a loving household.

Now I must pose the main question of this chapter: "May we use the term *theonomy*?" In view of the above, the answer must be yes. The word theonomy is simply a combination of the Greek words for God and law, *theos* and *nomos*. It refers, in the context of this book, to the rule of God through his law. As we have seen, the Scriptures teach that Christians are to obey the will of God and that this will is expressed in his law. Christ himself joined love for himself with keeping his commands. This is important to remember as we observe modern theologians refusing to say that love can be commanded or insisting that there is at best a tensionful, dialectical relationship between love and law. The life of man as a whole is subject to an order, a lawful order, which holds for him and for his relationships. If this is true, then the use of the term *theonomy*, or a synonym for it, is not only allowed but is necessary.

If one uses the term *theonomy*, however, he should be clear as to what he means, more particularly, what he means by God's law. We have seen that law, as understood in the Scriptures, has several levels: (1) the central commandment of love toward God and one's neighbor; (2) the explication of what this love means, as we find this in the Ten Commandments; and (3) the legally qualified prescriptions, which were elaborated in order to regulate the life of the people and to lead them to Christ. As we have seen, we may also speak of God's law in the sense of (4) the order that God has placed in the cosmos. If one uses the term theonomy to refer to the rule of God through his law, he must indicate what kind of law he has in mind, so that he can make it clear what he means by the rule of God in any particular context.

It is only when we have distinguished the various meanings of "law" and understood how law functions in various ways in God's dealings with people that we can answer the question as to what laws apply in the church today. If we do not do this, we are likely to repeat errors of the past, falling, e.g., into antinomianism or legalism.

As we have distinguished various kinds of law, we have observed that there is continuity as well as discontinuity between the old and new dispensations. We cannot discover an adequate criterion, however, if we think only in terms of continuity and discontinuity. We cannot, for instance, anchor continuity in the nature of God, saying that God's law is an expression of his will and is unchanging, just as God is unchanging. This statement is true, taken by itself; but it is true of God's law only in its central meaning. In view of the teachings of the Bible, it is inconceivable that the commandment of love will ever be abrogated. It is also inconceivable that there will be any changes in the meaning of God's law as expressed in the Ten Commandments. But this does not at all apply to the manner in which these commandments have been worked out (some would say "positivized") in the various arrangements that God himself has established. As we have seen, the legally qualified form that the law took in the old dispensation was not at all unchanging; it had a purpose, and when that purpose was fulfilled, it was set aside. In seeking an answer to the question as to what laws are valid today, we should avoid what, for this purpose, are abstract criteria. We can understand the continuity and discontinuity between the two ages only as we have distinguished the various meanings of law and have understood how law has various functions in God's dealings with human beings.

Thus, we may not assume that every law in the Old Testament age without exception continues to apply until it has been revoked. The sharp disjunction between the old and the new ages will not allow us to assume this. The legally qualified provisions we find in the old dispensation cannot be dealt with on the above basis. The dispensation of the law, which I have likened to a chrysalis, has been set aside; the new age has come. Any specific, legally qualified provision of the Old Testament may be applied in this new age only if it fits. The criterion for its usefulness will be a New Testament one.

In answering the question as to what laws apply today, one must take into full consideration the teaching of the Scriptures themselves as to the nature of law and its relation to the Old Testament and New Testament economies. Remember in this regard that New Testament believers are sons and daughters, not servants, and the church should be zealous to preserve the freedom that its members have in Christ. Attention must be focused on instilling in them a deep love for the One who loved them and gave himself for them and a consuming desire to serve him according to what he has commanded. And, as he said, his commandments are not burdensome.

The authority of Christ is preeminent in the church; it is unlimited. But the church itself, as an institution, has limited authority, even over the lives of those who are its communicant members. It may not seek to have authority over the life of the Christian in every respect. It should not overregulate. It should faithfully perform the task that Christ has given to it. Within its sphere, it has the glorious opportunity of exercising spiritual persuasion, seeking to bring men and women to a knowledge of Christ and to the service of Christ with their entire selves. In doing this, the church will call men and women to obey Christ's commands. But if the church falls into legalism, it will constrict rather than expand the lives of its members in their service of Christ. It should seek to inculcate a deep respect for law in the various forms it has taken in redemptive history; but in guiding its members it should have a firm grasp of what it means that the law was given through Moses, but that grace and truth came through Jesus Christ.

Chapter Two

God's Law and Mosaic Punishments Today

Tremper Longman III

Tremper Longman III

Tremper Longman III (Ph.D., Yale University) is Associate Professor of Old Testament at Westminster Theological Seminary (Philadelphia). With other degrees from Ohio Wesleyan University and Westminster Theological Seminary, he has taught at Westminster since 1980. He is the author of *Literary Approaches to Biblical Interpretation* (Foundations of Contemporary Interpretation Series) and *How the Read the Psalms*.

Chapter Two

God's Law and Mosaic Punishments Today

God's law (theonomy) or man's law (autonomy)? This is the choice that the classic texts of theonomy[1] place before the Christian public. Divine revelation or human subjectivity? Which do Christians want to guide them in their civic life? With the question put in these terms, Christians do not hesitate to give an answer. Of course, we want God's law and divine revelation to direct us in all aspects of our lives.

The extensive literature of theonomy, however, proclaims that God's law for society is the Mosaic law in its entirety (except in those rare instances where the New Testament explicitly discontinues its observance).[2] Most disturbing to those who are introduced to theonomy for the first time, it seems, is its advocacy, not only of the Mosaic case law, but also of its system of punishments. The death penalty for murder is one thing to the contemporary Christian; death for homosexuality, intercourse with one's wife during her period, adultery, and blasphemy is another.

Theonomists, however, challenge Christians to recon-

---

[1]Theonomists have produced tens of thousands of pages of written material in the past two decades. The best-known and most frequently cited texts are R. J. Rushdoony, *The Institutes of Biblical Law* (Nutley, N.J.: Craig, 1973); idem, *Law and Society* (Vallecito, Calif.: Ross House, 1982); G. L. Bahnsen, *Theonomy in Christian Ethics* (Nutley, N.J.: Craig, 1977); idem, *By This Standard: The Authority of God's Law Today* (Tyler, Tex.: Institute for Christian Economics, 1985).

[2]Bahnsen would include what is traditionally called the ceremonial law among the laws no longer observed in the New Testament period; cf. Bahnsen, *Theonomy*, 207–16. Rushdoony disagrees with Bahnsen on this point.

sider their reaction. "Remember," they say, "these are God's laws and God's punishments. Don't let your 'Christian' feelings let you get soft in the heart. God commanded them; therefore they are just."

However, before giving in to the logic of this argument we need to take a close look both at theonomy's position on penology as well as the teaching of Scripture. Perhaps there is something to the typical Christian "gut reaction" to theonomy. Although often not thought through, Christians' ideas are shaped by principles that may at least in part be defensible, since they are gained through study of the Bible. But first, what is a theonomic penology?

THEONOMIC PENOLOGY

As is pointed out in this book, theonomy is no longer a monolithic movement. There are many points of disagreement among people who use the term to describe their position. This chapter analyzes the views found in the seminal works of Greg Bahnsen and Rousas Rushdoony. Even these men do not always agree in detail, and their own views have progressed since they completed these works. However, their books are the most systematic expositions of a theonomic position in general and on penology in particular and are arguably the best known and most widely used books written from a theonomic perspective.

On the surface, a theonomic penology is quite clear-cut: We must return to a Mosaic system of punishments, and the Old Testament gives us the just penalty for all punishable offenses. To depart from God's law on this point is to introduce human, sinful subjectivity into the process. This will result in either a lenient penal code that will produce a rampant criminal society or a rigid penal code and its attendant tyranny.

What would the penology advocated by theonomy look like?

Restitution

In today's society, it is often the case that crime does pay and the victim suffers the penalty. In the Bible the principle of restitution counteracts both of these evils. For instance, a thief must restore to the victim what he stole and pay a penalty (Ex 22:1, 4). In this way, the criminal does not profit (provided he is caught), and the victim is compensated for his loss. In contemporary society, the criminal may pay a fine (in addition to a jail term), but that money is paid to the state. Victims must have recourse to the costly civil court system if they are to recover their losses. A further evil of contemporary practice is the large insurance premiums we pay to protect ourselves against theft.[3] This protection, according to Bahnsen and Rushdoony, should come from the principle of restitution.

What happens if the criminal can't make restitution? The Bible again provides the answer: "A thief must certainly make restitution, but if he has nothing, he must be sold to pay for his theft" (Ex 22:3). Rushdoony comments, "This means today some kind of custody whereby the full income of the convicted thief is so ordered that full restitution is provided for."[4] Elsewhere he doesn't mince words: "A man who abuses his freedom to steal can be sold into slavery in order to work out his restitution; if he cannot use his freedom for its true purpose, godly dominion, reconstruction, and restoration, he must then work towards restitution in his bondage."[5]

In the modern setting, one might wonder how cooperative a teenager who has been stealing to support his crack habit might be with such a program. Once again the answer of theonomy is simple: habitual criminals, particularly those who rebel against the restitution principle, must be put to death. Quoting Deuteronomy 21:18–21, Rushdoony asserts, "A criminal community cannot be allowed to exist. In terms of Biblical law, the habitual criminal must be executed, as well as the incorrigible delinquent. The community of the atonement cannot tolerate habitual criminals."[6]

The Prison System

Rushdoony finds no place for a prison system in a biblically based penology. After all, prison terms are never

---

[3]Rushdoony, *Institutes*, 277.
[4]Ibid., 460.
[5]Ibid., 485.
[6]Rushdoony, *Law and Society*, 86; cf. 240.

sanctioned by biblical law. According to Rushdoony, prisons support criminals and hurt honest taxpayers.[7] Our prisons are overcrowded with men and women who should be executed for their crimes, working to pay off their victims,[8] or physically punished.[9]

Death Penalty

Certainly the most controversial aspect of a theonomic penology is its advocacy of the death penalty for a variety of crimes. Most Christians agree that the death penalty is still in effect for murder, but Bahnsen and Rushdoony extend the list of capital offenses in line with the Mosaic law.

Bahnsen lists the following crimes as worthy of the death penalty: "murder, adultery and unchastity, sodomy and bestiality, homosexuality, rape, incest, incorrigibility in children, sabbath breaking, kidnapping, apostasy, witchcraft, sorcery, and false pretension to prophecy, and blasphemy."[10] Rushdoony adds offering human sacrifice, propagating false doctrines, sacrificing to false gods, rejecting a decision of the court, and failing to restore bail.[11] He believes that the death penalty for sabbath breaking is no longer in effect.[12]

Rushdoony argues that a consistent use of the death penalty will radically reduce crime by eliminating the criminal element from our society and also by providing a deterrent. In order to heighten the deterrent value of capital punishment, he would like to have public executions.[13] In addition, minors, the insane, and the mentally deficient all are treated like anyone else in the courtroom and are eligible for the death penalty if convicted of a capital crime.[14]

---

[7]Rushdoony, *Institutes*, 276.

[8]Bahnsen, *Theonomy*, 439.

[9]Rushdoony, *Institutes*, 228, 515.

[10]Bahnsen, *Theonomy*, 445. I have excluded the scriptural references that Bahnsen provides, since I don't dispute them.

[11]Rushdoony, *Institutes*, 235.

[12]Ibid., 28–58.

[13]Rushdoony, *Law and Society*, 699–700.

[14]Rushdoony, *Institutes*, 231.

Motivation for Penology

Modern liberals often speak of rehabilitation as a primary motivation for penology. In the past twenty years many have been disillusioned by the poor results achieved by such "enlightened attitudes." Rehabilitation doesn't work. Rushdoony and Bahnsen argue that rehabilitation never motivates biblical penology. The guiding principles are "retribution, restitution and compensation,"[15] not rehabilitation.

ASSESSMENT

There simply isn't space to treat the following points fully. My object in this section is to demonstrate the problems of a theonomic penology. The approach sounds clear and simple enough—just apply the laws and penalties of the Old Testament—but in practice such a procedure is very difficult. Even though Bahnsen and Rushdoony oversimplify the biblical data, we can observe the difficulty even in their own writings.

Fundamental Tension

My first point has to do with the approach of adherents of theonomy to law in general. Of course, their approach to the law is integrally connected with their approach to penology. Many of the chapters in this volume critique theonomy's application of the Mosaic law to today's society. These arguments are also telling against its application of Old Testament penalties as well. In this context, however, I wish to point out what I believe is a fundamental tension in the writings of Bahnsen and Rushdoony. At many points they make it clear that they believe that our modern civil law should simply be the Mosaic code in its entirety. At times they remind their readers that they do not mean only the Ten Commandments, but the Old Testament law in its entirety. For instance, Bahnsen inveighs against those "who balk before the *extent* of God's law and decide to recognize only the decalogue as applicable" (emphasis his).[16]

---

[15]Bahnsen, *Theonomy*, 438.
[16]Ibid., 313.

However, what is the Mosaic case law but the application of the Ten Commandments to the nation of Israel? None of the civil or moral laws is independent of the Ten Commandments; they are all summarized in them. The case laws are specifications of the general principles of the Ten Commandments.

As we then seek to apply the Old Testament case laws and penalties to our own situation, we need to ask, In what ways are we like Israel and in what ways are we different? How does this affect our application of the law and its penalties?

Bahnsen understands this occasionally, and the result is the tension to which I refer. For example, in his discussion of Deuteronomy 22:8 (concerning the law to build a parapet around the roof of a house), Bahnsen correctly identifies a cultural gap between ancient Israel and modern America. The Israelite law was an extension of the principle of the sixth commandment. Since the roof of a house was used as living space in ancient Israel, the law was given in order to protect life. Most houses in America don't utilize the roof as a living area. Bahnsen correctly applies the principle of the law by saying that it mandates fences around swimming pools.[17] By making this move, however, he is doing precisely what he appears to forbid others to do. He has really applied the sixth commandment to contemporary society, using the contextualization of that commandment in Deuteronomy 22 as a guide, and no more.

But a further step must be taken: we must recognize that there is more than a cultural difference between Israel and America; there is also a difference in their respective places in redemptive history.

Israel: God's Chosen Nation

There is apparently little problem with the fact of cultural differences. In applying the law and penalties of the Old Testament to modern societies, Bahnsen and Rushdoony recognize the need to bridge the cultural distance between Israel and modern times. Deuteronomy 22:8 does not require modern home-builders to construct a parapet around their

---

[17]Ibid., 445, 540.

roofs, but it does mean that a swimming pool must be bordered by a fence. In the area of penology, I don't think that either of the two theonomists would object to replacing stoning with the electric chair, a firing squad, or some modern equivalent in order to carry out an execution.[18] It's the principle that counts, and these principles are summarized in the Ten Commandments. As we apply the law and the penalties to contemporary society we must first inquire into the cultural differences between ancient Israel and modern America.

However, once we accept this point (and Bahnsen and Rushdoony write as if they do), we must ask why we shouldn't take into account an even more fundamental difference between Israel and any modern nation. Israel *as a nation* was chosen by God "out of all the peoples on the face of the earth to be his people, his treasured possession" (Dt 7:6). No other nation of the ancient or modern world is like Israel in its place in redemptive history.[19] Even if a majority of American citizens were sincere Christians—or even if everyone were—America would not be like Israel in terms of God's redemptive history.

It would seem to follow that there is at least the possibility that Israel's civil law might undergo some adaptation as it is applied to contemporary society. Rushdoony recognizes this fact in connection with the death penalty for Sabbath breaking (a view not shared with Bahnsen) when he writes:

> Does this mean that, in the modern world, Sabbath-breaking is punishable by death, or should be? The answer is, very clearly and emphatically *no*. The modern state is not in covenant with God but is an enemy of God. Sabbath-breaking has no specific penalty of death, just as there is no death penalty for adultery (Hos. 4:14), because the nations are not in covenant with God and are

---

[18]Although apparently Gary North wants to retain stoning as the proper mode of execution in modern society as well; see Gary North, *The Sinai Strategy: Economics and the Ten Commandments* (Tyler, Tex.: Institute for Christian Economics, 1986), quoted in T. Ice and H. W. House, *Dominion Theology: Blessing or Curse?* (Portland, Ore.: Multnomah, 1988) 73–74.

[19]In this connection, it is significant to note that in the holiness law of the Book of Leviticus God presses obedience upon Israel because of their special redemptive status. Note Leviticus 11:45 as an example.

therefore under sentence of death. Because of this general
and central indictment, the lesser offenses have no place.
Covenant offenses are one thing, enemy offense another.[20]

In another place Rushdoony gives a more theoretical expression to this idea when he says, "The covenant people are
doubly God's property: *first*, by virtue of His creation, and,
second, by virtue of His redemption. For this reason, sin is
more personal and more than man-centered. It is a theological offense" (emphasis his).[21]

Before applying a case law from the Old Testament
today, therefore, we must consider not only cultural adaptations but also discontinuities that result because of the
difference in redemptive status between Israel and any
modern society. How, for instance, would the difference in
redemptive status between Israel and America change the
laws that concern the divine-human relationship? Since God
chose Israel as a nation to be his elect people, it was
intolerable that a blasphemer or idolater or witch could be
allowed to live. God caused his special presence to rest in the
midst of Israel; his holiness would not allow such blatant
rebellion to continue. However, God has not chosen America
as a nation. He does not dwell on the banks of the Potomac
as he did on Mount Zion. It seems strange to seek legislation
by which witches, idolaters, apostates, heretics, or blasphemers would be executed in the United States or even to
hope for a time when such legislation would be enacted.[22]

As has been traditionally recognized, the proper ana-
logue to the nation of Israel is the Christian church. God
chooses to make his special presence known in the assembly
of the saints. He will tolerate no blasphemy, heresy, or
idolatry in the midst of his priestly people. God has given
spiritual weapons to his spiritual people to fight a spiritual
enemy. The church does not seek the death of blasphemers
who are in the church but their excommunication.

It is not a simple thing to apply the Old Testament law
and its penalties to the New Testament period. We must take

---

[20]Rushdoony, *Law and Society*, 685.
[21]Ibid., 28.
[22]Bahnsen, *Theonomy*, 445, 540; idem, *By This Standard*, 152; Rushdoony, *Institutes*, 38.

into account not only cultural differences, but also redemptive-historical differences. The latter will have a definite
impact on how Old Testament civil laws, which have to do
with the relationship between God and Israel, will be
brought over into modern society. Each law and each penalty
needs to be studied in the light of the changes between Israel
and America, the old covenant and the new covenant.
Theonomy tends to grossly overemphasize continuity to the
point of being virtually blind to discontinuity.[23]

SUBJECTIVITY IN PENOLOGY

Theonomy fears subjectivity in lawmaking and in the
administration of penalties.[24] Human autonomy is something
to be feared because of man's sinfulness, and in the area of
law it can be downright dangerous. The results of human
autonomy are either leniency and a criminal society or
tyranny and a criminal state. According to Bahnsen and
Rushdoony, the only way to avoid autonomy and achieve
theonomy is to simply apply the entire Old Testament law
and its penalties to modern society. If there is no penalty in
the Bible for a given act, then modern societies have no right
to impose one. Such an act may be sinful, but it is not
criminal. Further, human governments may not lessen or
increase a biblical penalty.

While I too fear human autonomy and subjectivity and
while I recognize that lawmaking has produced chaotic and
tyrannical societies throughout history and today, the claim
that theonomy would alleviate this problem is simply
misleading. What is especially frightening about such an
attitude is that the subjectivity of the theonomic interpreter is
pressed upon us as the Word of God. Rushdoony in
particular seems unaware of the enormity of the subjective
side of theonomic interpretation and quite often presents his
exegetical results as if they are without doubt the Word of
God for today. Perhaps this in part explains the rather

---

[23]For a good, clear statement of the continuity and discontinuity between
the covenants, refer to O. Palmer Robertson, *The Christ of the Covenants*
(Grand Rapids: Baker, 1980).

[24]Rushdoony, *Law and Society*, 668.

dogmatic and condescending style that characterizes his writing.

It has been correctly observed that the application of the Old Testament law to contemporary society would necessitate a new scribal caste that would produce a new Mishnah. Why is this the case?

In the first place, Old Testament law does not always provide a set penalty, but requires the human judges to decide the severity of the punishment. An instance of this is found in Deuteronomy 25:1–3:

> When men have a dispute, they are to take it to court and the judges will decide the case, acquitting the innocent and condemning the guilty. If the guilty man deserves to be beaten, the judge shall make him lie down and have him flogged in his presence with the number of lashes his crime deserves, but he must not give him more than forty lashes. If he is flogged more than that, your brother will be degraded in your eyes.

This passage illustrates the complexity and difficulty involved in applying Old Testament penology to the present situation. In the first place, we are left in the dark concerning the type of dispute under consideration here. It would have been clear to the original audience of this legal code, but it is not clear to us. This type of interpretive ambiguity is not infrequent and renders the theonomic application more difficult than either Bahnsen or Rushdoony is willing to admit. But the main reason I have cited this passage is to illustrate the responsibility placed on the human judge to determine the extent of the punishment. There is a significant difference between receiving two and receiving forty lashes with a rod,[25] and the decision was the responsibility of the *human* judge with all the subjectivity that would involve. Surely, according to the biblical ideal (as opposed to historical reality), the judges of Israel would be men who showed themselves blessed by godly wisdom, but this fact does not entail infallibility. In any case, Bahnsen and Rushdoony make it clear that they fear permitting anyone, Christian or not, to make such a decision.

---

[25]That is, if it is a rod that is meant. This would be another interpretive ambiguity as this Old Testament punishment is brought over into the New Testament period.

However, even when there is a clear Old Testament penalty for a crime, the subjectivity of the human interpreter comes into play. A prime example of this is Sabbath breaking. Bahnsen believes the death penalty still holds; Rushdoony believes there is clear biblical evidence against such a view.[26]

A further illustration comes from the law of restitution in case of a theft. I, for one, agree that restitution is a basic biblical principle of justice. But theonomists are very careful to apply the details of the penalties in the modern period. Now, according to Exodus 22:1, a thief must restore four sheep for one he has stolen and disposed of but five oxen for an ox. Why the difference? The Bible never says. How do we apply this principle today? If a thief steals my car, do I get four cars in return, or five? Rushdoony provides a wonderful example of modern midrash to argue that the victim gets fewer sheep because they reproduce so fast[27] but how does this apply to my car? Going further, what if I don't want four or five cars, can I receive the cash equivalent? If so, who will determine the present value of the car?

I would not be surprised if Bahnsen and Rushdoony would agree that the human interpreter is heavily involved in these decisions. However, the impression they give in their writings is that it is possible to avoid human subjectivity (which they refer to with the emotive word *autonomy*) by simply applying the laws and penalties of the Old Testament to the New Testament period.

It is my opinion that Bahnsen, Rushdoony, and their followers are more frightened than they have a right to be about Christians making legal and moral judgments guided by the principles of Scripture rather than by the explicit statements of the Old Testament. There is no doubt that the judgments of the law of the Old Testament were perfectly just in their Old Testament context. But God has given Christians the spirit of wisdom, not to make infallible judgments, but responsible ones. Indeed, he requires Christians to make judgments of this sort:

---

[26]This is by inference from Bahnsen, *Theonomy*, 228, 445, and Rushdoony, *Law and Society*, 685.

[27]Rushdoony, *Institutes*, 459–60.

I tell you the truth, whatever you bind on earth will be bound in heaven, and whatever you loose on earth will be loosed in heaven (Mt 18:18). Do you not know that we will judge angels? How much more the things of this life! (1Co 6:3)

FLEXIBILITY IN OLD TESTAMENT LAW

In reading the standard works of theonomy, one can easily get the impression that Old Testament laws are simple and clear-cut. We have already seen evidence to dispute this, at least from the perspective of the modern interpreter. In the same vein, one also gets the impression that there is one and only one just penalty for a crime. A closer look at the Old Testament, however, exposes flexibility in the application of penalties.

A clear example of such flexibility is in the law of the goring ox (Ex 21:28–32). According to this law, if an ox gores and kills a second time after a warning, the owner is to be put to death. However, there is the possibility that he can pay a ransom if it is demanded of him. Thus this law at least is flexible. Two further points may be made from these verses. Once again, we witness the difficulty of interpretive ambiguity. Ransom is a possibility, it appears, if "payment is demanded of him" (v. 30). But demanded by whom? The judge? The victim's family? We don't know, and if we apply this law to the present day, who is going to make the decision? The second point to bring out is the difference in severity between the two alternatives. No matter how high the ransom is, I doubt that anyone ever turned it down in favor of the death penalty. Rushdoony, in particular, insists that a biblical penalty is always perfectly proportionate in severity to the crime. The principle is always, in his opinion, "an eye for an eye" (the *ius talionis*). However, here we have a law that envisions two possible penalties of vastly different levels of severity. The flexibility of this law plus an examination of other penalties in the Old Testament lead me to believe that the *ius talionis* (Ex 21:23–24) is setting a limit to the severity of the punishment allowed, not mandating in every case the maximum allowed.

This insight leads us to another interesting passage, one that was suggested to me by an article written by James

Jordan.[28] "Do not accept a ransom for the life of a murderer, who deserves to die. He must surely be put to death. Do not accept a ransom for anyone who has fled to a city of refuge and so allow him to go back and live on his own land before the death of the high priest" (Nu 35:31–32). It appears from these passages that ransoms were a possibility for many other crimes. Rushdoony, I believe, would argue that this law specifically appeals to the goring-ox law, which we have just studied and which explicitly provides the possibility of a ransom.[29] However, this approach seems very unlikely because the law in Numbers 35 implies that there are a number of exceptions. If the goring-ox law were the only exception, who would need Numbers 35:31–32 to clear up any possible misunderstanding?

CONCLUSION

Many other texts and examples could be cited to support the points I have made. Further, there are other arguments that could be brought forward to critique the form of penology advocated by Bahnsen and Rushdoony. For instance, we could demonstrate that they have not successfully countered John Murray's interpretation that the New Testament does not recognize the death penalty for adultery.[30] Jesus speaks of divorce rather than the death penalty in cases of adultery (Mt 5:31–32). Bahnsen is so blinded by his idiosyncratic translation and interpretation of Matthew 5:17 that he can't see that Jesus, as the Son of God, does indeed introduce adaptations of the Old Testament law for a new redemptive situation. In the same vein, James Jordan has also cited the fact that Joseph was going to quietly divorce Mary when he believed that she had committed fornication.[31] Significantly, while narrating Joseph's plan, Matthew calls him a righteous man (Mt 1:19).

But let's conclude on a positive note and an agenda for

---

[28]James Jordan, "The Death Penalty in the Mosaic Law: Five Exploratory Essays" (Biblical Horizons Occasional Paper No. 3, 1988), 10.

[29]Rushdoony, *Institutes*, 230.

[30]John Murray, *Principles of Conduct: Aspects of Biblical Ethics* (Grand Rapids: Eerdmans, 1957), 54; see Bahnsen, *Theonomy*, 458–62.

[31]Jordan, "The Death Penalty," 10.

the future. The above criticisms should not be taken as a complete rejection of theonomy's insight into the law and its penalties. The distortions produced by theonomy result from its advocates' strong concern about Christians who overemphasize the situational and personal aspects of biblical ethics and also the discontinuity of the covenants. However, they have swung the pendulum too far in the direction of the normative character of the law and the continuity of the covenants. Nonetheless, some very helpful and important themes are presented by Rushdoony and Bahnsen, if one can see through the bombast. For instance, the time *is* ripe for a reconsideration of the use of imprisonment as the primary punishment for crime. Further, restitution and the needs of victims must be taken into account in a just system of penalties.

Perhaps the most significant contribution of theonomists, however, is simply their pointing to the Bible as crucial to the whole issue of just punishments. Although it is not the clearcut blueprint that theonomic rhetoric makes it out to be, there is deep wisdom and necessary guidance to be found in the principles of law and punishment contained in the Old Testament. Old Testament laws must be studied individually and sensitively to see precisely how they should be applied to our modern societies. Such studies are presently underway,[32] but they are only a beginning to a much needed and long-neglected study of God's law. We can be grateful to theonomy for forcing the church to take these issues seriously.

---

[32]Two examples are Jordan, "The Death Penalty" and Vern S. Poythress, "Understanding the Law of Moses: The Revelation of the Messiah Through Moses and Its Benefits" (unpublished manuscript, 1990).

PART TWO

THEONOMY AND BIBLICAL THEOLOGIES: SYSTEMATIC APPROACHES

In assessing theonomy it is helpful to see it in contrast to other systems of biblical theology. In this section Bruce Waltke critically appraises the contrast of Reformed theology with dispensationalism on the one hand and theonomy on the other with regard to the moral law. Both John Frame and Vern Poythress compare the theonomic approach of Greg Bahnsen with the contrasting approach of Meredith G. Kline, offering some criticisms of both approaches. Frame expresses hope for reconciliation of theonomists (as represented by Bahnsen) and antitheonomists (as represented by Kline) by means of fresh exegesis of Scripture. Poythress develops an argument for employing three perspectives on Old Testament law: the normative (God's standards for conduct), the personal (an attitude motivated by love for God), and the situational (promoting the glory of God in our situation).

Chapter Three

Theonomy in Relation to Dispensational and Covenant Theologies

Bruce K. Waltke

Bruce K. Waltke

Bruce K. Waltke (Th.D., Dallas Theological Seminary; Ph.D., Harvard University) is Professor of Old Testament at Westminster Theological Seminary (Philadelphia). With other degrees from Houghton college and Dallas Theological Seminary, he as taught at Dallas Seminary and Regent College, and at Westminster since 1985. He is the author of *Creation and Chaos, Intermediate Hebrew Grammar, Micah* (Tyndale Commentary Series), and co-author of *Biblical Criticism : Historical, Literary and Textual* and *An Introduction to Biblical Hebrew Syntax.*

Chapter Three

Theonomy in Relation to Dispensational and Covenant Theologies

In 1749 Jonathan Edwards said, "There is perhaps no part of divinity attended with so much intricacy, and wherein orthodox divines do so much differ as stating the precise agreement and differences between the two dispensations of Moses and Christ."[1] About a century later dispensationalism resolved the tension between them by divorcing them, and more than two centuries later theonomy remarried them. Meredith Kline observed:

> This theory of theonomic politics stands at the opposite end of the spectrum of error from Dispensationalism. The latter represents an extreme failure to do justice to the continuity between the old and new covenants. Chalcedon's error, no less extreme or serious, is a failure to do justice to the discontinuity between the old and new covenants.[2]

In this chapter I aim to appraise critically the views of dispensationalism, Reformed theology, and theonomy with regard to the role of the law in social ethics, including its role to define the duty of government officials and to inform civil legislation. One cannot appraise these views without also

---

[1]Jonathan Edwards, "Inquiry Concerning Qualifications for Communion," in *The Works of President Edwards*, 4 vols., 8th ed. (New York: Leavitt & Allen, 1858), 1:160. Cited by Daniel P. Fuller, *Gospel & Law: Contrast or Continuum?* (Grand Rapids: Eerdmans, 1980), 5–6.

[2]Meredith G. Kline, "Comments on an Old-New Error," *Westminster Theological Journal* 41 (1978): 172–73.

taking into consideration their views of the church-state relationship and of eschatology. I will present the views of each theology, a brief presentation of some arguments supporting it, and finally an evaluation of some of its strengths and weaknesses.

DISPENSATIONALISM

Views

Dispensationalists believe that God is pursuing three distinct programs: one for the Jews, one for the church, and one for the nations. Paul, they argue, by distinguishing these three groups in 1 Corinthians 10:32, implies these separate economies: "Do not cause anyone to stumble, whether Jews, Greeks, or the church of God." The touchstone of dispensationalism is its conviction that God's dealings with Israel are totally separate from his dealings with the church. According to dispensationalists, God administered Israel by the law, and the church by grace. C. I. Scofield wrote:

> The most obvious and striking division of the word of truth is that between Law and Grace. Indeed, these contrasting principles *characterize* the two most important dispensations—Jewish and Christian. . . . Scripture never, in *any* dispensation, mingles these two principles (emphasis his).[3]

According to dispensationalists, the law of Moses is a unity and was meant for *the distinct people*, Israel, for *a distinct time*, from Sinai (Ex 19:1) until it was nailed to the cross and was canceled by the death of Christ (Col 2:14), and for *a distinct place*, "in the sworn-land" (Dt 6:1).

The grace-administered church, according to dispensationalists, began at Pentecost and will cease at its rapture prior to the millennial reign of Christ.

Opponents of dispensationalists often accuse them of being antinomian. The charge is largely both uncharitable

---

[3]C. I. Scofield, *Rightly Dividing the Word of Truth* (Findlay, Oh.: Fundamental Truth Publishers, 1940), 5.

and untrue.[4] Dispensationalists include the "higher teachings" of the New Testament for the church as part of the grace principle. R. Laird Harris rightly censures theonomist Greg Bahnsen on this point:

> It is hardly fair to charge dispensationalists with being antinomian . . . , for they speak of being "inlawed to Christ." Dispensationalists do emphasize the ethical teachings of the New Testament and the example as well as the commands of Christ. It is obvious also that dispensationalists, like other true Christians, lead lives of admirable probity and high moral standards. They are not against God's law in this age, but rather believe that God's law in Moses' age was a unified code which is transcended today.[5]

Dispensationalists normally do not discuss either the relationship of the church and the state or God's mode of administering the nations, a principle concern of theonomists and the focus of this chapter. Surprisingly, even in his essay "A Dispensational Response to Theonomy," Robert Lightner does not clearly set forth his own views on these matters.[6] It can be inferred, however, from their system of theology and from observation that dispensationalists separate church and state after the radical model of Roger Williams and regard states as being governed by the eternal moral law, which, in contrast to Reformed theologians, they do not equate with the Ten Commandments. In their view, though the nations are a part of God's universal kingdom, they belong to the "world," which stands in black-and-white opposition to the church and are under the rule of Satan (Lk 4:5–6). Using H. Richard Niebuhr's models of analyzing Christ and culture, many dispensationalists follow the model in 1 John and Tertullian, that of "Christ Against Culture."[7] Nevertheless, in this view, though the church and culture,

---

[4]R. J. Rushdoony uses even more inflammatory, divisive, and unchristian rhetoric when he falsely asserts: "Dispensationalism is . . . either evolutionary or polytheistic or both" in *The Institutes of Biblical Law* (Nutley, N.J.: Craig, 1973), 18.

[5]R. Laird Harris, "Theonomy in Christian Ethics: A Review of Greg L. Bahnsen's Book," *Presbyterion* 5 (1979): 4–5.

[6]Robert P. Lightner, "A Dispensational Response to Theonomy," *Bibliotheca Sacra* 143 (1986): 228–45.

[7]H. Richard Niebuhr, *Christ and Culture* (New York: Harper & Brothers, 1951), 45–82.

including the state, stand in opposition to one another, the state is part of God's universal kingdom, administering justice according to natural law (Ro 13). In summary, dispensationalists are concerned with saving the church out of the world before the Rapture rather than with transforming culture. When a ship is sinking, they popularly argue, one does not shine the brass but puts out the lifeboats.

Finally, with regard to eschatology, dispensationalists believe that after the church is raptured, God will once again restore Israel in the "sworn-land" for a thousand years. At this time the church will reign with Christ over the Jews, the subjects of the kingdom. This kingdom of God will be administered according to the provisions of the new covenant, which contains the substance of the unified Mosaic law, including its ceremonies, but differs from it in containing better promises and better provisions. In this millennial kingdom the nations will subject themselves to the rule of perfected Israel.

Argumentation

The dispensational system of theology is founded on the "plain, normal" sense of Scripture. Even the hermeneutical principle, the analogy of faith, cannot supplant this foundation. Charles Ryrie explains their rule: "This means interpretation which gives to every word the same meaning it would have in normal usage. . . ."[8] In Micah 4:1, for example, "the mountain of the Lord's temple" must refer to the mount dominated today by the Dome of the Rock and cannot refer to the heavenly Jerusalem. Likewise, "Israel" means Abraham's physical seed and not the church. With this hermeneutical tool dispensationalists discern God's distinct programs for Israel and the church. Ryrie says, "Normal interpretation leads to clear distinction between words, concepts, peoples, and economies."[9]

The distinction between Israel and the church now turns around to become itself the hermeneutical principle in rightly dividing the Word of truth. J. N. Darby wrote that the

---

[8]Charles Caldwell Ryrie, *Dispensationalism Today* (Chicago: Moody, 1965), 86.

[9]Ibid., 98.

distinction between Israel and the church is the "hinge upon which the subject and the understanding of Scripture turns."[10] The whole is greater than the sum of its parts, and so specific Scriptures are "pigeonholed" as belonging to either Israel or the church. The law, it is concluded, belongs to the Jew and not to the church. Lewis Sperry Chafer taught:

> The Bible student must recognize the difference between a primary and a secondary application of the Word of God. Only those portions of Scripture which are directly addressed to the child of God under grace are to be given a personal or primary application. . . . It does not follow that the Christian is appointed by God to conform to those governing principles which were the will of God for people of other dispensations.[11]

Strengths

One may commend dispensationalists for recognizing that laws are mutable according to the end for which they were designed. If the objectives and situations for which a law was originally designed cease or are changed, then the law either ceases or may be changed. The New Testament clearly teaches that Christ inaugurated a new age, an age in which God no longer deals primarily with the Jews in the sworn-land but with Gentiles in the world and that he no longer administers his elect by the law of Moses to the extent that it was written for Israel's existence in the land. The apostle Paul clearly teaches in a number of passages that God is not administering the church by the law and that the law has been done away with (Ro 6:14; 7:4–7; 2Co 3:6–13; Gal 3:17–25; 5:18). Moreover, our Lord implied the coming of the new situation when he set aside both divorce, which had been allowed by Moses (Mt 5:31–32; 19:1–12), and Israel's dietary laws (Mk 7:18–19). The Jerusalem council set aside circumcision and "the law of Moses" (Ac 15:5—probably a reference to Israel's judicial and ceremonial laws) except that

---

[10]J. N. Darby, "Reflections Upon the Prophetic Inquiry," *The Collected Writings of J. N. Darby, Prophetic, No. 1*, ed. William Kelly (London: CAPS, reprint 1962), 18.

[11]Lewis Sperry Chafer, *Major Bible Themes* (Philadelphia: Sunday School Times, 1926), 97–98.

the people were enjoined "to abstain from food polluted by idols, from sexual immorality [probably a reference to Israel's laws of consanguinity], from the meat of strangled animals and from blood" (15:20). Correlatively, dispensationalists are to be commended for carefully distinguishing the specific situations for which specific texts were written and for distinguishing carefully between their primary interpretation and their secondary application to other situations.

They are also to be applauded for not depreciating the role of natural law and conscience. Before the Law was given at Sinai, the *Torah* implies the operation of conscience. Cain was found guilty of murder and sentenced (Ge 4), while Enoch and Noah were found righteous and rewarded (5:24; 6:8–9). Centuries before the Law was given at Sinai, Abraham asked in connection with the righteous people living in Sodom and Gomorrah: "Will not the Judge of all the earth do right?" (Ge 18:25), and later in connection with the moral atmosphere of Abimelech's court, which he judged as subnormal, he said, "There is surely no fear of God in this place, and they will kill me because of my wife" (20:11). In the New Testament Paul explicates the implication of these texts:

> Indeed, when the Gentiles, who do not have the law, do by nature things required by the law, they are a law for themselves, even though they do not have the law, since they show that the requirements of the law are written on their hearts, their consciences also bearing witness, and their thoughts now accusing, now even defending them. (Ro 2:14–15)

Weaknesses

On the other hand, dispensationalists commit a fundamental hermeneutical blunder when they simplistically base their views on an ill-defined notion of "the normal, plain" meaning of Scripture and, even worse, against its own fundamental principle, disallow the analogy-of-faith principle that could correct their errors. Vern Poythress brilliantly perceives that they read the text not "plainly" but "flatly," failing to see adequately the symbolic import.[12] For example, the temple on Mount Zion always participated in the heavenly reality and cannot be distinguished from it (cf. Heb 12:22). Moreover, dispensationalists fail to appreciate fully the significance that the church has become fellow heirs of Israel's covenants through its union with Abraham's Seed, Jesus Christ (cf. Ro 4:16–17; 11:11–24; Gal 3:26–29; Eph 2:19). Paul's illustration of the one olive tree in Romans 11 suggests that the elect comprise one covenant community rooted in the Patriarchs, and not two, and that the covenant community is essentially not a national group, because the Gentiles, who are not treated as political states, are grafted into it.

With regard to their handling of the law, dispensationalists, while tacitly acknowledging such verses as Romans 3:21 and 7:12, in practice give inadequate attention to the truth that the law is "holy, righteous, and good." Furthermore, they tend to obscure the truth that today Christ is the mediator of the new covenant (Heb 8:6), a covenant that assumes the provisions of the law (cf. Jer 31:33–34) but is superior to it because, unlike the old covenant, which Moses wrote on stone depending on Israel's faithfulness, Christ with the Spirit of the living God writes on the fleshly tablets of the heart (2Co 3:3). The new covenant is also superior because it depends on God's faithfulness to fulfill the law for his elect saints (Heb 8:6). In this connection we should note that dispensationalists also slight the truth that the church, composed of both Jews and Gentiles, is baptized into our Lord Jesus Christ, who is Abraham's physical seed, and so, in a very real sense, both Jews and Gentiles are Abraham's seed (Gal 3:26–29). The Lord Jesus Christ is the true "Israel" and "Judah" (cf. Jn 15:1), and so his body, the church, is the "Israel" and "Judah" with whom the new covenant is made (Jer 31:31). Then, too, dispensationalists fail to note that "the law" itself distinguishes between the moral law, the judicial law, and the ceremonial law, as we shall see, and that only the last two types are conditioned in time and space. Finally, the New Testament strongly implies that the church is bound, albeit through the power of the Spirit, to fulfill the

---

[12]Vern Poythress, *Understanding Dispensationalists* (Grand Rapids: Zondervan, 1987).

moral law (cf. Ro 13:8–10; Eph 6:2) and the general equity of its other laws (cf. 1Co 9:8–10). The moral law condemns sinners—note Paul's application of the Ten Commandments to his sinful generation in 1 Timothy 1:8–10—and so drives them to Christ for his justification that saves them from its condemnation and for his sanctification that fulfills its righteousness.

Dispensationalism is also to be censured for its lack of concern about the lordship of Christ over all society. This indifference can be seen in its failure to address the questions of church-state relationships and of the ethical principles that ought to guide the state. Following the model of Roger Williams, they relegate religion to the chapel and neglect the transforming power of Scripture to guide society in education, music, art, science, and politics. They restrict Christ's lordship because they fail to grasp the changing circumstances of the church from an oppressed minority in New Testament times to a reigning majority in later church history.

With regard to eschatology, dispensationalists commit the fundamental error of leaving the Reformed principle that unclear texts must be interpreted in the light of clear ones, and, instead, they interpret the clear texts of the New Testament epistles in the light of the unclear symbols of apocalyptic works such as Daniel and Revelation. Not one clear text in the New Testament teaches either that Israel will be restored to the land, or that Israel will be restored as a nation, or that there will be a millennial reign of Christ after this age, which is called by the apostles "the last days" (i.e., the last stretch of historical time) (Ac 2:16–17; Heb 1:2). No word in Scripture depicts the consummate glory of Christ as an earthly King ruling over the restored nation of Israel. This silence, after the Lord had promised that the Spirit would guide the apostles into all truth and bring glory to Christ (Jn 14:26; 16:12–15), is deafening! The New Testament teaches that the new covenant is in effect now (Heb 8) and that the shadows of the Old Testament law have been done away with forever (Heb 9–10). The attempt to link the Golden Age anticipated by the prophets with the millennium envisioned in Revelation 20 is a desperate one. None of the characteristics of the apocalyptic millennium—resurrected martyrs judging, living, and reigning with Christ in heaven—link it with the Old Testament kingdom promises, a remarkable absence in the New Testament book that shows more links with the Old Testament than any other book.

REFORMED THEOLOGY

Views

Reformed theologians confess that the elect participate in a covenant of grace that transcends dispensations. In this covenant, according to the Westminster Confession of Faith, "God freely offered unto sinners life and salvation by Jesus Christ, requiring of them faith in him that they may be saved."[13]

Reformed theologians regard the nonelect as standing under condemnation for having failed to keep the covenant of works made with Adam, humankind's federal head. According to the Westminster Confession of Faith, "the first covenant made with man was a covenant of works, wherein life was promised to Adam, and in him to his posterity, upon the condition of perfect and personal obedience."[14] Humankind, however, fell in Adam and can find salvation only through the gift of faith whereby it accepts the covenant of grace.

In this system the law has a two-fold purpose. On the one hand, for the nonelect, much like the covenant of works, it reiterates God's demands. The law says: "Keep my decrees and laws, for the man who obeys them will live by them" (Lev 18:5). The Westminster Confession says,

> God gave Adam a law, as a covenant of works, by which he bound him and all his posterity to personal, entire, exact, and perpetual obedience; promised life upon the fulfilling, and threatened death upon the breach of it. . . . This law, after his fall, continued to be a perfect rule of righteousness; and as such was delivered by God upon

---

[13]"The Westminster Confession of Faith, A.D. 1647," *The Creeds of Christendom*, ed. Philip Schaff, 4th ed. (New York: Harper & Brothers, 1877), 3:617; 7:3. Hereafter WCF.

[14]WCF, 2:2.

Mount Sinai in ten commandments. . . . The moral law
doth forever bind all . . . to the obedience thereof.[15]

On the other hand, for the elect, whom the Spirit of
Christ subdues and who are enabled "to do that freely and
cheerfully which the will of God, revealed in the law,
requireth to be done,"[16] the law functions as an aspect of the
covenant of grace. The Confession puts it this way:

> Although true believers be not under the law as a
> covenant of works, to be thereby justified or condemned;
> yet is it of great use to them, as well as to others; in that,
> as a rule of life, informing them of the will of God and
> their duty, it directs and binds them to walk accordingly;
> discovering also the sinful pollutions of their nature,
> hearts, and lives; so as, examining themselves thereby,
> they may come to further conviction of, humiliation for,
> and hatred against sin; together with a clearer sight of the
> need they have of Christ, and the perfection of his
> obedience.[17]

In summary, according to covenant theology, the law,
on the one hand, cannot justify the ungodly on account of
their sinful nature, but instead, condemning them, drives
them to the covenant of grace; on the other hand, the law is
useful in the sanctification of the elect in whom God works
both to will and to do his good pleasure.

Moreover, Reformed theologians traditionally analyze
the law as consisting of three parts: moral, ceremonial, and
judicial. The moral law, summarized in the Ten Commandments, is eternal, but the ceremonial and judicial laws,
though of eternal value for their typology and of eternal force
to the extent that they express the moral law in relative
situations, are abrogated. The Westminster Confession says,

> Besides this law, commonly called moral, God was
> pleased to give to the people of Israel, as a church under
> age, ceremonial laws, containing several typical ordi-
> nances, partly of worship, prefiguring Christ, his graces,
> actions, sufferings, and benefits; and partly holding forth
> divers instructions of moral duties. All which ceremonial
> laws are now abrogated under the New Testament. To

---

[15]WCF, 19:1, 2, 5.
[16]WCF, 19:7.
[17]WCF, 19:6.

them also, as a body politick, he gave sundry judicial
laws, which expired together with the state of that people,
not obliging any other now, further than the general
equity thereof may require.[18]

Since the ceremonial and judicial laws comprise most of
the law, and Reformed theologians regard them as canceled,
and since dispensationalists note that the Ten Commandments, with the exception of keeping the Sabbath, are
repeated in the New Testament, it may seem as though the
difference between Reformed theologians and dispensationalists comes down to the fine point of whether or not to keep
the Sabbath. In fact, however, this is not so; the two
theologies fundamentally differ in their attitudes toward the
law. Dispensationalists, concentrating on its spiritually debi-
litating effects through man's sinfulness, negate it; Reformed
theologians, moving beyond its weakness to its spiritual
value in conjunction with the Spirit, validate it. Dispensationalists pit law against Spirit; Reformed theologians combine them.

With regard to the relationship of the church and the
state, Reformed theologians are not agreed. Keith Pavlischek
traces Reformed theology's development of thought regarding the relationship of church and state and the toleration of
confessional pluralism into a "conquest-compromise-with-
drawal" paradigm. The radical Presbyterians, who prevailed
in the early seventeenth century, without reservation advocated a purely Calvinistic established church. The Independ-
ents and moderate Presbyterians, who had to contend with
civil war and growing sectarianism in the middle of that
century, compromised on the issue, making the issue of
"toleration" dependent on their historical situation. The
Baptists, represented by Roger Williams as the foremost
Baptist theorist, rejected the notion of a National Establishment and advocated instead a withdrawal from the pollu-
tions and corruptions of the political world.[19] Pavlischek
himself advocates toleration along the lines laid out by the
Reformed theologians Abraham Kuyper and Herman Dooy-

---

[18]WCF, 19:3–4.

[19]Keith Pavlischek, "In Critique of Theonomy: A Reformational Case for
Pluralism" (Th.M. thesis, Westminster Theological Seminary, Philadelphia,
1986), 97.

eweerd in their theory of sphere sovereignty. Nevertheless, although not agreed about church-state relationships, Calvinists are agreed that Christ is not to be pitted against culture but in Niebuhr's terms is "Christ the transformer of culture."[20]

Reformed theologians are also not agreed with regard to eschatology. Amillennialists identify the church as the fulfillment of the Old Testament promises after Christ's advent into the world, first in the flesh at Bethlehem and then in the Spirit at Pentecost. Historic premillennialists see the kingdom promises of the Old Testament as being fulfilled in the church after the first advent of Christ and consummated in restored national Israel after the second advent of Christ. Postmillennialists believe the second coming of Christ will be after the millennium, which is to come as the result of the Christianization of the world without miraculous intervention. Nevertheless, all Reformed theologians agree that the law is binding today in the sense that it is a means used by the Spirit to sanctify the elect.

Argumentation and Strengths

Scripture consistently asserts that the moral law of God, which is embodied in the Ten Commandments, is eternal. "Long ago," says the psalmist, "I learned from your statutes that you established them to last forever" (Ps 119:152). The positive Reformed attitude conforms to that of both Testaments. Psalm 119, the "golden ABC" (Luther), speaks of the law as righteous (v. 7, passim) and true (v. 142) along with many other spiritual virtues. The law from God's mouth is more precious to him than thousands of pieces of silver and gold (v. 72) and sweeter than honey to his mouth (v. 103). Paul also refers to the law as holy, just, good, and spiritual (Ro 7:12ff.). Although it is a deadly sword for sinners (Ro 7:9–11; 1Co 15:56), the law transforms saints into living trees (Ps 1:1–3).

Moreover, the law itself suggests the appropriateness of the Westminster Confession's tripartite analysis of it. In the Book of Exodus, the Ten Commandments (Ex 20:1–17) are plainly distinguished from the judicial commands designed

---

[20]Niebuhr, *Christ and Culture*, 190–229.

for the land and collected in the Book of the Covenant (20:18–23:19). Moses, reflecting on the two distinct revelations of the law on Mount Sinai, one to all Israel and the other to him (cf. Ex 19:24–20:17 with 20:18–23:33), said of the former, "Then the LORD spoke to you out of the fire. You heard the sound of words but saw no form; there was only a voice. He declared to you his covenant, the Ten Commandments, which he commanded you to follow and then wrote them on the two stone tablets" (Dt 4:12–13). Concerning the later judicial and ceremonial laws mediated to Israel through him he adds, "And the LORD directed me at that time to teach you the decrees and laws you are to follow in the land that you are crossing the Jordan to possess" (4:14). In Deuteronomy 5 Moses reinforces the distinction between the primary Ten Commandments, which are not restricted to time and place, and the secondary ordinances mediated through him and related to the land. After recounting the Ten Commandments, which are called the "covenant made at Horeb" (5:2), Moses says about them:

> These are the commandments the LORD proclaimed in a loud voice to your whole assembly there on the mountain from out of the fire, the cloud and the deep darkness; and he added nothing more. Then he wrote them on two stone tablets and gave them to me. (Dt 5:22)

He thereupon supplements this covenant and relates it to the land in the rest of Deuteronomy. After rehearsing the people's request that God no longer speak directly to them but through a mediator (5:23–29), the lawgiver reminds them of God's instructions: "Go, tell them to return to their tents. But you stay here with me so that I may give you all the commands, decrees and laws you are to teach them to follow *in the land* I am giving them to possess" (vv. 30–31). Moses then warns the people to obey carefully "so that you may live and prosper and prolong your days *in the land* that you will possess" (vv. 32–33). He commences giving the commands for the land in Deuteronomy 6:1:

> These are the commands, decrees and laws the LORD your God directed me to teach you to observe *in the land* that you are crossing the Jordan to possess, so that . . . you may enjoy long life . . .so that it may go well with you

and that you may increase greatly *in a land* flowing with milk and honey. . . . (Dt 6:1–3; emphases mine)

To be sure, these commands are informed by the Ten Commandments and are consistent with them so that they have binding force to the extent that they represent "the general equity," but they are specifically for the time Israel was in the land. The Torah plainly distinguishes the Ten Commandments from the rest of the law in at least the following ways: They have priority through the chronology of revelation, through the manner of revelation, and through their unrestricted extension. The Ten Commandments are uniquely uttered by the voice of God himself out of smoke and fire on a mountain in the hearing of all, and are uniquely written with the finger of God (Ex 31:18). They are uniquely housed in the Holy of Holies (Dt 10:1–6), the copy of heaven itself (Ex 25:9). Finally, they are uniquely to be kept without restriction to time or place.

The law also plainly distinguishes cultic legislation from the Ten Commandments and the judicial ordinances in three ways. First the cultic legislation is given in Exodus 25–40 and Leviticus, "The Handbook of the Priests," and not in Deuteronomy, addressed to the people as a whole, except to the extent that people are involved in the practice of this legislation, such as going up to Jerusalem three times a year. Second, the cultic legislation is given only after the Book of the Covenant had been ratified in a separate ceremony recorded in Exodus 24. Finally, throughout Scripture priority is always given to the religious and ethical laws over the cultic. In a chronology reflecting their relative importance, the covenant is first given, then the mostly judicial instructions in Exodus 21–23, and finally the cultic legislation in Exodus 25:1–40:38. When the people sin in connection with the Golden Calf (Ex 32:1–6), God, interrupting his giving of instructions regarding the tabernacle, instructs Moses to get down off the mountain (v.7). Samuel, the first prophet, expresses the prophetic ideal: "Does the LORD delight in burnt offerings and sacrifices as much as in obeying the voice of the LORD?" (1Sa 15:22).

In conclusion, laws are mutable or immutable relative to the abiding nature of the situation for which they were intended. Richard Hooker said:

In a word, we plainly perceive by the difference of those three laws which the Jews received at the hands of God, the moral, ceremonial, and judicial, that if the end for which and the matter according whereunto God maketh his laws continue always one and the same, his laws also do the like; for which cause the moral law cannot be altered: secondly, that whether the matter whereon laws are made continue or continue not, if their end have once ceased, they cease also to be of force: as in the law ceremonial it fareth: finally, that albeit the end continue, as in that law of theft specified and in a great part of those ancient judicials it doth; yet forasmuch as there is not in all respects the same subject or matter remaining for which they were first instituted, even this is sufficient cause of change: and therefore laws, though both ordained of God himself, and the end for which they were ordained continuing, may notwithstanding cease, if by alteration of persons or times they be found unsufficient to attain unto that end. In which respect why may we not presume that God doth even call for such change or alteration as the very condition of things themselves doth make necessary?[21]

Weaknesses

The fourth commandment calls into question the equation of the Ten Commandments with the eternal moral law. That command is mutable, for if the Reformers are right, it has been changed from the seventh day to the first. Nevertheless, the principle behind it is immutable. Also, Reformed theology should recognize the unity of the law, which, as a way of administration, has been changed. The New Testament, reflecting this change of administration, contains no collection of commandments such as are found in the Torah. Finally, Reformed theologians need to stress the role of the Spirit in keeping the new covenant, which has replaced the older, lest the untaught fall into legalism.

Reformed theology is also obviously weak in its failure to define convincingly church-state relationships and in deciding decisively the millennial question.

---

[21]*The Works of That Learned and Judicious Divine, Mr. Richard Hooker*, revised by R. W. Church and F. Paget (Oxford: Clarendon, 1888), 1:387; 3:x, 4.

THEONOMY

Views

"The theonomy movement," writes David Watson, "is composed of several groups of people whose ultimate goal is to reconstruct 'Christian' nations according to the model of Old Testament Israel."[22] Watson tersely summarizes the history of the movement:

> The first person to promote successfully this goal in the twentieth century was Rousas J. Rushdoony. . . . Rushdoony combined: 1) the philosophical presuppositionalism of Cornelius Van Til . . . ; 2) a "positive," postmillennial eschatology; 3) and a belief that the civil laws of the Mosaic covenant were still binding on the modern magistrate into his own unique blend of "Christian conservativism."

"In the early 1960's," Watson continues, "Rushdoony gained two brilliant young disciples, Gary North and Greg Bahnsen, and through the next decade, these three prolific theonomic authors built up the movement's theoretical foundations."[23] Although theonomists are not agreed in the details of their views and arguments, it is generally conceded that Bahnsen's book *Theonomy in Christian Ethics* lays the theory's cornerstone, and so I will interact primarily with this book.

Bahnsen states his view thus:

> Central to the theory and practice of Christian ethics, whether personal or social, is every jot and tittle of God's law as laid down in the revelation of the Older and New Testaments. The Christian is obligated to keep the whole law of God as a pattern of sanctification, and in the realm of human society the civil magistrate is responsible to enforce God's law against public crime.[24]

---

[22]David K. Watson, "Theonomy: A History of the Movement and an Evaluation of Its Primary Text" (M.A. thesis: Calvin College, Grand Rapids, Michigan, 1985), vi.

[23]Ibid.

[24]Greg Bahnsen, *Theonomy in Christian Ethics* (Nutley, N.J.: Craig, 1977), xiii. His book *The Authority of God's Law Today* (Tyler, Tex.: Geneva, 1983) popularly explains theonomic ethics.

Like dispensationalists, theonomists insist on the integrity of the law, resisting any *relevant* distinction between the Ten Commandments and specific judicial ordinances. Against dispensationalists, however, Bahnsen writes, "The Older Testament commands are not mere artifacts in a religious museum, nor are they ideals suspended over an age of parenthesis. . . ."[25] Against the Westminster Confession's article that the judicial laws are binding only to the extent that they express "general equity," though Bahnsen in contrast to Rushdoony denies he is in conflict with the Confession, Bahnsen reasons that because God loves us in a very extensive and specific fashion, "He did not deliver to us merely some broad and general moral principles."[26] Rather, "*every* single stroke of the law must be seen by the Christian as applicable to this very age between the advents of Christ."[27] "Does Scripture . . . limit the law which is binding upon Christians to the ten commandments?" he asks. To which he replies: "Our Lord definitely did not; according to His word, *every jot* and *every tittle* has abiding validity (Matt. 5:17)."[28]

Bahnsen's specific agenda is to bring back the penal sanctions of the Older Testament. The civil magistrate, he argues, is responsible to discharge fully the specific details of the law, both the positive demands of the law and its penal sanctions. The law of God commands not only "the full discharge of its precepts but also the infliction of the appropriate penalty for all infractions." Unless both of these elements are heeded "the law of God is *not* being met," Bahnsen says.[29] This means the death penalty is to be applied by the civil magistrate to violations both against the purity of the God-man relationship (e.g., idolatry, witchcraft, Sabbath breaking, apostasy, sorcery, blasphemy, and false pretension to prophecy), against the purity of the home (e.g., adultery and unchastity, homosexuality, rape, incest, and proven

---

[25]Bahnsen, *Theonomy*, 34.

[26]Ibid., 35.

[27]Cited by Rodney Clapp, "Democracy as Heresy," *Christianity Today* (February 20, 1987), 18.

[28]Bahnsen, *Theonomy*, 314.

[29]Ibid., 435.

incorrigibility of children), and against the purity of person-to-person relationships (e.g., murder and kidnapping).[30]

Theonomists, however, do not think this theonomic ethic should be applied to politics immediately. "Most theonomists," explains Pavlischek, "maintain that these laws should only be enacted when there is some sort of Christian consensus."[31] Bahnsen, with Rushdoony, believing that "God's law should not be imposed with force on a recalcitrant people or society," holds that "only when those Christians work out their adherence to God's Son in their various life involvements—including political and social ethics—will the statutes of God's law become the law of the land."[32] Theonomists are not revolutionaries willing to overthrow legitimate governmental authorities in order to usher in their own view of government. For this reason theonomists are also postmillennialists with the new twist that the future millennial kingdom will be administered according to the theonomic ethic. In theory postmillennialism is not essential to the system; in practice, however, it is, for otherwise the goal of theonomists appears hopeless. Like dispensationalists they see the Mosaic law once again in force in a millennium, not in a Jewish millennium, but in a Christian one.

Argumentation

What are some theses on which theonomy rests?[33] First, theonomists argue that the law in its entirety reflects the unchangeable, righteous character and standards of God for the actions and attitudes of all people in all areas of life, including politics, Bahnsen reasons:

> Since God is the living Lord over all creation and immutable in His character, and since all men are His

---

[30]Ibid., 445.

[31]Pavlischek, "Critique of Theonomy," 3.

[32]Bahnsen, "God's Law and Biblical Prosperity: A Reply to the Editor of the *Presbyterian Journal*" (privately distributed), 30, cited by Pavlischek, "Critique of Theonomy," 3.

[33]Cf. Bahnsen, *Theonomy*, 2nd ed. (Phillipsburg, N.J.: Presbyterian and Reformed, 1984), xvi-xvii; idem, *By This Standard: The Authority of God's Law Today* (Tyler, Tex.: Institute for Christian Economics, 1985), 345–47.

creatures and morally accountable to Him, we are led to believe that God's law (as reflecting the righteousness of God) applies to every man irrespective of his position in life, situation in the world, nationality, or place in history.[34]

Elsewhere he says the law's "standards of justice have remained immutable."[35] When D. James Kennedy, who denies he is "a theonomist as such," was asked by *Christianity Today*, whether it would be desirable for every nation to be theonomic, he replied, "Well, I think it would be presumptuous for me or anyone else to disagree with God, don't you?"[36]

Second, theonomists argue on the basis of Matthew 5:17, their Golden Text, that the Mosaic laws continue to be morally binding in the New Testament, unless they are rescinded or modified by further revelation. The new covenant, it is argued, does not abrogate the content of the older but reinforces it through its surpassing glory, power, and finality.

Third, Bahnsen recognizes a distinction between "positive" law, which is restricted to a specific situation such as God's command to Adam in the Garden not to eat the forbidden fruit, and "standing" law, which is unrestricted; he contends that the integrated Mosaic law is standing law. He discusses this important point, however, almost as an aside.

Fourth, theonomists are convinced that natural law is an unacceptable standard in guiding nations because it is "simply a projection of autonomy."[37] To be sure, Bahnsen, tips his hat to the statements in Scripture about natural law,[38] but that concession is irrelevant to his thesis.

Fifth, theonomists agree with Reformed theologians that the law serves many functions, including, for example, declaring God's character and demands, defining sin, exposing infractions, inciting sin, and guiding sanctification. They uniquely argue, however, that it also functions as a perfect

---

[34]Bahnsen, *Theonomy*, 339.
[35]Ibid., 398.
[36]Clapp, "Democracy as Heresy," 21.
[37]Bahnsen, *Theonomy*, 399.
[38]Ibid., 279–306, 345–55.

model of social justice for all cultures, even in the punishment of criminals. Bahnsen finds support for this thesis in
Moses' encouragement: "Observe the decrees and laws
carefully, for this will show your wisdom and understanding
to the nations, who will hear about all these decrees and say,
'Surely this great nation is a wise and understanding people'
(Dt. 4:6)." Bahnsen also appeals to Isaiah's and Micah's
vision in precisely the same words: "Many nations will come
and say, 'Come, let us go up to the mountain of the LORD, to
the house of the God of Jacob. He will teach us his ways, so
that we may walk in his paths' (Mic 4:2; Isa 2:3)."[39]

Sixth, Bahnsen sees no difference between church-state
relationships in the Older Testament and in the New. With
regard to the Old Testament he radically divorces the
priestly-cultic sphere (i.e., the Israelite "church") from that
of the kingly-civil sphere (i.e., the Israelite "state"). With
regard to the New Testament he just as radically unites the
ecclesiastical sphere (i.e., "the church") and the civil sphere
(i.e., "the state"). As a result there is no difference between
Israel's kings and other nations' civil magistrates, and the
Old Testament theocracy and the New Testament Christocra-
cy both combine state and church in expressing God's
kingdom. He recognizes that Israel is a theocracy, but that
admission he notes is irrelevant to theonomic ethics. Among
other arguments for equating Israel's king with the civil
magistrates in the surrounding nations he notes seven
characteristics identifying pagan kings as occupying the
same position in God's theocracy/Christocracy as Israel's
kings: God sovereignly appoints and removes both; neither
in nor outside Israel are rulers to be resisted; both bear
religious titles—for example, David's sons are called
"priests" and the uncircumcised Cyrus is called "Messiah"
and "Shepherd," while Paul refers to the civil magistrates of
Rome as "ministers." Both vicegerents are avengers of his
wrath, must deter evil but honor the good, and must rule
according to God's law.

Finally, Bahnsen argues that the death penalties of the
Older Testament are part of God's immutable, eternal law:

> Knowing that God's standard of righteousness (which
> includes temporal, social relations) is as immutable as the

---

[39]Ibid., 362.

character of God Himself, we should conclude that crimes which warrant capital punishment in the Older Testament continue to *deserve* the death penalty today.[40]

Strengths

We commend theonomists for their conviction, with Reformed theologians, that the law is a compatible servant of the gospel, to be delighted in, and is a useful tool in the Spirit's hands for sanctification. We also celebrate the theonomists' efforts to give concrete expressions to the confession that Christ is Lord of all and their high regard for the written Word. Westminster folk applaud them for basing themselves squarely on Cornelius Van Til's apologetics. Moreover, we applaud their fresh insights into many texts of Scripture and for alerting us to the hubris of the state in deifying itself rather than recognizing its derivative authority from God. Finally, we commend theonomists for putting theologians in the heuristic position to think through both the entailments of "general equity," on the one hand, and their eschatology and their understanding of the church-state relationship, on the other.

Weaknesses

The theonomists' particular way of cutting through this briar patch of problems, however, is neither theoretically sound nor practically workable. First, they cannot carry through the theonomic ethic consistently. Bahnsen must agree in the light of the clear teachings of the New Testament (e.g., Ac 15 and Heb 7–10) that the ceremonial laws cannot be continued. He attempts to salvage his thesis by noting that "the meaning and intention of these laws is equally valid under the Older and New Covenants, even though the former manner of observation is now 'out of gear.'"[41] But this way of putting the matter does not do justice to the New Testament. Bahnsen disallows the full force of the apostle's words: "'How can you desire to be enslaved again to the weak and worthless rudiments of the [ceremonial] law?' (cf.

---

[40]Ibid., 442.
[41]Ibid., 212.

Gal 4:9f)."[42] The writer of Hebrews links the law with the Levitical priesthood and asserts in no uncertain terms that it has been replaced by the Melchizedekian priesthood of Christ. Moreover, although Bahnsen attempts to define ceremonial law and what is situationally conditioned, he fails to do so, as shown by the many differences among theonomists. Bahnsen damagingly admits, "Theonomists will not necessarily agree with each other's every interpretation and ethical conclusion. For instance, like me, many do not affirm R. J. Rushdoony's view of the dietary laws, Gary North's view of home mortgages, . . . or David Chilton's attitudes toward bribery and 'ripping off' the unbeliever."[43] These differences, in fact, are only the tip of the iceberg once the various theonomists attempt to apply the law to hundreds of details. Rodney Clapp rightly noted:

> Reconstruction does not actually provide the clear, simple, uncontestably "biblical" solutions to ethical questions that it pretends to. . . . Reconstructed society would appear to require a second encyclopedic Talmud, and to foster hordes of "scribes" with competing judgments, in a society of people who are locked on the law's fine points rather than living by its spirit.[44]

Second, although Bahnsen acknowledges some difference between the Ten Commandments and other laws, that admission is irrelevant to his ethic. Also, although he makes a distinction between temporary positive law and enduring standing law, he fails to appreciate Hooker's point that the judicial and ceremonial laws, in contrast to the Ten Commandments, are meant for a specific situation and therefore are mutable, relative to changing purposes and situations. As noted, these laws were meant for Israel as long as they were in the Promised Land.

Third, the Golden Text of theonomy, Matthew 5:17, cannot aim to establish a theonomic ethic. Paul Fowler, Watson, Poythress, and others have pointed out Bahnsen's faulty exegesis of this verse. [45] Here I want to underscore that

---

[42]Ibid., 211.

[43]Bahnsen, *Theonomy*, 2nd ed. (1984), xix.

[44]Clapp, "Democracy as Heresy," 23.

[45]Paul B. Fowler, "God's Law Free from Legalism: Critique of *Theonomy in Christian Ethics*." Unpublished paper, n.d.

Bahnsen contradicts himself with regard to this text, for he must admit that in some cases Christ actually does abrogate the law. Although our Lord reinforces Moses when he says that the law is a matter of the heart, he replaces the older teaching of "eye for eye, and tooth for tooth," with his own authoritative teaching, "Do not resist an evil person. If someone strikes you on the right cheek, turn to him the other also" (Mt 5:38–42). He also negates dietary laws (Mk 7:19; cf. Ac 15:19–20) and certain provisions for divorce (Mt 19:3–9). Bahnsen will not concede the obvious point that in Matthew 5:38–42 Christ abrogates the principle of immediate justice; Christ will bring justice in the *parousia*. Bahnsen dodges the issue in Matthew 19:3–9. But our theonomist friend cannot shout down the obvious abrogation of the dietary laws in the New Testament. Here he appeals to the principle of the Reformers that distinguishes moral law from ceremonial law. With regard to Mark 7:19 he reluctantly concedes: "It is noted that the parenthetical inference of Mark 7:19 deals with the ritualistic law; hence this thesis suffers nothing in admitting that the ceremonies are no longer useful after Christ. The abiding validity of the *moral* law is our concern here."[46] Regarding Acts 15:19–20 he similarly concedes: "It does not imply that believers are obligated to keep the ceremonial provisions of the Mosaic law as such."[47] Bahnsen complains that his critics fail to note that he allows that "God has the authority and prerogative to discontinue the binding force of anything He has revealed,"[48] but what he fails to realize is that his concessions undermine his thesis. Jesus cannot be establishing every jot and tittle of the law, as Bahnsen's thesis declares, and at the same time abrogate some of the laws. The many specific changes of the law in the New Testament seriously undermine the thesis that the burden of proof rests on the interpreter to show that the law is not in force.

Fourth, Bahnsen distorts the purpose of the law when he alleges that one of its primary functions is to serve as a model of legislation for the nations. The law was written above all for the redeemed community to make them a

---

[46]Bahnsen, *Theonomy*, 228.
[47]Ibid., 131.
[48]Ibid., 2nd ed. (1984), xiv.

treasured possession, a priestly kingdom, a holy nation (Ex 19:5–6). The Sermon on the Mount was delivered not to the unbelieving world but to the disciples; in fact only Jesus' disciples can keep it. Christ summarizes his teaching in the abstract principle of the Golden Rule: "Therefore in everything, do to others what you would have them do to you, for this sums up the Law and the Prophets" (Mt 7:12). As is well known, similar sayings, though in the negative, are found in the rabbis (Tob 4:15 and Hillel) and in the philosophers (Isocrates, Philo, and the Stoics). What distinguishes it from these other precepts is the preceding *logion* to which the inferential particle *'oun* introducing the Golden Rule partially points: "Ask and it will be given to you; seek and you will find; knock and the door will be opened to you. . . . If you . . . know how to give good gifts to your children, how much more will your Father in heaven give good gifts to those who ask him!" (Mt 7:7–11). The morally good gift in view, as the parallel in Luke 11:13 shows, is the Holy Spirit, who enables believers to keep his commandments. Our Lord intends nations to come under his sway, not apart from the Gospel but through it (cf. Mt 28:18–20). Isaiah and Micah present the nations as converts to the true religion by representing themselves as overhearing the strong nations exhorting one another to go up to the temple so that they may learn to walk in his paths. Moses' statement in Deuteronomy 4:6 entails little more than the fact that "righteousness exalts a nation, but sin is a disgrace to any people" (Pr 14:34).

Fifth, as Meredith Kline brilliantly noted,[49] Bahnsen distorts Scripture by likening the separation of the ecclesiastical and civil roles with the separation of church and state in the New. In order to support his thesis, Bahnsen alleges, for example, that "the only time the *priests* were involved in *political* matters were *exceptional* cases" (emphasis his).[50] He goes on to argue that their involvement at Jericho is "exceptional." Elsewhere he argues that the succession of Israel's kings was based on popular choice: "The will of the people or human arrangements were foundational to the selection or election of a king."[51] In fact, however, the

[49]Kline, "Comments on an Old-New Error," 176–78.
[50]Bahnsen, *Theonomy*, 405.
[51]Ibid., 409.

involvement of priests in battle was normative. The law instructed, for example, that the priest should encourage the army before battle, promising them the Lord's presence; and one of the ways God initiated battle was through the Urim manipulated by the priests (1 Sam 28:6). To be sure, sometimes the *vox populi* put the king on the throne, but Yahweh complains, "They set up kings without my consent; they choose princes without my approval" (Hos 8:4). God indicated his approval through prophetic oracles. Bahnsen also does violence to Scripture when he suggests that Cyrus' role as Messiah is representative of the surrounding nations. In fact, however, Cyrus was uniquely given his titles because, functioning in the place of Israel's exiled Shepherd-king, he miraculously led Israel in a second exodus back to the sworn-land and rebuilt its temple. Bahnsen throws together so many unexegeted texts in the chapter entitled "Separation of Church and State" that the reader pushes away the indigestible potpourri.

His argument regarding church and state is not only exegetically flawed, it is also logically defective. Similarities between Israel's anointed kings and uncircumcised pagan kings do not establish their equivalence. One must also note the many dissimilarities between these kings. For example, Israel's magistrates, participating in the holy redemptive nation in contrast to the civil magistrates of the merely preservative states, had to follow rules of holy war that radically distinguished them from pagan rulers. According to the rules of holy war, for example, Yahweh's warriors had to hamstring their military might to the extent that they could not win apart from Yahweh's help. The LORD, for example, reduced Gideon's army from 32,000 men to 300. By contrast, Jesus assumes that pagan kings must match troop for troop (Luke 14:31–33). A spiritual chasm, not a mere crack, separates Israel's kings from pagan rulers, disallowing Bahnsen's equation. His seven similarities between the rulers of Israel and the rulers of the surrounding nations do not support Bahnsen's thesis but illustrate that God is the ruler of the universe as well as Israel's ruler. Ockham's razor, the maxim that assumptions introduced to explain a thing must not be multiplied, validates my contention that no other explanation is necessary.

His thesis is also theologically marred. Kline cogently

notes that the Chalcedon theory desacralizes Israel and sacralizes the nations.[52] In a brilliant essay on the politics of the kingdom—must reading for everyone in this debate— Edmund Clowney rightly notes:

> To suppose that the body of Christ finds institutional expression in both the church and state as religious and political spheres is to substitute a sociological conception of the church for the teaching of the New Testament. Christ does not give the keys of the kingdom to Caesar, nor the sword to Peter before the *parousia*. The church is the new nation (1Pe 2:9).[53]

Sixth, Bahnsen underestimates the role of natural law, which is sufficient to either commend a person toward God or condemn him before God (Ro 2:15). Harris has scriptural warrant for his contention that common grace and general revelation are "not so fragile as Bahnsen supposes."[54] Harris also has historical warrant. In fact, the Book of the Covenant probably draws heavily from the Code of Hammurabi, and without controversy the Book of Proverbs finds inspiration in Egyptian sapiential literature. The Ten Commandments give cause for obeying the first four commandments—note "for" (= "because") in Exodus 20:5, 7, 11—but none for the last five, probably because the former are unique in ancient Near Eastern literature and the latter are found commonly. No society that does not protect the life, home, property, and reputation of its citizens can endure. I suggest, however, that Luther went too far in 1525 in his treatise *Against the Heavenly Prophets*, in which he maintained that whatever in the law of Moses exceeded natural law was binding only on the Jews and not on Christians.[55]

Seventh, the law explicitly states that capital punishment for various offenses is not part of an eternal law. Cain's blood was not shed in *lex talionis* for Abel's blood, which cried out for justice, but in fact was protected (Ge 4:15).

---

[52]Kline, "Comments on an Old-New Error," 178.

[53]Edmund P. Clowney, "The Politics of the Kingdom," *Westminster Theological Journal* 41 (1978–79): 306.

[54]Harris, "Theonomy," 10.

[55]Cited by Peter Alan Lillback, "The Binding of God: Calvin's Role in the Development of Covenant Theology" (Ph.D. dissertation, Westminster Theological Seminary, Philadelphia, 1985), 1:122.

Capital punishment for religious offenses is specifically denied an unrestricted status with respect to the time and place of the offense and the people involved in it. When the son of Shelomith blasphemed, the people were confused as to what to do, showing that capital punishment for that crime did not exist before Israel became a nation. Only after they had put him in custody did the Lord make his will known to the people (Lev 24:10–16). Similarly, the law did not stipulate what should be done in connection with breaking the Sabbath. Once again, lacking prior precedent, the people put the unfortunate man who had gathered wood on the Sabbath day into custody until the Lord gave direction that he must die (Nu 15:32–36). These religious laws were appropriate for Israel's unique situation; they are not appropriate in a pluralistic society.

Moreover, postmillennialists mistakenly hope for a kingdom of perfect justice apart from the *parousia*. Most Christians, however, do not expect to establish a perfectly just kingdom apart from the Lord's coming in power. May the church boast in its weakness, not in its might! "We boast," says Paul of the Thessalonians, "about your perseverance and faith in all the persecutions and trials you are enduring. . . . As a result you will be counted worthy of the kingdom of God, for which you are suffering. God is just: He will pay back trouble to those who trouble you. . . . This will happen when the Lord Jesus is revealed from heaven in blazing fire with his powerful angels. He will punish those who do not know God and do not obey the gospel of our Lord Jesus" (2Th 1:4–8). May the church not hope for a kingdom apart from its sufferings with its Lord on the cross, lest it no longer have in mind the things of God but the things of men (Mt 16:21–23).

Finally, and above all, theonomists err by putting saints back under administration by the Mosaic law rather than by leaving them under administration by the Spirit of Christ.

CONCLUSION

Dispensationalism, by its overzealous negation of the law and by its radical separation of church and state, has left the state without the light of the law. On the other hand, theonomy, by its overkill application of the law to the state

and by its unholy alliance of church and state, would
ultimately take the light of the church out of the world and
would leave the world in its great darkness just as surely as
Judaism did. The debate, however, has the heuristic effect of
making the lamp of Reformed theology shine more brightly.
Dispensationalism by its emphasis on the Spirit fills that
lamp with oil, and theonomy by its attention to the specifics
of the law trims its wick.

Chapter Four

The One, The Many, and Theonomy

John M. Frame

John M. Frame

John M. Frame (A.M. M.Phil., Yale University) is Professor of Apologetics and Systematic Theology at Westminster Theological Seminary in California. With other degrees from Princeton and Westminster Theological Seminary, he has also been a minister in the Presbyterian Church in America. He is the author of *Doctrine of the Knowledge of God* and *Medical Ethics: Principles, Persons, and Problems*.

Chapter Four

The One, The Many, and Theonomy

"The Abiding Validity of the Law in Exhaustive Detail"[1] surely sounds like "a fine, brash hypothesis"![2] We hear that the theonomists advocate modern use of Old Testament civil penalties: capital punishment for adultery, homosexuality, idolatry, and blasphemy. We read that they advocate, on the basis of the Old Testament civil law, elimination of state education, the use of "hard money," reinstitution of slavery, elimination of graduated income and property taxes, elimination of prisons.[3]

I suppose that the greatest appeal of the Christian reconstruction movement, or theonomy, lies in the simplicity and radicalism of its proposal. Radical, to be sure: theonomists advocate a social order sharply different from what is common today; but that kind of radicalism can be presented as an advantage. God's wisdom contradicts the wisdom of the world, and so we would expect a Christian political program to contradict common standards. And, at first glance, the idea is also a simple one: theonomists want us simply to read the law and do it! It is the word of God, and

---

[1]Greg Bahnsen, *Theonomy in Christian Ethics* (Nutley, N.J.: Craig, 1977), 39, from the title to chapter 2.

[2]Alluding to a phrase of Antony Flew. See his "Theology and Falsification," in A. Flew and A. MacIntyre, eds., *New Essays in Philosophical Theology* (London: SCM, 1955), 97. The parallel to our present issue is instructive.

[3]See, e.g., Rodney Clapp, "Democracy as Heresy," *Christianity Today* 31, 3 (Feb. 20, 1987): 17–23.

therefore it is clear and unchanging.[4] If you don't accept it, your problem is not intellectual; it is unbelief and cowardice. If this is true, then it is exciting. Christians have a complete social program they never knew they had! And it is spelled out clearly, unproblematically, from the mouth of God himself!

I am trying here to catch something of the rhetorical spirit of the reconstructionist literature. This spirit exists somewhat more in R. J. Rushdoony and Gary North than in Greg Bahnsen, whose tone is more academic. The reader can see how their rhetoric can often become nasty. These authors find their position to be so plain and obvious that only a stupid, trifling, or heretical person[5] would take issue with them. Thus, in their literature, argument can degenerate into name calling. This tendency, however, may be even stronger on the anti-reconstructionist side, as I will indicate.

So simple and obvious does this teaching appear to the convinced theonomist that he tends to regard anyone who disagrees as antinomian; that is to say, such a one is really unwilling to obey God's law. The reconstructionists apply the antinomian label rather frequently to their opponents. Rushdoony describes a writer as antinomian merely on the ground that that writer disagrees with Rushdoony's exegesis of Exodus 21:22ff. Bahnsen also applies "latent antinomian" with a broad brush,[6] though he has said (contrary to my impression) that he never intended to characterize all nontheonomists in that way.

"Just read the law and do it!" appears to be the admonition of theonomists. One might expect, then, that such theological radicalism would push even further: to reinstitute animal sacrifices, yearly feasts in Jerusalem, sabbatical years and jubilee, the levirate, distinctive garb for God's people, and so on. But no. Rousas Rushdoony, to be sure, does speak sympathetically (but with uncharacteristic

---

[4]The unchangeability of God is a major argument for theonomy: Bahnsen, *Theonomy*, 141, 252. But if God's unchangeability is compatible with changes in the applicability of ceremonial laws, as it is for Bahnsen, why may it not also be compatible with such changes among the judicial laws?

[5]For these and other epithets, see R. J. Rushdoony, *The Institutes of Biblical Law* (Nutley, N.J.: Craig, 1973), 9, 14, 546, 551, 653, 682, 764, 819, 842. He uses these to attack thinkers such as John Calvin and John Murray.

[6]Bahnsen, *Theonomy*, 279ff., esp. 306–14.

inconclusiveness) about the continuing observance of passover and sacrifice.[7] Bahnsen, however, and most others in the movement relegate these to the "ceremonial" category. The same is true for the sabbatical years, jubilee, and distinctive garb. On the dietary laws and the levirate, as well as on long-term loans and some other matters, there are differences within the movement.

So "the abiding validity of the law in exhaustive detail" isn't quite what it may appear to be at first glance. Theonomy teaches that a large amount of Old Testament legislation falls within the "ceremonial" or "restorative" category.[8] Even that legislation has an "abiding validity in exhaustive detail" but only in the sense that we rest on Christ who has carried it out in our place. Therefore to the theonomist much of the Old Testament law, though its validity abides in exhaustive detail, is no longer, shall we say, *literally* applicable.

Besides the ceremonial laws, there are also laws that fail to apply literally today because of cultural factors. Rushdoony comments that Old Testament provisions against mixed marriage could not be simply applied to marriage in Gentile cultures, since for the latter the form of marriage was "atomistic" or "noncovenantal."[9] Bahnsen suggests that the Old Testament demand for rooftop parapets presupposes a culture in which guests were entertained on the roof. He says that the "underlying principle" of the law (our obligation to take safety precautions) "has abiding ethical validity."[10] Evidently, however, the literal meaning of the law does not.

Thus theonomy is not quite as radical as one might have initially supposed. Like the more traditional Reformed theologians, the reconstructionists find much in the Old Testament law that we cannot follow literally today.

And for the same reasons, their position now also appears to be less simple. For they, like the nontheonomists, must wrestle with the difficult question of what does, and what does not, fit into the "ceremonial" category. For both theonomists and nontheonomists, the ceremonial category is

---

[7]Rushdoony, *Institutes*, 794, 782–83.

[8]Bahnsen, *Theonomy*, 207ff.

[9]Rushdoony, *Institutes*, 412–13.

[10]Bahnsen, *Theonomy*, 540–41.

broader than what is *literally* ceremonial. Dietary laws, for example, are not about ceremonies, but both nontheonomists and some theonomists (e.g., Bahnsen) place these under the ceremonial rubric. It is also true (as James Jordan pointed out to me in recent correspondence) that some principles that *do* pertain to literal ceremonies have been considered literally applicable by Reformed theologians of theonomist and nontheonomist persuasions: the broad principles pertaining to public and private worship, especially the "regulative principle." But this means that "ceremonial" is not a clear rubric. Determining what is ceremonial is often as difficult as determining what is literally inapplicable. Often, indeed, these two determinations are the same; to some, "ceremonial" *means* "literally inapplicable." At other times, we (both theonomists and nontheonomists) reason, not from ceremonial to literally inapplicable, but the reverse. The "ceremonial" category, therefore, is itself problematic and does not help us much in determining literal applicability. And even if the conceptual vagueness of "ceremonial" could be cleared up, we would still face the question of which laws fall under that category and which ones do not. Is Deuteronomy 22:12, which mandates the wearing of tassels, a ceremonial law?[11]

And theonomists must also, like their nontheonomist brethren, determine to what extent cultural change affects the application of the statutes. The disagreements and divisions within the reconstructionist movement itself indicate that these tasks are not at all simple. We can see that fact also from the highly complicated arguments in the theonomic literature to the effect that this or that law is or is not literally normative today.

We will return to theonomy shortly, but for now I would like to present for purposes of comparison the position of Meredith G. Kline, who, of all the opponents of theonomy, has developed the most complete theological alternative.[12]

---

[11]Bahnsen does prefer to speak of "restorative" law, rather than "ceremonial." That is helpful in showing more clearly, I would say, the theological function of the concept. But there is still room for much argument about which laws belong to that category.

[12]This is, of course, an advantage Kline has over other would-be critics of theonomy. Most of those critics are rather unclear as to what they would put in the place of theonomy. I believe that in dealing with Kline, therefore, I am dealing with the antitheonomic position in its best form. Other antitheonomists may not be subject to all the criticisms I bring against Kline, but that

Kline also offers us what sounds like a "fine, brash hypothesis." As a slogan, we might take his statement that "the Old Testament is not the canon of the Christian church."[13] At first glance and out of context, the proposal sounds almost Marcionite. It sounds as if we may dispense with the Old Testament altogether.

Kline is, however, quick to disown any such notion. As it turns out, his concept of canon is a rather technical one, which he sharply distinguishes from inspiration. The Old Testament is inspired; it is God's word, and therefore infallible.[14] Its doctrinal teachings are profitable, indeed, normative for New Testament faith. Apart from these Old Testament teachings, we cannot rightly comprehend the New.[15] He continues:

> If to be normative for faith were what qualified for canonical status, the Old Testament would belong to the canon of the Christian church. However, the *sine qua non* of biblical canonicity, canonicity of the covenantal type, is not a matter of faith-norms but of life-norms. More specifically, inasmuch as the nuclear function of each canonical Testament is to structure the polity of the covenant people, canonicity precisely and properly defined is a matter of *community* life-norms. (emphasis his)[16]

One may well question whether biblical covenants (and hence "canons," in Kline's narrow sense) are as exclusively focused on life-norms as opposed to faith-norms, or community norms as opposed to individual norms, as Kline thinks they are. I doubt myself whether life can ever be separated from faith, or community from individual, in the way that Kline proposes. But what is presently most relevant is that Kline's "fine, brash hypothesis," like the corresponding theonomic hypothesis, turns out to be less radical than it appears at first glance. It is, as it turns out, only the

---

is usually because they have not thought out the questions to the degree that Kline has.

[13]Meredith G. Kline, *The Structure of Biblical Authority* (Grand Rapids: Eerdmans, 1972), 99.

[14]Ibid., 100.

[15]Ibid., 101.

[16]Ibid., 101–02.

"community life-norms" that are no longer currently normative. This category does, to be sure, appear broader than the
ceremonial law of the theonomic and the more traditional
Reformed theology. But a follower of Kline is likely to have
some problems determining just what does, and what does
not, fall under that category.

Kline, like the theonomists, sometimes speaks as if it
were all perfectly simple. In his review of *Theonomy*,[17] Kline
says that theonomy is "a delusive and grotesque perversion
of the teaching of scripture," rejected as "manifestly unbiblical" by "virtually all other students of the scriptures." The
issues, he says, are "big and plain and simple." The
theonomists miss a "simple message . . . written large across
the pages of the Bible so that covenant children can read and
readily understand it."[18] Since the matter is so simple to him,
he can use highly insulting terminology to describe his
opponents, for he evidently believes that they are either
intellectual dolts or evil heretics. I am reminded of the
reconstructionists' use of "antinomian."

But, as with the antinomian issue, this one is simply not
that simple. Kline's concept of canon, far from being
immediately obvious, is an original, controversial, and
debatable idea, supported by complicated and sophisticated
reasoning. It certainly cannot be said that there is any
evangelical, or even Reformed, consensus in favor of it. The
same may be said of his concept of "common grace," built on
the theory that the Noahic covenant establishes a religiously
neutral system of government, i.e., one in which no religion
is to have an advantage over any other. In his view, that
system was temporarily set aside in favor of the Israelite
theocracy, which was uniquely typological of the eschatological kingdom; but after Jesus had accomplished redemption,
the theocracy itself was set aside, so that all present-day

---

[17]Kline, "Comments on an Old-New Error," *Westminster Theological Journal*
41, 1 (Fall 1978): 172–89.

[18]Ibid., 172, 173, 175, 176. See also 177, 188–89. For Bahnsen's response,
see Greg Bahnsen, "M. G. Kline on Theonomic Politics," *Journal of Christian
Reconstruction* 6, 2 (Winter 1979–80), 199–200; cf. *Theonomy*, 576, which cites
other debatable "appeals to the obvious" in Kline's writings. Bahnsen is
understandably insulted by the allegation that he knows less than any
covenant child. Is Kline questioning Bahnsen's salvation? Doubtless he
doesn't intend to, but he has let his rhetoric get the better of him.

governments must reflect the Noahic "common grace order," an order that excludes any theonomic use of the Old
Testament penalty structure. Is this not a bit much to read
out of Genesis 8 and 9? Is it, in any case, really so obvious?

Consider the following matters: (1) Kline's theory mandates to the civil government a kind of religious neutrality,
which a Reformed reading of Scripture denies to every other
sphere. (2) Romans 13 sees the civil ruler, not as religiously
neutral, but as a minister of God. (3) Religious neutrality is
not only a wrong goal but also impossible in the nature of the
case. All crime comes from false religion; thus the work of a
righteous civil magistrate will inevitably repress false religions and encourage the true. (4) The Israelite theocracy is
not simply a picture of the final judgment. There is common
grace, divine longsuffering in Israel, both toward God's own
people who resist his word and toward pagans living in
Israel ("strangers") who are tolerated and protected within
certain limits. I cannot here argue in detail these objections to
Kline's system; but don't they at least call its "obviousness"
into question?

And, as we noted problems in determining what does
and does not fall under the theonomic/traditional concept of
ceremonial law, so it is not obvious what falls under Kline's
concept of "community life-norms." What about the dietary
laws, or the levirate, or the mandatory wearing of tassels, or
the prohibition of beard trimming, or the usury ordinances,
or slavery? Certainly it is arguable whether these fit under
the individual or the community category of life-norms.

And there are some laws that *do* seem to fall under the
"community life-norms" category, laws that most of us
would be unwilling to regard as abrogated. We must, for
example, ask again about the Old Testament teaching
concerning public worship. What about the regulative principle that worship is by divine command? It would surely
seem that this principle would fall under the category of
community life-norms. Is Kline, then, ready to dispense with
it for the New Testament church?

What about Old Testament death penalties for incest
and bestiality? Many nontheonomists say that God does not
require capital penalties for these crimes in modern societies;
but they do want to insist that, since the New Testament
church fulfills the Old Testament theocracy, the church ought

to practice excommunication against those who are guilty and unrepentant of these practices. In this connection, they cite 1 Corinthians 5:1–5. On Kline's view, however, the Old Testament penalty structure is simply abrogated. It is a community life-norm for a society other than the New Testament church. Therefore the New Testament church has no biblical guidance at all concerning these practices.

Then there is the interesting case of the statute in Exodus 21:22-25, which Kline discusses in an article.[19] On Kline's exegesis, the statute provides a death penalty for the destruction of an unborn child, though with the possibility of redemption. He concludes that this statute serves as a model for modern society. But we may well ask, Why? Certainly the death penalty for this crime is as much a community life-norm as the death penalty for any other crime in the Mosaic covenant. Kline's response to this question is that the death penalty for murder is not *distinctive* to the Mosaic covenant, but goes back to the Noahic covenant (Ge 9:6). Hence another qualification: the community life-norms that are no longer binding are those *distinctive* to the Mosaic covenant. But it is likely that much of the legislation found in the Torah antedates the Mosaic covenant itself. Certainly much of the Mosaic legislation is essentially application of the ordinances given in creation such as labor, marriage, and Sabbath. James Jordan has argued thus concerning the slavery laws.[20] Might not some of the Mosaic *penalties*, other than the death penalty for murder, also go back to earlier covenants, of which our Bibles contain incomplete transcripts? Or might they simply republish the natural revelation of God's ordinances mentioned in Romans 1:32?

Some years ago a student of mine who strongly claimed that he was not a theonomist, argued for the continuing normativity of the Mosaic statutes that mandate double restitution as a penalty for theft (Ex 22:4, 7, 9). In his view, this particular penalty was not based on anything distinctive to the Mosaic theocracy. It did not have a typological function. In the student's view, it simply represented the

---

[19]Meredith G. Kline, "*Lex Talionis* and the Human Fetus," *Journal of the Evangelical Theological Society*, 20, 3 (September 1977), 193–201.

[20]James B. Jordan, "Slavery in Biblical Perspective," Th.M. Thesis, Westminster Theological Seminary (Philadelphia, 1980).

eternal, unchanging *justice* of God: the thief loses what he had hoped to gain. He pointed out also that the typical modern penalty, imprisonment, is unbiblical, expresses liberal humanism rather than biblical realism, and has proved to be counterproductive in the fight against crime. His argument was that the Mosaic statute was rooted in something more permanent than the Mosaic covenant— whether the creation ordinances, the Noahic covenant, or natural revelation—and was therefore normative. Is that move open to a follower of Kline? I am not sure. At least it would seem to be a sensible modification of Kline's system, doing more justice to the diversity of origins and functions of the Mosaic laws than does Kline's leveling approach, which simply denies normativity to all community life-norms.

But if this is possible, then the door is open, within a basically Klinean orientation, to find a great many laws, indeed civil penalties, that have a continuing normativity. One might even find so many of them as to be mistaken for a theonomist!

Similarly, a theonomist may relegate so many Mosaic penalties to the restorative or ceremonial category that he will be mistaken for a Klinean!

I am certainly not saying that the positions of Kline and Bahnsen are indistinguishable, or anything of the kind. There are genuine theological differences here. Nor am I saying that their theological schematisms are irrelevant to the exegesis of the law. Indeed, their broad theological para- digms do influence their exegesis and application of individ- ual laws: Bahnsen's paradigm leads him to expect literal applicability most of the time; Kline's leads him not to expect it.

But neither theological position is clear or rich enough to *determine* the answers to all questions of exegesis and application. Indeed, after we have chosen sides in the debate (or have chosen not to choose, which may be the best course!) *all* the exegetical work remains to be done! Neither broad theological proposal, taken in itself, requires or forbids the continuing normativity of any biblical law. That question must be answered by exegesis of individual texts.

And once we get down to individual texts, Bahnsenian and Klinean exegetical procedures don't differ much from each other. Both will seek to read the text as God's word.

Both will assess the purpose of the text in relation to the history of redemption. Some laws will be seen to be given for a particular situation that does not now exist (Bahnsen's ceremonial laws, Kline's community life-norms).[21] Others will be seen as presently normative. Bahnsen will have a certain bias toward continuity, Kline toward discontinuity. But good exegetes try to resist their biases at a certain level.

My own suggestion would be that since we have reached something of an impasse in the theoretical debate between theonomists and nontheonomists, an impasse that has led to a lot of ugliness and division in the church, it might be best to set the theoretical debate aside for a while and put most of our effort into the exegesis of specific texts. Frankly, modern evangelicals (including the Reformed) do not know the Mosaic law very well. Since we seem to have more common ground in the area of exegetical method than on the broader theological questions, and since we really need to get to know the law better before seeking answers to the broader questions, let us carry out a joint study of biblical law. Let us try to ascertain the function of each statute and whether that function enables it to be literally normative today—and, if it does not, what we can positively learn from it. Perhaps we will find that many more laws are literally normative today than we would have guessed; and that discovery would be an impetus toward a theonomist position. Or perhaps we will discover some large class of laws (community life-norms? ceremonial laws?) that are not currently normative at all, suggesting the validity of an approach more in Kline's direction.

Some thoughts of Cornelius Van Til, a thinker much respected by both Kline and Bahnsen, may help to put the issue into perspective. Van Til pointed out that the search for an exhaustive system describing all reality is an apostate search. Only God has such a system, and we must be content to know as much of that as he has chosen to reveal, while working piecemeal to understand those fragments of the creation that he has made accessible to our human thought. Epistemological apostasy may take the form of a search for ultimate continuity (a perfect unity or system of

---

[21]At least, those community life-norms that are distinctive to the Mosaic covenant and further its distinctive purposes.

relationships) within creation ("rationalism"), or it may take the form of a search for the ultimate discontinuity (the ultimate particles of reality that are each totally unrelated to anything else: "irrationalism"). The rationalist seeks the ultimate "one," as Van Til puts it; the irrationalist, the ultimate "many." But neither search can succeed, for (1) God alone is the ultimate one and the ultimate many, the ontological Trinity. (2) He has created the world in his image so that there is no unity without plurality or vice versa. (3) Therefore God alone has an ultimate, exhaustive understanding of reality. When we seek an ultimate oneness without the constraints of such a biblical epistemology, we reach only a "blank identity," a oneness that does not have anything to unite. When we seek autonomously the ultimate many, we reach only meaningless particulars.[22]

The temptation for theonomists is to think they have discovered a perfect oneness in the relation between the testaments—a oneness without diversity. In practice, they know that such is impossible; but in their rhetoric, they often talk as if they had achieved that goal. The temptation for antitheonomists is to think that they have reached some kind of irreducible diversity, with no fuzzy boundaries, no ambiguity. In their hearts they know better, but their rhetoric still reflects an unseemly arrogance. In seeking reconciliation, it is important to admit frankly that such pretensions are sinful in God's sight. We do not have the final solution to the relation between the testaments, and we are unlikely to find one that is utterly without difficulty. Beginning at that point, we can greatly help others (even those favoring different paradigms from ours), and they can be of equal help to us.

---

[22]See, e.g., Cornelius Van Til, *The Defense of the Faith* (Philadelphia: Presbyterian and Reformed, 1955), 40–67.

Chapter Five

Effects of Interpretive Frameworks on the Application of Old Testament Law

---

Vern Sheridan Poythress

Vern Sheridan Poythress

Vern S. Poythress (Ph.D., Harvard University; D.Th., University of Stellenbosch) is Professor of New Testament Interpretation at Westminster Theological Seminary (Philadelphia). With other degrees from the California Institute of Technology, Westminster Theological Seminary, and the University of Cambridge, he has taught at Westminster since 1976. He is the author of *Philosophy, Science and the Sovereignty of God, Symphonic Theology: The Validity of Multiple Perspectives in Theology, Understanding Dispensationalists,* and *Science and Hermeneutics: Implications of Scientific Method for Biblical Interpretation* (Foundations of Contemporary Interpretation Series).

Chapter Five

Effects of Interpretive Frameworks on the Application of Old Testament Law

A group of Christians called theonomists are convinced that the Old Testament law even in its details is applicable to modern society. Some of their opponents are convinced that the life, death, and resurrection of Christ introduced a new era in which the Old Testament law is no longer directly binding.[1] The issue is not easy to resolve, because it depends partly on the hermeneutical frameworks and the sets of questions that one has when one approaches texts of the Old Testament. For simplicity I confine myself to comparing theonomy with only one kind of antithetical position, namely the "intrusionist" ethics of Meredith G. Kline.[2] Kline argues that Old Testament social and political law is not

---

[1]The literature on these issues is extensive. The standard argument in favor of theonomy may be found in Greg L. Bahnsen, *Theonomy in Christian Ethics* (Nutley, N.J.: Craig, 1977) and in revised form in idem, *By This Standard: The Authority of God's Law Today* (Tyler, Tex.: Institute for Christian Economics, 1985). Some of the sharpest opposition to theonomy is represented by Meredith G. Kline, "Comments on an Old-New Error," *Westminster Theological Journal* 41 (1978–79): 172–89; and idem, *The Structure of Biblical Authority* (Grand Rapids: Eerdmans, 1972). Bahnsen's reply to Kline is found in "M. G. Kline on Theonomic Politics: An Evaluation of His Reply," *Journal of Christian Reconstruction* 6, 2 (Winter 1979–80): 195–221. The theonomic viewpoint is part of a larger movement called Christian reconstruction, but not all people in the movement hold to theonomic distinctives.

[2]See Kline, *Structure of Biblical Authority*, expecially 154–71.

immediately applicable to us because it was tailored to the special situation of Israel. Israel as a holy nation prefigured the holiness of God's heavenly kingdom and the holiness belonging to the consummation of all things. For example, the wars against the Canaanites prefigured the Second Coming, when Christ will wage a final war against all his enemies (Rev 19:11–21). Special penalties may be appropriate for Israel because of its unique role as a prefigurement of Christ's kingdom. Ethical practices belonging most properly to the kingdom of God in its final manifestation "intruded" in certain ways into the practice of Israel.

AN INTRODUCTORY EXAMPLE: LEVITICUS 19:19

To see in action the differences between these two systems, let us consider a particular example. Leviticus 19:19 says, "Do not plant your field with two kinds of seed." This commandment is part of the Bible. It is God's expression of his character and his will for us. The commandment is therefore relevant to us, as part of the totality of the expression of the will of God. But just how is it relevant? Does it perhaps express a universal standard for human agricultural procedure, based on the creational principle that God made each kind of plant a distinct kind? Or does it symbolically express one element of the holy separation that Israel was to practice as a distinct "kingdom of priests" (Ex 19:6)? Israel's observance of special distinctions between clean and unclean foods and the observance of special festival days functioned to mark Israel as a holy nation, specially set apart for God's blessing and called to a special holy service. Does Leviticus 19:19 function as one instance of this special separation? If so, the statute has a lesson for the church, since the church is "a royal priesthood, a holy nation, a people belonging to God" (1Pe 2:9). The food laws that separated Jew from Gentile have ceased to function on a literal plane as the symbolic mark of the holy community (Eph 2:11–22), but the same principle of holy separation still binds the church (2Co 6:14–18). We are not to mix good and evil. The way in which we observe the principle of Leviticus 19:19 is simply adapted to the new circumstances introduced by the life, death, and resurrection of Christ (Eph 2:16).

How do we decide how Leviticus 19:19 applies to us?

The hermeneutical framework advocated by theonomy tells us to expect the whole Old Testament law to be binding on us. God's character is always the same, and Jesus explicitly affirms the abiding validity of the law (Mt 5:17–20). The hermeneutical framework advocated by Kline and other intrusionists tells us that the Mosaic law as a total system is no longer binding on us. The Mosaic law was specially designed as an instrument to convey typological truth concerning Israel as a holy nation. Since this typological function is fulfilled in Christ and in the consummation of all things, the literal observance of the law in its details is abrogated (Eph 2:15).

Actually, both theonomic and intrusionist interpretation, when understood in their very best form, include important qualifications. Bahnsen in advocating theonomy takes note of the changes due to differences in culture and to the advance in the redemptive plan of God.[3] Kline in advocating an intrusionist approach indicates that there is continuity in the faith-norms of the Old Testament, in some of its life-norms, and in the principles of God's justice.[4] But such qualifications are sometimes minimized or forgotten by enthusiastic followers of these approaches. For the sake of illustration, it is actually better for us to deal to some extent with more stereotyped, popularized versions of the two positions. We thereby expose the general tendencies of the positions without concerning ourselves immediately with all the details.

Neither of these frameworks by itself can solve all our problems. Theonomy rightly insists on continuity based on the unchanging moral character of God. And in principle it recognizes that the New Testament explicitly declares that some laws (e.g., food laws) need no longer be observed literally because they have been fulfilled in Christ.[5] But because its up-front emphasis is so heavily on continuity, many theonomists find themselves under heavy pressure to insist on straight-line continuity of application for all the Mosaic laws except those that are explicitly altered in the New Testament. Leviticus 19:19 is never explicitly altered in

---

[3]Bahnsen, *Theonomy*, 207–32; *By This Standard*, 7, 345–47.
[4]Kline, *Structure*, 101–2, 160.
[5]See Bahnsen, *Theonomy*, 204–16.

the New Testament, and so by this reasoning we must assume that it remains in force.

In fact, however, Bahnsen and many other theonomists think that Leviticus 19:19 is not to be literally observed.[6] My point is merely that their explicitly articulated hermeneutical principles push in the other direction. For example, in a summary Bahnsen lists this as one basic principle: "We should presume that Old Testament standing laws continue to be morally binding in the New Testament, unless they are rescinded or modified by further revelation."[7] Strict, wooden application of this principle would appear to imply the continuation of Leviticus 19:19 in force.

But it could also be argued that Leviticus 19:19 is to be included with the food laws as a ceremonial ordinance. Bahnsen indicates his awareness of this possibility in principle when he says, "The New Covenant also supercedes [sic] the Old Covenant shadows, thereby changing the application of sacrificial, purity, and 'separation' principles, redefining the people of God, and altering the significance of the promised land."[8] Doubtless Bahnsen would consider the principles of Leviticus 19:19 to be among the "separation" principles whose application is altered. But how do we tell in practice what counts as a "separation" principle? How do we tell what elements in Mosaic statutes are shadows and in what way they are shadows? How do we tell what is ceremonial and what is moral? We get some significant clues concerning these questions from the New Testament, but what do we do in a case like Leviticus 19:19, to which the New Testament does not explicitly refer?

For several reasons it is not sufficient merely to observe that keeping types of seed separate is one kind of separation. For one thing, all the laws in Leviticus 19, including those that are most obviously permanent and moral in character, function in some way to mark Israel as holy and separate from the other nations (18:1–5; 19:2). Second, it would be quite easy to argue that keeping the types of seed distinct is a

---

[6]However, Rushdoony asserts that "hybrids are clearly a violation of this law" (Rousas J. Rushdoony, *The Institutes of Biblical Law* [Phillipsburg, N.J.: Craig, 1973], 255).

[7]Bahnsen, *By This Standard*, 345–46.

[8]Ibid., 346.

principle of separation based on creation and therefore of permanent validity. Third, the immediate context of Leviticus does not provide decisive information about the permanency of this statute. Verse 19 contains two other statutes with similar concerns. But the same possible questions arise concerning the permanence or temporary character of all three statutes. Leviticus 19 as a whole contains a large number of ordinances by which Israel is to be holy (see v. 2). Israel's holiness was partially of a symbolical, ceremonial kind; and, sure enough, we find some ordinances in Leviticus 19 that have usually been regarded as ceremonial (e.g., vv. 5–8, 23–25, 26a, 27–28). But Israel's holiness also involved moral purity. Mixed in with these ceremonial ordinances are other ordinances partly of a practical kind (vv. 9–10; of course with moral implications) and partly of a moral kind (vv. 15–18, 26b, 29). In the verse immediately preceding verse 19 is the great command to love one's neighbor as oneself.

Finally, some of the penal laws given to Moses might well involve a principle of separation: the punishment for false worshipers, false prophets, and blasphemers maintains the purity and separation of Israel as a holy community from idolatry. The punishment for homosexual acts preserves before Israel the separation of sexes in their roles toward one another. The key book *Theonomy in Christian Ethics* assures us that the Mosaic penalties for such practices are universally binding.[9] But how do we know that some distinction among penalties regarding special purity and penalties regarding general offenses might be at work here just as it might be at work among the statutes of Leviticus 19?

Bahnsen in one place distinguishes "between laws reflecting God's *justice* and those based upon His *redemptive* purposes—i.e., moral law and restorative law, the former *defining* sin while the latter aims at salvation from sin."[10] The former laws are permanent, whereas the latter change in

---

[9]Bahnsen, *Theonomy*, 445–46. I have learned from recent oral conversation with Bahnsen that he is not sure whether the penalties for false worship ought to be literally carried over. But for many people the theonomic position is associated with the definite-sounding position enunciated in his earlier book.

[10]Ibid., 214.

form with the changes in redemptive epochs. This distinction is useful up to a point in that it provides a biblically based rationale for why some rules are permanent and others are not. But the distinction is not always easy to use in practice. Bahnsen himself indicates that we are not dealing here with a "watertight" distinction but only with a significant diversity in "first order functions of the two classes of commands."[11] Typically Mosaic laws involve both purposes in inextricable unity. All the laws point forward to Christ, i.e., both to his justice and to his redemption. Every law, including Leviticus 19:19, defines some sin at least with respect to Israel. Every law expresses God's justice, inasmuch as the special ceremonial laws all express in symbolic form the absolute holiness of God and the necessity of separation from evil. In a broad sense every law has redemptive purpose, because the law is intended to be a slave master leading to Christ (Gal 3:24–25). Laws that are primarily moral may include a note about salvation (Dt 5:15).

To distinguish their primary function Bahnsen notes that God's moral standards reveal our condemnation, while ceremonial law shows "the means of salvation *per se*."[12] But this legitimate distinction about first-order functions helps us least in just those cases where there might be doubt. For example, if refraining from sowing with two kinds of seed is indeed a universal agricultural principle, then it primarily functions to set forth a definition of sin and to condemn us for its violation. If on the other hand it expresses a principle of Israel's special separation for holiness, it primarily functions to point to the holiness of Israel and the holiness of the tabernacle, which in turn points to the final holiness of Christ in his sacrifice. To which category does this statute actually belong? If we know beforehand how to classify it, the classification will tell us its function. But in actual practice we tend to determine the classification of the statute by first understanding its function.

I think that Bahnsen understands his distinction in the same way that I do. We are supposed to determine the classification of any statute by first understanding its primary function. Understanding its function reveals whether it

---

[11]Ibid., 215.
[12]Ibid., 214.

primarily defines sin in a universally binding way or whether it primarily articulates the way of salvation in a way conditioned by the redemptive-historical context. We thereby determine in what respects it is permanently relevant to our redemptive-historical situation. The primary remaining difficulty is that it is not always easy to determine the primary function, particularly because several functions may sometimes be interwoven.

Theonomy at its best takes considerable note of discontinuities introduced by redemptive history and in particular by the coming of Christ. But because it is so interested in learning abiding principles of justice from the Old Testament, it focuses primarily on those aspects that are unchanging. The burden of proof is then placed on the person who would assert that there is change. When a framework of this kind rigidifies, as it sometimes does among followers of the movement, people insist on carrying over whatever is not decisively shown to be altered.

If we follow a rigid form of theonomic hermeneutical framework, we cannot evade the conclusion: no one text in the Old Testament or New Testament explicitly or decisively indicates the abolition of the literal observance of Leviticus 19:19, and therefore it continues in force. We are bound to observe it. But the real question is not whether we observe it but how. What does the text enjoin? For what purpose? Does God express a permanent agricultural principle or a principle of Israelite symbolic holiness? No one text in the Old Testament or the New Testament explicitly or decisively indicates the answer in *either* direction. In particular, nothing proves conclusively that this statute is *not* ceremonial. The principle of preserving distinctions and separations here may be of the same ceremonial order as the principle of clean and unclean foods.

The fact that the distinction of seeds has some basis in creation does not really count against this possibility. When Israel maintained distinctions between clean and unclean foods, she had to depend every moment on the order of creation that guaranteed the existence and preservation of distinct kinds of animals. But the separation between clean and unclean was nevertheless a temporary measure reexpressing a principle of creation on a heightened symbolic plane until the coming of fulfillment. Of course, in the case of food laws we are confident that we have understood correctly because there are some explicit New Testament passages on the subject (Mk 7:19; Col 2:21; 1Ti 4:3–5). But what about other Old Testament laws? Can we be sure that the New Testament will mention explicitly every case where an alteration of observance of law is appropriate? Might not there be room for deciding some issues on the basis of a more general context of Old Testament and New Testament teaching together? We presume to dictate to God the form that the New Testament must take if we rigidly require the New Testament to mention every case before we are ready to admit that it may be ceremonial.

In the light of this example, we might think that the safest course is to follow the intrusionists in denying the direct applicability of the Old Testament. But difficulties of a converse kind await us. Does our hermeneutical principle say that no Mosaic statute is binding unless specifically reiterated in the New Testament? It follows that Leviticus 19:19 is not binding. But then it becomes all too easy to miss the binding principle exemplified in Leviticus 19:19, namely the principle of separating from evil (2Co 6:14–18). Crudely used, this framework threatens to forbid us access to the divine wisdom and justice displayed in the Old Testament. Moreover, it makes us unable to follow the apostles when they argue ethically on the basis not of their own immediate God-given authority but of the Mosaic law (for example, Eph 6:2).

In the argument above I made a rigid form of theonomic hermeneutics look bad by choosing Leviticus 19:19 as the test case. But I might make rigid intrusionist hermeneutics look bad by choosing some other passage. Some passages like Leviticus 18:23 and 19:15 that are not directly reiterated in the New Testament express abiding principles, and it would be too easy for our sinful nature to evade their requirements if we eliminated them and tried to deduce everything from the two great commandments of loving God and neighbor.

THREE PERSPECTIVES ON ETHICS

How do we avoid some of the dangers that have cropped up in this examination of Leviticus 19:19? Let us stand back from the particular example and reflect on the general principles involved in arriving at conclusions in matters of ethics.

We may start with one of the theses of theonomy. God's word is the proper standard for evaluating all human action, including the actions of government officials and the laws made by civil legislators. This particular thesis deserves the support of all Christians, for a very good reason. Confessing the lordship of God necessarily implies bowing to his will and realizing that he, rather than any human being, is the sovereign, all-wise judge of the world. As John M. Frame has argued, God's lordship implies that he specifies the standards for all evaluation, that he is always personally present to us as the One to whom we must respond in a personal relationship of love, and that he controls our situation so as to create opportunities and responsibilities toward our environment.[13]

Corresponding to these three ways in which God rules over us are three perspectives in terms of which we may approach ethical questions. The first perspective, the normative, focuses on the rules in Scripture, God's norms for human conduct. The second perspective, the attitudinal or personal, focuses on personal attitudes. The third, the situational perspective, focuses on what is best for our situation.[14] From the normative perspective, we must conform to God's standards as expressed in Scripture. From an attitudinal or personal perspective, we must be motivated by love for God. From a situational perspective, we must promote the praise and honor of God in our situation.

Within a biblical worldview these three perspectives ultimately harmonize with one another, because God is the source of all. Moreover, each perspective when rightly understood encompasses the others. The normative perspective encompasses the personal, because God's law (the norm) instructs us concerning the importance of the heart and the motivation of love. The normative perspective

---

[13]See John M. Frame, *The Doctrine of the Knowledge of God* (Phillipsburg, N.J.: Presbyterian and Reformed, 1987), 15–18.

[14]See John M. Frame, "The Doctrine of the Christian Life," classroom syllabus for Westminster Theological Seminary, 1979; Vern S. Poythress, *Symphonic Theology: The Validity of Multiple Perspectives in Theology* (Grand Rapids: Zondervan, 1987), 34–36.

encompasses the situational, because God's norms instruct us on the necessity of taking account of the situation (for example, 1Co 8:7–10). The situational perspective encompasses the normative, because God is the most significant person in our situation and God's laws are the most significant ethical facts about our situation. We cannot possibly honor God in our situation without taking into account what he says about it. The situational perspective encompasses the personal because our own dispositions as well as the existence of other people and their needs are part of the situation to which we are called to respond.

Although the three perspectives harmonize in principle, human beings in their sinfulness have a tendency to distort the truth, and the possibilities for distortion are enhanced when they use only one perspective. For example, modern situation ethics blatantly distorts biblical truth. It one-sidedly uses a situational perspective to deny that God's norms are part of the definition of our situation and that only by paying attention to the norms may we rightly judge what the consequences of our actions will be for the honor and praise of God. By contrast, the Pharisees of Jesus' day one-sidedly used a normative perspective. They appealed to a constant norm, the Sabbath law, in order to show that Jesus broke the law. They failed to understand that the true intention of the Sabbath law involved an adaptation in the case of special circumstances of human need (Lk 6:9–11; 13:15–16) and special authority (6:1–5).

The same dangers confront us. When using the normative perspective, we may rightly observe that God's moral character is unchangeable and that therefore the moral norms are always the same. But then it is easy to overlook the fact that the special character of Israel as a holy nation involved the observance of ceremonial ordinances that expressed God's character and norms in a way adapted to a unique situation. Thus theonomists run the danger of using the appeal to unchanging norms in order to prejudice the question of whether the great bulk of Mosaic legislation is adapted to the unique situation of Israel. In other words, they put in the background the situational perspective, and this move may make them underestimate the difficulty and complexity of disentangling the abiding principles from the particularity of their application to Israel.

Conversely, when using the situational perspective, we may rightly observe that all of God's word given to Israel was adapted to Israel's needs and situation. The Israelites lived with an agricultural, preindustrial economic and civic organization. But most of all they lived in a situation before the coming of Christ, when they needed to enjoy the benefits of salvation in symbolic form before the salvation itself had been definitively accomplished or consummated. In such a redemptive-historical situation the entire geopolitical structure of the nation typologically embodied anticipations of Christ; covenant, king, priest, and Israel's corporate status as son (Ex 4:23) all foreshadowed Christ's unique holy role. But when we concentrate on the situationally unique position of Israel, it is easy to overlook the fact that these very special arrangements foreshadowed a universally binding pattern, a permanent norm, namely the pattern of Christ's own righteousness and perfect fulfillment of the law. Thus the special character of the Israelite law simultaneously expresses universal norms. Intrusionists run the danger of using the appeal to the special situation of Israel in order to prejudice the question of whether we can find principles of universal justice in Mosaic statutes.[15]

We should mention one more danger, the danger of relying too much on so-called "natural law," the natural sense of right and wrong impressed on our consciences. To do so is to misuse the personal perspective. It is true that even human beings without access to the written word of God have a sense of right and wrong (Ro 1:32). But Scripture nowhere indicates that they thereby know more ethical principles than those revealed in the Bible. In fact, the opposite is the case. The Jews by their access to the written law know God's will in a privileged way (2:17–22). We must recognize that human sin distorts our attitudes and our "natural" feelings. We must be ready to submit ourselves to Scripture over and over again as a remedy for sin.

---

[15]I should make it clear that I regard the outstanding representatives of the positions, Greg L. Bahnsen and Meredith G. Kline, as intelligent and sophisticated interpreters of the Old Testament. A close reading of their positions shows that they are well aware of both continuity and discontinuity between the two Testaments. They are aware of the relevance of both norms and situations. But tendencies at work in their positions get exaggerated by their followers.

EFFECTS OF PERSPECTIVES ON INTERPRETATION OF DEUTERONOMY 4:6-8

We may show the effects of perspectives by examining the interpretation of Deuteronomy 4:6-8.

> Observe them carefully, for this will show your wisdom and understanding to the nations, who will hear about all these decrees and say, "Surely this great nation is a wise and understanding people." What other nation is so great as to have their gods near them the way the LORD our God is near us whenever we pray to him? And what other nation is so great as to have such righteous decrees and laws as this body of laws I am setting before you today?

Theonomists commonly appeal to this text to show that the Mosaic law has worldwide relevance.[16] It is obvious why theonomists should think that this text supports them. According to these verses, the other nations and not only Israel can recognize the wisdom of these statutes and admit that they are "righteous" (4:8). The righteousness of Mosaic ordinances thus pertains not only to Israel but also all other nations. When other nations have their eyes opened to the truth, they will want to have just such righteous laws and they will express admiration for Israel's wisdom. Mosaic laws thus express standards binding on all nations and not merely on Israel. Micah 4:2 picks up this same theme in the context of eschatological prophecy. "In the last days" the house of the Lord will be established as the most prominent mountain, the nations will come to learn the law, and "the law will go out from Zion, the word of the LORD from Jerusalem" (Mic 4:1-2). What the nations might potentially enjoy according to Deuteronomy 4 they come actually to enjoy in the time of fulfillment.

This argument looks very convincing until we realize that the framework of assumptions of theonomy has had a large input in influencing what we notice in these texts.[17] To concentrate on the normative perspective is to concentrate on the norms, standards, or rules. By definition, norms or

---

[16]See, for example, Bahnsen, *Theonomy*, 356.

[17]For further discussion of hermeneutical frameworks, see Vern S. Poythress, *Science and Hermeneutics: Implications of Scientific Method for Biblical Interpretation* (Grand Rapids: Zondervan, 1988).

rules are the same in every situation. Hence when we operate in this framework, we are already predisposed to assume primarily continuity in space and time. Continuity in space implies that the same laws bind other places, that is, other nations besides Israel. Continuity in time implies that the same laws bind people at all times—past, present, and future.

But now suppose that we approach the same texts using the framework of intrusionists and their emphasis on the situational perspective. Immediately we have in the forefront of our minds the unique situation of Israel: Israel is the unique holy nation and a kingdom of priests with its shadowy typological institutions pointing forward to fulfillment. Within this hermeneutical framework, Deuteronomy 4:6–8 appears to mean something quite different. The other nations admire Israel not only for the righteousness of her laws (4:8) but also for the God who is so near to Israel whenever they call on him (4:7), for the wisdom expressed as God reveals his character and salvific purposes uniquely to Israel, and for the land that God gave Israel as a gift (4:5). That is to say, the nations do not notice the commandments merely as rules standing by themselves but as an expression of God's special communion with Israel. They understand the rules as what is wise for this special holy people Israel. The nations are pictured, not as saying, "We should have these same laws for ourselves," but "What a special God Israel has, what a special grace God has shown to Israel, and what wise statutes God has given them for their special situation. We would certainly want to have laws just like that if we were the special chosen nation. But unfortunately we are not the special chosen nation, so it is not immediately clear that we should have precisely these laws in every case." A radical discontinuity in space exists between Israel and the other nations.

When the intrusionist framework comes to Micah 4:1–2, another difference is introduced. The "last days," as the time of eschatological fulfillment, means the revelation of the glory of God in a surpassing form (Isa 40:5). Shadows are superseded by realities, and whatever is shadowy in the Mosaic law will find fulfillment in transformed fashion. In the New Testament era the fulfillment comes and the light of the revelation of the glory of God has shined in the face of

Jesus Christ (2Co 4:6). It is clear that the "word of the LORD" going forth from Jerusalem is preeminently the word of the Gospel, the word concerning the life, death, and resurrection of Jesus Christ (Lk 24:44–49; Ac 1:8). The righteousness of the law is fulfilled in Christians as they live in union with Christ (Ro 8:4). The whole Old Testament, including the Mosaic law, is to be interpreted in the light of the Christocentric character of fulfillment (Lk 24:44–46). Thus a radical discontinuity arises in time through the coming of Christ. Taken together, the discontinuities in space and time prohibit us from carrying over Old Testament statutes directly to ourselves.

Thus the same two texts, Deuteronomy 4:6–8 and Micah 4:1–2, look very different, depending on our hermeneutical framework. If our framework stresses norms and continuity, we see the implications of continuity. If our framework stresses the different redemptive-historical situations and therefore discontinuities arising from differences in situation, we see the implications of discontinuity. In my judgment, neither framework finds any difficulty with these particular texts. Neither framework forces an unnatural sense on the texts or is forced to overlook a phrase that is difficult to harmonize.[18]

In fact if we are already thoroughly committed to one of the frameworks, our interpretation of these and many other texts looks obvious. Our whole position is obviously right, and only someone insensitive to the obvious or sinfully resisting the clear teaching of Scripture could fail to agree with us. A certain dogmatism and harshness toward opponents can creep in unawares because we are not fully aware of how much the prechosen framework has influenced our conclusions. The arguments have more circularity in them than is commonly understood.

Of course, Deuteronomy 4:6–8 and Micah 4:1–2 still have relevance to the debate. We should not just throw up

---

[18]Some people might reject as "unnatural" the intrusionist transformation of Micah 4:1–2. But to undermine such an interpretation one must reject the intrusionist's global hermeneutical theory about shadows and fulfillment and the possibility of Old Testament prophetic literature expressing itself in the symbolic language of shadow appropriate to an audience living under Mosaic structures. See the discussion of this issue in Vern S. Poythress, *Understanding Dispensationalists* (Grand Rapids: Zondervan, 1987).

our hands and say that both positions are right or that no one can know which is right. We must look again at these passages and others to try faithfully to understand all their implications. But initial impressions are not enough. We must be patient in trying to understand the whole warp and woof of God's revelation, and not merely quote a passage like this in isolation because we can see how it supports our position when interpreted against the background of that position. It is too easy to read into a passage what we afterwards read out.

UNIQUENESS AND UNIVERSALITY IN DEUTERONOMY 17

The interpretation of Deuteronomy 17:2–13 may further illustrate the interaction of frameworks with texts. Verses 2–7 articulate principles for dealing judicially with false worship. Whereas Deuteronomy 4:6–8 superficially might appear to affirm the complete universality of all Mosaic law, Deuteronomy 17:2–13 superficially appears to affirm its special character. Intrusionists sensitive to the special status of Israel will immediately point out all the indications of ways in which the penalty for false worship is connected with the unique Israelite situation. The actions take place within the land given by God (17:2, 4). False worship involves transgression of God's covenant, that is, the covenant made especially with Israel in a unique historical event at Mount Sinai (v. 2). Execution is by stoning (v. 5), which may be analogous to the production of stone memorial altars testifying to God's history with Israel (cf. Ge 28:18; Jos 22:10–34). The execution redemptively purifies the community (v. 7). Difficult cases are to be referred to the priests in the place that God will choose (v. 8).

But theonomists can also point out how this unique Israelite situation is a model embodying principles of universal application. The land of Palestine is a special, holy land given by God, but it is thereby a symbol of the fact that all the earth is owned by God (Ps 24:1) and given to human beings as he chooses (Ac 17:26). Israel is under special covenant with God, but this covenant is analogous not only to the covenant made with all human beings through Adam but also to the new covenant whose rule will extend to all

nations (Mt 28:18–20). Execution by stoning may have no
special significance, since it is apparently the common
method of punishment for capital crimes. Even if it has the
significance of memorializing, it embodies the general principle of remembering the Lord's past dealings with his people
(Ps 77:11). With regard to the note of purification (17:7), just
acts of the civil government are among the means by which
national well-being is maintained and enhanced and the
wrath of God turned away (cf. God's judgment on nations in
Amos 1–2). Hence the text 17:7 embodies a general principle.
The procedure for consulting with the priests in 17:8
expresses the general principle of having a system of appeals
(cf. Ecc 5:8–9) and being able to consult people knowledgeable in the law.

As before, the real question is not whether Deuteronomy 17:2–13 is relevant to us or binding on us, but how is it
binding? More precisely, what changes take place as we
expand the application of the Mosaic law from Israel to the
nonholy nations and as we expand its application in time
through the changes introduced by the coming of fulfillment
in Jesus Christ? What is permanent principle and what is
adaptation to a unique situation in time and space?

Some verses of the Old Testament express a general
principle pretty much as they stand (e.g., Lev 19:4). Other
verses express a principle in the form of a foreshadowment
(e.g., v. 8). *As a matter of degree* we may therefore classify
many of them as primarily "moral" or "ceremonial." But we
oversimplify if we say merely that one verse is specific to
Israel and another verse is universal. In fact all the verses are
God's personal covenantal communication to Israel first of all
and are colored by their unique redemptive-historical context. At the same time all the verses express God's character
and his abiding principles of justice.

To put it another way, all the verses point forward to
Christ. They point forward to the uniqueness of his incarnation, death, and resurrection once and for all and hence have
a unique redemptive-historical coloring. Simultaneously they
point forward to the universality of the principles of justice
by which he reigns. Hence they express in some way God's
character and are generalizable into rules with universal
bearing.

Deuteronomy 17:8–20 is a particularly good illustration

of this dual reality. If we read these verses from a theonomic framework, we are on the lookout for unchanging principle. So we notice the practical wisdom of a system of appeals and the necessity and justice of dealing radically with a person who would destroy the very foundations of authority by contumacy (17:12–13). If we read Deuteronomy 17:8–20 from an intrusionist framework, we immediately recognize the typological status of the high priest, the judge, and the king as special officers foreshadowing Christ. Hence we see the passage as speaking of the necessity of listening to the voice of God in Christ and the penalty for rebellion against Christ. In fact both of these readings are true as far as they go. Israel is a nation among nations, and so of course God's political wisdom for Israel will embody lessons for all government. All governments are subject to God's rule. At the same time Israel is a nation filled with typological symbols, and so of course there is a fruitful analogy between Israel's system of government and the government of Christ. But we are in danger of missing something if we consistently adopt only one of these frameworks. What we miss may sometimes be crucial to understanding the Old Testament in depth and therefore crucial to applying it rightly in changed circumstances. For example, if we rigidly applied a principle of continuity, with no understanding of the typological role of the high priest, we would be forced to set up a contemporary earthly high priest for ourselves. If we rigidly applied a principle of discontinuity, we would simply learn nothing about principles for organizing a modern state.

In the case of Deuteronomy 17 it is comparatively easy to see some of the basic insights to be derived from each of two perspectives. In such a case, a typical reader operating within one perspective might still notice complementary truths. But what happens when we come to more difficult cases? Then the reader is all the more tempted to stop short simply with the answers obtained from one perspective.

PENAL LAW

Old Testament penal laws, where the notorious disagreements arise, involve some of the same difficulties that we have just seen. Penal laws clearly involve a principle of justice and fit punishment and hence embody permanent

principle. Some penal laws just as clearly involve restoration
(for example, the thief repays what he has stolen and the
manslaughterer is free to return to his home after the death
of the high priest, Nu 35:9–28). Does such restoration
foreshadow the coming of Christ? If we have decided
beforehand that a particular penal law (e.g., Ex 21:14) is
moral, its function is primarily to define sin and restrain evil.
If we have decided beforehand that a particular penal law
(e.g., Lev 20:2–3; Nu 1:51; 3:10) is ceremonial and is based on
the special holiness of Israel, its function is partly to assert
the special holiness of Israel as a foreshadowing of the
holiness of Christ, the holiness of the church, and the
cleansing from sin by Christ's substitutionary penal death.
But it is wiser not to impose our classification at all, lest we
compress the richness of the passage or prejudge the limits
of its implications. Instead we should patiently try to
understand the function of the particular law in its context
and on this basis discern how it applies—perhaps in a
variety of respects—in the New Testament era.

Bahnsen and many other theonomists maintain as a
general principle that the penal laws are all moral, that is,
that they all express permanent, universal principles.[19] At a
minimum, such an assertion may mean only that every law
expresses universal principles by revealing God's justice.
Such is in fact the case, as we can see from the uniform
biblical testimony to the holiness and goodness of the law
(e.g., Ps 119; Ro 7:14; 13:8–10), the unchangeable character
of God, and the fact that God's word is always consistent
with every aspect of his character, including his justice. The
examples above illustrate these truths.[20] But theonomists
appear to be saying something more. At a maximum they are
claiming that penal laws require no substantial adjustments
because of the coming of Christ. Theonomy as popularly
understood involves such a maximalist position, but it is
more accurate to say that Bahnsen's general statements

---

[19]See Bahnsen, *By This Standard*, 3–4, and 347, principle #10.

[20]The Westminster Confession of Faith (XIX,iv) gives confessional status to
this principle when it affirms that "to them [Israel] also, as a body politic, He
gave sundry judicial laws, which expired together with the State of that
people; not obliging any other now, further than the general equity thereof
may require." The phrase "general equity" implies recognition of permanent principles of justice.

concerning penal law are qualified by the places where he says that we should presume continuity unless we have biblical evidence to the contrary.[21]

Bahnsen and others have much to say in favor of this general principle concerning penal law. But their most powerful arguments and proof texts deal with the fact that universal principles of God's justice are embodied in all God's statutes whatsoever. If their arguments point to pure permanence for all laws whatsoever, they prove too much, because food laws clearly do not fit. If their arguments allow (as in fact they do) for changes in the form of application due to advance in redemptive history, such changes may also affect some of the penology (such as Ex 30:33, 38; Lev 23:29; Num 35:28). Which parts are affected and how? That remains to be seen. But then we must look at the penal law statute by statute, context by context, and try to understand its functions. We do not merely assume that no changes can ever be entertained. Bahnsen instructs us to examine patiently the particular texts and warns us of the complexities involved.[22] Popularized theonomy needs to pay attention.

Bahnsen's advocacy of a presumption of continuity is understandable in a Christian atmosphere given to ignoring the Old Testament in general and its penology in particular. He is summoning the troops to awake from their slumber and their compromises with the evil world around and to recognize the wisdom of the Old Testament. I am uncomfortable with his stance because I am attacking a different evil, namely, the presumption that we know what sort of literature we will find in the Old Testament before we read it. Theonomists run the danger of presuming that the Mosaic law consists in blueprints for modern economics and politics, while intrusionists run the danger of presuming that the Mosaic law consists only in typological truths about purely spiritual redemption in Christ. Both of these moves flatten Mosaic literature in one direction and so hinder the rich understanding that we need to do the job accurately in political ethics and in Christological understanding. Bahnsen himself shows sensitivity to this danger when he writes:

---

[21]Bahnsen, *By This Standard*, 6, 345–46.
[22]Ibid., 7.

> We need to be sensitive to the fact that interpreting the Old Testament law, properly categorizing its details (for example, ceremonial, standing, cultural), and making modern day applications of the authoritative standards of the Old Testament is *not an easy or simple task*. It is not always readily apparent to us how to understand an Old Testament commandment or use it properly today. So the position taken here does not make everything in Christian ethics a simple matter of looking up obvious answers in a code-book. Much hard thinking—exegetical and theological homework—is entailed by a commitment to the position advocated in these studies. (emphasis his)[23]

We will have to do our homework to understand the whole Bible in depth. Some theonomists' simple arguments to the effect that the Old Testament law is confirmed in the New Testament and therefore must be kept now in a literal and straightforward way are not adequate. Some intrusionists' simple arguments to the effect that many laws are not found outside of the Mosaic era and therefore may safely *not* be kept are equally inadequate. Both of these routes are the lazy way out in the sense that they do not come to grips with the full richness of Old Testament revelation. We have to work to understand what God is saying—and that means understanding in indissoluble and harmonious unity both how God dealt uniquely with Israel to foreshadow Christ and how God constantly revealed his eternal justice as an aspect of the wisdom that is found in Christ (Col 2:3). When we neglect to use both normative and situational perspectives (and for that matter the personal perspective) to supplement our understanding, we flatten out the depth of Old Testament revelation.

The best representatives of both theonomy and intrusion are of course not so simplistic. But I think that even they may be able to learn by some more sensitive listening to the other side. And I would appeal to the followers on the two sides not to be so swallowed by the persuasive rhetoric associated with an admittedly insightful framework that they are unable to see nuances that come readily to light only by adopting another point of view. It would be a shame if the theonomists' commendable attempt to evaluate politics, economics, and civil government in the light of the standard of God's

---

[23]Ibid.

written word should fail to produce godly fruit. But our labors will be corrupted if Christian infighting takes over or if overconfidence in a hermeneutical framework makes us stop short of deep penetration into God's word. If we stop short, we may be in possession of unjust principles that we think just.

If we are largely ignorant of the Old Testament, we have a heavy responsibility to become familiar with it. As we become knowledgeable, our knowledge of the Old Testament gives us more weighty responsibility to apply it. But we also have a responsibility not to dishonor the name of God by inordinately dogmatic claims by which we put forward as God's justice what in some cases may turn out afterwards not to be so.

PART THREE

THEONOMY AND COVENANT CONTINUITY: NEW TESTAMENT EVIDENCES

The continuity of the Old Testament law, which is a major emphasis of theonomy, has always been a teaching of Reformed theology. But the nature and character of this continuity must be decided on the basis of New Testament evidences. In this section Dan McCartney explores the New Testament's references to the Pentateuch and finds a stress on Christology and covenantal relationship, from which ecclesiastical and ethical implications flow, for Christians in particular rather than for the world in general. Moisés Silva takes a new look at Paul's concept of the relationship between law and promise, old covenant and new in Galatians 3:21, and reaffirms the traditional Reformed view that the law, while not opposed to the promise, was never intended to be the source of righteousness and life. Dennis Johnson provides a New Testament perspective on the law's penal sanctions, showing that in the Epistle to the Hebrews the sanctions are cited to maintain the purity of the covenant community (rather than the state).

Chapter Six

The New Testament Use of the Pentateuch: Implications for the Theonomic Movement

Dan G. McCartney

Dan G. McCartney

Dan G. McCartney (Ph.D., Westminster Theological Seminary) is Assistant Professor of New Testament at Westminster Theological Seminary (Philadelphia). With other degrees from Carnegie-Mellon University and Gordon-Conwell Theological Seminary, he has taught at Westminster since 1983. He has contributed to the *New Geneva Study Bible, Inerrancy and Hermeneutic: A Tradition, A Challenge, A Debate,* and *Technology and the Seminary.*

Chapter Six

The New Testament Use of the Pentateuch: Implications for the Theonomic Movement

It is a postulate of the so-called theonomic movement that the law of God as revealed in the Old Testament is relevant and applicable in all ages, because the God who gave the law does not change. With this tenet we have no quarrel. At issue is the way in which the Old Testament is applied to people today. Theonomists argue that ideally the civil law of the Old Testament, including its sanctions, should be implemented by the civil authority in this age, because it represents God's own addressing of the problem of civil government. Theonomists, as well as other Reformed believers, recognize that all the Old Testament is fulfilled in Jesus. However, some theonomists also fail to follow through on the implications of this fact—at least they follow through in a different way than the writers of the New Testament did. My contention is that the New Testament's use of both legal and nonlegal material in the Old Testament should inform our hermeneutic and determine the way in which we apply the law to ourselves and our society.

LAW IS CHRISTOLOGICAL AND COVENANTAL

A conscious thesis of the New Testament is that the Old Testament is Christological. With regard to the law specifically, Romans 10:4 tells us that "Christ is the end of the law." Theonomists, as well as most Reformed Christians, are quite right in pointing out that this does not mean that Christ is the *termination* of the law but that he is its goal. The Old Testament *points to* Christ and finds in Christ its ultimate purpose.

This is not to say that everything in the Old Testament is a direct prophecy of Christ in the modern sense of the word *prophecy*, but that the Old Testament as a whole is focused on Christ. Jesus taught his disciples in Luke 24:46–47: "This is what is written: The Christ will suffer and rise from the dead on the third day, and repentance and forgiveness of sins will be preached in his name to all nations." Peter learned this lesson and echoes his Lord in Acts 10:43, where he tells Cornelius that "all the prophets testify about him that everyone who believes in him receives forgiveness of sins through his name" (cf. Ac 3:18, 24). Many years later Peter still stresses this function of the Old Testament. He informs his hearers that "the prophets, who spoke of the grace that was to come to [them], searched intently and with the greatest care, trying to find out the time and circumstances to which the Spirit of Christ in them was pointing when he predicted the sufferings of Christ and the glories that would follow" [1Pe 1:10–11]. The term *prophets* undoubtedly means not just the second part of the Old Testament canon, but the entire Old Testament.[1] The implication of these passages is that to understand any part of the Old Testament, it must be related to this overall Christocentric purpose of God.

The New Testament writers, like their contemporaries, did not distinguish between legal and nonlegal material in the Old Testament, particularly in the Pentateuch. It was all Torah. For example, in Galatians 4, Paul says, "Are you not aware of what the law says," and then proceeds to cite *narrative* material from Genesis. Law was the revelation of God's will, which included his purposes in history. Thus Genesis, which contains very little legal material, was still Torah, and in fact it was the foundation for Torah because it defined the relationship with God that was the context of the law. This formal definition of relationship is what we call

---

[1]Cf. J. R. Donehoo, *The New Testament View of the Old Testament* (Philadelphia: Westminster, 1900), 75, or (in reference to 2Pe 1:20) E. J. Young, *Thy Word Is Truth* (Grand Rapids: Eerdmans, 1957), 24.

"covenant." Torah, or *nomos*, was not just a collection of rules but a covenant, a definition of the nature of the relationship God was forming with his people.

The Mosaic law was a further covenant with God's people. It was God's unique gift to a *particular* group. This covenant was not made with the world at large. This is not to say that the principles of the law were not good for the world around them. Deuteronomy 4:6 implies that the nations will marvel at the justice of Israel's laws. But the Old Testament legal package cannot be extricated from its covenantal, that is to say particularistic, context.

According to the New Testament, a right relationship with God is possible only through Jesus Christ (e.g., Ro 3–4, Gal 3, Heb 9). Because the purpose of the Old Testament is to define the relationship of God to his people, Jesus in Luke 24 says that the Old Testament, which is the written "constitution" for the people of God, has its ultimate focus in himself and his redemptive work. The way in which the New Testament uses Old Testament passages dealing with Israel and applies them to Christ, for example, the application in Matthew 2:15 of Hosea 11:1 ("Out of Egypt I have called my son"), is simply an outworking of this focus.

The principle of covenantal representation is at work here as well (cf. Ro 5). Jesus died for the sins of *his* people, taking upon himself the curse of the law which was due them (not the curse on the world at large).[2] If the Old Testament is about Christ, then it is certainly true that the *law* aspect of the Old Testament is also about Christ. Paul explicitly cites the Pentateuchal curse, "Anyone who is hung on a tree is under God's curse" (Dt 21:23) and applies it to Christ (Gal 3:13).

EXAMINATION OF EXPLICIT PENTATEUCHAL CITATIONS

It would be instructive to examine all the uses of the Old Testament by the New Testament to show how this principle of covenantal Christocentrism is worked out, but clearly this task would occupy volumes rather than a few pages. Most of

---

[2]Except in the sense that people throughout the world are scheduled for inclusion among God's people (1Jn 2:2).

the citations in the New Testament are from the Psalms and Isaiah. But for the purposes of this study, which is concentrating on the law, let us focus on the New Testament's citations of the Pentateuch.

Pentateuchal quotations for the most part occur in a few clusters. The largest of these is Acts 7, where Stephen cites the Pentateuch thirteen times, along with other books, in tracing the history of early Israel. Paul refers to Genesis and Exodus ten times in Romans 9–11. In Galatians 3 he refers to the Pentateuchal books six times. Jesus refers to the law of Moses at least six times in Matthew 5. Hebrews either cites or alludes to Genesis several times in Hebrews 11, with three more citations in chapters 12–13. And James cites the Pentateuch three times in chapter 2, as does Peter in Acts 3, Paul in Romans 4, and Jesus in Matthew 4/Luke 4.[3] Both clusters and individual citations can be classified according to certain types of use, which I have named (1) covenantal-historical, (2) ecclesiastical, and (3) ethical. The first of these might also have been called "doctrinal," because doctrine is based on history and flows from the covenant, and the recounting of history is for doctrinal purposes.

Historical or Covenantal Use of the Pentateuch

By far the largest number of clusters (all but one) and most individual citations deal with the nature of God's relationship with his people. The citations give definition to and a historical context for what God did in Jesus Christ's death and resurrection, and for what he is doing in his people now. It is in this category that the New Testament conviction that the Old Testament is about Christ is most evident.

Very soon after the resurrection of Jesus, his disciples began to apply the principle of Jesus' hermeneutic and to read the Old Testament, including the Pentateuch, from a Christological perspective. Both Peter's speech at Solomon's porch (Ac 3) and Stephen's speech in Acts 7 focus on the eschatological "prophet like Moses," indicating that Jesus was this prophet and that he was *greater* than Moses (cf.

---

[3]The only books where several independent (nonclustered) Pentateuchal citations occur are 1 and 2 Corinthians and Hebrews.

Heb 3). Peter's audience probably included Sadducees, and thus the citations of Acts 3 are limited to the Pentateuch. He uses these passages Christologically, hinting first at the Resurrection by using the same texts that Jesus used in Matthew 22 (Ex 3:6, 15), then referring to Jesus as the Christ, who had been foretold through all the prophets (3:18), who was the prophet like Moses, whom Moses himself predicted, and disobedience to whom would mean being cut off from God's covenant people (Peter combines Dt 18:15, 19 with Lev 23:29). Finally Peter ties this all together as the fulfillment of the Abrahamic covenant (v. 25), the covenant foundational to the people of God, referring as well to the worldwide blessing that was intended by God in his calling of Abraham (citing Ge 22:18; 26:4).

Stephen's speech, which includes the largest number (thirteen) of Pentateuchal citations of any chapter in the New Testament, recounts a great deal of Israel's history. His sermon too leads up to the announcement of the "prophet like Moses" of Deuteronomy 18:15. This recounting of the history of God's previous dealings with his people is typical of covenant establishment and renewal. The Book of Deuteronomy, which as a whole is in the form of a covenant, starts out with a lengthy recounting of the historical background, with some emphasis on Israel's failure (Dt 1–3). Stephen in much the same way gives the covenantal background for his analysis of Israel's present rebellion and need.

The great apostle to the Gentiles also recognized this character of the Torah. The chapters that are arguably the most important in understanding Paul's theology are replete with Pentateuchal citations.

Galatians packs six Pentateuchal references into chapter 3 and has an additional reference in each of the two following chapters. The use is very similar to what takes place in Romans 4, but with greater stress on the problem of works-righteousness. Paul starts with Abraham (citing Ge 15:6, and also 12:3 [= 18:18]) and draws the conclusion that it is by faith that a relationship with God is formed and maintained, not by external obedience to rules. "Faith" is a covenant word; it implies commitment, trust, and faithfulness. So Paul is showing here the futility of a noncovenantal relation to the Old Testament law (i.e., a non-Christological relation).[4] Paul then goes on to show the ultimate relation of the law to Christ. The Torah functions in two ways in this passage: as establishing the covenant relationship and securing the promise (v. 8, citing Ge 12:3) and as indicating the curse that comes because of disobedience (v. 10, citing Dt 27:26 [Septuagint]—"cursed be everyone who does not do everything written in the law"). Both of these are fulfilled in Christ, who is the seed (singular) of Abraham (v. 16, citing Ge 12:7), and who takes the curse (v. 13). As Christ is the seed, the covenant applies supremely and first of all to him, with its curse as well as its blessing. Paul has Deuteronomy 21:23 give the Christological answer to the problem of Deuteronomy 27:26! But if one attempts to go to the law directly rather than through Christ by faith, if one attempts to bypass God's foundation of the promise covenant in Christ, then the law serves only to condemn.

Paul also refers to the Pentateuchal history in Galatians 4:21–31 (the contrast of Sarah and Hagar), again emphasizing the covenantal nature of the revelation in the Torah, and God's sovereignty in its application through Christ. Hagar represents the Sinaitic covenant, which brings slavery; Sarah the Abrahamic, which is freedom. This is a reversal of what most Jews would have thought, since Jews regarded the Sinaitic covenant as the path to freedom. But Paul's point is that the covenant promises were fulfilled through the son who came by way of God's sovereign intervention (Isaac), not by way of man's activity (Ishmael).

Romans represents a more deliberate construction of argument than Galatians, but some of it deals with similar matters. Chapter 4 deals with the question of Abraham's relation to law and faith and cites Genesis 15:6 ("Abram believed the LORD, and he credited it to him as righteousness") three times (Ro 4:3, 9, 22). Paul also refers to the preceding verse in Genesis (15:5) in 4:18, along with the promise of Genesis 17:5 that Abraham would be the father of

---

[4]The questions of whether "faith *of* Jesus Christ" in 3:16 is a subjective or objective genitive, and whether *pistis* means "belief" or "faithfulness," do not have to be answered here. Whichever way it is taken, the point is that it is through the covenant relationship with Jesus that a person is justified, whether that covenant relationship be viewed from the standpoint of its sovereign ratification and administration by Jesus, or from the standpoint of the commitment of the believer to that covenant.

many nations. This use of the Torah establishes both the covenantal nature of the Gospel and the precedence of this covenantal Gospel over the Mosaic legislation. We do not have to solve here the question of the degree of continuity of the Abrahamic covenant with the Mosaic; even those who make the sharpest distinction will have to admit that the Mosaic legislative covenant would be impossible without the more foundational covenant in Abraham, and those who draw the closest continuity will agree that the promise aspect is more fundamental than the legal application in Moses.

This covenantal concern also lies behind the discussion of national Israel in Romans 9–11. The burning question in these chapters is precisely God's faithfulness to his covenant. The Pentateuch is cited ten times in a more or less serial fashion[5] to demonstrate the sovereignty of God in his election and how that election relates to the people of Israel and the present church. God's covenant is sovereignly administered. As such he can include whomever he wants to include, even Gentiles.

Further, the right relationship with God (righteousness) is, as in Romans 4, a covenantal matter. Israel tried to obtain it by obeying the legal details, i.e., by treating the law not as a matter of covenant relationship established by God himself but as an economic transaction, with the Mosaic legislation as currency with which one could purchase the relationship.

Deuteronomy 32 (the Song of Moses) appears to be very important in Romans. The Song is Moses' farewell to his people, and in it he outlines certain aspects of God's intentions for Israel's future. Deuteronomy 32:21 is cited in Romans 10:19 as evidence that God's intention to use the acceptance of Gentiles as a goad to Israel has always been part of the plan. Similarly, 32:43 occurs in Romans 15:10 ("Rejoice, O Gentiles, with his people"). Finally, that citation of Deuteronomy 32:35 in Romans 12:19 ("It is mine to avenge. . .") occurs in a context where Paul is giving general ethical guidance. This citation should not be taken as a "contextless" citation; rather, the reference shows that there

---

[5]The progression from Romans 9:7 through 11:8 follows roughly a canonical order (Ge 21:12; 18:10; 25:23; Ex 33:19; 9:16; Lev 18:5; Dt 4:1; 30:12–14; 32:21; 29:4). Perhaps there is something like a historical prologue here, as in Stephen's speech in Acts 7.

is in Paul's mind a connection between the covenantal relation of God with his people (the main theme of Dt 32) and the ethical matter of not taking personal vengeance but allowing the Lord to judge his people.[6] Ethics *grows out of* God's covenant relationship with his people.

In 1 Corinthians 15:45 Paul cites Genesis 2:7 in order to draw the analogy between Adam and Christ. The covenantal representation of all men by Adam in Paul's understanding of Genesis is more thoroughly explicated in Romans 5 (which does not actually *quote* Genesis) but is certainly operative here as well.

Hebrews has some kind of reference to the Pentateuch in virtually every chapter, with explicit citations in all, except chapters 2, 3, and 5. Chapter 1, which shows the superiority of Christ over angels, cites the Septuagint version of Deuteronomy 32:43 ("Let all God's angels worship him"). It is debated whether Hebrews takes this as referring to Christ's first coming, second coming, or exaltation at his ascension, but in any case the "him" is certainly taken to be Christ. This is from the same verse that Paul cited in Romans 15:10 and marks the exaltation of God by the nations. Deuteronomy 32 is also cited in Hebrews 10:30 as part of the scriptural reminder that God will enforce his covenant. Both verses 35 and 36 of Deuteronomy 32 are cited, which shows the particularistic orientation of this "repaying"—the Lord will judge his people.

Most of the other Pentateuchal citations in Hebrews are related to Hebrews' concern with the superior covenant. Hebrews 6:13–14 cites Genesis 22:16–17 ("I will surely bless you") to emphasize the certainty of God's covenant promise. The discussion of the covenant contrast in chapters 8 and 9 cites Exodus twice: 25:40, where Moses is instructed to follow a heavenly pattern in the construction of the tabernacle, and 24:8, which specifies the use of blood in sanctifying the people. In chapter 11 there are several allusions to and three citations of Genesis (5:24; 21:12; 47:31), which trace the history of faith in God's promises, i.e., in the better covenant. Exodus 19:12–13 (a beast that touched the moun-

---

[6]Such a connection is also apparently seen by the author of Hebrews, who cites this same verse in Heb 10:30, climaxing his development of the implications of the covenant he has expounded in the preceding chapters.

tain was to be stoned) and Deuteronomy 9:19 (Moses said, "I feared the wrath and anger of the LORD") are presented as a contrast to the new covenant of grace in 12:20–21.

Hebrews 13:5 constitutes a simple hortatory use of Deuteronomy 31:6–8, where God promises, "I will never leave you nor forsake you." And Genesis 2:2 is cited in Hebrews 4:4 as part of the exegesis of Psalm 95:11, where the primary focus is on Israel's disobedience in the wilderness.

Hebrews thus cites the Pentateuch to present the contrast between the Mosaic covenant and the promised future covenant, to show the new covenant's superiority and greater ultimacy, to show the superiority of the new covenant's mediator, and to encourage and exhort his readers. Although Hebrews does not actually cite the Pentateuch in its description of the sacrificial system, the argument is certainly based on the information of the Pentateuch, focusing as it does, not on the temple, but on the tabernacle. That this tabernacle worship is treated as only a shadow of the heavenly realities involving Christ points again to Christ as the goal and purpose of the law.

This same conviction is operative in the Gospel of John, where John identifies Jesus as the antitypical Passover Lamb. Although the Gospel of John contains many allusions to the Old Testament, the only *citation* of the Pentateuch occurs in John 19:36, which cites Exodus 12:46 (Nu 9:12) to show the connection between Jesus Christ, none of whose bones were broken, and the Passover Lamb. The Torah, as much as the rest of the Old Testament, is understood as focusing on Christ first of all.[7]

There are a couple of additional cases in the New Testament where the Pentateuch is used to establish doctrine, but where covenant is not so much in the forefront, namely Matthew 22:32 (Mk 12:26; Lk 20:37) and Acts 3:13. Both of these passages refer to Exodus 3, where God declares himself as the God of Abraham, Isaac, and Jacob. Jesus deduces from this that there is a resurrection, since God is a God of the living, not the dead. In Acts 3 Peter cites this same verse in preparation for his declaration of Jesus' resurrection. As already noted, since Peter was addressing a

---

[7]This is very evident in the abundant allusions to Exodus in John, e.g., in the "Bread of Heaven" discourse in John 6.

group that probably included Sadducees, he used their canon, the Pentateuch, to demonstrate the doctrine they denied.

Even these have a covenantal basis, however, since God's relationship to Abraham, Isaac, and Jacob is covenantal, and it is this very strength of covenant relationship that seems to demand the necessity of a resurrection.

In summary, Torah, as much as the Old Testament as a whole, is understood not as a collection of rules but as a covenantal constitution, material that functions as an instrument of establishing relationship. Since Christ is the ultimate focus of that relationship, for only he is by nature a son, the covenant is ultimately about him and has him as its focus. But those who are united to him, both those who by faith were part of his people before his coming and those who by faith are now part of his people, share in the covenant by virtue of his identification with them.

Ecclesiastical Use of the Pentateuch

The second category is closely related to the first in that it flows from the covenantal nature of the Old Testament revelation. Paul and Peter share the conviction that since the Old Testament is about Christ, it is also therefore about the people who are in Christ, the church. This can be seen in Galatians 3, for example, where Paul makes a point of the word *seed* in the Abrahamic promise being singular and thus referring to Christ (vv. 16, 19). But Paul then goes on to indicate in verse 29, "If you belong to Christ, then you are Abraham's seed, and heirs according to the promise." This is why Paul can take a messianic prophecy like 2 Samuel 7:14 (cf. Heb 1:5) and apply it to believers (2Co 6:18). Similarly 1 Peter 2 speaks of the living Stone of the Old Testament prophecies (vv. 4, 6–8) and then says, "You also, like living stones, are being built into a spiritual house"(v. 5).[8]

Most applications of the Old Testament to believers, like most Christological applications, involve quotations from the

---

[8]The first epistle of John actually uses the term *anointing* of those who are covenantally united to the Anointed One; e.g., 1 John 2:27: "The anointing you received from him remains in you . . . his anointing teaches you about all things." (Cf. 1Jn 2:20; 2Co 1:21).

prophets or Psalms, but Paul, particularly in the Corinthian letters, uses also the Torah as a means for comprehending the present life of the church. Israel of the Pentateuch is paradigmatic for church life.

In 1 Corinthians 9:9 Paul cites Deuteronomy 25:4 ("Do not muzzle an ox while it is treading out the grain") and applies it *a minore ad maius* to the right of a minister of the gospel to be supported by the church. Paul's argument here is interesting in that he evidences a concern with the principle lying behind the law, not the specific literal case. In fact he even denies that the literal case is the one uppermost in God's mind. Paul's concern is exclusively with the application of the principle to the church. This use of Deuteronomy 25:4 recurs in 1 Timothy 5:18.

In 1 Corinthians 10:7 Paul quotes Exodus 32:6 ("The people sat down to eat and drink and got up to indulge in pagan revelry"). The context is very informative regarding Paul's understanding of the Torah. This Torah does not provide a covenantal context for Israel only; it does so also for the *church*. Indeed, the purpose of Israel's history being recorded in the Torah was to serve as "warnings for us, on whom the fulfillment of the ages has come" (10:11).

In 2 Corinthians 6:16 Paul declares that "we are the temple of the living God," and cites in proof three passages, all of which can be traced to more than one Old Testament location. The first of these ("I will live with them and walk among them, and I will be their God, and they will be my people") is first stated in Leviticus 26:12. Paul's principle is that God's dwelling among his people (v. 16) is foundational to their holiness (v. 17) and sonship (v. 18). This is the context of the citation of 2 Samuel 7:14 mentioned earlier, which Paul applies to the church. As the Old Testament applies to Christ, it applies to us by virtue of our being in Christ.

An application of the principle of 1 Corinthians 10 that Israel's history is for the church occurs in 2 Corinthians 8:15, where Paul refers to the situation of Israel in the wilderness (Ex 16:18) in informing his readers of the mutual dependence of the Corinthian Christians and those in Judea.

Ephesians 5:31 refers to Genesis 2:24 ("the two shall become one flesh") in relation to the marriage question, following the lead of Jesus (see below). Paul's use of it is interesting because he calls it a "mystery" and applies it to Christ and the church. Even institutions of the creation covenant have their utimate focus in Christ. In this sense everyone has *some* covenantal connection with God, because everyone shares in the covenant with Adam, and even with Christ, who is the mediator of all creation. Christ is head of his church, the firstborn from the dead (Col 1:18), and he is also the firstborn over all creation (v. 15). But God's particularistic covenant, which has to do with a *filial* relationship with God, pertains only to those who are particularistically "in Christ," who have "become one" with him.

In 2 Timothy 2:19 Paul refers to Numbers 16:5: "God's solid foundation stands firm, sealed with this inscription: 'The Lord knows those who are his.'" God's affirmation to Israel in Numbers is taken as a promise to the church, which serves as a seal of God's foundation. God's relationship with his people begins with his knowledge of them. The context in Numbers is interesting—it is where Moses tells Korah that God will indicate whom he has chosen and who is holy by allowing that person to approach him.

Paul is not unique in this use of the Old Testament law. Peter begins his call to ethics with a citation of Leviticus 19:2 in 1 Peter 1:16—"Be holy, because I am holy." First Peter has only two Pentateuchal references within its panoply of Old Testament citations. The first is foundational, however. "Be holy, because I am holy" is the basis for the entire ethical development of the epistle. Peter can quote the mandate to Israel and apply it to the church, not because the mandate applies to all mankind but because the church now stands as Israel. This is propounded in 2:5–10, which includes the collation of material from Exodus 19:6 and Isaiah 43:21 in 2:9: "You are a chosen people, a royal priesthood, a holy nation, a people belonging to God." As this whole section makes clear, especially verses 4–5, the flow of thought is that Old Testament Israel finds its fulfillment in Christ, and those who come to Christ become the new nation of God.

A special application of the Israel paradigm is that church discipline is informed by the Torah. Here is the only application of the Old Testament where sanctions come into view. The tone is set in Acts 3, where we noted Peter's reference to the "prophet like Moses" of Deuteronomy 18, disobedience to whom meant being "cut off." This is the basis for sanctions in the New Testament. The punishment of unrepentant wickedness in the church is removal from covenant fellowship. Two passages in particular are relevant and cite the Pentateuch.

In 1 Corinthians 5:13, in dealing with the incestuous relationship in the church of Corinth, Paul cites Deuteronomy 17:7: "You must purge the evil from among you." It is cited in summary of Paul's mandate that the church apply discipline not to outsiders but to those within the church. Paul applies the sanction to those who are in the church, not to the world at large.

In 2 Corinthians 13:1, where Paul is facing the possibility of coming to Corinth in judgment of the church, he cites Deuteronomy 19:15—"Every matter must be established by the testimony of two or three witnesses." The biblical rules of evidence pertain in church courts. Again, this is not to deny that the *principle* is applicable to secular courts, but Paul will have nothing to do with the secular courts and does not try to apply biblical law to them.

In summary, because the people of God are covenantally united to Christ, the spiritual description and function of Israel under the old covenant now pertain to the church. In particular, the spiritual sanction of being cut off from God's people now applies to the church, which is obligated to discipline its members, not by civil power but by removal from fellowship.

Ethical Use of the Pentateuch

The interrelationship of the covenantal-historical and ecclesiastical uses of the Old Testament should clue us in to the further interrelationship of the ethical uses of the Pentateuch.

Most of the strictly ethical references to the law occur on the lips of Jesus. In the synoptic gospels, all references to the Pentateuch except for Luke's explanation of the consecration in the temple (Luke 2:23) are found on the lips of Jesus. Most of these are in legal contexts:

1. Jesus cites Deuteronomy to refute the devil in Matthew 4 (Luke 4). It is interesting to note that Jesus refuses to allow a Christologically explicit text (Ps 91, cited by Satan)

to overturn an ethical principle (not testing God). By no means does the covenantal-Christological understanding of the Old Testament vitiate the ethical force of the law of God. Rather, it *focuses* it. Jesus, as the ultimate focus of the covenant, also sustained its maximal ethical demand.

2. Jesus contrasts the limiting casuistic approach to the Pentateuchal requirements with the extensive internal demands that are truly implied in them. The words "you have heard that it was said . . . but I tell you. . ." (Mt 5) serve not as a correction of the law, but as a correction of its interpretation and use. This kind of correction also prevails in Matthew 15:4 (Mk 7:10), where Jesus shows how the Pharisaic casuistry undermines the true intent of the law.

3. Perhaps something similar to this is also going on in Matthew 19:18–19 (Lk 18:20), the story of the rich young man who thinks he has kept the "second table" of the law (including the love of neighbor!) since his youth, but Jesus shows him that his heart is a different matter.

4. In Matthew 19:4–5 (Mk 10:6–8) Jesus cites Genesis 1:27 and 2:24 to give the true divine outlook on divorce, which had been lost sight of in the Jewish discussions of what constituted "grounds" for divorce. Again, Jesus is correcting the interpretation and use of the law, which is not intended to justify departures from God's character but to demand conformity to it.

5. When asked about the greatest commandment (Mt 22:37; Mk 12:29; Lk 10:27), Jesus cites Deuteronomy 6:5 and Leviticus 19:18, both stressing the inward heart nature of obedience that the law requires.

These are all in contexts where some question of the application or intent of the Torah is in view, and in each case Jesus drives his hearers beyond a superficial casuistic reading to grasp the divine intention. In none of these cases does the question of sanction or appropriate punishment arise, and in no instance does the issue of state involvement or enforcement appear. This is partially because the state was not a theocracy. More to the point perhaps is that *Jesus does not seem to be concerned with the civil application or civil enforcement of the Mosaic legislation.*

The textually dubious incident of the woman caught in adultery (Jn 8) may yet be an authentic tradition; here Jesus points away from the law's sanction to the relationship to God. The state is not in view, except perhaps as part of the box into which Jesus' questioners were trying to put him, but his approach to Old Testament sanctions is instructive. Where legal questions arise, he is concerned with the law's internal application, not its external enforcement.

Other New Testament ethical discussions that include references to the Torah follow lines similar to these set forth by Jesus. Most frequently Leviticus 19:18 ("Love your neighbor") is presented as encapsulating the intent of the law with respect to human interactions (Ro 13:9; Gal 5:14; Jas 2:8). By its very nature, such law is not something the civil authority, even in a theocracy, could enforce.

In addition to these three, Romans 7:7; 1 Corinthians 6:16; Ephesians 6:2–3; and James 2 make ethical citations of the Pentateuch.

In Romans 7:7 the command Paul singles out as having produced the awareness of sin is "Do not covet," an internal matter.

In 1 Corinthians 6:16 Paul refers to Genesis 2:24 to demonstrate the seriousness of sexual relations.

Ephesians 6:2–3 mentions the fifth commandment as the basis for Christian children's obeying their parents (as well as for other relationships having to do with authority structures). This too has a covenantal aspect, for it is identified as the first command with a promise. This promise was "so that you may live long in the land the LORD your God is giving you." The reference to the Abrahamic covenantal promise in Genesis is clear. It is equally clear that Paul was not referring to the literal acquisition of the land. The conclusion must be that Paul was intimating a connection between the obedience of children (a Christian ethic) and the covenantal promises to Abraham, which are now being fulfilled in the church.

James 2:11 refers to the sixth and seventh commandments as coming from the same God, demonstrating that a violation of a part of the law is a violation of the whole law. But the more interesting citation is in verse 23, where James refers to Genesis 15:6, the very passage so central to Paul in his focus on Abraham as the paradigm for justification by faith. James also uses Abraham as a paradigm, to show that a true faith that justifies is one that issues in obedience.[9] Although this quotation does not constitute an ethical application of an Old Testament mandate, it does point to the fact that there is an inseparability to the covenantal foundations in the sovereign purpose of God and the obedience of those included in the covenant. True commitment to the covenant (faith) implies covenant faithfulness (obedience).

In summary, the most basic use of the Pentateuch in the New Testament is to establish the covenantal nature of the gospel. Since the law is covenantal, it is the inward obedience of the heart stemming from the relationship to God that determines the New Testament's positive use of the law. The ecclesiastical and ethical applications of the law to the church all flow from this covenantal basis, inasmuch as the only contact between the Gentile church and the law of Moses is through Christ, the covenant mediator.

Perhaps we could have divided these into texts where ethics is uppermost and texts where doctrine is uppermost. But this would obscure the fact that ethics and doctrine are so closely related in the New Testament that the one always implies the other. What should be apparent from these texts is (1) that the ethical use of the Pentateuch is dependent on its covenantal fulfillment in Christ and (2) that the application of the law to believers—as to who they are (ecclesiology), what they are to believe (doctrine), and how they should live (ethics)—is predicated on the grounds of their covenantal identification with Christ. Therefore the law is applied *only* to believers, and the only sanction ever in view is removal from fellowship.

THE THREE ASPECTS OF THE LAW

All Reformed Christians agree that the Old Testament law applies to believers, because it applied to Christ. But all

---

[9]Certainly James was aware that Abraham's belief in God and consequent justification (Ge 15) *preceded* his obedience in offering Isaac (Ge 22). His point is simply that Abraham's faith was not an idle one. There is thus no conflict with Paul, who in 1 Corinthians 6:9–10 informs us that "neither the sexually immoral nor idolaters nor adulterers nor male prostitutes nor homosexual offenders nor thieves nor the greedy nor drunkards nor slanderers nor swindlers will inherit the kingdom of God."

also agree that the sacrificial cultic mandates, which point to Christ's once-for-all death, apply to believers only indirectly or spiritually, as elucidating the meaning of Christ's death and our own physical and spiritual death in Christ. The law provides an understanding of the nature of sin and the nature of God's dealing with it, along with an understanding of the covenant and its solemnity and significance; i.e., it teaches doctrine. But no one supposes that believers should engage in sacrifices, not only because we have no tabernacle or temple but also because the whole system was fulfilled in Christ. On the other hand, all Reformed Christians also agree that the moral principles set forth in the law reflect the very character of God and thus provide the Christian with a clear and unambiguous indication of the ethical behavior God expects of his people.

This recognition of the nonapplication of sacrificial mandates in the church, coupled with a recognition of the continued importance of the moral principles, has resulted in a traditional perception of the law as having three aspects—a moral, a cultic or sacrificial, and a civil. These distinctions may not be too helpful in an initial examination of the New Testament; the New Testament does not explicitly make such distinctions. But the distinctions are often used to delineate the problem with respect to the theonomic controversy, which focuses on the question of the applicability of the civil aspect of the law. It is important to bear in mind, however, that in the New Testament *all* a the law apply only to believers and only through the mediation of Christ. This is because all aspects of the law are understood *covenantally*.

Our examination of New Testament citations has shown that the new covenant application of the moral, civil, and cultic aspects of the law is in terms of ethics, discipline, and doctrine of the church. Not once in the New Testament is the civil aspect of the Old Testament law applied to the civil authority as an ideal. So far as I can determine, there are in the New Testament only two citations that make reference to civil aspects of the law. The first of these is Jesus' dealing with the question of divorce (Mt 19 and parallels, and Mt 5), where reference is made to the certificate that Moses mandated. This was a civil matter, but it was being used to infer that there were moral grounds for divorce. Jesus corrects this by showing that the moral principle is derived from Genesis 2 and that the certificate was *only* a civil matter. There is little interest in the civil matter as such.

The second is the mention that the testimony of two or three witnesses is necessary in the case of Paul's having to judge the church in Corinth (2Co 13:1). As we have seen, there is indication elsewhere (e.g., 1Co 5; 2Co 10:6) that Paul sees some application of civil law as a paradigm for discipline within the church, but there is here of course no wielding of civil power.

On the other hand, where the New Testament does touch on the relationship of Christians with the state, no reference is made to the Old Testament law (Mt 22:17; Ro 13; 1Pe 2).

THE PURPOSE OF LAW

The purpose of the law, like that of all Scripture, is to communicate the knowledge of God and institute and maintain a relationship with him. This includes knowledge of his character and knowledge of his plan. The covenant contains both; God's character and his plan are bound up together. Therefore there is no easy division between moral, civil, and ceremonial law, or even between law, prophecy, praise, history, and wisdom, because they are all bound together. The Old Testament as a whole must be understood as it is in the New Testament, as focused on Christ.

Therefore the New Testament's approach to the Old Testament is not an attempt to readapt or contemporize case law, in the way the Rabbis did. The law, or rather the Old Testament as an entirety, is focused on Christ, and *through him* it becomes applicable to believers. Thus case law is not *directly* applicable, even to believers; it is applicable only as a working out of God's moral principles, an expression of God's character revealed in Christ.

SANCTIONS AND FALSE GODS

The theonomic controversy frequently swirls around two practical questions, that of whether the state should enforce true religion (as the original Westminster Confession stated) and that of the applicability of the Torah's prescribed negative sanctions (punishments).

Regarding the first question, it is perhaps worth noting that Paul never urges people to break the *physical* idols of non-Christians, as a direct application of Old Testament civil law would have us do. We are rather to tear down the *intellectual* foundations, "demolishing *arguments* and every pretension that sets itself up against the knowledge of God, taking every *thought* captive to make it obedient to Christ" (2Co 10:5). With all the New Testament's emphasis on the *internality* of true religion, it would be odd indeed to find a New Testament writer suggesting that an external imposition of religion would accomplish anything.

The covenantal Christological approach understands the sanctions as applicable to Christ. He became the curse for us (Gal 3:12–13) and so his death was an enactment of the ultimate sanction for all law violation. As we have noted, the New Testament gives no indication of the law's sanctions as applicable to any except Christ and, through him, his people. But for those who are in Christ the ultimate sanction has already been delivered. There may indeed be punishment for people *within the church* (2Co 10:6), but this does not involve civil authority or those outside the church (1Co 5:12), and its only form is various degrees of removal from fellowship (being "cut off" from the people).

It is true that God does maintain a covenant relation with all mankind in Adam, but God's covenant with mankind as a whole is very general. It really consists of one primary mandate: submit to divine sovereignty. The only sanction applicable is death, which is administered by God himself. Perhaps the Noahic covenant (Ge 9:1–17; cf. esp. vv. 9–10) applies to the world at large. But here the agency of man in applying a sanction is invoked only with regard to murder. This means that the only sanction required of all civil government by God's covenant with all mankind is the death penalty for murder.

THE NEW TESTAMENT—OUR CHURCH

The New Testament situation is our own: the church is not the state; a distinction must be made between our citizenships. The Old Testament situation is unlike our own in that the church was the state, and the heavenly realities were depicted only in shadows in the physical life of national

Israel. Therefore the way the New Testament applies the Old Testament to the state is the way we ought to do it. That is, it does not, so we should not.

Christians desire just laws, and in a civil situation where a Christian has some civil power he ought to argue for just laws, laws that will reflect the character of God and his demand that we love our neighbor. But to apply *directly* any part of the law, moral or ceremonial as well as civil, to the non-Christian world at large, or to a society other than the church, is to treat the Old Testament *non*-Christologically, as divorced from its covenantal context. This is not to say that Old Testament law does not apply to unbelievers, but only that it does so very indirectly, inasmuch as it is an expression of the moral character of God, and man falls short of this demanded perfection. The explicit sanctions of Old Testament civil law thus apply only insofar as they are an underlining of God's holiness. Their specific implementation is not directly applicable any more than are the dietary proscriptions or the division of the land. Unbelievers die, not because of a negative relation to the Mosaic law, but because of their general position of being in Adam and thus in rebellion against God (Ro 5). It is in Adam that people die, not in Moses.

CONCLUSION

The Bible says that Christians are strangers and sojourners (Heb 11:13; 1Pe 2:11). It reminds us that this earth is not our home; our faith is that of Abraham who looked forward to a city whose builder is God. This all stems from the covenantal understanding of the Pentateuch as applied through Christ to the church, and it points away from any expectation of civil authority implementing the covenantal obligations. I fear that the theonomists are spending a great deal of effort on a venture that would, if successful, only serve to draw Christians away from God's kingdom, since the contrast between the world and God's kingdom would then be blurred.

I realize this may sound to those of theonomic persuasion like the kind of isolationism that characterized fundamentalism for many years. I am not, however, advocating a withdrawal from civil matters. Christians need to seek to clarify the ethical principles lying behind God's administration of his people under the old covenant and to strive to see the righteousness represented in those principles implemented. But neither should we seek to make the state into the church or vice versa, or expect the state to secure righteousness on earth.

Recently some theonomists have taken to heart the statement of 1 Peter that "judgment begins with the house of God," and have consequently focused their attentions on applying the law of God to his people. This is a promising development because it brings the Old Testament back into its proper covenantal context. It also may well help to stem the tide of antinomianism and lack of fear of God which pervades the *church* in our time. It is to his people that God says, "Be holy, because I am holy."

Chapter Seven

Is the Law Against the Promises? The Significance of Galatians 3:21 for Covenant Continuity

Moisés Silva

Moisés Silva

Moisés Silva (Ph.D., University of Manchester) is Professor of New Testament at Westminster Theological Seminary (Philadelphia). With other degrees from Bob Jones University and Westminster Theological Seminary, he has taught at Westmont College, Fuller Theological Seminary, and Trinity Evangelical Divinity School, and at Westminster since 1978. He is the author of *New Testament Survey*, *Biblical Words and Their Meaning*, *Philippians* (Wycliffe Exegetical Commentary Series), *Has the Church Misread the Bible?* (Foundations of Contemporary Interpretation Series), and *God, Language, and Scripture* (Foundations of Contemporary Interpretation Series).

Chapter Seven

Is the Law Against the Promises? The Significance of Galatians 3:21 for Covenant Continuity

The current debates on theonomy and related movements can be viewed—indeed *must* be viewed—as part of a much larger issue: What is the relationship between the old and the new covenant? Does the newness of the gospel suggest a breach between it and the Sinaitic covenant? Or to use Paul's provocative language in Galatians, "Is the law opposed to the promises?" That the question should occur at all to the apostle is itself a significant clue. Clearly, Paul recognized that the two covenants represented two *distinct* administrations, and no one is likely to argue that they were identical in character or function.

Unfortunately, any attempt to define the relationship more precisely runs against an apparent ambiguity in the biblical data. Paul, in particular, can formulate the relationship in a sharply antithetical style, as in Galatians 3:12, "the law is not based on faith" (*ho nomos ouk estin ek pisteōs*). On the other hand, his frequent appeals to the Old Testament itself in support of his gospel message, to say nothing of his positive comments on the law in several passages, create the presumption that the old covenant is of a piece with the new.

As is well known, the Reformers' concern with the doctrine of justification by faith alone led some groups to emphasize the differences between the two covenants. The

Lutheran tradition in particular has consistently held up the
law-grace contrast as one of its most distinctive teachings.
From a different perspective, modern dispensationalism too
has been zealous to stress the antithesis between the Mosaic
administration and the "age of grace."

The Reformed tradition, in contrast, has been concerned
to minimize the antithetical elements, to assert the coherence
of God's gracious provisions in both dispensations, and to
stress the continuing validity of God's law for the Christian.
Some writers, such as John Murray, have sought to highlight
the unity among the various covenants beyond what one
finds in the standard Reformed formulations.[1] Those sympathetic to the theonomist movement would want to go even
beyond Murray by drawing out in considerably greater detail
the significance of the whole Mosaic legislation for the
church today.[2]

To be sure, one very important strand in the Reformed
tradition has sought to guard carefully the distinctions
beween law and promise. Meredith G. Kline, for example,
focuses on Galatians 3 and states, "Paul found the difference
between two of the Old Testament covenants to be so radical
that he felt obliged to defend the thesis that the one did not
annul the other (Gal 3:15ff.)."[3] The reason for such a radical
assessment, Kline suggests, is that in Paul's view "the
Sinaitic Covenant had been ratified by human oath alone.
Promise was present as well as law in this covenant but it

---

[1]See especially Murray's article, "The Adamic Administration," published
in his *Collected Writings*, vol. 2 (Carlisle, Pa.: Banner of Truth, 1977). For a
critique of Murray, cf. Mark W. Karlberg, "Reformed Interpretation of the
Mosaic Covenant," *Westminster Theological Journal* 43 (1980): 1–57.

[2]In his book *Theonomy in Christian Ethics* (Nutley, N.J.: Craig, 1977), Greg
L. Bahnsen puts it succinctly: "The Christian is obligated to keep the whole
law of God as a pattern of sanctification and . . . this law is to be enforced by
the civil magistrate where and how the stipulations of God so designate"
(p. 34).

[3]Meredith G. Kline, *By Oath Consigned: A Reinterpretation of the Covenant
Signs of Circumcision and Baptism* (Grand Rapids: Eerdmans, 1968), 22. He
continues, "The Sinaitic administration, called 'covenant' in the Old
Testament, Paul interpreted as *in itself* a dispensation of the kingdom
inheritance quite opposite in principle to inheritance by guaranteed promise:
'For if the inheritance is by law, it is no longer by promise' and 'the law is
not of faith; but, He that doeth them shall live in them' (Gal 3:18a, RSV, and
v. 12, ASV; cf. Lev 18:5)."

was only the law that had been covenantally solemnized." In any case, "the unquestionable fact emerges in Galatians 3 that Paul saw in the Old Testament alongside the covenant of promise another covenant which was so far from being an administration of promise as to raise the urgent question whether it did not abrogate the promise."[4]

Kline's incisive way of putting the question will help to place the concerns of the present chapter in proper focus. What is in fact the difference that Paul sees between the two covenants? Does the difference arise out of the very character of these covenants or out of the situation in which Paul writes his epistle? Considering the logic of the apostle's argument in Galatians 3, what then is the significance of the rhetorical question in verse 21?

ASSUMPTIONS

Any attempt to expound Paul's argument in this remarkable passage is greatly complicated by the bewildering variety of approaches to the subject. Pauline scholarship, of course, has always been preoccupied with the apostle's statements regarding the law, but the past decade or two have witnessed a staggering number of publications that, while seeking to guide the reader out of the exegetical maze, themselves become additional labyrinthine passageways— not seldom in the form of blind alleys. It would be foolhardy to ignore the substantive contributions made by modern scholarship, but there can be no question in this brief article of surveying the whole field or of attempting to engage every pertinent proposal.[5] The reader, therefore, is entitled to know that I am working with four major assumptions. They are the following:

1. Being committed to the full authority of Scripture, I cannot accept the common view that Paul's statements about the law contain irreconcilable elements. Even apart from the doctrine of inspiration, I would hold to the axiom that formal contradictions (i.e., apparent discrepancies) by *any* writer

---

[4]Ibid., 24.

[5]For a superb review of the options, see Stephen Westerholm, *Israel's Law and the Church's Faith: Paul and His Recent Interpreters* (Grand Rapids: Eerdmans, 1988); cf. my review of this book in *WTJ* 51 (1989): 174–77.

should be interpreted, whenever possible, as materially consistent—especially if they involve a fundamental question, such as the law is for Paul. One must of course avoid easy, artificial solutions and recognize that certain problems may lie beyond our ability to solve them. Moreover, we should resist the temptation to think that consistency equals flat uniformity. Widely differing contexts may well have led the apostle to bring out significantly different strands in his teaching. Nevertheless, I approach the text assuming that the apostle is consistent with himself and that parallels from his other letters may legitimately be brought to bear on the interpretation of Galatians.[6]

2. I assume the basic Reformed understanding that, while Christ came to fulfill the law and his death abrogated the Jewish sacrificial system in particular, there is biblical warrant for distinguishing ceremonial from moral elements in that law and that the moral precepts (summarized preeminently in the Decalogue) continue to provide divine guidance and must be obeyed. Within such parameters, as we have already noted, Reformed theologians have debated the precise relationship between the Mosaic law and the Gospel, between the binding nature of divine covenants and the gracious character of God's promises. The present article will address a few of those areas of debate, but no attempt will be made to demonstrate the more basic principles on which wide agreement exists among Reformed scholars.

3. Similarly, this chapter assumes the classic Protestant understanding of Galatians and its teaching of justification by faith. Recent scholarship has challenged this interpretation from various angles, arguing that Luther read his introspective concerns into the text,[7] or that the traditional opposition between Jewish "legalism" and Paul's doctrine of justification is a modern construct,[8] or that Paul's focus is not

---

[6]I have touched on this question elsewhere; cf. my review article, "Betz and Bruce on Galatians," *WTJ* 45 (1983): 371–85, esp. 383.

[7]Krister Stendahl, "The Apostle Paul and the Introspective Conscience of the West," *Harvard Theological Review* 56 (1963): 199–215. For an important critique of Stendahl's position see John M. Espy, "Paul's 'Robust Conscience' Re-examined," *New Testament Studies* 31 (1985): 161–88.

[8]Cf. E. P. Sanders, *Paul, the Law, and the Jewish People* (Philadelphia: Fortress, 1983). Note the critiques by Thomas R. Schreiner, "Paul and Perfect Obedience to the Law," *WTJ* 47 (1985): 245–78, and especially Robert

so much on our faith but on Christ's faith(fulness),[9] and so on. No doubt, the Reformers' exegesis of Galatians 3 can stand some nuancing—such as a greater appreciation for Paul's overarching concern with Abrahamic sonship—but their basic insight is, to my mind, irreproachable.

4. Finally, I accept the propriety—indeed the necessity—of tying our exegesis to the historical context of the passages being examined. The writing we refer to as Galatians did not arise from speculative thought in a private study but from urgent problems faced by a living church. Because our information about that living context derives largely from the text itself, we cannot avoid a certain amount of "mirror reading," though this approach has come under criticism in recent years.[10] Since Galatians states explicitly and unambiguously that the writing of the letter was made necessary by certain troublemakers in the churches being addressed (Gal 1:6–7; 5:7–12), we surely must avoid interpreting Paul's words in isolation from that historical reality.

THE FUNCTION OF GALATIANS 3:21

Given those assumptions, I wish to argue that Galatians 3:21 deserves a great deal more attention than it has received. The significance of this verse lies not only in the key it provides for sorting out the argument developed by Paul in this chapter but also in its implications for our understanding of the apostle's thought as a whole.

H. Gundry, "Grace, Works, and Staying Saved in Paul," *Biblica* 66 (1985): 1–38.

[9]Note Richard B. Hays, *The Faith of Jesus Christ: An Investigation of the Narrative Substructure of Galatians 3:1–4:11*, Society of Biblical Literature Dissertation Series, No. 56 (Chico, Calif.: Scholars, 1983), and my critique in *Philippians*, Wycliffe Exegetical Commentary(Chicago: Moody, 1988), 186–87.

[10]See especially George Lyons, *Pauline Autobiography: Toward a New Understanding*, Society of Biblical Literature Dissertation Series, No. 73 (Atlanta: Scholars, 1985), who wishes to understand the peculiarities of Galatians as rhetorically motivated. Fatal to Lyons' thesis, however, is the fact that he gives no attention at all to the obvious presence of opponents in Galatia. For some believers, incidentally, an emphasis on the epistle's historical setting is suspect in that it appears to hand over the interpretation of Scripture to the scholar; I deny this inference and would argue rather that the alternative is to hand it over to the arbitrary whim of the reader.

This verse is translated smoothly and accurately by the NIV: "Is the law, therefore, opposed to the promises of God? Absolutely not! For if a law had been given that could impart life, then righteousness would certainly have come by the law." What needs emphasis is that the apostle here encapsulates his assessment of the law by specifying in what respects the law may be viewed positively and in what respects negatively. The positive element can be readily inferred from Paul's forceful exclamation (*mē genoito*): the law is harmonious with God's saving purposes, that is, with the Abrahamic promise. The negative element is expressed by a contrary-to-fact conditional sentence that in effect constitutes a twofold denial: (1) the law cannot impart life (*zōopoiēsai*)—it certainly was not given (*edothē*) for that purpose; and (2) righteousness is not by the law (*ek nomou*). We may argue that nowhere else does Paul specify quite so clearly and crisply just what it is about the law that draws his polemical remarks.

Note, however, the logical function of this conditional sentence, which is introduced by a causal conjunction (*gar*, "for"): it plainly sets forth the *reason* for Paul's emphatic assurance that the law is not opposed to the promises. And this reason takes the form of pointing out *under what conditions* the law would have to be regarded as being opposed to the promises, namely, if righteousness came by the law. If the law were a source of righteousness (i.e., if it could impart life), then it would certainly be in competition with the promises, and a fundamental antithesis would exist between the two. But in point of fact the law cannot impart life. God did not give the Israelites a law that, by providing an alternate source of righteousness, thwarted the promise. Quite the contrary, the law *aided* the promise by shutting, imprisoning, locking up everyone under sin (vv. 22–23).

Paul's use of the words "law" (*nomos*), "could" (*dynamenos*, lit. "being able"), and "life" (in *zōopoiēsai*, "to make alive") in close connection with each other is strongly reminiscent of Romans 8:2–3:

> . . .through Christ Jesus the law of the Spirit of life [*ho nomos tou pneumatos tēs zōes*] set me free from the law of sin and death. For what the law was powerless to do [*to gar adynaton tou nomou*] in that it was weakened by the sinful

nature [*en hō esthēnei dia tēs sarkos*], God did by sending his own Son in the likeness of sinful man to be a sin offering.

The parallel is not merely lexical but substantive. Two principles are contrasted in the Romans passage: one is the Mosaic law, which is closely associated with sin, as it is in Galatians 3:22–23; the other is the life-giving principle of the Spirit, which corresponds to the saving promise of Galatians 3:14 (*tēn epangelian tou pneumatos*).[11]

Moreover, Romans 8:3 makes explicit what is only implicit in the Galatians passage: the weakness of the flesh is the obstacle that makes the law impotent for salvation. People are dead in their trespasses and sins, and so the commandments do not avail—what we need is life. Apart from spiritual life, we cannot do what is written in the Book of the Law and so we come under a curse. This point needs to be stressed, since a few writers have denied that the universality of sin plays a role in Paul's argument in Galatians 3:10.[12]

---

[11]The precise reference of *tou nomou tēs hamartias kai tou thanatou* in Romans 8:2 is debated by scholars. For the view that Paul has in mind the Mosaic law, see C. K. Barrett, *A Commentary on the Epistle to the Romans*, Harper's New Testament Commentaries (New York: Harper & Row, 1957). One could argue that *nomos* in this phrase merely refers to the "principle" of sin described in the previous chapter. At the very least, however, Paul must be using a word play to communicate one of his more fundamental theological convictions, namely, that the commandment provides the occasion for sin and issues in death (Ro 7:8–11), so that the law may be regarded as the power of sin (1Co 15:56).

[12]Most commentators recognize that Galatians 3:10 contains an implied premise. The explicit premise is the quotation from Dt 27:26: "Cursed is everyone who does not continue to do everything written in the Book of the Law." The implied premise is that no one perseveres in doing everything written in the law. The conclusion is then: "All who rely on observing the law [*hosoi ex ergōn nomou eisin*] are under a curse." Building on some suggestions by R. Bring, Daniel P. Fuller has argued that the implied premise is different, namely, "Anyone wishing to earn his salvation through his works is trying to bribe God, an offense that deserves a curse" (see his book *Gospel and Law: Contrast or Continuum* [Grand Rapids: Eerdmans, 1980], 87–88; for a critique, see the review of Fuller by Douglas J. Moo in *Trinity Journal* 3 NS [1982]: 99–103). Strangely, Fuller's main argument against the traditional view is that such a view needs to add a proposition (regarding the universality of sin) to the Galatians text. Fuller's solution, however, entails adding *two* propositions to Paul's argument: (1) works' salvation is bribery; (2) people who bribe are under a curse. And while the implied premise required by the traditional interpretation is fundamental for Paul's

THE RELEVANCE OF GALATIANS 3:18

The contrary-to-fact conditional clause of Galatians 3:21 is paralleled in substance (though not formally in its syntax) by verse 18, "For if the inheritance depends on the law [*ek nomou*], then it no longer depends on a promise [*ex epangelias*]." What verse 21 describes as righteousness and life, verse 18 expresses with the term "inheritance" (*klēronomia*; cf. the ringing affirmation of verse 29 that Christians are *klēronomoi* according to the promise). The fact that in verse 18 Paul uses what some grammarians call a "real" condition must not mislead us into thinking that the apostle accepts the reality of the condition in view: the very point of the verse is that inheritance *cannot* depend on the law, else the promise would be annulled (v. 17, *eis to katargēsai tēn epangelian*).[13]

We must come to grips with this correspondence between verses 18 and 21. Unless we think that the apostle could have contradicted himself blatantly in the space of a few verses, we must recognize that verse 21 is a more specific restatement of the argument of verse 18. The only alternative left would be to argue that the subject matter of these two verses is quite different—hardly a credible solution.

If my understanding of the argument is correct, then it appears that we cannot really appeal to verse 18 in support of the contention that Paul sees a "radical opposition of the law covenant of Sinai to the principle of inheritance by promise."[14] In fact, it can plausibly be argued that the very burden of the passage is to deny any such opposition. Kline's reading of Galatians 3 appears to be that *Paul's own view* of

theology and explicit elsewhere in his writings, nowhere does Paul (or any other Jewish writer, to my knowledge) actually describe legalism as bribery.

[13]It is true that if a speaker or writer believes the condition is fulfilled he is likely to use a real or first-class conditional clause, but the inverse does not follow. Satan may well have known that Jesus is the Son of God, but that fact cannot be inferred (contrary to a common argument) from the use of a first-class condition in Matthew 4:3. Note in particular that Paul uses the same syntactical construction in places where he clearly views the condition as impossible (Gal 2:21; 1Co 15:12–19, 29–34). Cf. also Michael Winger, "Unreal Conditions in the Letters of Paul," *Journal of Biblical Literature* 105 (1986): 110–12.

[14]This quotation comes from Kline, *By Oath Consigned*, 23. The appeal to Galatians 3:18 is on p. 22.

the opposition between law and promise raised "the urgent question" of whether the one annulled the other. But here precisely is where we must inquire into the historical context that called forth the epistle to the Galatians, since the polemic tone of the passage makes plain that Paul is responding to accusations from his Judaizing opponents.

Reconstructing the Judaizers' argument calls for a cautious approach. Having no direct access to what Paul's opponents were saying in Galatia, we are forced to read between the lines, and such a technique can become progressively treacherous as we move further and further away from what the text actually says. But it is no less dangerous to interpret Paul in a vacuum, and the effort must be made to identify those elements to which he is responding.

We could hardly be accused of falling into speculation, for instance, if we should argue that *the Judaizers insisted on the compatibility between the Abrahamic and Sinaitic covenants.* This rather obvious point, however, has seldom affected our reading of Galatians 3 the way it ought to. When we read in verse 17 that the law "does not set aside the covenant previously established by God," we tend to deduce (perhaps unconsciously) that, according to the Judaizers, the Sinaitic administration did indeed set aside the Abrahamic promise and that Paul is therefore refuting an explicit Judaizing proposition.

But such an interpretation is untenable. We have no evidence whatever that the Judaizers argued for the annulment or even the alteration of the Abrahamic covenant. Quite to the contrary. Every indication we have—considering the thrust of the argument in Galatians 3:7, 29, as well as Romans 4:9–17—is that the Judaizers wanted the Gentiles to participate in the Abrahamic inheritance. This blessing could be received, in their understanding, only by the Gentiles' submitting to circumcision and thus becoming Jews (cf. Ac 15:1, 5). Paul's insistence that Gentile Christians must not be circumcised, and that on the grounds that the inheritance was based on the promise to Abraham, is in fact what raised a question regarding the compatibility between the two covenants![15]

We may therefore infer, with only a modest amount of speculation, that this issue became a point of controversy in Galatia. If so, the Judaizing forces may well have argued that *Paul* was the one guilty of pitting the two covenants against each other, that his theological use of the Abrahamic promise involved a nullification of the Mosaic law (an inference explicitly denied by him in Ro 3:31), and that his polemic undermined the unity of God's administration. To put matters differently, we may say that Paul is on the defensive as he writes chapter 3 of Galatians.

The apostle, however, proceeds to defend his position by taking the offensive: it is the Judaizers who are guilty of opposing law and promise! By failing to understand the gracious character of the Abrahamic promise, the Jews in general and the Judaizers in particular have raised law keeping to a level that it was never intended to occupy. By failing to grant to believing Gentiles the Abrahamic inheritance, it is the Judaizers who treat the Sinaitic covenant as an unlawful addition to the previous covenant. Though it is certainly not their avowed intention, they thereby set aside (*akuroō*) and do away with (*katargeō*) the promise (v. 17).

We are now in a better position to understand the logical function of verse 18, which is introduced with the conjunction *gar* ("for"). What is the connection between verses 17 and 18? More specifically, what does verse 18 explain or give the reason for? It seems remarkable that most commentators have not pointed out the problem raised by Paul's implied accusation in verse 17, namely, that according to the

---

[15]Similarly, it was *Paul's* emphasis on grace that raised the question whether Christians may continue in sin (Ro 6:1); it was *Paul's* preaching of a message rejected by Jews that raised the question whether God's word had failed (9:6); and so on. Cf. Hans Dieter Betz, *Galatians: A Commentary on Paul's Letter to the Churches in Galatia* (Hermeneia; Philadelphia: Fortress, 1979), 174, on Galatians 3:21: "It may be that this argument is directed against accusations made by opponents against the Apostle. These accusations would object to Paul's construct of a total dualism between the Torah of Moses and the promise to Abraham. Paul defends himself by an attack: a contradiction between the Torah of Moses and the promise to Abraham can be perceived only if the Torah retains its traditional Jewish role. This is done by his opponents, not by Paul himself. If, therefore, there is such an objection against him, it is based upon a misunderstanding of his theology."

Judaizers the law does away with the promise. Only Betz appears to focus on the precise issue: "Who could think of such an absurd possibility?"[16]

Since the Judaizers would certainly have denied that their teaching destroyed the Abrahamic covenant, the implied charge of verse 17 needs demonstration. In providing the necessary proof, Paul reveals what is the basic point in the dispute with these words: "If the inheritance depends on the law" (*ei ek nomou hē klēronomia*). Paul has assumed throughout his argument that this principle constitutes the Judaizing premise, and that is precisely the point that the apostle will not concede.

Why not? Because such a premise is in complete antithesis with the scriptural principle (supported earlier by Hab 2:4) that the inheritance "depends on a promise" (*ex epangelias*). Note again that the antithesis is not between law and promise merely, but rather between inheritance-by-law and inheritance-by-promise (the preposition *ek* is critical). It is not the law in some undifferentiated sense that Paul inveighs against but the law as life-giving source, to use the language of verse 21. Since the two principles are absolutely antithetical, it follows that the inheritance must come either by promise or by law, not by both. And since the apostle has already proved that it comes by promise, then it certainly cannot come by law. The conclusion of verse 18 is resounding: *tō de Abraam di' epangelias kecharistai ho theos*, "but God in his grace gave it to Abraham through a promise."

THE PROBLEM OF GALATIANS 3:12

One serious and well-known exegetical problem remains: the meaning of verse 12: "The law is not based on faith [*ek pisteōs*]; on the contrary, 'The man who does these things will live by them [*zēsetai en autois*].' " Paul here quotes Leviticus 18:5 and sets it in antithesis to Habakkuk 2:4 (quoted in the previous verse). Does the apostle regard these two passages of Scripture as setting forth different and mutually exclusive principles of justification? One more look at verse 21 may help us treat this problem.

Paul's explicit denial in verse 21 that the law produces

---

[16]Ibid., 158.

life (*zōopoiēsai*) seems at first blush to be a blatant contradiction of the Leviticus 18:5 promise (*zēsetai en autois*). Moreover, it is not at all clear that Leviticus 18:5, in its context, sets forth a legalistic way of righteousness. Many expositors would want to argue that the verse is a gracious promise, namely, the path of obedience is a path of life, since God's command (= his word) is life. And as if to complicate matters, Paul himself can describe the law as *hē entolē hē eis zōēn*, lit., "the commandment unto life" (Ro 7:10 [literal trans.]; cf. in verse 14 the use of *pneumatikos* to qualify *nomos*).

A recent attempt to solve this difficulty is the argument that Leviticus 18:5 is indeed a gracious statement and that Paul accepts it as such, but that the Judaizers used the verse as their legalistic motto. According to this view, Galatians 3:12 does not represent the law but rather the Judaistic misunderstanding of the law. As we will see, there may be a measure of truth in this approach, but in the end it faces some insuperable objections.[17]

It is indeed reasonable to suppose that the Judaizers appealed to Leviticus 18:5 in support of their teaching. If so, one would expect Paul's treatment of the verse to reflect their misuse of the biblical text. As Herman Ridderbos points out, Paul's negative statements regarding the law arise out of his conflict with Judaism. It would thus be surprising if his polemic did not reflect Judaism's understanding of "the law before Christ and the law without Christ."[18]

While we may therefore agree that Galatians 3:12 is *colored* by Paul's assessment of contemporary Jewish thought, the evidence does not permit us to say that *ho nomos* in that verse really means "the Jewish misunderstanding of the law." This solution is too simple and appears contrived. But we are not forced to the opposite extreme, namely, to the

---

[17]See Moo's review, mentioned above, n. 12.

[18]H. Ridderbos, *Paul: An Outline of His Theology* (Grand Rapids: Eerdmans, 1975), 154. Note that Galatians 1:14, with its reference to "the traditions of my fathers" (*tōn patrikōn mou paradoseōn*), focuses the reader's attention not on the Written Torah simply but on the Oral Torah, the traditions of the elders that our Lord so harshly condemned. Cf. Mark 7:8–9 and my article "The Place of Historical Reconstruction in New Testament Criticism" in *Hermeneutics, Authority, and Canon*, ed. D. A. Carson and J. W. Woodbridge (Grand Rapids: Zondervan, 1986), 109–33.

view that the term means the Mosaic Law pure and simple. Surely the context allows and even directs us to take a middle way. In verse 11 Paul had focused attention on a specific function (whether real or only supposed) of the law—the law as justifying agent (*en nomō oudeis dikaioutai para tō theō*). The text gives no indication whatever that the apostle moves beyond that framework to speak of broader aspects of the law. On the contrary, as we have seen, he goes on to contrast law and promise explicitly when these are viewed as instruments or sources of inheritance, life, and righteousness (vv. 18, 21).

On the basis of Paul's positive statements about the law,[19] I wish to argue that the apostle did indeed regard the law as leading to life—but not as life generating!—and that therefore he would have affirmed the truth expressed in Leviticus 18:5. On the other hand, he vigorously denied that the law could be the *source* of righteousness and life; indeed, he denied not merely that the law could be such but also the view that God had given it (*edothē*, 3:21) with such a purpose (otherwise, it would be opposed to the promise).

Now in the context of his polemic with the Judaizers, who argued that the works of the law could justify and who supported their claim with an appeal to Leviticus 18:5, Paul sets up an antithesis between Leviticus 18:5 and Habakkuk 2:4 to demonstrate precisely that the law cannot justify. Paul nowhere concedes that the law claims to be able to justify. Possibly what bothers us as modern interpreters is that we would want the apostle to argue explicitly: "The Judaizers have misused Leviticus 18:5." It should give us pause that the New Testament writers seldom, if ever, use that line of argument in refuting theological error. Jewish literature contemporary to the New Testament shows a similar hesitation to score points by refuting the opponent's use of Scripture. And the later rabbinic scholars, as a rule, refuted an argument based on Scripture by counteracting with a different passage, not by demonstrating faulty hermeneutics.[20]

---

[19]Harmonious with promise, 3:21; worthy of being fulfilled, 5:14; also Romans 7:10, 12; et al.

[20]Cf. Rimon Kasher, "The Interpretation of Scripture in Rabbinic Literature," in *Mikra*, Compendia Rerum Iudaicarum ad NT, 2/1, ed. M. J. Mulder

A satisfactory exegesis of Galatians 3:12 would require a much longer treatment than is possible here—and one that brought fully into the picture Paul's discussion in Romans 10:5. My concern here has been merely to alleviate the apparent problem by considering these points: (1) The clarity and forcefulness of Galatians 3:21 must play a much greater role than it has so far in the discussion of verse 12. (2) The consistency with which the whole context focuses on the source of inheritance/life/righteousness must color our reading of verse 12. (3) The likelihood that Leviticus 18:5 was introduced into the first-century debate by the Judaizers rather than by Paul must be taken seriously.

CONCLUSION

Readers who are familiar with the history of the interpretation of Galatians 3 may find my treatment of verse 12 annoyingly traditional. And indeed I am satisfied that the mainstream of Reformed interpretation has read this passage accurately even if it has not been able to answer all the questions raised by it.

More to the point, close attention to the significance of verse 21 has reaffirmed in my mind the validity of the way in which Reformed theology has handled the concept of law broadly considered. Over against orthodox Lutheranism and classic dispensationalism, the Reformed tradition has understood clearly that the Pauline critique of the law has reference only to its soteriological function: in this respect it was preparatory, not life-giving.[21]

If so, we may argue that Galatians 3—that is, the

(Assen: Van Gorcum; and Philadelphia: Fortress, 1988), 547–94, esp. pp. 581–82, which mention a few exceptions to the pattern.

[21]It is worth pointing out that Kline, in spite of his emphasis on the antithetical character of law and promise in Paul's writing, would hardly deny that the antithesis has a soteriological focus. In *By Oath Consigned*, page 30, where he incidentally alludes to Galatians 3:21, Kline makes explicit that his real concern is "law as a principle of inheritance." Therefore he can add on page 33, "Far from being annulled by the covenants mediated through Moses, the promise was renewed in them." By the same token, we should note that Bahnsen, while stressing the unity between the covenants, uses strong antithetical language when he distinguishes specifically between the promise-principle and the law-principle: they "are directly contradictory" (*Theonomy*, 512).

Pauline passage that most directly addresses the question of covenant continuity—gives no support to recent attempts among Reformed scholars to redefine the relationship between the old and new covenants. Paul's argument is, on the one hand, quite consistent with the reluctance of the Westminster Confession of Faith to enforce the Mosaic civil laws (though admittedly there is nothing in the argument that would forbid such an enforcement). On the other hand, this passage does not allow us to radicalize the distinction between law and promise—unless it be in answer to the very precise question: Are both law and promise life giving? *Mē genoito*!

Chapter Eight

The Epistle to the Hebrews and the Mosaic Penal Sanctions

Dennis E. Johnson

Dennis E. Johnson

Dennis E. Johnson (Ph.D., Fuller Theological Seminary) is Associate Professor of New Testament at Westminster Theological Seminary in California. With other degrees from Westmont College and Westminster Theological Seminary he has been a minister in the Orthodox Presbyterian Church. He is the editor of *Foundations of Christian Education: Addresses to Christian Teachers by Louis Berkof and Cornelius Van Til.* He is a former moderator of the General Assembly of the Orthodox Presbyterian Church and is the former acting president and former academic dean of Westminster Theological Seminary in California.

Chapter Eight

The Epistle to the Hebrews and the Mosaic Penal Sanctions

A FLASHPOINT OF CONTROVERSY

Among the most controversial aspects of theonomic ethics is its insistence on the continuing application of the penal sanctions of the Mosaic law. Critics of Christian reconstructionism's stress on the contemporary political relevance of the Old Testament law express alarm at the prospect of a "Christianized" state wielding "the sword" against the unrighteous, executing the advocates of false religion, those guilty of sexual sins, defiant children, and others. On the other hand, on the very issue of penology theonomists believe that other Christians have disregarded God's law and capitulated to the modern secular ideal of toleration. God's law, they reason, reveals God's justice; God's justice is unchanging; governments must administer God's justice; therefore governments must enforce the standards of justice delivered by God through Moses, and those unchanging standards specify the punishments that various crimes deserve.

Thus theonomy's critics see in its advocacy of the Mosaic penal sanctions a signal of theonomy's dangerous hermeneutical and theological error. Its advocates, on the other hand, see in the "penal sanctions question" a litmus test of fidelity to and love for God's law. It is no wonder that, despite the large area of common ground between theonomists and other Reformed and evangelical Christians, when the discussion turns to the status of the penal sanctions, positions become polarized, the emotional pitch rises, and rhetorical bombardment escalates. We might conclude that if we want light, not mere heat, concerning the issues raised by theonomy, we had better stay away from the question of the penal sanctions.

But we cannot simply avoid this question. Christians are bound to acknowledge the lordship of King Jesus in the political arena as in all other dimensions of life. Therefore we must consider *how* the Word of the Lord, which structured the social life of his people before Christ's coming, should guide our response to Jesus' lordship in our redemptive-historical and socio-political setting. Certainly one dimension of that question is the issue of public justice, including the use of government's coercive powers to suppress injustice. Advocates of theonomy, while acknowledging that exegetical and theological reflection remains to be done, offer a confident and straightforward answer to the question, How should government's coercive powers be used in the interests of justice? They believe that governments should see to it that criminals receive the punishments specified for their crimes in the judicial laws of Moses. The critics, on the other hand, are not persuaded that the sanctions expressed in the Mosaic judicial laws were intended by God as a blueprint for modern legal codes.

CONTINUITY, DISCONTINUITY, AND BURDEN OF PROOF

What separates the two groups seems to be largely a difference in approach to the continuity and discontinuity between the Old Testament and the New, between the old covenant order of promise and the new covenant order of fulfillment inaugurated in Christ's death and resurrection.

Both theonomists and their critics acknowledge continuity and discontinuity between the old covenant and the new. Although theonomists lay great stress on ethical continuity between the Mosaic order and the new covenant age, no theonomist of whom I am aware actually contends that the law's applicability remained utterly unchanged by the coming of Christ.[1] Greg Bahnsen, for example, writes of the

---

[1]Some statements of theonomy do indeed seem to allow for *no change whatsoever* in the relevance and application of the law as a result of the

progress of revelation, insisting that the New Testament must interpret the Old Testament for us, and that we must not simplistically equate Old and New Testament ethics.[2] And besides this large-scale redemptive-historical transition (which has affected particularly the ceremonial/sacrificial aspects of the law), Bahnsen also sees between ancient Israel and our situation other discontinuities that affect the applicability of the law's specific commands: "localized imperatives" (such as the command to exterminate the Canaanite nations in the conquest), "cultural details" (e.g., accidental killing by a flying axhead), and "administrative details" (form of government, location of capital) are not to be carried over directly into our social and political context.[3]

On the other hand, theonomy's critics acknowledge, to one degree or another, a continuity in the disclosure of God's holiness and justice through the Mosaic law and through the New Testament. To be sure, some in dispensational circles would argue that principles of the law are not binding in our age unless they are repeated in the New Testament; but they also acknowledge that the central demands of righteousness revealed in the Ten Commandments have in large measure been repeated in the New Testament. Reformed covenant theologians acknowledge an even greater degree of continuity.

So the difference between theonomists and nontheonomists is not that one group sees nothing but continuity between the Mosaic order and the new covenant, while the other sees nothing but discontinuity. *Both* groups acknowledge *both* continuity and discontinuity.

And yet, there is a difference. It is a difference in predisposition, and it shows itself in differing assumptions about where the *burden of proof* lies in questions concerning the applicability of Old Testament law. In general, theonomy

---

coming of Jesus the Messiah: "The advent of the Savior and the inauguration of the New Age do not have the effect of abrogating the slightest detail of God's righteous commandments." Or again: "To lay aside any of God's law or view its details as inapplicable today is to oppose God's standards of holiness." Greg L. Bahnsen, *By This Standard: The Authority of God's Law Today* (Tyler, Tex.: Institute for Christian Economics, 1985), 38, 51. However, these statements are qualified at other points in the same book. See below.

[2]Ibid., 4–5.

[3]Ibid., 5–6.

argues that the burden of proof rests on any contention that
a particular Mosaic stipulation does *not* apply now as it did
for Israel. In principle, of course, it is possible that the
coming of Christ has changed significantly the application of
a particular Mosaic stipulation; but such a change must be
proven exegetically. Apart from such explicit proof, the
presumption should be in favor of the law's continuing,
unchanged application.[4]

At the opposite extreme, some critics of theonomy hold
that the burden of proof rests on the view that Mosaic laws
do continue to apply in our postresurrection situation. Since
God's new creation in Christ gives rise to a new people of
God, the (international, interethnic) church, we should
assume that the laws given to Israel in the age of preparation
have fallen away *unless they are explicitly reaffirmed in the New
Testament.*

To put it another way, theonomists and their critics
interpret the *silences* of the New Testament differently. Since
the New Testament has relatively few explicit statements
with reference to the penal sanctions (see below), each side
of the debate tends to base its case partially on what the New
Testament does *not* say. Theonomy's approach views the
New Testament silences as tacit *reaffirmations* of the Mosaic
case laws: since God's holiness and justice do not change, we
should assume no change in his righteous demands *unless
later revelation specifically announces change.* Moreover, general
New Testament statements about God's justice or God's law
can be assumed to include the specifics of the penal
sanctions announced in the judicial laws. After all, the
apostolic writers saw no need to repeat in detail the
standards of righteousness that God had already made clear
to Israel.

At the opposite extreme, dispensationalism's stress on
discontinuity leads its adherents to "hear" in the New
Testament's silences a tacit *repeal* of the unmentioned aspects
of the Mosaic law. New Testament statements that speak

---

[4]"What is important is the *presumption* of continuing validity taught
elsewhere by Christ (Matt. 5:19) and Paul (Acts 25:11; Rom. 13:4; 1 Tim.
1:8–10; cf. Heb 2:2). Silence cannot defeat that presumption, for the
presumption can be turned back only by a definitive word of abrogation."
Ibid., 283.

generally of grace replacing law, of the law's weakness, etc., are understood to erase the judicial laws and (sometimes) much more as guidance for the life of God's new people. In effect, Christ's coming wiped the slate of God's ethical instruction clean, and only what is now reinscribed by the teaching of Jesus and the apostles binds the New Testament church.

But such generalized appeals to "burden of proof" or interpretations of the New Testament's silences do not help us understand the *precise character of the continuity and discontinuity* in God's revelation of his will through the history of redemption. The variety of ways in which the New Testament applies Old Testament laws (e.g., 1Co 5:6–8; 9:9–10) should caution us against presuming a particular understanding of continuity or discontinuity as our starting point. On this issue the burden of proof rests on all views—theonomic, nontheonomic covenantal, dispensational, and all the shades and variations in between. Arguments from silence are notoriously subjective, because there may be many explanations for the fact that an author does not mention a particular topic. To understand accurately the role of any aspect of the Mosaic Law in the age of the new covenant, we must rest our convictions on the statements, not the silences, of the New Testament. We must also pay careful attention to the specific ways in which the New Testament writers comment on the judicial laws before we draw sweeping conclusions from the New Testament's general statements.

CATEGORIES OF LAWS

If we are to let the New Testament guide our understanding of the Old, therefore, we must pay attention to the complexity of the New Testament's teaching on the law, being careful to note both its broad principles and its specific qualifications. We will need to exegete carefully any New Testament passage in which a particular judicial law may be quoted, alluded to, or commented on. But at the same time we cannot approach the judicial laws atomistically. They are part of a systematic order by which the Lord exerted his covenantal dominion over every sphere of Israel's thought and behavior.

As part of this system, certain laws can be grouped together into categories, since together they reinforce particular aspects of God's lordship over Israel. For example, the ceremonial laws demanding separation in diet, clothing, and agricultural practices operated in concert to underscore God's call to holy separateness in every sphere of life.[5] Although the New Testament neither repeals nor reaffirms the Mosaic prohibitions against sowing different grains in the same field and against wearing clothing made of different materials, when we recognize the *category* to which such laws belong, we can see that the fulfillment of the dietary laws (Mk 7) has implications for these other laws as well. Therefore we will also need to be alert to the *categories* of judicial laws within the Mosaic order and to the way the New Testament handles these categories.

Certain penal sanctions belong to categories of laws that set Israel apart from all the noncovenantal nations as a holy people, with God's temple in their midst. This high privilege entailed heightened responsibility to stay separate from *all* that would render a worshiper unfit to enter God's presence, whether "moral" or "ceremonial." Thus the law demanded that not only those guilty of incest but also those who had eaten a fellowship offering after the third day be "cut off from their people" (Lev 18:6–18, 29; 19:5–8). Since the coming of Christ, God's covenant people are no longer a single nation that uses physical force and penalties as means to maintain the community's purity and integrity. The church is international, and its discipline is maintained through the proclamation and application of Christ's Word by his undershepherds. Discipline must maintain the purity of the people of God no less in the new covenant than in the old; but this discipline is now wielded through the sword of the Spirit rather than by the physical "sword." To discern the significance of the Mosaic penal sanctions today we must discover how and to what extent these sanctions functioned within the categories of laws that set Israel apart as a holy people and how the "fulfillment-form" of the church under the new covenant affects these laws.

[5]Leviticus 11:1–47; 19:19; Deuteronomy 22:9–11.

NEW TESTAMENT REFERENCES
TO THE PENAL SANCTIONS

Only a few specific references to the Mosaic penal
sanctions are found in the New Testament.[6] Below I will

[6]In this connection it is helpful to bear in mind the variety of acts for
which the death penalty—the most extreme penal sanction available to
human government—was specified in the Mosaic judicial laws: premedi-
tated murder (Ex 21:12, 14); attacking or cursing parents (21:15, 17; Lev 20:9);
kidnapping (Ex 21:16; Dt 24:7); failure to restrain an animal known to be
dangerous, though a redemption price is allowed (Ex 21:29–32); sorcery
(22:18); bestiality (v. 19; Lev 20:15); worshiping a false god (Ex 22:20; Dt
17:2–7); working on the Sabbath (Ex 30:12–17); offering children to Molech
(Lev 20:2–3); adultery, including sexual relations with an engaged virgin,
unless it takes place in the open country or she is a slave (Lev 20:10; Dt
22:13–27; Lev 19:20–22); having sexual relations with father's wife, daughter-in-law, a woman and her daughter, or a man (homosexuality) (Lev
20:11–14); consulting mediums (20:27; see v. 6); blasphemy (24:13–16);
seducing members of the covenant to worship other gods, whether by a
prophet or by a close relative or by a whole city (Dt 13, especially vv. 5, 9,
15); showing contempt for a judge or priest (Dt 17:12); falsely accusing
someone of a capital offense (19:16–21); being a rebellious and profligate son
(21:18–21).

In addition, those found guilty of certain acts must be "cut off from their
people." In some instances this may possibly entail banishment, "shun-
ning," or excommunication from the congregation of Israel; but in many
cases it clearly refers to the death penalty, as the overlap with acts listed in
the previous paragraph demonstrates. Leviticus 18:6-23, 29 requires that
"such persons must be cut off from their people"; i.e., those who have
sexual relations with mother, stepmother (note 20:11 above), sister, granddaughter, stepsister, aunt, daughter-in-law (note v. 12 above), brother's
wife, a woman and her daughter or granddaughter (note v. 14 above),
wife's sister, *one's own wife during her menstrual period* (see also v. 18),
neighbor's wife (see v. 10 above), a man (see v. 13 above), an animal (see
Ex 22:19; Lev 20:15 above). Also to be "cut off from their people" are those
who offer their children to Molech (Lev 18:21; see 20:2–3 above); those who
eat the fellowship offering after the third day (19:7–8); and those who
consult mediums (20:6). We should probably also include here the failure of
a male member of the covenant to receive circumcision (Ge 16:14).

Concerning two other sexual liaisons (with uncle's wife and brother's
wife) it is said that "they will die [or be] childless" (Lev 20:20–21). If this is,
as it seems to be, a different sanction from being cut off from the people, it
may refer either to a directly imposed divine curse of barrenness or,
possibly, a humanly executed sterilization.

Finally, those who exploit widows and orphans are threatened: "I will kill
you with the sword; your wives will become widows and your children
fatherless" (Ex 22:22–24). It seems likely that this curse envisions the Lord's
use of a human intermediary in executing his wrath, but it is not clear

argue that among the most significant of these are the passages in the Epistle to the Hebrews that compare and contrast the Mosaic penalties to the judgment awaiting those who repudiate the new covenant inaugurated by Christ. A brief survey of the other New Testament references to the penalties of the Law of Moses will, I believe, demonstrate how important the passages in Hebrews are.

In the Sermon on the Mount Jesus cites the law's requirement that murderers be brought to judgment; then he asserts that not only murder but also unjustified anger brings liability to judgment, and anger expressed verbally brings *eternal condemnation* (Mt 5:21; Lev 24:17).[7] Jesus cites the law's "eye for eye, tooth for tooth" principle, only to tighten further its restriction on vindictive retaliation (Mt 5:38; cf. Ex 21:24; Lev 24:20; Dt 19:21). Thus, on the one hand, Jesus announces a more severe penalty than the Mosaic law: under Moses, murder was grounds for the judgment of execution; but for Jesus' disciples a cross word or taunt becomes grounds for *eternal destruction*. Yet, on the other hand, Jesus restricts his disciples' right to inflict on others the penalties provided in the Torah. Are Jesus' teachings in the Sermon on the Mount *intended to function* as a guide to new covenant jurisprudence in the political sphere? Learning from Jesus that the insult is a far more serious offense than any of us would have imagined, should Christians urge their government to make it a capital crime? If so, are we then forbidden by Jesus' word in Matthew 5:38 from pressing charges against the perpetrators of this and other misdeeds? The implied argument from lesser sin/punishment to greater confirms that the law reveals God's justice; but Jesus' treatment of the penal sanctions poses difficulties for us if we assume that biblical statements about God's justice in interpersonal relations[8] are always intended to define the role of civil government as "God's agent of wrath" (Ro 13:4).

---

whether this human instrument is to be the regular judicial system of Israel or a chastising invasion by a Gentile nation.

[7]Scholars debate whether Jesus intends to contrast the new, heightened ethics of his kingdom with the written law contained in Scripture or with the oral Torah transmitted through rabbinic tradition. At this point, however, there would be no real distinction in *content* between the written law and the oral law.

[8]A distinction between sins of the "hand" (action) and sins of the "heart" (attitude, motivation) is sometimes used to delimit the government's

Other accounts of Jesus' earthly ministry reaffirm the appropriateness of the penal sanctions as expressions of God's disfavor toward sin. Jesus underscores the value that God placed on showing honor to parents when Jesus cited the judicial law demanding execution of one who curses father or mother (Mt 15:4, par. Mk 7:10; see Ex 21:17; Lev 20:9). Zaccheus signals his repentance by offering fourfold restitution to those whom he has defrauded in his tax collecting (Lk 19:8; see Ex 22:1). On the other hand, Jesus is falsely accused of blasphemy worthy of death (Mt 26:66, par. Mk 14:64; Jn 19:7; cf. Lev 24:13–16; see also Jn 10:33). He undergoes the penal sanction of being hanged on a tree, but for our offenses, not his own (Gal 3:13; Ac 5:30; see Dt 21:22).

In the account of the woman caught in adultery (Jn 7:53–8:11), the woman's accusers appeal to the law requiring death by stoning for this sin (Lev 20:10). But for two reasons this passage makes little contribution to our understanding of the New Testament's stance toward the penal sanctions: (1) Probably this passage was not part of the original text of the fourth gospel. It does not appear in the oldest and best manuscripts of John's gospel. Therefore, since its place in God's Word is questionable, it is precarious to rest any doctrinal weight on this text. (2) Jesus' response, "Let the one without sin cast the first stone," is ambiguous. Would Jesus be repealing the death penalty as the sanction against adultery? Or (since no executioners will be perfectly sinless) for any and all crimes? Or would he simply be requiring that the witnesses, who must cast the first stone, be innocent of the sin with which they are accusing the woman—endorsing the law's penalty but indicting the hypocrisy of his opponents? Even if the text is an authentic part of God's Word, it gives us no clear guidance on the question of the continuing significance of the Mosaic penalties.

Two New Testament passages that speak of actions "worthy of death" have sometimes been thought to contain

---

legitimate sphere to punishing actions that are verifiable by external evidence. According to this distinction, however, the insulting speech forbidden by Jesus in Matthew 5:22 is a public action that would fall under the oversight of civil government—if Jesus were treating either the Old Testament commandment or his own intensification of it as a general pattern for penology.

appeals to the penal sanctions of the Old Testament. In Romans 1:32 Paul climaxes a catalog of sins with the comment: "They know God's righteous decree that those who do such things deserve death. . . ." The expression "deserve death" (axios thanatou) may be an allusion to Deuteronomy 21:22,[9] and some of the sins listed by Paul (homosexuality, murder, disobedience to parents, and sometimes slander) in the preceding context carried the penalty of death under the Mosaic law. Therefore some have concluded that Paul here appeals to the Mosaic penal sanctions to show that the sins listed ought to be punished by physical death and that the punishment should be carried out by human government. It seems more likely, however, that Paul's reference is to a punishment *more severe* than physical death, a punishment *beyond the power of human government* to inflict. Not all of the sins in Paul's preceding list (vv. 29–31) were in fact punished by physical execution under the Mosaic laws, in part because many of the sins Paul mentions (greed, envy, arrogance, insensitivity, and lack of compassion) are actions of the "heart" rather than the "hand." Even external sins such as gossip and slander were punishable by death only in the case of false witnesses who accused an innocent party of a capital crime against an innocent party. Moreover, although Paul began this section speaking of the present revelation of the wrath of God (Ro 1:18), he is making the transition to the final revelation of God's wrath (2:5–6); and it is this ultimate display of divine wrath in eternal condemnation that is the most natural referent of the phrase "deserve death" in this context (see 6:23).

In Acts 25:11 Paul protests his innocence before the Roman governor Festus by saying, "If. . .I am guilty of doing anything deserving death, I do not refuse to die. But if the charges brought against me by these Jews are not true, no one has the right to hand me over to them." Is Paul here making a direct appeal to the Mosaic judicial laws as defining crimes that cause one to be "deserving of death"? Certainly Paul does claim not to have violated the law of the Jews

---

[9]In the Hebrew Scriptures (*mišpat mawet*) and the Septuagint (*krima thanatou*) the expression is: "[receiving a] judgment of death." Thus our New Testament passages do not contain a direct verbal echo of Deuteronomy 21:22.

(v. 8), but it is pressing his words further than the context will allow to argue that Paul expects the pagan Festus to understand the complexities of the Torah (see footnote 6) well enough to find Paul's appeal intelligible and persuasive. On this point it is most natural to suppose that Paul is appealing to Roman law.

In 1 Corinthians 5:1–13 we find more relevance to the question of the continuing applicability of the penal sanctions. The Corinthian church has boasted in its "freedom" to the point of condoning a man's cohabitation with his father's wife, a violation not only of divine law but also of pagan propriety. Paul exhorts the church to expel the man from their midst, in the hope that such severity of judgment may bring repentance and rescue in the day of the Lord (vv. 2, 5). Does this excommunication replace the Mosaic penalty of death for adultery? Not necessarily, since it could be argued that Paul is instructing the *church* regarding what it should do, without addressing the question whether a *further* penalty should be imposed by the civil government. But it is noteworthy that Paul seals this discussion with a formula quoted from the Mosaic penal sanctions: "Expel the wicked man from among you" (v. 13; see Dt 17:7, 12; 19:19; 21:21; 22:21, 24; 24:7). His wording follows that of the Septuagint so closely that his intent to appeal to this Old Testament formula is unmistakable. In the Deuteronomy contexts this formula, whenever it appears, refers to the execution of those committing deeds "worthy of death": idolatry, contempt for judges, false witness, persistent rebellion toward parents, adultery, and kidnapping. These offenses against God and the covenant community introduce an infectious pollution (v. 6) that must be excised. The old covenant community was granted a governmental-political structure that "bore the sword" and had the authority to purge the community through the physical execution of offenders. Paul applies the *same terminology* to the new covenant community's judging/purging act of *excommunication*—a judgment that is both more severe (since it is "handing this man over to Satan," an anticipation of the final judgment), and more gracious (since it envisions a saving outcome to the temporal exercise of church discipline, which may bring about repentance that will lead to rescue from eternal judgment) (v. 5).[10]

We come, then, to two sections in the Epistle to the Hebrews (2:1–4; 10:26–31) that refer explicitly to the penal sanctions of the Mosaic law, and at the same time place these sanctions in the context of a broad theological analysis of the relationship of the law to the new covenant order established with the sacrifice of Christ.

THE PENAL SANCTIONS IN THE EPISTLE TO THE HEBREWS

These two passages (Heb 2:1–4; 10:26–31) are part of an overarching structure in which the author to the Hebrews contrasts the old covenant order established through the Law of Moses with the new covenant inaugurated through the death of Jesus Christ. We are prepared by the prologue to view all of history in terms of a contrast between the past, in which God spoke through prophets, and "these last days," in which he has spoken in a Son (1:1–2). The argument then advances in four phases, each centering on a particular Old Testament Scripture:[11]

1. Jesus is superior to the angels, the heavenly mediators of the law (1:1–2:18). The central passage is Psalm 8:5–7, which indicates that humanity's subordination to the angels (through the angelically mediated law of Moses) was only temporary, now that Jesus has been crowned with glory and honor.

2. Jesus is superior to Moses, the earthly mediator of the law (3:1–4:13). The central Old Testament text, Psalm 95:7–11, indicates that the "rest of God" which the wilderness generation failed to enter was not simply the territory of Palestine (later conquered under Joshua, Heb 4:8), but rather a greater Sabbath-rest that still stands open to us, to be entered by faith.

3. Jesus is superior to Aaron and the priesthood that the

---

[10]As Christ's servants faithfully proclaim and apply his word, their discipline of the church has heavenly ramifications (Mt 16:19; Jn 20:22–23).

[11]This analysis of the structure of Hebrews was clarified for me by "The Structural Function of the Major Quotations," an unpublished paper by my former colleague, Allen Mawhinney.

law established (4:14–7:28). Psalm 110:4 is central here, for there the psalmist announced the future coming of a priest-king who would minister forever, never prevented by death (as were Aaron and his descendants) from continuing in office.

4. Jesus is superior to the covenant—centered in the sanctuary and the sacrificial system—that the law inaugurated (8:1–12:29). Jeremiah 31:31–34, quoted in Hebrews 8:8–12 and again more briefly in 10:16–17, by announcing the coming of a new and better covenant, clearly implied the obsoleteness and inadequacy of the Mosaic covenant.

Throughout the epistle the superiority of the new order to the old is reinforced by the repeated use of the word "better" (thirteen times in Hebrews) and by a series of *a fortiori* ("how much more") arguments that reason from the *value* of the Mosaic order to the *greater value* of the order established by Jesus (2:2–3; 9:13–14; 10:28–29; 12:25). The same logic lies behind the comparison of Moses and Jesus in the second section of the epistle: Moses was faithful as a *servant in* God's house, but Christ was faithful as a *son over* God's house and is therefore worthy of greater honor (3:3–6). During Moses' ministry the wilderness generation responded to God's voice with unbelief, and so they failed to enter the land. Their sobering example alerts us to the greater danger—the greater "rest" to be lost—if we fail to mix our hearing with faith as God's voice now addresses us in Jesus (see Heb 12:25–29).

Now, it is obvious that the Epistle to the Hebrews approaches the Mosaic Law from the perspective of its sanctuary and sacrificial system. For Hebrews, the tent of meeting and the ceremonies that were carried on there were at the very heart of the old covenant, for they symbolized the *goal* of the covenant (communion with God) and they provided the *means* to that goal through the covering of sinful impurity.[12] For the same reasons the center of the new covenant is the heavenly sanctuary in which our Great High Priest leads us (now "perfected" by his sacrifice) in wor-

---

[12]Geerhardus Vos, "Hebrews, Epistle of the Diatheke," in R. B. Gaffin, Jr., ed., *Redemptive History and Interpretation* (Phillipsburg, N. J.: Presbyterian and Reformed, 1980), 183–85.

ship.[13] We are not surprised, then, to find that much of Hebrews' discussion of the new covenant replacing the old focuses on the sacrificial-ceremonial aspects of the Mosaic Law. Of course, even as Hebrews announces that the old order has given way to the new, the epistle also reaffirms the *principles* (holiness, substitutionary death for atonement, intercession, etc.) underlying the redemptive structures of the Mosaic order. The implicit conviction that "drives" the argument is that the old covenant atonement structures were finally dependent on the atoning death of Christ: the types derived their form and significance from the Antitype who was to come.

Nevertheless the coming of the Great Priest has brought significant changes in the law delivered by God through angels to Moses. The author of Hebrews says as much in his discussion of Jesus' right of priestly appointment in Hebrews 7. He knows very well that the Mosaic Law concerning priestly appointment mandated that only those of the family of Aaron, of the tribe of Levi, might enter the sanctuary as priestly mediators on behalf of their brothers. Concerning the tribe of Judah, from which our Lord was descended, Moses spoke nothing concerning priests (Heb 7:14). The Word of God, however, announced (in Ps 110:4) the coming of another priest, *appointed on the basis of a different criterion* than that of genealogical connection to Levi. The new priest would hold his office by virtue of his indestructible life ("you are a priest forever," 7:16–17) and by virtue of a direct and personal oath taken by God ("the Lord has sworn and will not change his mind," 7:20–21).

Now, the introduction of this new principle of priestly appointment when the new priest (Jesus) undertakes his office *demands a change in the law*. This is so because *on the basis of* the Levitical priesthood the people were given the law (Heb 7:11).[14] In some sense—probably in the sense that

---

[13]"The Epistle considers the Christian state as in the main a *cultus*. Christianity is not a *douleia* [slavery], but a *latreia*, that is, a direct worship of God. This is intended in the sense of drawing near to God and worshiping Him. . . . It is a service in a sanctuary, with priest, altar and sacrifice. The idea of sacrifice is wider, therefore, than that of atonement. Its essence is proper worship of God in His presence." Geerhardus Vos, *The Teaching of the Epistle to the Hebrews* (Grand Rapids: Eerdmans, 1956), 43.

[14]The Greek reads *ho laos gar ep' autēs nenomothetētai*. The antecedent of the pronoun *autēs* is "the Levitical priesthood" (*tēs Leuitikēs hierosynēs*). The use

Geerhardus Vos has identified for us (see note 12), that the sanctuary stands at the center of the covenant, signifying the presence of the Lord and the atoning means necessary for Israel to enjoy it—the priesthood of Aaron and his sons is the very foundation of the law given through Moses to Israel.[15] Therefore when the principle of priestly appointment is changed (from genealogical connection with Levi to the power of an indestructible life and an inviolable divine oath), an accompanying change in the law, which rests on the priesthood, must take place (7:12). How sweeping is this change in the law?

1. Minimally, the immediate context of Hebrews 7 demands that the change in the law entail the *abolition of the "fleshly commandment" that priests can come only from Aaron's family tree.* (The genealogical law was, after all, a tacit acknowledgment of the weakness of the old order, since it presupposed that death would prevent each generation of priests from continuing in their service, 7:23.)

2. The broader context of the epistle makes it clear that the change also embraces the *sacrifices* required to effect atonement and reconciliation. As the psalmist had announced, the day has arrived when God is not pleased with the slaying of animals as sacrifices and offerings, whole burnt offerings and sin offerings: the Son has entered the world to do the Father's will by offering up the body prepared for him as the once-for-all sacrifice of atonement (Ps 40:6–8, cited and interpreted in Heb 10:5–10).

3. But this means that the *focus of cleansing for God's presence,* which is accomplished by the new priest, is not external and cultic but internal, dealing with the *conscience* (Heb 9:13–14).

4. This leads us to the question of the relation of the Mosaic *penal sanctions* to the priesthood and sanctuary, the

---

of *epi* to introduce the legal basis on which a covenantal arrangement depends is found also in 8:6 (see footnote 15).

[15]Note the other use of *nomotheteō* "to give law, establish legally" in 8:6: The new covenant has been legally established (*nenomothetētai*) upon the better promises (*epi kreittosin epangeliais*) announced in Jeremiah 31:31–34 (cited in Heb 8:8–12). A new covenantal/legal foundation has been established, replacing the Levitical priesthood and rendering the old covenant obsolete (v. 13).

heart of the covenant. Has a change in application also been introduced here?

Hebrews 2:2 affirms the justice of the Mosaic penal sanctions, as a basis for the *a fortiori* argument that neglect of the great eschatological Word of God, the word of salvation spoken through the Lord himself, will justly bring even more severe punishment than that meted out to Old Testament violators of the law. "Every trespass of unwillingness to hear[16] received a just reward" (literal trans.).[17] For God, then, to prescribe the penalties of the Mosaic Law for those members of Israel who disregarded his covenant word, given through angels, was unquestionably a display of his justice.

But we should also note that these penalties are mentioned here specifically in the context of the *contrast between the old order and the new*. They are one element in the old order that vividly demonstrates "how much more" important is the new order announced by the Lord Jesus.

At first glance we may be inclined to think that there is only a tenuous connection at one point in the comparison. The *content* of the divine revelation spoken of in verse 2 is *commands*, prohibitions, legal requirements; but the content of the divine revelation spoken of in verse 3 is "such a great salvation." Why are these very different words from God brought together? At the heart of the author's concern is the *justified right of the covenant Lord to expect an appropriate response from his covenant people when he speaks*, whatever the content of his speech to them. When God speaks, he has the right to expect his people to hear, to believe, to obey, to draw near in

---

[16]*Parakoē*, a significant word-choice in the light of the coming exposition and application of Psalm 95:7–11: "Today if you hear his voice. . . ." (Heb 3:7–22). See Hebrews 4:2. B. F. Westcott, *The Epistle to the Hebrews* (1892; repr. Grand Rapids: Eerdmans, 1970), 38, goes so far as to say on 2:2: "The discipline and punishment of the wilderness (c. iii. 16ff.; 1 Cor x. 6ff.) furnished the typical illustration of this teaching which extends to the whole Jewish life: c.xii. 25, x.28f."

[17]"Reward" (*misthapodosia*) appears twice elsewhere in Hebrews (10:35; 11:26) in a positive sense—the great reward of faith—and nowhere else in the New Testament. "Rewarder," again in a positive sense, appears only in Hebrews 11:6. "Just" (*endikos*)—"based on what is right . . . deserved" (Bauer/Arndt/Gingrich, *Greek-English Lexicon of the New Testament* [Chicago: University of Chicago, 1957], 262)—appears only here and in Romans 3:8 (concerning those who slander Paul's gospel and whose condemnation is deserved) in the New Testament.

response to his invitation. And the greater the grace revealed in his words to his people, the greater their liability should they disregard his voice. Thus the justice of the punishments meted out to violators of the Mosaic Law belongs within the context of God's gracious covenantal address. At issue is not divine justice in the abstract as a model for political jurisprudence, but the Lord's just expectation in view of his people's covenantal obligations to him.

This covenant-context of the Mosaic penal sanctions is made more explicit in Hebrews 10:26–31. The author of Hebrews here reinforces his exhortation to approach God in faith, to hold fast the confession of our hope, to assist and encourage one another in the battle of perseverance. He raises the negative possibility that some may be "sinning deliberately after having received the knowledge of the truth" and declares, as he has in different language in Hebrews 6:4–12, that for such people what is left is no sacrifice for their sins, but only the terrifying anticipation of condemnation. The Mosaic penal sanctions underscore the severity of God's demand: "Anyone who rejected the law of Moses died *without mercy* on the testimony of two or three witnesses" (Heb 10:28). Again the Mosaic Law is the launching point of the argument that establishes the greater privilege and glory of the new covenant: *"How much more severely* do you think a man deserves to punished who has trampled the Son of God under foot, who has treated as an unholy thing the blood of the covenant that sanctified him, and who has insulted the Spirit of grace?"* (Heb 10:29) This summary of that new covenant offense (trampling God's Son, scorning his blood, insulting the Spirit), corresponding to a capital offense under the old, shows that the author is not thinking of *every violation* of the Mosaic Law when he speaks of one "who rejected the law of Moses." Violation of the *fundamental demand of loyalty* to the Sovereign is the focus of the penalty in view in Hebrews 10:28–29. John Calvin rightly notes that nothing less than apostasy from the faith is the issue being addressed here:

> The apostle describes as sinners not those who fall in any kind of way but those who forsake the Church and separate themselves from Christ. . . . There is a great difference between individual lapses and a universal

desertion of this kind which makes for a total falling away from the grace of Christ. . . . It is clear from the context that the apostle is referring here only to apostates.[18]

Moreover, Calvin finds support for his conclusion specifically in the author's appeal to the Mosaic Law:

> The Law did not punish any kind of transgression by death but only apostasy when a man departed completely from his religion. The apostle has referred to the passage in Deut. 17:2–5, which says that if anyone transgresses the covenant of your God to serve other gods you shall take him out of the gate and stone him to death.[19]

It is possible that Calvin is deliberately leaving out of account the many other offenses for which, according to the Mosaic Law, death was the requisite penalty (see footnote 6); but it could be that, though referring explicitly only to Deuteronomy 17, Calvin is thinking of *all* the sins for which the Mosaic Law mandated capital punishment as *various forms of the law against apostasy*—expressions of covenantal infidelity at its most fundamental level. In a sermon on Deuteronomy 17:2–7 (November 18, 1555) he makes it clear that he understands this text to address *not* the sin of idolatry generally, but rather the specific sin of willful apostasy: "God's speaking here is only of such countries or cities as have had the grace to have the true religion established among them, so that He is worshipped there, *and they have all consented to submit to God's order*" (emphasis added).[20] A following analogy to an oath of allegiance taken to a human magistrate shows that this universal "consent to submit to God's order" is the significant factor for Calvin. In this respect (though he may have envisioned the political out-workings differently from the contributors to this book) Calvin has grasped an important component of the divine

---

[18]John Calvin, *The Epistle of Paul the Apostle to the Hebrews and the First and Second Epistles of Peter*, trans. W. B. Johnston (Grand Rapids: Eerdmans, 1963), 146.

[19]Calvin, *Hebrews*, 148. P. E. Hughes, *A Commentary on the Epistle to the Hebrews* (Grand Rapids: Eerdmans, 1977), 421, adds Deuteronomy 13:8 to illustrate the prohibition against showing mercy to apostate covenant violators.

[20]John Calvin, "Sermon 103. 18 November 1555. Deuteronomy 17:2–7," republished in *Calvin Speaks* (Geneva Divinity School) I, 3 (September 1980): 3.

justice revealed in Deuteronomy 17 and in Hebrews 10 (with respect to the Mosaic punishments generally).

The concern of Hebrews is with an offense that can be committed only by a member of the covenant, by one "sanctified" by identification with Jesus' sacrificial blood in baptism (Heb 10:29). Although all disobedience, even by those who are confronted only with God's general revelation, is without excuse (Ro 1:20), it is precisely the status of *covenant privilege* that makes apostasy so heinous and its severe punishments (in Old Testament and New Testament) just and righteous. In fact, the greater privilege of the new covenant age mandates that those who now treat the covenant's Lord and Mediator with contempt receive an even greater punishment than any human court can execute—eternal judgment at "the hands of the living God" (Heb 10:31).

This conclusion illustrates the difficulty of using the Mosaic penal sanctions as a pattern for modern jurisprudence. Both theonomists and their opponents acknowledge that the redemptive work of Christ has changed the political structure of the covenant people. Under the new covenant the purity of the covenant community is maintained not by physical sanctions but by spiritual discipline: excommunication, not execution, is the method by which the covenant people are to "expel the wicked man" from among them (1Co 5:13).

Where does this leave the civil government today, which (though it is a minister of God's justice, Ro 13:4) does not have the same *covenantal* role as that fulfilled by the city elders, judges, and anointed kings of Old Testament Israel? Since the justice of the Mosaic sanctions presupposed the offender's privileged status and prior commitment as a member of the Lord's covenant, for a civil government today to apply such sanctions *justly* would require the state to take into account the status of the offender in relation to God's covenant. The state should then execute church members who apostatize but not Hindus who persist in their ancestors' idolatry. Such a scenario, however, would inject the physically coercive power of the civil government into virtually every aspect of the church's discipline of its members.

Moreover, such a view of the Mosaic penal sanctions

overlooks the redemptive-historical place assigned to them by the Epistle to the Hebrews. The punishments of the Mosaic Law belong clearly to the old order, and thus they point ahead to the higher privilege and the resultant higher accountability of the new covenant order established in Jesus. Although these penalties are not precisely labeled "types" in Hebrews, the epistle nevertheless leads us to see that they are fulfilled and heightened in the sanctions of church discipline that point to the ultimate horror of separation from God and affliction under his jealous wrath (Heb 10:27, 30–31). The justice of these sanctions is specifically qualified by the covenant bond that has been violated, the relationship between the offender and the Lord, which has been severed irreparably.

It is clear that the author to the Hebrews is not answering the question of how to set up a Christian political system, which interests many North American Christians today. His readers were in no position to need or to implement whatever counsel he might have offered on such a topic. Thus his reference to the justice of the Mosaic penalties ought not to be taken out of the context of his argument, as though he were authorizing the use of these sanctions as a universal pattern of penal codes to be carried out by noncovenantal governments. The author of Hebrews presents the penalties of the Mosaic Law as covenant sanctions, visited justly on those who violate covenant with the Lord. Thus during the period of promise they reflected on a lesser scale the far more severe consequences of repudiating the greater disclosure of the Lord's holiness and grace in the priestly work of Jesus Christ, which has taken place "in these last days" (Heb 1:1–2).

CONCLUSION

Ultimately the New Testament must be our guide in determining how the various categories of commandments in the Law of Moses function as God's authoritative Word to the postresurrection church. The character of the continuity and the discontinuity between the old covenant and the new is such that we cannot rely on arguments from silence or generalized statements if we are to understand and apply correctly in this age the revelation of God to Israel through Moses.

The specific statements of Hebrews 2:2 and 10:28 sum up the impression gleaned from other, less explicit New Testament passages: the Mosaic penal sanctions belonged in the context of the discipline and purity of the covenant community. They pointed toward the exclusion of apostates, whose lives and words showed contempt for the Lord of the covenant, from the community of the people of God.

The question whether the penal sanctions should also instruct the state as it is charged to administer justice to persons within and without God's covenant is not explicitly addressed in the New Testament. This silence of the New Testament regarding the possible applicability of the Mosaic Laws in the civil-political sphere is no doubt partly attributable to situational factors surrounding the composition of the New Testament books: first-century Christians were in no position to attain or wield political power as a bloc. But this situation is itself significant; for God is the Lord of history, who determined to bring about the accomplishment of redemption and the climax of redemptive revelation at just such a time—"when the time had fully come" (Gal 4:4)—when his true people were politically powerless. It is no accident of history that the New Testament speaks more often and more explicitly regarding the responsibilities of subjects to political authorities (Mt 5:41; Ro 13:1–7; 1Ti 2:1–2; Tit 3:1; 1Pe 2:13–17; et al.) than it does regarding the responsibilities of political rulers (Ro 13:4). Rather, this is a reflection of God's sovereign and wise design of his Word, the standard for our faith and life.

The New Testament's minimal direction to governmental officials does not support the view that the Mosaic penalties should be enforced by a noncovenantal governmental structure on a noncovenantal people. Christians who find themselves with governing responsibilities in such a situation may indeed search all of God's Word for reflections of his justice that will aid them in their task, made so difficult by the mixed situation of "the present evil age" (Gal 1:4). But they should also recognize that the mere fact that a penalty was prescribed in the law of Moses for Israelites who had scorned their covenant privilege does not automatically authorize a modern state to purge its populace with equivalent punishments.

If anything, the New Testament's interpretation of the penal sanctions in a covenant context and the New Testament's divinely purposed silence regarding the specifics of civil jurisprudence in the new covenant age should humble the political aspirations of the North American church. In what it says and in what it does not say, the New Testament reminds us that the saving rule of God's kingdom spreads among the nations through his weak but faithful servants, who proclaim the folly of the cross in the hidden power of the Spirit. And it calls us, even as we pursue evangelism and justice in the present age, to look ahead to the only perfect disclosure of the kingdom's righteousness, at the coming of the King, Jesus Christ.

PART FOUR

THEONOMY AND TRIUMPHALIST DANGERS: SPECIFIC CONCERNS

Even to some sympathetic observers of theonomy the most troubling aspect of the movement, beside its application of the penal sanctions of the Old Testament judicial law, is the triumphalist tone of much of its rhetoric. This is related to some extent to a postmillennial eschatology, and it manifests itself in theonomic views of church-state relations, in the way in which theonomy makes its appeal to modern American culture, and in Christian reconstruction's approach to the poor in society.

In this section Richard Gaffin expresses concern that contemporary postmillennialism has deeschatologized the present, replacing the church's suffering in the present interadvental period with triumphalism and removing the watchfulness required by the imminent return of Christ. With regard to church-state relations William Barker finds that Jesus' teaching concerning the tribute money supports the idea that it is not the Lord's intention for the civil government to promote the true faith, but only to allow freedom of religion in this era of the carrying out of the Great Commission. John Muether describes theonomy as attractive to our late-twentieth-century culture because it contains sociological traits that are distinctively American, evangelical, and modern. Timothy Keller takes issue with Christian reconstructionists such as Gary North and David Chilton with regard to poverty and how to deal with it biblically.

Chapter Nine

Theonomy and Eschatology:
Reflections on Postmillennialism

Richard B. Gaffin, Jr.

Richard B. Gaffin, Jr.

Richard B. Gaffin, Jr. (Th.D., Westminster Theological Seminary) is Professor of Systematic Theology at Westminster Theological Seminary (Philadelphia). With other degrees from Calvin College and Westminster Theological Seminary, he has taught at Westminster since 1965. He is the author of *The Centrality of the Resurrection* (previously published as *Resurrection and Redemption*) and *Perspectives on Pentecost*. He is the editor of *The Shorter Writings of Geerhardus Vos*.

Chapter Nine

Theonomy and Eschatology: Reflections on Postmillennialism

Essential to the emergence of theonomy/(Christian) reconstructionism has been a revival of postmillennialism.[1] Among current postmils, to be sure, there are some who are not reconstructionists, but all reconstructionists—whatever their differences—consider themselves postmils. Or so it would have seemed until just recently with the unanticipated and apparently growing impact of reconstructionist viewpoints in circles whose eschatology is characteristically premil. Still, for reconstructionism's leading advocates, postmillennialism is plainly integral—whether logically or psychologically—to their position as a whole. Nonreconstructionist postmils would naturally deny any such connection.

This chapter provides some partial, personally tinged, yet, I hope, not entirely unhelpful reflections on the resurgent postmillennialism of the past twenty to twenty-five years. My reservations lie in at least four areas.

DEFINING POSTMILLENNIALISM

A large element of ambiguity cuts across much of today's postmillennialism. Before trying to specify that ambiguity it will be helpful, historically, to give some attention to the fact that in the past, too, postmillennialism

---

[1]This renaissance, unless I've overlooked something, has been taking place almost entirely within the English-speaking, especially American, Reformed community; nothing more than scattered traces are present in non-Reformed contexts or, for that matter, in the rest of the Reformed world—Holland, South Africa, and elsewhere.

has not been the clearly defined, unambiguous position that some of its contemporary proponents make it out to be.

It is fairly common to point out the inadequacy of our conventional designations *pre*, *post*, and *a*. But no less commonly, in ensuing discussion that recognition recedes. As a result, efforts to distinguish, for one, between the postmil and amil positions get confused—usually, as it turns out, more than a merely terminological confusion.

Who coined the term *amillennial*, and when did it first begin to be used? Perhaps I've missed it somewhere, but the usual sources don't seem to know or at least don't say. At any rate, in 1930 Geerhardus Vos, for instance, viewed today as an amil, still seems to distinguish only between a premil and postmil position and to include himself in the latter.[2] And as late as 1948, a year before his death, again in contrasting the two positions, he distances himself, apparently, not from postmillennialism as such but only from "certain types" of it.[3] Similarly, in a 1915 article B. B. Warfield, besides characterizing "premillennial" and "postmillennial" as "unfortunate," "infelicitous" terms, seems to recognize only those two positions.[4]

More representatively, the original (1915) and revised (1929/30) editions of the *International Standard Bible Encyclopaedia* have no entry for amillennialism, and under "Millennium, post-millennial view" simply refer the reader to Vos's

[2]*The Pauline Eschatology* (1930; reprint Grand Rapids: Baker, 1979), 226. This passage is from a chapter virtually identical with an article ("The Pauline Eschatology and Chiliasm") originally appearing in *The Princeton Theological Review* 9 (1911): 26–60 (see p. 26).

[3]Geerhardus Vos, *Biblical Theology* (Grand Rapids: Eerdmans, 1948), 406; cf. 405. This seems a more accurate assessment of what Vos says than that of Greg Bahnsen, "The *Prima Facie* Acceptability of Postmillennialism," *The Journal of Christian Reconstruction* 3, 2 (Winter 1976–77): 55–56 (Bahnsen quotes from unpublished class notes identical with the passage from *Biblical Theology* cited above). In "The Second Coming of Our Lord and the Millennium," in *Redemptive History and Biblical Interpretation. The Shorter Writings of Geerhardus Vos* (Phillipsburg, N.J.: Presbyterian and Reformed, 1980), 419, Vos appears to distance himself from "the mind of the most pronounced pre- or post-millenarian" (this article first appeared in 1916). As far as I have been able to discover, Vos never calls himself or his views "amillennial."

[4]*Selected Shorter Writing* (Nutley, N.J.: Presbyterian and Reformed, 1970), 1:349.

(decidedly amil) article "Eschatology of the New Testament."[5]

To note a couple of other related examples: On the millennium passage (Rev 20:1–10), Warfield adopts what almost everyone today would consider an amil view.[6] And the late John Murray, though often claimed (mistakenly, I believe) as a postmil, sets forth, in what in my judgment is the clearest extant statement of his overall eschatological outlook, a position that—if we are to choose one of the standard labels—is best designated amillennial.[7] Murray's exegesis of Romans 11 no more makes him a postmil than Warfield's exegesis of Revelation 20 makes him an amil.

(By the way, can anyone who has carefully read Murray's 1968 address on Matthew 24–25 seriously question its amillennial thrust?[8] It may be somewhat speculative on my part, but hardly unwarranted, to detect in this address— it does not refer explicitly to the work of others—a refutation of the characteristic postmil treatment of Matthew 24, advanced around that time, for instance, by J. Marcellus Kik, particularly the notion that everything up through verse 35 is fulfilled in the fall of Jerusalem and the destruction of the temple.[9] With typical incisiveness Murray shows that the passage covers history down to its consummation and that the decidedly non-"golden" element of tribulation for the

[5]The recent (1986–89) revision of ISBE discusses all three positions in a single article, "Millennium," by J. W. Montgomery (3:360–61), who cites Vos as a representative amil.

[6]"The Millennium and the Apocalypse," in *Biblical Doctrines* (New York: Oxford University Press, 1929), 643–64 (originally published in *The Princeton Theological Review* 2 [1904]: 599–617). Vos cites this article with (tacit) approval in his ISBE article, "Eschatology of the New Testament," reprinted in *Redemptive History and Biblical Interpretation*, 45.

[7]"Structural Strands in New Testament Eschatology," a paper read at the seventh annual meeting of the Evangelical Theological Society in December 1954 and decisively influenced, in my judgment, by Vos, especially pages 36–41 of *The Pauline Eschatology*. Regrettably, for whatever reasons, this paper has not been reprinted in Murray's *Collected Writings*. It can be found in the library of Westminster Seminary, Philadelphia.

[8]"The Interadventual Period and the Advent: Matthew 24 and 25," *Collected Writings of John Murray* (Edinburgh: Banner of Truth Trust, 1977), 2:387–400.

[9]*The Eschatology of Victory* (1948; reprint Nutley, N.J.: Presbyterian and Reformed, 1971), 30–40, 59–173, esp., e.g., 158. The 1971 edition includes a lecture series given at Westminster Seminary in 1961.

church "is represented as characterizing the interadventual period as a whole," p. 389.)

In the past, then, especially over against premillennialism, "post" appears also to have covered what, in effect, was "a." The possibility for that sort of usage lay in the obvious (though sometimes overlooked) consideration that the amil view is postmillennial in the sense that for both views Christ will return after the millennium; all amils are postmil.

What prompted invention of the word *amillennial*? While the precise origins of the term may be uncertain, the reason for its emergence seems plain enough. Eventually those who did not share a "postmil" emphasis on the millennium as purely future felt the need to have a label for their view. "Amillennial" has functioned, at least characteristically, not necessarily to deny that the millennium is on earth (although some "amils" have no doubt taken such a position) but to maintain the identity of the millennium and the interadvental period. The "a" negates in two directions: (1) the millennium is the interadventual period, not an interregnum following it (the premil view), and (2) the millennium is the interadventual period in its entirety, not just an era toward its close (the postmil view).

By now enough has been said to remind us all that, measured by church-historical standards, the threefold pattern of designation (*a, post,* and *pre*), which we tend to consider traditional, is, after all, a fairly recent innovation. More importantly, "a" and "post" do not distinguish differing viewpoints with long, clearly delineated traditions well-established in the church's past, as some seem to think. So it is somewhat misleading simply to speak—as I, for instance, did at the start—of a revival of postmillennialism in connection with the recent emergence of Christian reconstructionism. There are undoubtedly genuine continuities with earlier "postmillennial" viewpoints, but to assert confidently that current postmillennialism has rediscovered "the historic Reformed eschatology" is surely gratuitous.

For my part (though I remain open to discussion), I am not ready to abandon the historical judgment of none other than Warfield, reported by his friend (and fellow postmil) Samuel G. Craig: "He himself [Warfield] freely admitted that a-millennialism, *though not known in those days under that name,* is the historic Protestant view, as expressed in the creeds of the Reformation period including the Westminster Standards" (emphasis added).[10] For bygone generations of the church, for instance, to have expressed (more or less unbounded) optimism about the spread of the Gospel or to have believed that Romans 11 teaches a future mass conversion of Jews hardly makes them postmils in a later or contemporary sense.

The ambiguity in earlier postmillennialism, which I have suggested gave rise to the label *amillennial* as an effort to clarify, has been further compounded by the fact that presently a sizable number of postmils (especially in reconstructionist circles, it seems) consider the millennium to be coextensive with the *entire* interadvental period. This is surely a departure, in the main, from previous postmillennialism, and in that respect such postmils are amillennial. In the present situation, then, we have "postmil amils" (all amils) and "amil postmils" (some postmils).

How are we to assess this development? Does it perhaps indicate that these postmils at least have drawn close to amils and that a basis for eschatological common cause exists between them? It is attractive and challenging to think in that direction, and I, for one, least of all want to be guilty of missing or failing to capitalize on existing elements of unanimity. However, it has to be noted that the postmils in view still wish to remain identified as *postmils*. That, I take it, is not merely incidental or an indifferent matter of terminology but, as I will try to make clear below, reflects the instinct that their deepest affinity, despite the amil corrective made, is still with earlier ("nonamil") postmillennialism.

My comments so far should have made clear, if anything, that "postmillennialism" is hardly a simple or monolithic entity. My reservations, then, are not with all that has fallen under that name in the past (or, for that matter,

---

[10]In the editor's introduction to B. B. Warfield, *Biblical and Theological Studies* (Philadelphia: Presbyterian and Reformed, 1952), xxxix. The emphasized clause provides knowledgeable confirmation for the relatively recent origin of the term *amillennial*. Note also the assessment of L. Berkhof, *Systematic Theology*, 4th ed. (Grand Rapids: Eerdmans, 1962), 708: "the name [*Amillennialism*] is new indeed, but the view to which it is applied is as old as Christianity. . . . It has ever since [the ancient church fathers] been the view most widely accepted, is the only view that is either expressed or implied in the great historical Confessions of the Church, and has always been the prevalent view in Reformed circles."

continues to do so at present) but with what, it seems to me, are certain characteristics prominent in much current (and earlier) postmillennialism. That proviso needs to be kept in mind in what follows.

ESCHATOLOGICAL STRUCTURE

My primary reservation, in a word, is that, like premillennialism, postmillennialism—distinguished from amillennialism—"de-eschatologizes" the present (and past) existence of the church. Postmils misperceive the basic structure of New Testament eschatology and so, in a fundamental way, devalue Christian life and experience in the present (and the past) as well as for the immediate, foreseeable future. How does that happen?

1. Nothing has been more characteristic of current postmillennialism than its emphasis on the kingship of the ascended Christ; nothing fires the postmil vision more than that reality. Yet it is just this reality that postmillennialism effectively compromises and, in part, even denies. Postmils especially will no doubt find this last statement startling, maybe even outrageous, so let me try to explain.

Nothing is more distinctive to the postmil vision than its expectation of promised "victory" for the church, a future "golden age," before Christ's return. That golden era is variously conceived; in its reconstructionist versions, for example, it is to be a period of global supremacy and control by Christians over every area of life. But all postmil constructions—past and present, and all of them marked (as postmil) in distinction from other eschatological viewpoints—have in common that the millennial "gold"/"victory" (1) is expected before Christ's return and (2) up to the present time in the church's history, apart from occasional anticipations, has remained entirely in the future.

Here, then, is where a problem—from the vantage point of New Testament teaching, a fundamental structural difficulty—begins to emerge. Emphasis on the golden era as being entirely future leaves the unmistakable impression that the church's present (and past) is something other than golden and that so far in its history the church has been less than victorious. This impression is only reinforced when, typically in my experience, the anticipated glorious future is pictured just by contrasting it with what is alleged to be the church's presently dismal state (the angle of vision seldom seems to include much beyond the church scene in the United States!), usually with the added suggestion that those who do not embrace the postmil vision are "defeatists" and contribute at least to perpetuating the sad and unpromising status quo.

The New Testament, however, will not tolerate such a construction. If anything is basic (and, I'm inclined to say, clear) in its eschatology, it is that the *eschatological* kingship of Christ begins already at his first coming culminating in his resurrection and ascension. Already at and dating from Christ's exaltation, "God has placed all things under his feet and appointed him to be head over everything for the church" (Eph 1:22; cf. v. 20).

This is a key eschatological pronouncement (announcing the fulfillment in Christ in terms of Psalm 8:6 and 110:1). At least two observations bear on this and similar declarations (e.g., Ac 2:34, 36; Php 2:9–11; 1Pe 3:22): (1) The New Testament certainly teaches a new phase of Christ's kingship in the future. But that decisive, quantum transition is plainly associated with events concomitant with his personal, bodily return (note especially the application of the same two passages, from Psalms 8 and 110, to the resurrection hope of the church in 1Co 15:24–28), and not with some prior, intermediate point or set of developments leading up to his return. (2) The *entire* period between his exaltation and return, not just some segment toward the close, is the period of Christ's *eschatological* kingship, exercised undiminished throughout (through the eschatological, Pentecostal presence and power of the Holy Spirit in the church).

In other terms, for the New Testament the *entire* interadventual period, not just a closing episode, is the "golden age" of the church; that period and what transpires in it, as a *whole*, embodies the church's millennial "success" and "victory." To deny that by defining "golden"/"success"/"victory" (almost) exclusively in terms of the church's future (short of Christ's return), is either to deny the eschatological quality of the church's present existence (to "de-eschatologize" the present), or—what for the New Testament is no less problematic, as we will presently see—to deny the equation (for the period until

Christ returns) of what is "eschatological," on the one hand, and "victory," "success," etc., on the other.

On either of these alternatives the effect is the same: the present exercise of Christ's (eschatological) kingship, as presented in the New Testament, is decisively diminished. His kingship, in effect, is held in abeyance; rather than being a present actuality, it is largely a matter of potential, poised for its future, "golden" exercise.

2. At stake here is the basic *duality* of the eschatological fulfillment taught in Scripture. What from the Old Testament angle is a unitary, telescoped focus of eschatological hope (*one* coming of the Messiah, *one* Day of the Lord) turns out in the differentiation of its actual fulfillment, in the New Testament, to have a *dual* focus (not three or more foci). In other words, there are *two* comings (or, more accurately, two episodes of the one coming) of the Christ, but no more than that. In the terminology of then contemporary Jewish eschatology, taken over by Jesus and the New Testament writers, the "age-to-come"/kingdom, already present in Jesus' earthly ministry culminating in his exaltation, will also arrive in the future at his return, but not until then (and then not again and again).

Certainly within the first, "already" installment there is room for different stages or phases—marked off by epochal events like Jesus' baptism, his death, resurrection, ascension and Pentecost, and the fall of Jerusalem. But none of these events or some presumably still future event or development prior to Christ's return, no matter how momentous, can have categorical, definitive eschatological significance on a par with Christ's coming in its (past and future) duality. Pentecost, for instance, is properly understood as Christ's coming (to be with the church through the presence and power of the Holy Spirit; see, e.g., Jn 14:18–20; Ro 8:9–10; 1Co 15:45; 2Co 3:17). But it would be thoroughly misleading to view Pentecost on the same level as the incarnation and what the New Testament regularly calls the Parousia (e.g., 1Co 15:23; 1Th 2:19; 2Pe 3:4), so that the latter would then be the "third" coming of Christ.

(The fall of Jerusalem, by the way, is to be closely associated with the above-mentioned events [death, resurrection, ascension] *preceding* it; with them it is one in a unified complex of events. As such, like those other events, it does point to and anticipate the second coming—with which, from the unitary outlook of the Old Testament, the event complex of the first coming can even be said to be one event. But the fall of Jerusalem is decisively misunderstood unless we recognize that—even for the apostolic church, when it was still future—its primary affinities are not toward the future but the *past*, toward the first coming, as it marks the end of the brief transitional period from the old to the new covenant. It is a fundamental misreading to see the eschatological discourses of Jesus [Mt 24, Mk 13, Lk 21] and the Book of Revelation as fulfilled almost exclusively or even largely in the events of A.D. 70, as if those events were of major eschatological importance. The destruction of Jerusalem and the temple begins already on Good Friday, when God himself radically desecrates "the holy city" [Mt 27:53] in its inner sanctum. Already then the city is desolated at its vital center as the temple curtain is torn "in two from top to bottom" [v. 51; cf. Mk 15:38; Lk 23:45]. What happens in A.D. 70, despite the untold suffering and violence, is but the inevitable aftermath, nothing more than a secondary after-shock.)

The pivotal factor here, once more, is the *duality* involved. When—by contrasting it with the present (and past) condition of the church—an attempt is made to locate the climactic eschatological event(s) prior to Christ's return at a point still in the future for the church, then all that precedes necessarily (in terms of fundamental biblical struc-ture) forfeits its eschatological character. Alternatively, if we grant the eschatological significance of Christ's first coming taught in the New Testament, the future (prior to his return) cannot involve the introduction of anything substantively or constitutively new eschatologically; that future must be in continuity with and an unfolding of the eschatological reality already present and operative in the church.

If, as some charge, this position is "staticism," involving a "static" view of history, so be it. But it is not a staticism that eliminates real, meaningful progress in history. It is, we may say, the "staticism of eschatological dynamism," stati-cism in the sense of the kingly permanence of the exalted Christ being effectively manifested—in its full, diverse (and ultimately incalculable, unpredictable) grandeur—over the entire interadvental period, from beginning to end. What is constant throughout this period—the exercise of Christ's eschatological kingship—is more basic and constitutive than any of the variations and "success"/"progress"/"development" that have and may still result from that exercise. In other words, the "gold"/"victory" is already present and continually being realized.

To put my main concern here another way, any viewpoint for which the victory of the church on earth prior to the eternal state is (primarily) future is essentially "chiliastic," that is, by that focus on the future it denies (at least implicitly) or can maintain only inconsistently the New Testament emphasis that the *provisional* eschatological order has already been inaugurated at Christ's first coming.[11] Because, for the period prior to the new heavens and earth, postmillennialism effectively shifts the eschatological center of gravity into the future, it, no less than premillennialism, is a form of chiliasm. In opposition to what is common to these other two positions—their "chiliastic" preoccupation with the millennium as entirely future—the New Testament teaches "realized millennialism" (Jay Adams).[12]

3. But now, how about the "amil postmils" mentioned earlier? What about the fact that many (most?) contemporary postmils recognize that the millennium and the interadvental period are coextensive? Doesn't that fact make much of my preceding analysis and criticism, at least so far as they are concerned, inapplicable and irrelevant? So it might at first seem.

The issue here, however, is not whether there is agreement about the millennium beginning at Christ's first coming and spanning the whole interadvental period; nor is

---

[11]The comments of W. Rordorf concerning the historic Christian, Augustinian rejection of chiliasm are undeniably pertinent here: ". . .if the thousand-year kingdom is already present, it will not come a second time. A time of salvation which is only temporary ['provisional,' *'eine zweifache nur vorläufige Heilszeit'*] cannot occur twice. Conversely, if in opposition to Augustine we were to maintain belief in the future millennium, we should not hold that the thousand-year kingdom is already proleptically realized: the very same reason would lead us to this conclusion" (*Sunday*, [Eng. trans. Philadelphia: Westminster, 1968], 117).

[12]*The Time Is At Hand* (Nutley, N.J.: Presbyterian and Reformed, 1970), 9–11, passim; however, we may ask whether Adams, too, sufficiently appreciates the *eschatological* nature of the millennium/interadvental period.

it even the recognition that "the definitive cataclysm has already taken place," important as that recognition is.[13] Rather, the issue is what implications are drawn from this recognition (and from the kingship of the ascended Christ) for the present (and past) existence of the church: Is millennial "victory" defined so that it is realized only at the end or over the entire period? Is that victory only a future expectation or a present reality as well?

The answer given to this question is decisive, and, so far as I can tell, the former is the answer given more or less consistently by the postmils in view. Their deepest intention or instinct is revealed in continuing to call themselves postmils and in thinking of their position as a revival of postmillennialism (even though their recognition that the millennium and the interadvental period are coterminous was usually lacking in earlier postmils). "Amil" postmils are not really very amil after all; that factor appears to represent an exegetical concession that is not particularly influential in their overall viewpoint.

But they are inconsistent, in some cases perhaps even in fundamental tension, with themselves. You can't have it both ways. Either give up the hope of future "dominion," defined in contrast to the alleged disarray, the supposedly indecisive, ambiguous, noninfluential, "nonvictorious" condition of the church at present (and in the past), or, as the inevitable alternative, effectively abandon the present/past *eschatological* kingship of Christ as anything more than (largely unrealized) potential.

I should reemphasize my concern not to be involved here in unnecessary polarizing or in exaggerating differences. If that is happening, then I need (and want) to have it pointed out. Perhaps, despite everything said so far, the line between myself and some postmils will prove after all to be a

[13]I agree for the most part with the comments of David Chilton in "Orthodox Christianity and the Millenarian Heresy" and "Optimistic Amillennialism," *The Geneva Review* 19 (June 1985): 3; 20 (July 1985): 5–6. The entire statement, excerpted above, reads: "*The definitive cataclysm has already taken place, in the finished work of Christ*" (p. 3, emphasis his). It seems to me, however, that his vision of *Paradise Restored* (Tyler, Tex.: Reconstruction Press, 1985) is controlled by an eschatological structure substantially in tension with, even alien to that indicated in his helpful, often incisive articles.

rather fine one. If it is simply a matter of disagreement over specific exegetical questions like whether Scripture entitles us to optimism about the future spread and success of the Gospel (most emphatically yes, although my definitions of "optimism" and "success" may be somewhat different), or whether Romans 11 teaches a mass end-time conversion of Jews (most likely not), then the debate can continue without the differences having to be substantive eschatologically.

A problem, however, enters—and I become uneasy—when and where a particular set of answers to these (and related) questions (a certain notion of future millennial "victory") is elevated to be definitive for eschatology and so becomes perceived as a basic eschatological position supplanting all others. Then, with this (postmil) set of answers assuming such principial, constitutive proportions, the de-eschatologizing of the church's present, already noted, is virtually inevitable.

4. This, finally, is the place to make clear that what I have so far written about postmillennialism should not be read as a defense of amillennialism as a whole. From the angle under consideration, my criticism of the latter is in a way even more sweeping. If the postmil is to be faulted for de-eschatologizing the existence of the church prior to the anticipated era of millennial victory, the amil, too often, has been guilty of de-eschatologizing the *entire* interadvental period. The correct exegetical insight that the millennium can't be reduced to an era either within or following that period often has gone (and goes) hand in glove with a failure (along with post- and premils) to comprehend the true, eschatological dimensions of the interadvental period as a whole. Measured by the New Testament, much amillennialism has not really been an *eschatological* position at all. Whether or not "defeatist" is the best description of it, it is, let's say, "thoroughly de-eschatologized" millennialism. (By the way, should we want to throw around the charge of "defeatism": if amils are "defeatist" about the entire millennium [interadvental period], then postmils are guilty of being "defeatist' about what has turned out so far to be a substantial part of it.)

For me, a bottom line to much of the discussion so far is this: Biblical eschatology, especially New Testament eschatology, decisively corrects (and relativizes) our traditional eschatological debates. The New Testament presents an eschatological structure that is in fact "*pre*-millennial" (!)—in the sense of being prior to and more fundamental than any of the standard eschatological views. The church today will remain impoverished in understanding its true identity and its task in the creation, until it is grasped by the fully eschatological significance of Christ's death and resurrection and embraces the "realized" or "inaugurated" eschatology taught in the New Testament—what Vos, for want of a better term, calls the "semi-eschatological" nature of Christian existence in the period between Christ's resurrection and his return. What will challenge and activate and sustain the church (and give it "optimism") in its present calling is its perception, not of a presumed promise of future dominion before Christ's return, but of the real victory it already possesses in the exalted Christ.

What the New Testament announces in Christ's first coming, especially his exaltation, is nothing less than the actual beginning of the end—the great, long-awaited work of God bringing history to an end and inaugurating the new and final order for the creation (e.g., Mk 1:15; 2Co 5:17; Gal 4:4; Eph 1:10; Heb 1:2; 9:26). This order, from the *outset*, is so climactic that it cannot be superseded—other than by the eternal state of affairs beginning at Christ's return. There is no other "second" in eschatological order of magnitude than that state—precisely what Hebrews 9:28 teaches ("he will appear a second time. . ."; cf. v. 26). Any set of developments in the interim between Christ's resurrection and his return, however otherwise significant, perhaps even momentous, can be of no more than subordinate, derivative importance eschatologically. Any "hope" for what may yet transpire prior to his return cannot compare with what has already arrived in Christ *and* is already being realized in and through the church.

What Vos writes primarily with premillennialism in view applies as well to postmil constructions:

> Paul conceives of the present Christian state on so high a plane that nothing less nor lower than the absolute state of the eternal consummate kingdom appears worthy to be its sequel. To represent it as followed by some intermediate condition falling short of perfect heavenly life would be in the nature of an anticlimax. . . .

It is thus of the very essence of salvation that it correlates the Christian's state with the great issues of the last day and the world to come. . . .

The point we wish to emphasize in all this is that Paul throughout represents the present Christian life as so directly leading up to, so thoroughly prefashioning the life of the eternal world, that the assumption of a *tertium quid* separating the one from the other must be regarded as destructive of the inner organism of his eschatology. For . . . what the Christian life anticipates is . . . something of an absolute nature, something pertaining to the consummate state. No matter with what concrete elements or colors the conception of a Chiliastic state may be filled out, to a mind so nourished upon the firstfruits of eternal life itself, it can, for the very reason of its falling short of eternal life, have had little significance or attraction. [14]

This is the eschatology taught in the New Testament: a realized-eschatological and therefore decidedly optimistic amillennialism, optimistic about the victory—present (and past) no less than future—being realized in and through the church.

ESCHATOLOGY AND SUFFERING

I now come to my most substantial reservation. It concerns the understanding of Christian existence and of the role of the church in the world, until Jesus returns, that seems to characterize much contemporary postmillennialism, particularly within reconstructionism. Developing this point will serve to clarify and sharpen the formal, structural observations—by themselves necessarily somewhat abstract—already made. I confine myself here almost entirely to that dimension of my concern, as I see it, that is most critical and religiously sensitive ("practical," if you will).

The inaugurated eschatology of the New Testament is least of all the basis for triumphalism in the church, at whatever point prior to Christ's return. Over the interadven-

---

[14]"Eschatology and Chiliasm," 34–35; cf. *Pauline Eschatology*, 235–36. Cf. "Second Coming," 422: "The point may be made that . . . the present so directly leads up to, so thoroughly pre-fashions the eternal future as to leave no room for a third something that would separate the one from the other."

tal period in its entirety, from beginning to end, a fundamental aspect of the church's existence is (to be) "suffering with Christ"; nothing, the New Testament teaches, is more basic to its identity than that.[15]

1. Two passages, both in Paul, are especially instructive concerning this reality. Strictly speaking, they are autobiographical, but the immediate and broader context of both shows that they intend to provide a paradigm, not only for other apostles or his own generation but for all believers until Jesus comes.

a). 2 Corinthians 4:7—"But we have this treasure in jars of clay to show that this all-surpassing power is from God and not from us."

"This treasure in jars of clay" graphically captures the tension at the heart of this statement and of the apostle's overall understanding of the nature of Christian existence between the resurrection and the return of Christ. "This treasure" is the Gospel or, better, the content of the Gospel—the glory-light of the (exalted) Christ (v. 4), the eschatological, new-creation glory of God, revealed in Christ (v. 6). "Clay jars," in contrast, are believers—in all of their mortality and fragility. We have "this treasure," Paul says, but for now, until Jesus comes, we have it only in the "clay jars" that we are. Or, as he puts it elsewhere (Ro 6:12–13), believers are "alive from the dead," already resurrected, but they are that only "in the mortal body," as they are (in that sense) still unresurrected.

Verses 8 and 9 expand on this fundamental, resurrected/not-resurrected "dialectic" of the Christian life—by means of four pairs of pointedly formulated contrasts: as "clay jars," believers are "hard pressed on every side," "perplexed," "persecuted," and "struck down"; nevertheless (note the fourfold repetition of "but not")—as possessing "this treasure"—they are "not crushed," "not in despair," "not abandoned," and "not destroyed."

Verse 10 further describes this reality in summary fashion: we (believers) carry around in the body "the dying of Jesus" [*nekrōsis* here has in view death as an activity or

---

[15]For a more developed treatment of the discussion in this section, see my article "The Usefulness of the Cross," *Westminster Theological Journal* 41 (1978–79): 228–46, and the literature cited there.

process], so that "the life of Jesus" ["this treasure"] may be manifested "in our body" ["in clay jars"]. Verse 11 closely parallels verse 10 with slight explanatory variations: "always being given over to death for Jesus' sake, so that the life of Jesus may be manifested in our mortal flesh."

Even from this brief analysis of the passage there should be little difficulty in recognizing that in the summary description in verses 10–11 suffering (characterized as "the dying of Jesus" and "always being given over to death for Jesus' sake") and "the life of Jesus" are not separate sectors of Christian experience, as if the latter, by addition, somehow balances off and compensates for the former. Much less does Paul say that the tendency of the latter is to replace the former; in fact, he effectively distances himself from the (postmil-like) view that the (eschatological) life of (the risen and ascended) Jesus embodies a power/victory principle that progressively ameliorates and reduces the suffering of the church.

Rather, Paul intends to say, as long as believers are in "the mortal body," "the life of Jesus" manifests itself *as* "the dying of Jesus"; the latter describes the existence mode of the former. Until the resurrection of the body at his return Christ's resurrection-life finds expression in the church's sufferings (and, as will become clear presently, nowhere else—so far as the existence and calling of the church are concerned); the locus of Christ's ascension-power is the suffering church.

This, it should not be overlooked, involves an evangelistic or missiological reality of fundamental proportions— "death is at work in us, but life is at work in you" (v. 12; cf. v. 7: "that this all-surpassing power may be from God and not from us").

b). Philippians 3:10—"I want to know Christ and the power of his resurrection and the fellowship of sharing in his sufferings, becoming like him in his death."

This aspiration expresses essentially the same idea as 2 Corinthians 4:10–11. In the immediate context Paul is concerned for "the surpassing greatness of knowing Christ Jesus [his] Lord" (v. 8), knowledge that comes from being "found in him" (v. 9), that is, from being united with Christ. Verse 10, then, brings into view a fundamental component of this rich, experiential union–knowledge.

A key to the intended impact of verse 10 is to recognize that both "ands" (following "Christ" and "resurrection") are not simply coordinating but explanatory; they do not merely connect, they explicate. In step-wise fashion Paul progressively traces a single, composite notion: Knowing the power of his resurrection is not something in addition to knowing Christ, nor is knowing the fellowship of his sufferings a further addition to both. Rather, the controlling consideration is union with Christ in his death and resurrection such that to "know"/experience Christ is to experience the power of his resurrection and that, in turn, is to experience the fellowship of his sufferings—a total reality that can then be summed up as conformity to Christ's death.

By virtue of union with Christ, Paul is saying, the power of Christ's resurrection is realized in the sufferings of the believer; sharing in Christ's sufferings is the way the church manifests his resurrection-power. Again, as in 2 Corinthians 4:10–11, the locus of eschatological life is Christian suffering; the mark—the indelible, ineradicable impression—left on the existence of the church by the formative power of the resurrection is the *Cross*. And, further, this is not some merely temporary state of affairs incidental to the circumstances of the church in the apostle's own day but is for all—the whole church in whatever time and place—who aspire to the resurrection of the dead (v. 11).

c). This is also what Romans 8:17b has in view when Paul rounds off his immediately preceding teaching with a sweeping proviso—not a condition for the adoption just spoken of (v. 14b–17a) but a conditional element nonetheless, given with that adoption: "if indeed we share his [Christ's] sufferings in order that we may also share in his glory."

This correlation of future glory and present suffering is a prominent concern in the section that follows. At least two points are worth noting about "our sufferings" (v. 18): (1) their nature/breadth and (2) their terminus.

(1) Christian suffering ought not to be conceived of too narrowly. In the passages so far considered, and elsewhere in the New Testament (e.g., 2Co 1:5–10; 1Pe 4:12–19), suffering surely includes but is more than persecution and martyrdom (reserved primarily, say, for apostles and foreign missionaries).

Romans 8:18ff. especially discloses the breadth of what ought to be our conception of Christian suffering. Suffering has to be seen in the context of the "frustration"/"futility" (*mataiotēs*), the "bondage to decay" to which the entire creation has been subjected, not by the inherent nature of things but because of God's curse on Adam's sin (v. 20–21 are, in effect, a Pauline commentary on Ge 3). Suffering is a function of the futility/decay principle pervasively at work in the creation since the fall; suffering is everything that pertains to creaturely experience of this death-principle.

From this perspective, then, Christian suffering is literally all the ways in which this "weakness-existence" (v. 26) is borne, by faith, in the service of Christ—the mundane, "trivial" but often so easily exasperating and unsettling frustrations of daily living, as well as monumental testing and glaring persecution. Suffering with Christ is the totality of existence "in the mortal body" and within "this world in its present form [that] is passing away" (1Co 7:31), endured for his sake. What has to be reckoned with here is the pervasive "givenness" of Christian suffering—its constitutive nature for the existence of the church as a whole; suffering for Christ is the inseparable correlate of believing in him—the precise point of Philippians 1:29: "For it has been granted to you on behalf of Christ not only to believe on him, but also to suffer for him. . ." (cf. 2Ti 3:12: "In fact ["in the last days," v. 1, that is, until his return], everyone who wants to live a godly life in Christ Jesus will be persecuted").

(2) Romans 8:18ff. is no less clear as to the terminus of this comprehensive suffering. Together with the rest of the creation, Satan and his servants excepted, believers exist in hope (v. 20), in "groaning" (v. 22–23, cf. 26) anticipation (v. 19, 23) of "the revelation of the sons of God" (v. 19), of "the glorious freedom of the children of God" (v. 21). This revelation/liberation of believers (note: along with and inseparable from the liberation of creation as a whole) is the future dimension of their adoption and will take place at the time of the redemption (= resurrection) of the body (v. 23), not before. Until then, at Christ's return, the suffering/futility/decay principle in creation remains in force, undiminished (but sure to be overcome); it is an enervating factor that cuts across the church's existence, including its mission, in its entirety. The notion that this frustration factor

will be demonstrably reduced, and the church's suffering service noticeably alleviated and even compensated, in a future era before Christ's return is not merely foreign to this passage; it trivializes as well as blurs both the present suffering and future hope/glory in view. Until his return, the church remains one step behind its exalted Lord; his exaltation means its (privileged) humiliation, his return (and not before), its exaltation.

d). It bears emphasizing that what we are presently considering is not some subordinate, peripheral strand of New Testament teaching. That can be further appreciated from the fundamental structural observation that Paul and the other writers expound the teaching of Jesus and so the eschatological reality, central to that teaching according to the Synoptic Gospels, called the kingdom of God/heaven; the New Testament writers are basically interpreters of the kingdom-proclamation of Jesus (and, so, in turn, of the Old Testament as the roots of that proclamation).

The passages on suffering just considered, among others, expand on a fundamental dimension of Jesus' teaching on discipleship: The actual arrival of the eschatological kingdom in Jesus' coming means, until his return, suffering service. In the kingdom the measure of greatness is to be a servant (Mt 20:26; Mk 10:43); a key watchword of the kingdom is "very last and servant of all" (Mk 9:35). More specifically, Jesus announces as an absolutely requisite, "life-saving" condition of discipleship: "If anyone would come after me, he must deny himself and take up his cross daily and follow me" (Lk 9:23–24; cf. Mt 10:38; 16:24; Mk 8:34; Lk 14:27). Cross bearing is a comprehensive description of kingdom-discipleship, as the qualification "daily" makes explicit. In response to the disciples' request for prominent kingdom status—kingdom "dominion," if you will—the only promise Jesus has for them (and us), this side of his return, is the "fellowship of sharing in his sufferings" (cf. Php 3:10): "You will drink the cup I drink and be baptized with the baptism I am baptized with" (Mk 10:37, 39). John has got it just right: until Jesus comes again, the presence of the kingdom is bracketed by the realities of "suffering" and "endurance" (Rev 1:9; cf. 3:11; 22:7, 12, 20).

2. This mark—this *essential* mark—of the church's identity seems muted or largely ignored in much of today's

postmillennialism, measured by my reading and other contacts, which I take to be fairly representative. Its "golden" dreams appear to leave little place for Christian suffering—other than as a perhaps necessary, but temporary means for achieving those dreams, whose realization, in turn, will mean the virtual disappearance of suffering for the church.

Most assuredly, the eschatology of the New Testament is an "eschatology of victory"—victory presently being realized by and for the church, through the eschatological kingship of the exalted Christ (Eph 1:22). But any outlook that fails to grasp that, short of Christ's return, this eschatology of victory is an eschatology of suffering—an eschatology of (Christ's) "power made perfect in weakness" (2Co 12:9)—confuses the identity of the church. As Paul reminds the church just a few verses after the Romans 8 passage considered above (v. 37), *not* "beyond" or "[only] after" but "*in* all these things" ("trouble or hardship or persecution or famine or nakedness or danger or sword," v. 35), "we are more than conquerors." Until Jesus comes again, the church "wins" by "losing."

What has happened to this theology of the cross in much of contemporary postmillennialism? The picture of hope and progress that I get from reading the New Testament does not include, for instance, the unbeliever as a naked child scrambling for the crumbs falling from the bountiful, overladen table of the believer.[16] Is it really overreacting to say that such triumphalism is repugnant to biblical sensibilities? Some postmils at least—especially within reconstructionism, it seems—are spelling "success" and "progress" with an alphabet that cannot be found in the New Testament.

(Hermeneutical commitments of far-reaching importance are at stake at this point, although I cannot discuss them here at any length. Briefly, the basic issue is this: Is the

---

[16]So the picture on the front cover of Gary North's *Dominion and Common Grace: The Biblical Basis of Progress* (Tyler, Tex.: Institute for Christian Economics, 1987). That this is what the cover intends to convey is surely the impression left by the contents of the book itself, especially as the author elaborates his views of historical progress and the millennial outworkings of common grace.

New Testament to be allowed to interpret the Old—as the best, most reliable interpretive tradition in the history of the church (and certainly the Reformed tradition) has always insisted? Does the New Testament as a *whole*—as the God-breathed record of the [eschatological] end point of the history of special revelation—provide the *controlling* vantage point for properly understanding the entire Old Testament, including its prophecies? Or, alternatively, will the Old Testament, particularly prophecies like Isaiah 32:1–8 and 65:17–25, become the hermeneutical fulcrum? Will large reaches of the still-future eschatological outlook present in the New Testament, like the discourses of Jesus in Matthew 24 with its parallels and the bulk of Revelation, be effectively deprived of their continuing relevance for the eschatological outlook of the church today, by relegating their fulfillment to the past events of A.D. 70?[17] Will the vast stretches of Old Testament prophecy, including its recurrent, frequently multivalent apocalyptic imagery, thus be left without effective New Testament control and so become a virtual blank check to be filled out in capital, whatever may be its source, that is something other than the result of sound exegesis? To adopt this alternative is to be leading the church into a hermeneutical morass from which, only with difficulty, it will eventually have to extricate itself. We ought to spare ourselves that.)

Any outlook that tends to remove or obscure the (constitutive) dimension of suffering for the Gospel from the present *triumph* of the church is an illusion. The misplaced expectation, before Christ's return, of a "golden age" in which, in contrast to the present, opposition to the church will have been reduced to a minimum and suffering will have receded to the periphery for an (at last) "victorious"

---

[17]Do we really wish to risk staking the viability of our eschatological position on doubtful answers to questions of Special Introduction—questions that themselves, by the nature of the case (the lack of adequate canonical givens in many instances), admit to answers that are at best highly probable and are always, like all results of historical scholarship, subject in principle to review and revision? If I understand correctly, this appears to be the line being followed increasingly by some postmils in trying to argue for a rigorously consistent "preterism," based on the conclusion that all of the New Testament documents, particularly Revelation, were presumably written before the fall of Jerusalem and have a future outlook largely preoccupied with that fall as a key eschatological event.

Christendom—that misconception can only distort the church's understanding of its mission in the world. According to Jesus, the church will not have drained the shared cup of his suffering until he returns. The church cannot afford to evade that point. It does so at the risk of jeopardizing its own identity.

WATCHFULNESS FOR CHRIST'S RETURN

My final reservation is that postmillennialism deprives the church of the imminent expectation of Christ's return and so undermines the quality of watchfulness that is incumbent on the church. At issue here is not that there are imminence statements in Matthew 24 and its synoptic parallels, for example, that refer proximately to the fall of Jerusalem; some no doubt do. Rather, the issue is that not all such statements are fulfilled in that cataclysm and those that are, in their immediate contexts, ultimately point to the Second Coming. The *marana tha* of the New Testament is not nearly satisfied by the events of A.D. 70 (1Co 16:22; cf., e.g., Ro 13:11–12; Php 4:5; Jas 5:8; 1Pe 4:7; 1Jn 2:18; Rev 1:3; 22:20).

The overall message of the New Testament is that—given the death and resurrection of Christ, the coming of the Spirit at Pentecost, and the close of the apostolic era (including the destruction of Jerusalem), in their eschatological significance—the stage is set for Christ's return; the only event still outstanding in the history of redemption, as far as biblical prophecy reveals, is that return with its concomitants (see, e.g., 2Th 2:1–12). So, for instance, Paul sees the spreading, worldwide triumph of the Gospel as already fulfilled in his own day; through his own (apostolic) ministry, in part, "all over the world this gospel is bearing fruit and growing," and "the gospel . . . has been proclaimed to every creature under heaven" (Col 1:6, 23).[18] Similarly, the

---

[18]One reason I am inclined against the view that Romans 11:11ff. teaches a future mass conversion of the Jews is that Paul seems to see his *own* ministry to the Gentiles (with its jealousy-provoking, repentance-producing effect) as serving, *already* at that time, to bring about the *"fullness"* of the Jews (v. 11–15; cf. "all Israel," v. 26)—a fullness that throughout the passage *contrasts* with the elect "remnant" (v. 5), who were not "hardened" (v. 7) and did not "stumble" (v. 11); the Jews who repent through the apostle's activity are not added to the remnant but inaugurate the fullness, whose sum total will then be realized over the entire interadvental period.

Book of Acts does not leave the reader hanging, presumably waiting for "Part 3" to Theophilus or some other sequel for the final outcome. It tells a *complete* story; it documents the actual realization of the sweeping promise of 1:8—the universal spread of the Gospel through the *apostles* (see v. 2–3 for the apostolic antecedent of "you" in v. 8), expanding out from Jerusalem (the Jews) to "the ends of the earth" (Rome representing the world center of the Gentiles). In short, the first part of Jesus' pronouncement in Matthew 24:14 ("And this gospel of the kingdom will be preached in the whole world as a testimony to all nations, . . ."; cf. Mk 13:10) has an adequate fulfillment in the ministry of the apostles.

Certainly the New Testament anticipates and makes provision for the postapostolic future of the church, quite explicitly in the Pastoral Epistles especially; it recognizes that there is to be an ongoing superstructure erected on the once-for-all apostolic foundation (Eph 2:20). But it gives no indication as to the duration of that future, at least no calculable indications. A pivotal consideration, it seems, is that according to the New Testament, Christ *could* have returned at virtually any time since the ministry of the apostles; all the demands of prophecy, short of Christ's return and its sequel, have been satisfied by the course of redemptive history terminating with their ministry.

In other words, the universal circumference of the Gospel's triumph has been drawn by the ministry of the apostles. So far as God has revealed his purposes, the subsequent process of filling in that circle could have been and can be terminated at any time. That filling-in process is the church's "filling up what is lacking in Christ's afflictions," to use Paul's language describing his own ministry (Col 1:24; cf. Ro 8:17b). But the duration of that essentially missiological reality, just how long it will take to constitute the sum total of that suffering, lies hidden with God. The "day of salvation" (2Co 6:2), the New Testament announces, has not only arrived but is also at its end; the length of its gracious extension is known only to God, rooted in the unfathomable depths of his saving mercy.

It seems, then, that the New Testament does not warrant the kind of confidence that is prepared to assert, "This world has tens of thousands, perhaps hundreds of thousands of years of increasing godliness ahead of it, before the Second Coming of Christ."[19] Perhaps it may be that long, even longer, but then again, perhaps not. Perhaps it may be in our time, but then again, perhaps not. The New Testament calls us to a readiness, an (eager) longing (Ro 8:23, 25) that is not trapped by either extreme of reckoning.

The balance we ought to have is aptly expressed by the Westminster Divines in the words with which, take note, they chose to close their Confession of Faith:

> . . . so will He have that day unknown to men, that they may shake off all carnal security, and be always watchful, because they know not at what hour the Lord will come; and may be ever prepared to say, Come Lord Jesus, come quickly. Amen.

THE CHURCH IN THE WILDERNESS

It will not do simply to dismiss this chapter as the ramblings of someone who has betrayed his Reformed heritage—with its ennobling vision of life itself as religion and the whole of life to the glory of God—for an anemic, escapist Christianity of cultural surrender. Without question, the Great Commission continues fully in force, with its full cultural breadth, until Jesus returns; "teaching them to obey everything I have commanded you" is the mandate of the exalted Last Adam to the people of his new creation. We cannot measure the limit of that "everything" and its implications; of it we can only confess with the psalmist: "To all perfection I see a limit; but your commands are boundless" (119:96). That mandate, then, is bound to have a robust, leavening impact—one that will redirect every area of life and will transform not only individuals but, through them corporately (as the church), their cultures; it already has done so and will continue to do so, until Jesus comes.[20]

---

[19]Chilton, *Paradise Restored*, 221–22. This prediction, unlike the prophecies of Hal Lindsey et al., may be immune to embarrassment by the disconfirming possibilities of the immediate future, but it is on the same continuum of chiliastic calculation.

[20]This is a good place to register my reaction to typical reconstructionist rhetoric (that seems a not unfair description) that you can't expect people to work effectively for the success of the Gospel today unless they are convinced of the reconstructionist vision of eventual millennial victory; you can't and won't work for a goal, the argument runs, that you don't believe

But that intended impact will be realized only as the church lives out of the mind-set articulated by Paul in 1 Corinthians 7:29–31: "The time is short"—not temporally (or temporarily), say, until the events of A.D. 70 (a fairly typical postmil misunderstanding, apparently, that trivializes this passage and strikes at the heart of Paul's theology of Christian existence as a whole), but until Jesus comes—however long that may be. For that shortened, compressed time, he continues, "those who have wives should live as if they had none; those who mourn, as if they did not; those who are happy, as if they were not; those who buy something, as if it were not theirs to keep; those who use the things of the world, as if not engrossed in them." "For," he reasons, introducing a consideration of much more fundamental, far-reaching magnitude than the fall of Jerusalem ever had, "this world in its present form is passing away."

Reconstructionist postmillennialism, it seems, lacks or at least substantially mutes this Pauline "as if not" (*hōs mē*), this paradoxical tension of "fully involved detachment" or, if you will, "detached involvement" in the affairs of this world. In fact, its vision of millennial "gold" leaves little, if any, place for that tension.

This tension, it should not be missed, reflects an essential quality of the Gospel itself; it exhibits a dimension of that "offense" and "foolishness" that Paul earlier in this same letter tells us unbelief inevitably perceives the Gospel to be (1:23). Admittedly, the balance called for here is elusive and difficult to maintain; there are no easy formulas or self-evident regimens. The perennially demanding, often perplexing path the church is called to follow, until Jesus comes, can be negotiated only as "we live by faith, not by sight" (2Co 5:7).

That faith, in its mode as hope and eschatological optimism, perseveres—as the immediate context intimates in the light of Romans 8:18–25—toward the permanent,

---

will be realized. Assuming for a moment the legitimacy of any particular reconstructionist/theonomic vision and, apart from other considerations, that line of reasoning seems suspiciously akin, on a broader, corporate scale, to arguing that you can't expect the individual believer to be concerned personally for perfect holiness unless such personal perfection is attainable in this life. Presumably, reconstructionists will not want to maintain that in the light of Romans 6:1ff.; 1 Peter 1:15–16 et al.

perfected order for *this* creation (not some other heavens and earth), in all of its concreteness and full corporeality, to be established, without further delay, along with the bodily resurrection of believers at Christ's return.[21] In the meantime, such faith will remain on guard against being drawn off balance—whether by premillennial (or de-eschatologized amillennial) tendencies toward world-renunciation and neglect, or by the disposition, more pronounced in some postmils than others, toward world-absorption and seduction.

* *

The comprehensive outlook found in the Book of Hebrews provides a fitting close to these remarks. Two realities dominate the writer's marvelous exposition of God's eschatological, "last days" speech in his Son (Heb 1:2). The one reality is Jesus, the high priest in heaven (e.g., 4:14; 8:1). Fulfilling Psalm 110, the exalted Christ is "priest forever, in the order of Melchizedek" (e.g., 5:6; 6:20; 7:17); the New Testament contains no more impressive presentation of the realized eschatological dimension of his person and work than this.

But for whom is the exalted Christ high priest? Who is served by his sanctuary service (Heb 8:2) of eschatological intercession (7:25)? The answer to that question is the other reality in view—the church as a pilgrim congregation, a

---

[21]My surmise is that, for many, a significant factor disposing them toward either a premil or a postmil position stems from etherealized, even insipid, less-than-biblical understandings of the eternal state. Such rarefied, colorless conceptions give rise to the conviction—compounded by a missing or inadequate awareness of the realized eschatology taught in Scripture—that eventually God must somehow "get in his licks" and "settle things" in history, as distinct from eternity. But what is the eternal order other than the consummation of *history*, the historical process come to *its* final fruition? The new heavens and earth, inaugurated at Christ's return, will be the climactic vindication of God's covenant and, so, his final historical triumph, the ultimate realization of his purposes for the original creation, forfeited by the first Adam and secured by the last. Inherent in both a postmil and a premil outlook, it seems, is the tendency, at least, toward an unbiblical, certainly un-Reformed separation or even polarization of creation and redemption/eschatology. (As this chapter goes off to the editors, it strikes me that the whole might well have been developed from the angle of this footnote.)

people in the wilderness. Utilizing a broad covenant-historical analogy, the writer compares the church between Christ's exaltation and his return to Israel in the desert (see esp. 3:7–4:11): just as the wilderness generation delivered from Egyptian bondage (picturing realized eschatology) had not yet entered Canaan (a picture of still future eschatology), so the New Testament church, presently enjoying a real experience of the salvation promised in the Gospel, has not yet entered into the possession of that salvation in its final and unthreatened form ("God's rest").

Two basic perspectives emerge with these two realities. On the one hand, the writer's realized eschatology leaves no room for a premil position: Once Jesus "has gone through the heavens" (Heb 4:14) and has "sat down at the right hand of the throne of the Majesty in heaven" (8:1), his return for a provisional earthly rule, prior to the eternal heavenly order, would be retrograde for the writer, a step backward eschatologically. Christ's return will be the return of the *heavenly* high priest, not the appearance of Christ temporarily exchanging heavenly ministry for earthly duties. That return will mean the appearance on *earth* of the heavenly order/sanctuary where Christ is "a high priest forever" (6:20), the manifestation on *earth*, without delay at his return, of the "heavenly Jerusalem" (12:22), the "enduring city" (13:14), the eternal "rest"-order (4:11).

But the writer is no less indisposed toward a postmil outlook: Until Christ returns the church remains a wilderness congregation; like the Patriarchs in the land of promise, believers are "aliens and strangers on earth" (Heb 11:13). That tension is an essential dimension of their identity—aliens in the creation that is theirs by right and whose eschatological restoration has already been secured for them by their high priest and king.

There is no "golden" age coming that is going to replace or even ameliorate these desert conditions of testing and suffering. No success of the Gospel, however great, will bring the church into a position of earthly prosperity and dominion such that the wilderness with its persecutions and temptations will be eliminated or even marginalized. That would have to be the outcome if prosperity—understood, for instance, in the terms of Isaiah 65:17ff.—is to be at all meaningful. Such prosperity and blessing for the church are reserved until Christ returns.

The writer of Hebrews operates with a simple enough eschatological profile: the bodily absence of Christ means the church's wilderness existence; his bodily presence, its entrance into God's final rest. What he must confront in his readers is a perennial problem for the church, a primal temptation bound up with its wilderness existence: the veiledness, for the present, of messianic glory and of the believer's eschatological triumph; "at present we do not see everything subject to him" (Heb 2:8), with the longing as well as the promise that "at present" holds for the church. All of us, then, are involved in a continuing struggle— against our deeply rooted eschatological impatience to tear away that veil and our undue haste to be out of the wilderness and see the realization of what, just because of that haste and impatience, will inevitably prove to be dreams and aspirations that are ill-considered and all too "fleshly."

"For here we do not have an enduring city, but we are looking for the city that is to come" (Heb 13:14).

Chapter Ten

Theonomy, Pluralism, and the Bible

William S. Barker

William S. Barker

William S. Barker (Ph.D., Vanderbilt University) is Professor of Church History at Westminster Theological Seminary (Philadelphia). With other degrees from Princeton University, Cornell University, and Covenant Theological Seminary he has taught at Covenant College and Covenant Theological Seminary, and at Westminster since 1987. He was editor of the *Presbyterian Journal* and has contributed to the *Dictionary of Christianity in America*.

Chapter Ten

Theonomy, Pluralism, and the Bible

Ever since the late 1970s evangelical Christians in the United States have become increasingly active in politics. Particularly those who would term themselves fundamentalists have suddenly discovered what was widely held—if not always practiced—in Reformed circles: that our faith applies to all of life and thought. Of great, and evidently growing, appeal to such American Christians has been the movement in the Reformed camp known as theonomy. This movement, as represented for our purposes in the book *Theonomy in Christian Ethics*, by Greg L. Bahnsen,[1] seeks a restoration of God's law as the recognized basis for civil government. In making his appealing case for this theonomic approach to civil authority, Bahnsen admirably seeks to steer clear of some historic mistakes in church-state relations in a chapter entitled "Separation of Church and State" and particularly to avoid certain unwelcome connotations of the term "theocracy" as applied to American politics.[2] His argument is that there was a separation of church and state in Old Testament Israel, and that the same kind of distinction will serve as well today in a government operating according to God's law.

At the same time, Bahnsen's advocacy of the law of God

---

[1]Greg L. Bahnsen, *Theonomy in Christian Ethics* (Nutley, N.J.: Craig, 1977); the expanded edition, with a seventeen-page additional preface replying to critics, otherwise has the same pagination (Phillipsburg, N.J.: Presbyterian and Reformed, 1984). See also Greg L. Bahnsen, *By This Standard: The Authority of God's Law Today* (Tyler, Tex.: Institute for Christian Economics, 1985).

[2]Bahnsen, *Theonomy*, 427–32.

as the basis for civil government is clearly opposed to the modern concept of pluralism.[3] The term *pluralism* is used today in several senses. *Webster's Ninth New Collegiate Dictionary* defines pluralism as (1) "a state of society in which members of diverse ethnic, racial, religious, or social groups maintain an autonomous participation in and development of their traditional culture or special interest within the confines of a common civilization" and (2) "a concept, doctrine, or policy advocating this state."[4] In terms of civil rights for ethnic or racial minorities pluralism is so widely acknowledged in our American culture as to be accepted as commonplace. It is the idea of religious pluralism, however, that is of concern to Bahnsen. God's law as the basis for civil government, according to the theonomy movement, clearly militates against religious pluralism.

As this essay undertakes to answer the question "Is pluralism biblical?" in the affirmative, it is necessary to mention one kind of pluralism that clearly is contrary to Scripture. That is the concept, which has become increasingly favored in the churches most affected by secular and ecumenical trends, of pluralism of religious belief within Christianity.[5] This is not the variety of pluralism with which we are concerned here. Rather, we are concerned with the concept of the civil authority recognizing the freedom of religious belief and practice by a variety of groups—including theists, humanists, naturalists, and atheists—with no one such group established or favored by the state.[6] It is my

[3]Bahnsen, *By This Standard*, 340.

[4]Springfield, Mass.: Merriam, 1983.

[5]For an example, see Wilfred Cantwell Smith, *Religious Diversity: Essays by Wilfred Cantwell Smith*, ed. Willard G. Oxtoby (New York: Harper & Row, 1976). In the first essay, "The Christian in a Religiously Plural World," 3–21, Smith argues for what he terms the Christian value of acceptance of other people over against the value of doctrinal truth, citing favorably the United Church of Canada's declaration in 1966 that God works creatively and redemptively in various religions, not just through knowledge of Jesus Christ.

[6]For descriptions of religious pluralism in America, see Robert T. Handy, ed., *Religion in the American Experience: The Pluralistic Style*, (Columbia, S.C.: University of South Carolina Press, 1972), Introduction, xiv-xvi; Franklin H. Littell, *From State Church to Pluralism: A Protestant Interpretation of Religion in American History*, new ed. (New York: Macmillan, 1971). E. Clinton Gardner, *The Church as a Prophetic Community* (Philadelphia: Westminster, 1967)

contention that such religious pluralism within a society is our Lord's intention for this time in history and hence is biblical. Bahnsen's advocacy of God's law as the basis for civil authority, with essentially the same kind of separation of church and state that existed in Old Testament Israel, opposes this sort of pluralism.

A brief review of the history of church-state relations since New Testament times will give us perspective on this theonomic approach.

During its first three centuries in the Roman world, Christianity obviously did not enjoy favorable relations with the civil government, frequently experiencing its persecution and having little opportunity to exercise an active positive influence. Guided by New Testament teachings such as Romans 13:1–7; 1 Timothy 2:1–7; and 1 Peter 2:13–17, the early Christians kept the laws that did not require them to go counter to the commands of the Lord and prayed for their governors as rulers ordained by God.

A new complication arose when the Roman emperor himself identified with the Christian church. Constantine's conversion in the early fourth century put the church in a favored position, bringing it relief from the immediately preceding fiercest persecution of Emperor Diocletian and also adding to its numbers many with less commitment than that of the earlier martyrs. Doctrine was consolidated in the age of great ecumenical councils, but the secular rulers themselves exercised undue influence in ecclesiastical deci-

comments that "religious pluralism implies—indeed, presupposes—a secular society," but he makes a distinction between "secular" and "secularist": "A pluralist society is secular, but it is not secularist; for a secularist society is one in which secularism as an anti-theistic conception of reality has become the official world view" (p. 94). Certain dangers inherent in the American trends are described by Phillip E. Hammond, "Pluralism and Law in the Formation of American Civil Religion," in *America, Christian or Secular? Readings in American Christian History and Civil Religon*, ed. Jerry S. Harbert (Portland, Ore.: Multnomah, 1984), 205–29. He argues that law and the courts have replaced the church and theology as the basis of public morality with the coming of religious pluralism. Kathryn J. Pulley, "The Constitution and Religious Pluralism Today," in *Liberty and Law: Reflections on the Constitution in American Life and Thought*, ed. Ronald A. Wells and Thomas A. Askew (Grand Rapids: Eerdmans, 1987), 143–55, also points out such dangers; she comments on the tendency toward relativism inherent in religious pluralism.

sions as by the late fourth century the orthodox emperor Theodosius the Great established Christianity as the state religion.

Augustine sought to sort out the relative authority and power of church and state in the new situation in what became known as the "two swords" theory, especially as it was enunciated by Pope Gelasius I (492–496). Using a technical distinction of Roman law, Gelasius claimed that while the emperor in Constantinople had *potestas*, or power, the bishop of Rome had *auctoritas*, or authority. The church through its clergy was to declare the will of God, and the emperor and his civil magistrates were to carry it out.

The relative influence of Christian bishop and Christian king on matters of law and government ebbed and flowed through the centuries. The high tide of papal influence carried church-state relations to a new stage, however, in what might be termed the "ecclesiocracy" of such popes of the High Middle Ages as Gregory VII (1073–85) and Innocent III (1198–1216), who claimed ability to depose secular rulers and to launch the military campaigns known as crusades.

With the coming of the sixteenth-century Reformation there was an attempt to restore balance in church-state relations. Reformers like Luther and Calvin in their movements clearly curtailed the kind of political excess that characterized the medieval papacy. They tended, however, still to think in Augustinian "two swords" terms of an established church and were not able, as were the persecuted Anabaptists, to return to a pre-Constantinian consciousness, which more aptly suits a missionary situation. Calvin deserves credit for developing one side of church-state separation, the protection of ecclesiastical integrity against intrusion by the civil magistrate into essentially spiritual matters, such as admission to the Lord's Table. The Scottish Presbyterians likewise stressed the prerogatives of King Jesus in his church over against Erastian attempts to have the civil authority decide such matters.

It remained for American Protestantism, however, to conclude that disestablishment of the church would be in the best interests of Christianity as well as of the state. The Presbyterian Church of America expressed this sentiment in the first of the "Preliminary Principles" attached to its new Form of Government in 1789:

> I. That "God alone is Lord of the conscience; and hath left it free from the doctrine and commandments of men, which are in anything contrary to his word, or beside it in matters of faith and worship:" Therefore, they consider the rights of private judgment, in all matters that respect religion, as universal, and unalienable: They do not even wish to see any religious constitution aided by the civil power, further than may be necessary for protection and security, and at the same time, equal and common to all others.

It is important to be aware of this historical background in order to appreciate the need for a further distinction between church and state than that which is made by theonomy. Bahnsen does make a proper distinction, as Calvin does, between outward behavior, as the civil magistrate's area of responsibility, and sins of the heart, which are God's concern alone.[7] He refines this distinction thus: "While the church propagates the gospel of God's grace, the state maintains the standards of God's justice in social matters (matters of outward behavior, but not matters of the heart, conscience, or belief)."[8] Further on he says, "Thus the state cannot be a promoter of the gospel or personal Christian faith, and the church cannot use the sword of the state in its evangelism."[9]

This distinction, however, is regarded as "simply the reaffirmation and confirmation" of Old Testament separation of church and state functions. In Old Testament Israel there was a distinction of functions, but both the civil ruler and the priests were under the authority of God's law.[10] But herein lies a problem. For in the Old Testament, godly kings like David, Jehoshaphat, Hezekiah, and Josiah, while recognizing a distinction of function (see particularly Jehoshaphat's distinction in 2Ch 19:11), surely were concerned, and

---

[7]Bahnsen, *Theonomy*, 381–82.

[8]Ibid., 386.

[9]Ibid., 426.

[10]Ibid., 417, 420–21. In *By This Standard*, 166, 288, 289, 330, Bahnsen describes certain discontinuities between the old and new covenants in regard to church and state.

properly so, to use their authority not just for social matters, but for the propagation of God's saving truth and the promotion of personal faith. More was expected of even the civil ruler in a nation in covenant relationship with the Lord.

A further distinction between church and state is called for in our time than that which Bahnsen makes. It is a distinction between that part of the law summed up by what Jesus termed the first and greatest commandment and that part of the law summed up by what he termed the second commandment, which is "like it." Love of God and love of neighbor are of course intimately related, because our Lord scarcely mentions the one without also referring to the other, and on these commandments all the Law and the Prophets hang. But unless a proper distinction is made between them, confusion of function will result. In making his point that the Old Testament holds the nations surrounding Israel responsible for keeping God's law, Bahnsen appears to make no distinction between the first great commandment and the second: "When the Israelite, Daniel, assumed civil office in a nation which was not Jewish or located in the promised land, he apparently did not feel that the rules for leadership had changed from what God would have expected of a civil magistrate in Israel."[11] Yet just the sort of distinction I am concerned to make was followed by Daniel. He applied the principles of God's law as it affected relations between human neighbors, and he himself was diligent in his own relations to God. But, although he bore witness to the true God, he did not use his civil authority to enforce the true religion, in the sense of belief and worship, on a pagan society. Nebuchadnezzar eventually gave his personal testimony that the Lord is "the Most High God" (Dan 4:2) and "the King of heaven" (v. 37), but he said at the same time that Daniel "is called Belteshazzar, after the name of my god, and the spirit of the holy gods is in him" (v. 8). This is clearly not an exclusive commitment. In like manner Darius decreed that "people must fear and reverence the God of Daniel" (Dan 6:26), but there is no evidence that these kings destroyed the other religions as the civil ruler was required to do in God's covenant nation.

This further distinction, between the first great com-

---

[11]*Theonomy*, 358.

mandment and the second, as applied to church-state relations, is implicit in Jesus' statement concerning the tribute money in Matthew 22:15–22 (with parallels in Mk 12:13–17 and Lk 20:20–26). The position that I believe this passage indicates is that (1) the civil authority is ordained by God to function in the area of the second great commandment, namely, that of human relations, and that (2) in the area of the first great commandment, namely, our relation to God, the civil authority's responsibility is not to enforce the true faith, but to maintain freedom. With complete respect for the theonomists' contention that Jesus came not to abolish the Law and the Prophets but rather to fulfill them, I seek the answer to the questions, How does our King intend for the first great commandment to be fulfilled? and, How is our righteousness to surpass that of the Pharisees and the teachers of the law with regard to church-state relations?

Picture the scene as Jesus is asked about paying tribute to Caesar. It is the Tuesday of that last week between his triumphal entry into Jerusalem and his arrest and crucifixion. The religious and political leaders among the Jews are so deeply concerned about his growing following that the Pharisees and Herodians conspire together to trap him in his words. Luke says, "Keeping a close watch on him, they sent spies, who pretended to be honest. They hoped to catch Jesus in something he said so that they might hand him over to the power and authority of the governor"—that is, the Roman procurator Pontius Pilate.

In this sort of religio-political context, they ask a religio-political question: "Teacher, we know you are a man of integrity and that you teach the way of God in accordance with the truth. You aren't swayed by men, because you pay no attention to who they are. Tell us then, what is your opinion? Is it right to pay taxes to Caesar or not?"

Realizing their evil intent, Jesus charges them with hypocrisy and demands, "Show me the coin used for paying the tax." Mark adds, "and let me look at it." They bring him a denarius, and he asks them, "Whose portrait is this? And whose inscription?"

"Caesar's," they reply.

And Jesus says, "Give to Caesar what is Caesar's and to God what is God's." And all three synoptic Gospels record that the crowd was amazed at his answer.

The reason for their amazement at the wisdom of Jesus becomes apparent as we grasp the full dynamics of this situation. And as we do so, we see how, although this may not be the *locus classicus* in the New Testament for church-state relations, it provides the foundation on which such passages as Romans 13 and 1 Peter 2 build. The basic principles can all be inferred from Jesus' simple but profound statement.

First, it is important to see the horns of the dilemma on which Jesus' enemies sought to trap him. His questioners included disciples of the Pharisees along with the Herodians. These two groups might themselves give different answers to the question about paying the tax to the Roman regime. The Herodians were those associated with the Herods, the Idumean-Jewish rulers who were politically allied with the Roman regime. The Pharisees, on the other hand, were zealous for the prerogatives of the Jewish religion and were sensitive to anything that might compromise one's consecration to the Lord by recognition of pagan religion. In the audience there no doubt were the most extreme in this direction politically, the Zealots, who advocated revolution against the Roman regime.[12]

A yes-or-no answer was impossible. Either way, Jesus would offend some significant part of his audience. If he said no, the Herodians and those like them would have grounds for charging him with treason against the Roman government. If he said simply yes, the Zealots and many like the Pharisees would have grounds for claiming he could not be the Messiah, for he would recognize not only a pagan regime, but pagan religion.

The reason for this last point lies in the Roman denarius. Many of these coins from the reigns of Augustus and of Tiberius have been found, and the images and inscriptions on them are of a similar nature. Most likely the tribute money here is the silver denarius of Tiberius, which shows a

---

[12]For information on the Herodians, see Harold W. Hoehner, *Herod Antipas* (Cambridge: Cambridge University Press, 1972), Appendix X, "The Herodians," 331–42; H. H. Rowley, "The Herodians in the Gospels," *Journal of Theological Studies* 41 (1940): 14–27. Concerning the Zealots in this context, see Oscar Cullmann, *The State in the New Testament* (New York: Scribner, 1956), 20, 34–37, and his book *Jesus and the Revolutionaries* (New York: Harper & Row, 1970), 45–47.

bust of the emperor on the obverse with the inscription "TI (BERIUS) CAESAR DIVI AUG(USTI) F(ILIUS) AUGUSTUS" ("Tiberius Caesar, son of the deified Augustus, and Augustus"). On the reverse is a female figure, probably Tiberius' mother Livia, as Pax, with the inscription "PONTIF(EX) MAXIM(US)" ("Highest Priest").[13] Some scrupulous Jews regarded the minting of such coins as a violation of the first commandment because of the recognition of another deity in the inscription and also a violation of the second commandment because of the graven image. The holiness of third-century rabbi Nahum ben Simai of Tiberia is illustrated by the fact that he never allowed his eyes to look at the portrait on a coin.[14] Bar Kochba, the revolutionary who claimed to be the Messiah in the second century, "had the imperial *denarii* collected, the obnoxious portraits and inscriptions beaten out by hammers and replaced by Hebrew temple vessels and inscriptions."[15] In the third century Hippolytus, a Christian, reported that some of the Essenes would not handle such a coin.[16] Ethelbert Stauffer says of Tiberius' denarius that it "is the most official and universal sign of the apotheosis of power and the worship of the *homo imperiosus* in the time of Christ."[17]

---

[13]For pictures of the denarius of Tiberius, as well as discussion, see Stewart Perowne, *The Later Herods: The Political Background of the New Testament* (London: Hodder and Stoughton, 1958), Plate 10 (opp. p. 33); S. G. F. Brandon, *Jesus and the Zealots: A Study of the Political Factor in Primitive Christianity* (New York: Scribner, 1967), Plate I(a) (opp. p. 144) and 45–46, 347–48; H. StJ. Hart, "The Coin of 'Render unto Caesar. . . ,' " in *Jesus and the Politics of His Day*, ed. Ernst Bammel and C. F. D. Moule (Cambridge: Cambridge University Press, 1984), 241–48; Ethelbert Stauffer, *Christ and the Caesars: Historical Sketches* (London: SCM, 1955), trans. K. and R. Gregor Smith from 3rd German ed. of 1952, 112–37; Herbert Loewe, *"Render unto Caesar": Religion and Political Loyalty in Palestine* (Cambridge: Cambridge University Press, 1940), 97. See also J. Duncan M. Derrett, *Law in the New Testament* (London: Darton, Longman & Todd, 1970), especially chapter 14, " 'Render to Caesar. . . ,' " 313–38. For a contrasting point of view, see J. Spencer Kennard, Jr., *Render to God: A Study of the Tribute Passage* (New York: Oxford University Press, 1950), especially 139.

[14]F. F. Bruce, "Render to Caesar," in *Jesus and the Politics of His Day*, ed. Ernst Bammel and C. F. D. Moule (Cambridge: Cambridge University Press, 1984), 259; Stauffer, *Christ and the Caesars*, 126.

[15]Stauffer, *Christ and the Caesars*, 126.

[16]Hippolytus, *Refutatio omnium haeresium*, 9:26; English translation in *Ante-Nicene Fathers*, 5:136.

[17]Stauffer, *Christ and the Caesars*, 127.

With such Jewish scruples concerning this Roman coin no doubt present in Jesus' audience, it is significant that Jesus requested that they show him the coin that he might look at it. At a stroke he not only embarrasses his questioners, who might have wanted to avoid being implicated with those who carried the coin by making them fetch one, but he also demonstrates that the scruple is exaggerated by evidently taking the dime-sized coin into his own hands when he asks, "Whose portrait is this?"

But when Jesus gives his terse response to their sheepish answer, "Caesar's": "Give to Caesar what is Caesar's, and to God what is God's," the weight of his statement falls on Herodians, Pharisees, and all alike. His emphasis is clearly on the latter half of the statement, in such a fashion that the force of the recognition of Caesar's due in the former half is much diminished.[18] Yes, Jesus was willing to pay the tax to Caesar—who minted the coins, maintained defense, administered justice, and built the roads—because God had ordained civil government for such purposes. But no, Jesus would not render to Caesar what was God's alone, namely worship and ultimate obedience. And the significant point for our purpose here is that it was not a compromise of Jesus' commitment to the things of God to pay the tax to Caesar, even with Caesar's blasphemous religion on the coin. *In the New Testament situation, under a Gentile regime, he did not expect the civil authority to support the true religion.*

Jesus' recognition of a new political situation in the new era that was to dawn with the institution of the church is shown in the wider context of all three Synoptic Gospels. The challenge from the Pharisees and Herodians concerning the tribute money is preceded, evidently earlier on the same day, by Jesus' parable of the vineyard and its wicked tenants, which the chief priests and the Pharisees rightly understood as directed at them (Mt 21:45; Mk 12:12; Lk 20:19). This parable is so pointed in its conclusion, "Therefore I tell you that the kingdom of God will be taken away from you and given to a people who will produce its fruit," that it functions as a pronouncement of the end of the Old Testament

---

[18]Günther Bornkamm, *Jesus of Nazareth*, trans. Irene and Fraser McLuskey with James M. Robinson from 3rd German ed. of 1959 (New York: Harper and Brothers, 1960), 122.

theocracy. In Luke's account the people, not just the religious leaders, respond, "May this never be!" But Jesus looked directly at them and applied Psalm 118:22, "The stone the builders rejected has become the capstone" (Lk 20:16–17). It is as though a curtain is being drawn down on the earlier act of God's drama of redemption, later to be raised on a stage with a new political setting as the Gospel goes forth to those other people, the Gentile nations. In this new setting it will not be appropriate for the civil authority to support the true religion as it was in the Old Testament theocracy.

The wider context in Matthew and Mark also provides reinforcement for the idea that Jesus' response concerning the tribute money had in view the twofold division of the law. The statement itself, referring to "the things of Caesar" (who is, pointedly, a man) and "the things of God," already makes such a division explicit in the minds of those involved in the debate with Jesus. Then evidently at the conclusion of the same discussions, after Jesus had silenced the Sadducees concerning the resurrection, a representative of the Pharisees (Mk 12:28 says, "One of the teachers of the law came and heard them debating") asks him, "Of all the commandments, which is the most important?" Jesus replies: " 'Love the Lord your God with all your heart and with all your soul and with all your mind.' This the first and greatest commandment. And the second is like it: 'Love your neighbor as yourself.' All the Law and the Prophets hang on these two commandments."

In the same conversation in which his teaching concerning the civil government is uttered we have also his familiar division of the law of God concerning our obligation toward the Lord and our obligation toward fellow human beings. Clearly Jesus recognized Caesar's prerogatives in the latter area of human relations, but Caesar was not to infringe on our liberty, nor was he expected to enforce the true faith and worship, in the former area of our relation to God.

If we are indeed zealous for the application of God's law in society, our first question must be, What is our King's intention? Jesus' response to the question concerning the tribute money reveals that his intention is for the civil authority to apply God's law in the area of human relations in which God has ordained him to serve. In the area of our relation to God, not only is it not legitimate for the state to enforce its false religion on us ("Give to God the things that are God's"), but it is not even the proper function of the state to enforce religion ("Bring me a denarius and let me look at it")—even the true faith and worship.

This distinction became important as the Gospel went forth into the Gentile nations. All that missionaries could rightly ask of the civil authority was the freedom to preach the Gospel so that people might be freely persuaded by the word and by the Spirit. To have the state in any way coerce belief or worship could only compromise the free nature of the Gospel and contaminate the purity of the church.

The distinction that I propose is one that was recognized in the Westminster Confession of Faith. Chapter XIX,2, says of the law of God that it "was delivered by God upon Mount Sinai in ten commandments, and written in two tables; the first four commandments containing our duty towards God, and the other six our duty to man." Chapter XX,2, says of Christian liberty: "God alone is Lord of the conscience, and hath left it free from the doctrines and commandments of men which are in any thing contrary to his word, or beside it, in matters of faith or worship." Here we have two categories of human doctrines and commandments that must not infringe on our liberty: (1) those that are contrary to God's word in any area and (2) those that are even just beside God's word—that is, alongside it—in the areas of faith or worship. Faith and worship, the area of our relationship to God and of his unique prerogatives, are not to have any doctrines or commandments laid on our consciences apart from God's own word. In other areas the requirement is only that such doctrines and commandments not be contrary to God's word; and, as Romans 13:5 tells us, we are conscience-bound to obey the civil magistrate in such matters so long as they are not contrary to God's word.

Yet theonomy seems not to recognize such a distinction in its claims that the civil authority is responsible to carry out all of the law of God (although an important distinction is properly made between crime and sin). In the context of Old Testament Israel as the nation in covenant with the Lord, the civil ruler was responsible to exterminate false religion and support the worship of God. But with the close of the Old Testament theocracy and the spread of the Gospel among the

Gentile nations this is evidently no longer our Lord's intent for the civil authority. Bahnsen seeks to make a distinction between, on the one hand, outward behavior and justice in social matters and, on the other hand, matters of the heart, conscience, or belief; but his position of applying the whole law of God in the state, as in the Old Testament, does not provide sufficient basis for his own distinction and thus protect the liberty of conscience and belief of non-Christians under a Christian government or of Christians under an unbelieving government.

How would this distinction apply to some of the issues of our time? Abortion and pornography, for example, as violations of the sixth and seventh commandments and hence in the area of the second great commandment, would be proper concerns for the civil government to deal with. It is appropriate for Christians to address the conscience of unbelievers in such matters and to seek through the legitimate channels of government to restrain wickedness in outward behavior by law and its enforcement.

The kind of distinction I am making, however, would oppose the requirement of prayer or acts of worship in the public schools. This would be enforcing a matter in the area of relations to God by means of civil authority.[19] On the other hand, we should contend for the freedom to have theistic perspectives, as on the question of human origins, included with other possible perspectives in the teaching of the public schools, so that a specifically antitheistic doctrine is not forced on the children of our society.

A matter such as Sabbath observance raises even more complex questions since there are clearly issues related to the fourth commandment that fall under the second great commandment as well as the first. In a society that includes substantial numbers of Jews and Muslims, as well as Christians with different understandings of the Sabbath, what we should expect from the civil authority is a measure of freedom for people to observe their one day of the week for religious practices.

---

[19]Here I am essentially in agreement with Paul Woolley, *Family, State, and Church—God's Institutions* (Grand Rapids: Baker, 1965), 21–25, 26–29; and with Edmund P. Clowney, *The Doctrine of the Church* (Philadelphia: Presbyterian and Reformed, 1969), 33–34.

We can well ask about such a position as I outline, What standard is there, if not the law of God, for the secular government? The answer is that the law of God does function here, in the area of the second great commandment, explicitly for the Christian citizen or public official and at least implicitly for the unbeliever, whose conscience does to some degree—as Paul indicates in Romans 2:14–15—witness to him. Our responsibility as Christians is to have *our* consciences so well informed by the word of God that we live and testify in such a way that will influence the unbelieving society toward righteousness. Knowing that obedience to this second great commandment can flow ultimately only from obedience to the first great commandment, we cherish the freedom to appeal, as did Paul in the Roman Empire, to the God who raised Jesus from the dead as the one whose "eternal power and divine nature" people have no excuse for denying since the creation of the world (Ro 1:18–20). If it is indeed not our King's intention for the civil authority to enforce the first great commandment, then among the five alternatives that Bahnsen offers as possible standards for civil law, natural revelation as indeed "a sin-obscured edition of the same law of God" "suppressed in unrighteousness by the sinner"[20] is that to which we must appeal—on the basis of our own knowledge of special revelation and with the intent of bringing more of the unbelieving population to repentance toward God and faith in our Lord Jesus Christ. This is the way Paul operated in the Roman Empire and the way any Christian must operate in a missionary situation.

How then can the state avoid the idolatry of making itself God? Twentieth-century secularism shows that it is very difficult for a state to resist this tendency. It can, however, be checked whenever there is at least the recognition that in addition to "the things of Caesar" there are also "the things of God" and that, although these two areas can ordinarily function compatibly, there may be instances when for some citizens they will conflict and call for the primary allegiance to "the things of God" to take precedence. The ancient Roman state thus made some allowances for Jewish monotheism. In the American context we have been blessed, largely because of Christian influences through Western

---

[20]Bahnsen, *Theonomy,* 399–400.

civilization, with a sense of a "higher law" above and beyond even the U.S. Constitution. Whether this higher law be derived from custom, natural law, the will of the people, or the Scriptures, it has at least meant that those who govern are subject to the law, and the law itself is subject to the Constitution, which is interpreted to embody certain underlying, lasting principles. Obviously, much depends on who has the power to interpret the Constitution. Certainly we should seek to have officials who will bring a Christian understanding to such tasks. We can be thankful that the United States, in contrast to the Soviet Union, still recognizes theistic possibilities for an understanding of the higher law, and we should learn from the Soviet example the necessity to contend earnestly for the protection of that theistic expression.

Some Reformed friends ask me, in light of my view, how we are to understand such passages as Psalm 2:10–12, which calls upon the kings of the earth to "serve the Lord with fear" and to "kiss the Son, lest he be angry and [they] be destroyed in the way." The answer is that this is in the context of the nations raging and the rulers gathering together against the Lord and against his Anointed One. What we ask of the civil government is that it not oppose Christ but serve the Lord by following his law in the area of human relations and allowing his people the freedom to preach the Gospel. It is the missionary mandate and the freedom to pursue it that is the intention of our King.

Matthew weaves the discourses of Jesus together to form the tapestry of his gospel. The statement concerning the tribute money is integral to what is said in the beginning of the Sermon on the Mount and at the conclusion of the Great Commission. Our righteousness surpasses that of the Pharisees and of the teachers of the law when we have entered the kingdom through repentance and faith, being baptized into the name of the Father and of the Son and of the Holy Spirit, being disciples who recognize that all authority is given to Jesus Christ in heaven and on earth, and making disciples, teaching them to obey everything he has commanded. Among these things is to give to Caesar the things that are Caesar's and to God the things that are God's. It is not Caesar's prerogative to enforce the true religion. The kingdom of King Jesus comes through the faith that comes by the hearing of the word.

This was the testimony of Justin Martyr in his *First Apology* after referring Emperor Antoninus Pius and his sons to Jesus' statement about the tribute money: "So we worship God only, but in other matters we gladly serve you, recognizing you as emperors and rulers of men, and praying that along with your imperial power you may also be found to have a sound mind."[21]

This was the testimony of Tertullian in his *De Idolatria*: "The Lord . . . said, 'Render to Caesar what are Caesar's, and what are God's to God;' that is, the image of Caesar, which is on the coin, to Caesar, and the image of God, which is on man, to God; so as to render to Caesar indeed money, to God yourself."[22]

This was also the testimony of Daniel in his interpretation of Nebuchadnezzar's dream of the kingdoms and empires that would succeed his own:

> In the time of those kings, the God of heaven will set up a kingdom that will never be destroyed, nor will it be left to another people. It will crush all those kingdoms and bring them to an end, but it will itself endure forever. This is the meaning of the vision of the rock cut out of a mountain, but not by human hands—a rock that broke the iron, the bronze, the clay, the silver and the gold to pieces (2:44–45).

This is the history of the church. The victory of our King comes not through civil governments, but through his witnesses—people like Daniel, Justin, and Tertullian, and like you and me—those who testify that all authority is the Lord's.

---

[21]Justin Martyr, *First Apology*, ch. 17; English translation in Cyril C. Richardson, ed., *Early Christian Fathers*, Library of Christian Classics, vol. 1 (New York: Macmillan, 1970), 253.

[22]Tertullian, *De Idolatria*, ch. 15; English translation in *Ante-Nicene Fathers*, 3:70.

Chapter Eleven

The Theonomic Attraction

John R. Muether

John R. Muether

John R. Muether (M.A.R., Westminster Theological Seminary; M.S.L.S., Simmons College) was, at the time of writing, Librarian and Assistant Professor of Theological Bibliography at Westminster Theological Seminary (Philadelphia). Currently he is Librarian at Reformed Theological Seminary in Orlando, Florida. With a B.A. from Gordon College, he served at Westminster from 1985 to 1989.

Chapter Eleven

The Theonomic Attraction

The rise of the Christian reconstruction movement raises many issues for Reformed Christians. Some of the hermeneutical, theological, and historical issues are addressed in other chapters in this volume. Here I would like to raise a sociological question: If theonomy is the consistent teaching of Scripture and the Westminster Confession of Faith, why does it seem that we have discovered it only now, in late twentieth-century America? Why not, say, in seventeenth-century England or in nineteenth-century Holland?

What is it about the movement that is generating so much current interest? An examination of why theonomy is flourishing here and now, rather than in other places and in earlier times, will reveal features about the movement that will help us understand it. This chapter, then, aims to address the "theonomic attraction."

First, several introductory matters. In focusing on sociological questions I do not wish to minimize the theological issues at stake in the theonomy debate. While we can learn much from theonomy by sociological analysis, we readily concede that theonomy is first and foremost a *theological* question, and that ultimately it must be judged on that basis.

A related point is this: if theonomy is a "new kid on the block," a recent development in Reformed thought, that fact does not in itself constitute an argument against it. We believe that the Holy Spirit leads his people into the truth. I also believe that sometimes he does so only after many years, centuries, even millennia. All who claim to be heirs of the Protestant Reformation must acknowledge this.

Finally, this chapter will make several generalizations

about the theonomic mind-set. Theonomy is a diverse and an increasingly diversifying movement, with many internal differences. There is the Atlanta group, the Tyler group, the Vallecito group, and others. Their differences are significant, and some of these differences will come through in this discussion. Nevertheless, my reading of the literature of theonomy persuades me that the generalizations drawn here are legitimate.

In examining the theonomic attraction, I will divide the discussion into external factors (features about contemporary American culture) and internal factors (features within the movement itself).

EXTERNAL FACTORS

The Changing Landscape of American Religion

American religion as recently as the 1950s was a threefold pluralism aptly described by the title of Will Herberg's classic *Protestant, Catholic, Jew*.[1] But some observers have noted that post–World War II America wasn't truly pluralistic, because it didn't involve the coexistence of conflicting ideas. Instead there was a strong consensus among these faiths about America and its purpose in the world. America was a force for good in the world, democracy was the model the world was encouraged to imitate, and the Soviet Union was the evil empire. Further, among these faiths Protestantism enjoyed unchallenged cultural hegemony. Up until the middle of this century it was Protestantism that unofficially shaped the moral climate in America. Protestantism provided the "symbolic center" to American religious life despite the legal disestablishment of religion.

By the late 1980s, of course, the picture had changed dramatically. The reasons behind this change are familiar to us; certainly Vietnam is a giant symbol of that change.[2] There is now a profound disagreement, rather than essential unity,

---

[1] Will Herberg, *Protestant, Catholic, Jew: An Essay in American Religious Sociology* (Garden City, N.Y.: Doubleday, 1955).

[2] For an examination of the shift in American religious life see Robert Wuthnow, *The Restructuring of American Religion: Society and Faith Since World War II* (Princeton, N.J.: Princeton University Press, 1988).

regarding the question of America's moral purpose. Herberg's threefold pluralism has bifurcated into a clash of the
left and the right. Gone too is any sense of Protestant cultural
hegemony. No longer can we take for granted the role of
religion in American public life. Instead the forces of
secularism have attempted to establish what Richard John
Neuhaus has termed the "naked public square": the exclusion of religiously based values from public debate.[3]

The Cultural Crisis

The changing American religious scene has produced for
conservative Protestants a cultural crisis. Out of this cultural
crisis emerged a politicized fundamentalism led by Jerry
Falwell and his Moral Majority, Pat Robertson, and others. A
good analysis of these developments is found in Richard
John Neuhaus' article, "What the Fundamentalists Want."[4]

Fundamentalists, Neuhaus writes, did not just decide
one day to become politically involved. Their new engage-
ment was a response to an assault on their religious
freedoms. It was an "aggressive defense" against "government actions dictated by the 'secular humanists' in control of
American public life."[5] The government actions included
outlawing prayer in public schools in the early 1960s; the
increasing aggressiveness of the IRS and other government
agencies in interfering with the free exercise of religion; and
finally the infamous Supreme Court decision, *Roe v. Wade*,
and the legalization of abortion on demand.

Out of these events there developed a widespread
feeling among evangelicals that things were falling apart.
The state was morally bankrupt, and evangelicals were
searching for ways to reorder American society.

But notice something further: this cultural crisis has
manifested itself especially through *law*. It was through the
law (or more specifically, judicial activism) that the cultural

---

[3]Richard John Neuhaus, *The Naked Public Square: Religion and Democracy in
America* (Grand Rapids: Eerdmans, 1984).

[4]This article was originally published in *Commentary* (79, 5 [May 1985]: 41–
46) and was reprinted in Richard John Neuhaus and Michael Cromartie,
eds., *Piety and Politics: Evangelicals and Fundamentalists Confront the World*
(Washington, D.C.: Ethics and Public Policy Center, 1987), 3–18.

[5]Neuhaus, "What the Fundamentalists Want," 15–16.

shift took place. Since the law was the battleground, it was natural that conservative Protestants would focus on the law. Many Christians found their solution in the neatly packaged answer that theonomy offered: the civil law found in the Old Testament, God's blueprint for all governments in all times.

INTERNAL FACTORS

These external factors are important. The threat of an increasingly hostile and secularizing culture goes far to explain the current interest in theonomy. We have covered these factors only superficially.

But even more important than the external factors in explaining theonomy's popularity are some features about the movement itself. Theonomy is well suited to appeal to our contemporary culture because it is, in important respects, characteristically American, evangelical, and modern. Let us look then at these internal factors: theonomy as an American phenomenon, theonomy as an evangelical phenomenon, and theonomy as a modern phenomenon.

1. Theonomy as an American Phenomenon

AMERICA AS A CHRISTIAN NATION

Was America founded as a Christian nation? Whether or not America was or should be a Christian nation, it is clear that many Americans believe that it was and should be. Many Americans believe in America as the noble experiment, the "city on a hill." America, for many of its citizens, has deep religious significance, and their devotion to their country is tied to its Christian roots.

Another point that most will affirm is that America is not *now* a Christian nation. Many see it as a thoroughly secular nation. For those who want to restore a past they believe once existed, Christian reconstruction offers a "return to Christian America." Many theonomists who claim to be restoring a biblical civil government may be harboring dreams of a return to an America (real or imagined) of the past.

As they harbor these dreams, they attract other evangelicals with the same hopes. It is instructive to consider, in this connection, the outcome of the 1987 Consultation on "The Biblical Role of Civil Government" that was held at Geneva College. Four positions were represented (theonomy, principled pluralism, Christian America, and national Confessionalism), but participants report that it ended up more like a debate between two viewpoints: the pluralists against the other three who formed a coalition in support of the idea that America should be, in some sense, a Christian nation.[6]

MILLENARIANISM IN AMERICAN CULTURE

Millenarianism—the establishment of a timetable for the end of history and the return of Christ—has always played an important role in American religion. From the seventeenth-century Puritans to contemporary studies of biblical prophecy, from liberal postmillennialists who wanted to Christianize America through the social gospel to heretical sects like Jehovah's Witnesses, millenarianism continues to fascinate Americans.

In his book *The Pursuit of the Millennium* Norman Cohn points out that millenarianism flourishes particularly in times of social crisis.[7] This has been true throughout American history. The Great Awakening; the trauma of civil war; the social challenges of urbanization, industrialization, and immigration in the late nineteenth century all were heightened periods of millenarian thought in America. Similarly, the social upheavals of our day have also increased millenarianism among conservative Protestants. For many, it confirmed their dispensationalism, as prophets like Hal Lindsey clearly spelled out how near we are coming to Armageddon.[8]

Theonomy also appeals to the millennial expectations of evangelicals, but in a very different way. Rather than succumbing to a passive and pessimistic premillennialism, theonomy urges Christians to adopt an active, robust, and optimistic postmillennialism, an "eschatology of victory"

---

[6]The papers of the consultation have recently been published in Gary Scott Smith, ed., *God and Politics: Four Views of the Reformation of Civil Government* (Phillipsburg, N.J.: Presbyterian and Reformed, 1989).

[7]Norman Cohn, *The Pursuit of the Millennium* (Fair Lawn, N.J.: Essential Books, 1957).

[8]Hal Lindsey, *The Late Great Planet Earth* (Grand Rapids: Zondervan, 1970).

brought about by the rule of the righteous. This is an enticing message to its listeners, as Rodney Clapp pointed out:

> [Theonomy's] postmillennialism is important on the practical level because it emboldens its proponents. If D. L. Moody thought the world was a sinking ship from which souls should be rescued, the Reconstructionists want to commandeer the ship, repair it, and sail it toward their own destination.[9]

"AMERICA IN DECLINE"

Related to these first two points is the current concern over the decline of America. In his recent best-seller, *The Rise and Fall of the Great Powers*, Paul M. Kennedy argues that America, like European empires of the past, is a rapidly crumbling dynasty soon to be replaced by new empires from the orient.[10]

Whether or not Kennedy is right is not our concern. What is important is how Americans are reacting. The perceived "Britainization" of America is challenging the optimism characteristic of much of past American life. Americans are deeply concerned, convinced that they are living in America's twilight years and that their children will be worse off than they are.

Furthermore, the collapse of great powers of the past (Spain, France, and Britain) did not elicit great religious concern. The church managed to survive the decline of the state. But because of the popular understanding of America's place in God's plan, the perceived decline of America evokes great concern, and these concerns are addressed in theonomy. The answer, theonomy tells us, is not in better management techniques or in improved microchip technology. The answer is in national repentance, because God promises prosperity to the nation that obeys biblical law.

---

[9]Rodney Clapp, "Democracy as Heresy," *Christianity Today* (Feb. 20, 1987), 19.

[10]Paul M. Kennedy, *The Rise and Fall of the Great Powers: Economic Change and Military Conflict from 1500 to 2000* (New York: Random, 1987).

2. Theonomy as an Evangelical Phenomenon

DOMINION THEOLOGY AND
THE CHARISMATIC MOVEMENT

Reconstructionism proclaims a "dominion theology" that has strong affinities with the charismatic movement. Both urge believers to "name it and claim it"; to take control and have dominion over their lives.[11] Charismatics have tended to apply this thinking to their personal lives; it is for some charismatics the key to their health and wealth. Theonomy is teaching charismatics to extend dominion thinking to the political and social realm as well. Gary North, a professed convert to charismatic thought, writes:

> [Pentecostals] recognized that God moves in history to heal the sick and dying. Always in the back of any Pentecostal's mind is this nagging question: 'If God can heal a sick person, why can't he heal a sick society?'. . .
>
> Then in the late 1970's, a handful of Pentecostal-Charismatics discovered Christian Reconstruction. They finally got the answer they had been waiting for: God *can* heal a sick society. Better yet: God *will* heal a sick world through a great movement of the Holy Spirit. These men dropped dispensationalism, and adopted a world-and-life view that is consistent with the victories that charismatics have seen first-hand.[12]

And so the reconstructionists and the charismatics have discovered each other.[13] The result is a powerful and popular coalition that will be only slightly slowed by the demise of Pat Robertson's political aspirations in 1988. North goes on to describe the strength of this new coalition: "The critics [of this new alliance] worry about the fact that Pentecostalism's

---

[11]George Grant expresses the theonomic craving for dominion in this way: "[I]t is dominion that we are after. Not just a voice. It is dominion we are after. Not just influence. It is dominion we are after. Not just equal time. It is dominion we are after. World conquest." *The Changing of the Guard: Biblical Blueprints for Political Action* (Ft. Worth: Dominion, 1987), 50–51.

[12]Gary North, "Christian Reconstruction and Charismatic Renewal," *Christian Reconstruction* 12, 3 (May/June 1988): 2.

[13]It may be worthwile to note here that the two views share not only a gospel of dominion. They also share a common unwillingness to make important redemptive-historical distinctions. Just as the theonomist denies that the Old Testament civil law is no longer binding, the charismatic denies that the gift of tongues has ceased.

infantry is at last being armed with Reconstructionism's field artillery. They *should* be worried. This represents one of the most fundamental realignments in U.S. Protestant church history."[14]

Rousas J. Rushdoony shares North's assessment. He claims that charismatic reconstructionists number over 20 million.[15] Where they seem to be growing very vocal is at Pat Robertson's CBN (now renamed Regent) University, where reconstructionists are on the faculty and reconstructionist literature is used for textbooks.

The irony of believers in a restoration of biblical law uniting with charismatics was not lost on one observer. This critic of theonomy wrote:

> [Pat] Robertson is . . . a false prophet, according to the biblical definition. If you are a theonomist, you ought to know that the law exacts capital punishment for false prophets, it does not recommend that they be elected to office. In view of this, I think it strange that North, Chilton, and other theonomists have dedicated their books to Robertson.[16]

THEONOMY AS A DEMOCRATIC MOVEMENT

In the book *Evangelicalism and Modern America*,[17] church historian Nathan Hatch has a chapter entitled, "Evangelicalism as a Democratic Movement." In it he describes evangelicalism as a grass-roots movement with no hierarchy and no headquarters, but with a very sophisticated network of parachurch organizations. This is a "democratic" network of voluntary associations, Hatch writes, and he argues persuasively that this democratic character explains the success of evangelicalism. Theonomy seems to have grown in a similar way: it is intentionally parachurch, with a network of newsletters, conferences, publishing houses, TV shows, and even celebrities.

Hatch notes that as a parachurch, democratic movement, evangelicalism holds the institutional church in low

---

[14]North, "Christian Reconstruction," 2.

[15]Clapp, "Democracy as Heresy," 21.

[16]John Robbins, letter to *Journey* 2, 1 (Jan.-Feb. 1987): 12.

[17]George M. Marsden, ed., *Evangelicalism and Modern America* (Grand Rapids: Eerdmans, 1984).

regard. Again, this is a tendency of many theonomists. We have noted theonomy's relation to the charismatic movement. Gary North draws this startling conclusion about the "healing services" that his Tyler, Texas, church recently adopted: "[The healing] did not lead to tongues-speaking, but it did lead to a new willingness to accept the fact that no one ecclesiastical organization has all the answers."[18] This ecclesiastical relativism is astonishing from an allegedly Reformed author, but it is consistent with contemporary evangelicalism.

Consider also the words of theonomic pastor Joseph Morecraft. In a television special on theonomy hosted by Bill Moyers, Morecraft spoke positively about the union of the "light" of Reformed theology and the "heat" of the charismatic movement in the reconstruction alliance. Baptists, Methodists, Episcopalians, and Catholics are also joining the movement, he claimed. "Denominational affiliation means very little to the theonomic movement today. There is among these people, common principles and common faith."[19]

From another reconstructionist voice, Ray Sutton, comes this call for ecclesiastical pluralism:

> I think denominational diversity . . . has facilitated broader and deeper expansion of the Church. Also, I think it is naïve to assume that the Church would get along better and/or function better if it were all under the same "governmental" roof. Maybe Christians would fight more if they were all in the same Church.[20]

The indifference toward ecclesiastical authority on the part of Morecraft and Sutton suggests little concern for what obedience to God's law means for ecclesiology. On the one hand, theonomists prefer theocracy over pluralism in the political order. But on the other hand, they imply that, for pragmatic purposes, Christians should ignore God's law for

[18]North, "Christian Reconstruction and Charismatic Renewal," 2. I am told that North's "healing services" do not go beyond James 5. Perhaps we wouldn't use the term charismatic to describe him or his worship, but that he chooses to describe himself by that term is significant.

[19]"On Earth as It Is in Heaven" [television broadcast]. Bill Moyers, host. December 27, 1987. Public Broadcasting Service.

[20]Ray Sutton, "On the Road to Rome Again?" Geneva Review 21 (August 1985): 5.

his church. If so, where is the theonomy? Who then is the antinomian?

I have a friend who is fond of telling theonomists, "When it comes to the church, I'm a theonomist." Many theonomists seem to argue the opposite: they believe the regulative principle for the state, for the family, for education, indeed for all of life *except* for the church. (Not all theonomists feel this way, I should point out. James Jordan, for example, has written extensively on the institutional church and laments the "relatively low, Americanized view of the Church" that is characteristic of much theonomic thinking.)[21]

As we noted, this ecclesiology is consistent with Hatch's picture of American evangelicalism: a parachurch, interdenominational, and theologically tolerant movement. There is another irony here: among the more notorious claims of theonomy is that "democracy is heresy," because democracy asserts the will of man over the will of God. "Christianity," Rushdoony claims, "is basically and radically anti-democratic."[22] Yet, in the areas that Hatch describes, theonomy comes across as a thoroughly democratic movement.

THE BIBLICISM OF THEONOMY

Theonomy shares with contemporary evangelicalism a biblicist hermeneutic that depreciates the role of general revelation and insists on using the Bible as though it were a textbook for all of life.[23] This is a mind-set characteristic of contemporary evangelicalism, and it is not limited to one side of the political spectrum. Fundamentalists use the Bible as a textbook on geology, finding evidence of a literal six-day creation and a ten-thousand-year-old earth. Evangelical social activists like Ronald Sider see the Bible as a textbook on economics, claiming, for example, that in the Old

[21]*Geneva Review* 18 (March 1985): 3.

[22]Quoted by Moyers, "On Earth as It Is in Heaven."

[23]A fuller study of this phenomenon can be found in Dean C. Curry, "Evangelicals, the Bible, and Public Policy," *This World* 16 (Winter 1987): 34–49. Curry correctly faults evangelicals for denying that extrabiblical truth is available through God's common grace. But his analysis is flawed when he attributes part of the problem to the presuppositional epistemology of Cornelius Van Til.

Testament Jubilee we find instruction on economic redistribution.

Theonomic literature displays the same sort of hermeneutic. Dominion Press of Fort Worth, Texas, has published a multivolume series called "Biblical Blueprints." The titles in this series include the following:

Ruler of the Nations: Biblical Blueprints for Governments
Who Owns the Family? Biblical Blueprints for Family/State Relations
In the Shadow of Plenty: Biblical Blueprints for Wealth and Poverty
Honest Money: Biblical Blueprints for Money and Banking
The Children Trap: Biblical Blueprints for Education
Inherit the Earth: Biblical Blueprints for Economics
The Changing of the Guard: Biblical Blueprints for Political Action
Healer of the Nations: Biblical Blueprints for International Relations
Second Chance: Biblical Blueprints for Divorce and Remarriage

These "blueprints" offer specific biblical prooftexts for many contemporary issues. Why, for example, should the United States return to the gold standard? Because careful and prudent economic analysis suggests it will produce a healthier economy? No, because Deuteronomy 25:15 says that you shall have just weights and measures.[24]

3. Theonomy as a Modern Phenomenon

THE ILLUSION OF TECHNIQUE

William Barrett and Jacques Ellul[25] both have suggested that one hallmark of modernity is its obsession with technique. Technique is the key to modern life. All that is necessary to solve modern problems is the application of proper technique. This belief in the supreme power of technique is often termed "functional rationality."

Sociologist James Davison Hunter has pointed out that

---

[24]Note what is lacking in this series: there is no "biblical blueprint" on the church. This is further evidence of theonomy's low view of the church.

[25]William Barrett, *The Illusion of Technique: A Search for Meaning in a Technological Civilization* (Garden City, N.Y.: Anchor, 1978); Jacques Ellul, *The Technological System*, trans. Joachim Neugroschel (New York: Continuum, 1980).

functional rationality is an important ingredient to contemporary evangelicalism as well.[26] In fact, he argues that evangelicalism has survived the threat of modernity in large part because it has assimilated functional rationality. Examples he cites are the carefully quantified methods of church growth, evangelistic methodologies that urge the mastery of four spiritual laws, and the proliferation of "how to" and self-help books in Christian bookstores, offering step-by-step solutions to every human problem. Evangelical success is found increasingly in prepackaged techniques.

Recall the "Biblical Blueprint" series. The titles themselves represent a strategic marketing device. The very idea of "biblical blueprints" conveys the message that prosperity will come if Christians master the proper technique. This is functional rationality, and theonomists have mastered it.

THE POLITICAL ILLUSION

Charles Colson sees in theonomy another illusion characteristic of our day, the political illusion, which asserts that there is no problem except that which admits to a political solution.[27] This is a uniquely modern idea, and it finds expression in the myth that the problem of poverty is solved by massive economic redistribution, or that the problem of racism is cured by school busing. But evangelicals are not immune to these notions. Many evangelicals, including theonomists, seem to believe that homosexuality, AIDS, and abortion are social problems that are solvable once Christians take control of Washington.

Like most political conservatives, theonomists believe in a very limited federal government. Colson claims that theonomy would achieve exactly the opposite from what it hopes: rather than a greatly diminished federal government, "the imposition of biblical law on secular society would result in a much bigger government. Bringing the Kingdom of God by human means would require massive government, a massive army to restrain evil and bring about

---

[26]See his *American Evangelicalism: Conservative Religion and the Quandary of Modernity* (New Brunswick: Rutgers University Press, 1983) and *Evangelicalism: The Coming Generation* (Chicago: University of Chicago Press, 1987).

[27]As interviewed on Moyers, "On Earth as It Is in Heaven."

utopia."[28] The history of the twentieth century ought to be enough to dissuade Christians from the illusions of politics. All too often massive political programs aimed at addressing social inequities, no matter how noble their intentions, have turned totalitarian. But more importantly, the modern idea that politics is everything ought to be rejected because it is idolatry. Against this temptation the Catholic philosopher James Schall wisely reminds us: "The ultimate effect of Christianity upon politics is a limiting one, one that frees man by removing from politics what politics cannot deliver. In this way, politics is left to be politics and not a false religion."[29]

UTOPIANISM

The modern impulse to pick up the sword against a perceived social injustice is a sign of the politicization of the Gospel prevalent among both the religious left and the religious right. It is also indicative of another modern idea: political utopianism, or the idea that one can establish the kingdom of God in political form. Eric Voegelin has alerted us to the utopian temptation that characterizes modernity. In his words, modern man wants to "immanentize the eschaton."[30]

The utopian temptation, when combined with millenarianism, is one that modern Christians are particularly vulnerable to. There is a strong temptation among contemporary Christians to work toward a theocratic utopianism— the premature consummation of the kingdom of God in this world. The most notable example of politicized utopianism is liberation theology. But theonomy displays the same impulse, and for this reason Clark Pinnock has aptly described theonomists as "the liberation theologians of the Right."[31] The sad irony of this temptation is that many of the efforts of

---

[28]Ibid.

[29]James V. Schall, *Christianity and Politics* (Boston: St. Paul Editions, 1981), 92.

[30]Eric Voegelin, *The New Science of Politics: An Introduction* (Chicago: University of Chicago Press, 1952), 129–32.

[31]Quoted in Clapp, "Democracy as Heresy," *Christianity Today* (February 20, 1987), 21.

liberation theology have produced governments that are very poor guarantors of freedom, especially religious freedom.

CONCLUSION

We have seen that theonomy is attractive because it provides an answer to an external threat—that of an increasingly secular culture. We should applaud theonomists for speaking to this threat and for calling the attention of the church to it, even if we oppose their solution to it.

What about the theonomic solution? I have suggested ways in which theonomy resembles modern American evangelicalism. If this analysis is correct, then one should examine these elements carefully to determine how they affect the theonomic approach. Among the elements I have suggested are theonomy's rapport with the charismatic movement, its low view of the church, and its populist hermeneutic. I have also asked if the attraction to theonomy is linked with an obsession with the fate of America and the preservation of the American way of life. Christians must avoid a civil religion that confuses the kingdom of God with the American way of life, and we must be willing to recognize that the church can—and will—survive the fall of this country, should God bring it about.

This confusion of the kingdom of God and the fate of America has produced a politicized gospel that threatens the Reformed doctrine of the spirituality of the church. In an editorial endorsing church-organized pickets against abortion clinics, the *Counsel of Chalcedon*, a theonomic journal, explicitly rejected the idea of the spirituality of the church, suggesting that this concept was a major cause of our current predicament: "I believe that this 'spirituality of the church' doctrine . . . is one of the devil's greatest lies in recent years. And most of the so-called Bible-believing church has swallowed the lie hook, line and sinker."[32]

Against this view Edmund P. Clowney insists that the kingdom of God is a spiritual rule, and its weapons can only be spiritual: "Christ did not give the keys of the kingdom to Caesar, nor the sword to Peter." Clowney recognizes that the church will have a leavening effect on the state, but

---

[32]*Counsel of Chalcedon* 8, 9 (November 1986): 3.

"even the world-wide spread of the gospel cannot remove Christ's prohibition of the sword as a means of bringing in or maintaining his kingdom."

Clowney acknowledges the unpopularity of the classic Reformed position in our day of political activism:

> The Christian will be charged with other-worldliness, aloofness, non-involvement. He cannot forget his heavenly citizenship to be conformed to this world. He refuses to make patriotism or revolution or a socialist utopia his hope. He sees the naivete and the apostasy of secular hope.

To succumb to the present temptation, Clowney concludes, renders the church "in Babylonian captivity to secular goals and values."[33]

A similar point was made by sociologist Peter Berger. In challenging politicization of the church (a problem that he located across the theological spectrum), Berger went so far as to label the political activism of the church apostasy: "[No political agenda] belongs in the pulpit . . . or in any statements that claim to have the authority of the Gospel. *Any* cultural or political agenda embellished with such authority is a manifestation of 'works-righteousness' and *ipso facto* an act of apostasy."[34] While we may find the language of apostasy excessive, Berger is right when he argues that deep compromises of the Gospel inevitably result when the purposes of God are confused with a partisan political agenda.

Theonomy has properly reminded us of the responsibility of Christians to transform their culture. But there is always a reciprocal force at work, and that is the subtle way in which the culture transforms the Christian. How that subtle transformation takes place—along with its theological and cultural ramifications—ought to be the concern of anyone confronted with the attraction to theonomy.[35]

---

[33]Edmund P. Clowney, "The Politics of the Kingdom," *Westminster Theological Journal* 41 (1979): 291–310.

[34]Peter Berger, "Different Gospels: The Social Sources of Apostasy," *This World* 17 (Spring 1987): 13.

[35]Thanks are due to Kenneth A. Myers for many helpful suggestions throughout this chapter.

Chapter Twelve

Theonomy and the Poor: Some Reflections

Timothy J. Keller

Timothy J. Keller

Timothy J. Keller (D.Min., Westminster Theological Seminary) is Adjunct Professor of Practical Theology at Westminster Theological Seminary (Philadelphia) and is pastor of a Presbyterian church in New York City. With other degrees from Bucknell University and Gordon-Conwell Theological Seminary, he has taught at Westminster since 1984. A past director of Mercy Ministries for the Presbyterian Church in America, he is author of *Ministries of Mercy: The Call of the Jericho Road*.

Chapter Twelve

Theonomy and the Poor: Some Reflections

This chapter will look at the views of some writers in the Christian reconstruction school (of Geneva Ministries, Tyler, Texas) on the issue of the Christian's responsibility to the poor. There are three men whose writings on poverty offer some representative views: Gary North, David Chilton, and Ray Sutton. I will cite them, not to offer a point-by-point critique of each man's work, but to draw the outline of some basic positions and concepts that characterize broadly the reconstructionist movement. Then I will offer some responses to and reflections on those positions.

What should Christians do for the poor? That is the question. In any discussion of Christian concern for the poor, there are three thorny issues that must be addressed:

1. How shall we understand the *causes* of poverty?
2. Should there be *conditions* on our care for the poor?
3. What *strategies* should be used to care for the poor?

THE ISSUE OF CAUSE

Chilton and North see the roots of modern poverty as cultural and personal disobedience to God's law. They remind us so often that wealth is God's benediction on faithfulness to his law that they appear to be saying poverty is simply the result of sloth and sin.

North wrote in 1986:

> There is a tight relationship between wickedness and poverty. There is also a tight connection between right-

eousness and having enough to eat. God places the
unrighteous under covenantal judgment: *cursing.* Their
descendants are cut off. He places the righteous under
covenantal judgment, too: *blessing.* They are never found
begging, and their descendants inherit the earth.[1]

What does the term *tight relationship* mean? Is North
saying that most poor people are lazy and/or wicked? If he is
not teaching this, he does little to deter us from that
conclusion. In the same chapter he says, "Physical hunger is
a down payment from God on what lies ahead: spiritual
hunger for eternity. . . . People who don't produce anything
of value are going to starve, whether we legislate any tax-
financed welfare programs or not."[2] "Even God-haters can
benefit externally if they conform themselves outwardly to
these principles. These principles *work*, unlike people on
public welfare."[3]

David Chilton draws a similar view. When he discusses
"Third World" poverty, he clearly states that the cause is
God's curse on their unbelief:

> This is God's curse on men whenever they rebel: the land
> itself spews them out (Lev. 18:24–28; Isaiah 24). The curse
> devours productivity in every area, and the ungodly
> culture perishes (Deut. 28:15–26). They suffer terrible
> disease (Deut. 28:27), and are politically oppressed (Deut.
> 28:28–34). . . . The "Third and Fourth Worlds" are under
> the judgment of God.[4]

Here are some responses to these views of the root
causes of poverty:

1. *Biblically, the causes of poverty are more complex than these
writers acknowledge. There are at least three causes.*

One cause is "oppression" or injustice. One of the key
Hebrew words most often translated "poor" in the Old
Testament is *ani*, meaning "the wrongfully dispossessed."
Oppression is any social condition or unfair treatment that
brings a person to, or keeps a person in poverty. (See Ex

---

[1]Gary North, "Editor's Introduction," in George Grant *In the Shadow of
Plenty* (Ft. Worth: Dominion; Nashville: Thomas Nelson, 1986), xiii.

[2]Ibid., xii.

[3]Ibid., xiii–xiv.

[4]Chilton, *Productive Christians in an Age of Guilt-Manipulators*, (Tyler, Tex.:
Institute for Christian Economics, 1981), 116, 119.

22:21–27; Ps 82:1–8; Pr 14:31.) Examples of oppression include delayed wages (Dt 24:15), unjustly low wages (Eph 6:8, 9)[5], court and government systems weighted in favor of the great and wealthy (Lev 19:15), and high interest loans (Ex 22:25–27).[6]

A second cause of poverty is natural disaster or calamity, including crop failures; disabling injury; birth defects (physical handicaps); and victimization by criminals, floods, storms, and fires. Joseph's hunger relief program (Ge 47) helped those who were in poverty because of famine. God's social legislation assumes that there would be a steady stream of Israelites who would "wax poor" (Lev 25:25, 39, 47). Such passages seem to have in view the kind of poverty that is caused by circumstances.[7]

Third, poverty is caused by personal sin. A life of laziness (Pr 6:6–7) and problems of self-discipline (23:21) can bring about poverty. Expensive tastes and luxury seeking can also be reasons for economic trouble (21:17).

It is critical to recognize *all* of these causes. None of the reconstructionist writers seem to speak much of "calamity," the constant stream of factors in a fallen nature (Ro 8:18ff.)

---

[5]John Murray concludes that under God's law, even slaveowners were bound to pay just and fair wages. "And this means that bond-servants are to be compensated for their labor in proportion to the service rendered. The principle 'The laborer is worthy of his hire' is not suspended [in bond service]. This places the slavery which the New Testament recognizes in an entirely different perspective from what the word 'slavery' is liable to connote to us." (*Principles of Conduct* [Grand Rapids: Eerdmans, 1957], 99.)

[6]Richard Baxter names "oppression" as a sin in his *Christian Directory.* "Oppression is the injuring of inferiors who are unable to resist or right themselves." He especially mentions the oppression of servants by masters and of tenants by landlords. Richard Baxter, *A Christian Directory*, part 2, chap. 14, and part 4, chap. 20. "A good landlord will be familiar with the meanest of his tenants, and will encourage them to freely open their complaints, and will labour to inform himself who is in poverty and distress, and how it cometh to pass; that when he hath heard all, he may understand whether it be his own oppression or his tenants' fault that is the cause. . . ." In *The Practical Works of Richard Baxter*, 4 vols. (London: Henry G. Bohn, 1854), 1:848.

[7]It is interesting that Jonathan Edwards considers a lack of financial and administrative sense to be a natural disaster. He writes: "A want of a natural faculty to manage affairs to advantage, that is to be considered as his calamity. Such a faculty is a gift that God bestows on some, and not on others; and it is not owing to themselves." Jonathan Edwards, "Christian Charity" in *Works* (Edinburgh: Banner of Truth, 1974), 2:172.

that will bring poverty into our lives. (There are plenty of poor people who are neither sluggards nor oppressed.) Also, the "oppressors" of the poor in the Bible *are* the rich and the powerful. Of course, corrupt and ruthless government bureaucrats fit into this category; I do not doubt that the corruption of the federal bureaucracy has severely aggravated poverty in the United States. But the Bible also speaks about the tendency of the powerful to use their holdings greedily and to oppress the poor. Surely that is still happening today in the U.S. and elsewhere.

Richard Baxter and other Puritans applied these texts to contemporary economic injustices by the elite against the poor. Is it really possible that the rich today are not doing this anymore? Baxter, for example, noted that many rich persons, in charging "fair market value" rent to poor tenants were nonetheless oppressing them if it created severe hardship for the tenant families.[8] (See below for more discussion on this point.) If Christians have discovered oppression by the rich and powerful in every age, should we not expect to find it and denounce it in America today? We should criticize not only Big Government, but also Big Business for any violations of God's law.

It is also critical to remember all of these causes if we are to avoid uncritically adopting either the "liberal" or the "conservative" ideology toward the poor. The "liberal" tends to see all the poor as oppressed. Thus the *main* or only component in the social program of liberals is *legislation* to prevent victimization. But the "conservative" tends to see most of the poor as irresponsible, people who have not "pulled themselves up by their bootstraps." They believe that poverty has increased largely because government welfare has trained people not to work. Thus the *main* or only component in conservatives' poverty plans is *work programs*.

But simplistic analysis does not work. Many of the poor cannot get ahead in the work force because of horrendous upbringings in poor homes, where there is often abuse and where the parents make no effort to help their children get an education. These children are victims of "oppression," not only by the dependency-creating welfare system, but

[8]Baxter, *Christian Directory*, 849.

also by their own parents and by the affluent of the city who will not pay (either voluntarily through charity or even involunarily through taxes) to establish good schools and safe living conditions in poor areas. The roots of poverty are complex.

2. *It is unfair to intimate that the majority (or even a sizable minority) or the poor are "sluggards" who do not work.*

There were 32.4 million poor people in the United States in 1986 (7 million families).[9] These 32 million, roughly, can be broken down in this way:

    I. 12 million of the poor are *children*
   II. 20 million of the poor are *adults*
      A. 18 million "able-bodied" adults:
        1. 9 million are working poor
        2. 1 million are unemployed, seeking work
        3. 4 million are single parents at home
        4. 2 million are retired (elderly)
        5. 2 million are in school (e.g., teenagers)
      B. 2 million ill or disabled

These very basic figures instantly undermine a very common notion, namely, that "most (or many) of the poor are poor because they simply refuse to work." Some report that the fastest growing group of poor in the United States is the working poor. Of the 7 million families in poverty, more than half had at least one worker, and over 20 percent had two, but a minimum-wage salary is still just about $7,000 per year, not enough to lift a family out of poverty. The U.S. Conference on Mayors discovered in 1987 that 22 percent of all the homeless had jobs.[10]

When we look at the adults who are not working, we see that many have good reasons. Many are retired or disabled, while others are still teenagers in school. A swiftly growing

---

[9]The 1987 Census Bureau's report on family income and poverty reported in "Poverty Rate Dips as the Median Family Income Rises," *New York Times* (July 31, 1987): 1. Other figures in this paragraph are taken from *Statistical Abstract of the U.S. 1987*. (U.S. Bureau of the Census: Washington, D.C., 1986), 107th ed.; William O'Hare, "The Eight Myths of Poverty," *American Demographics* (May 1986); and *World Almanac, 1987* (New York: World Almanac, 1987).

[10]"Homelessness Up Sharply, Report Says," *Philadelphia Inquirer* (December 17, 1987), 39.

group of the poor are single female heads of households, who are often unskilled and cannot make enough money at a job to pay for child care.

In fact, a quick scan of the figures reveals how few of the poor are really "unaccounted for." Perhaps 500,000 to one million of the poor are able-bodied, mature (not elderly) adults without children who do not appear to be working. It is not fair to assume that all of these people are lazy. Many could be addicted to alcohol or drugs or be mentally ill. But even if we *did* count this group as the "shiftless" poor of the popular imagination, we see that it is only a small fraction of the massive group of needy Americans.

3. *It is unfair to (virtually) blame modern welfare programs for poverty in the United States.*

That is the overall impression made by the works of the reconstructionists and many recent conservative critics of American social policy whose theses and arguments are adopted liberally by reconstructionist writers.[11] We don't have scope in this article to comprehensively survey the critiques and defenses of the government's poverty programs. But here is a brief summary.

"Liberals" as a general rule will claim that poverty decreased during the 1960s but has increased during the last ten years. They will cite the growing homeless population as evidence that this is true. The conclusion drawn is that, under the Democrats, poverty was shrinking, but that since the Republicans came into power, since the Nixon years, poverty programs have been cut back and the poor have increased.

More recently, "conservatives" have launched a devastating barrage of criticism against the government's social-welfare institutions. In general, conservatives say that in the 1950s there was a lower poverty rate than in the 1980s after

---

[11]See, for example, Gary North's liberal citations of Thomas Sowell, *Knowledge and Decisions* (New York: Basic Books, 1980) and P. T. Bauer, *Equality, the Third World and Economic Delusion* (Cambridge, Mass.: Harvard University Press, 1981) in his article in *Wealth and Poverty: Four Christian Views of Economics*, ed. Robert G. Clouse (Downers Grove, Ill.: InterVarsity, 1984). See also Charles Murray *Losing Ground: American Social Policy 1950–1980* (New York: Basic Books, 1984); Lawrence Mead, *Beyond Entitlement: The Social Obligations of Citizenship* (New York: Free Press, 1986); and George Gilder, *Wealth and Poverty* (New York: Basic Books, 1981).

staggering increases in welfare spending. Usually, figures like the following are presented: 10–12 percent poverty rate in 1959–60, but 14–15 percent today.[12] The conclusion is drawn that "liberal" social policies increased poverty.

My own appraisal is that the statistics do not support any one ideology well at all. Poverty *did* significantly decrease under Kennedy and Johnson. (From 1950 until 1973, the percentage of the American population that lived in poverty fell from 30 percent to just over 11 percent.)[13] Then it increased under Nixon, Ford, and Carter. (Between 1973 and 1982 the rate went from 11 percent of the population to 15 percent.)[14] But finally, it decreased slowly (from 15 percent in 1982 to 13.6 percent in 1986) under Reagan, the most conservative of all the presidents.

But the Reagan conservatives cannot be too pleased at their record. While the overall percentage of people in poverty decreased, the Census Bureau reported in 1986 that there really is a growing gap between the haves and the have-nots—the poor are getting poorer.[15]

Also, the changes in the constituency of the poor are telling. One of the major changes in this period is in the status of the aged. The elderly have moved from the bottom to the lower middle of the income spectrum, being greatly aided by the inflation of housing costs and by inflation-indexed Social Security. While 35 percent of all elderly people were poor in 1959, just 12.4 percent were poor in 1986.[16] Instead, it is single-mother families and children who are now making up a greater and greater proportion of the poor. In 1986, for the first time, single-parent families were the leading category of poor households.[17]

In other words, neither the liberal whitewash of welfare

---

[12]See George Grant, *Bringing in the Sheaves* (Atlanta: American Vision, 1985), 45.

[13]William O'Hare, "The Eight Myths of Poverty," *American Demographics* (May 1986): 25.

[14]Ibid.

[15]Between 1978 and 1984, the gap between the average income of the poor and the poverty line grew from $3,772 to $4,141. See "Poverty Rate Dips as the Median Family Income Rises," *New York Times* 1,12 (July 31, 1987): 1.

[16]See Frank Levy, "Actually, We Are All Getting Poorer," *New York Times* 3,7 (May 3, 1987): 3.

[17]"Poverty Rate Dips as the Median Family Income Rises," *New York Times* 1,12 (July 31, 1987): 1.

nor conservative denigration is completely warranted. Poverty did not massively increase under liberal social policy, but neither has "supply side" economics significantly helped the poor.

Another conservative critique commonly asserts that the U.S. government is spending *hundreds of billions* of dollars on poverty programs.[18] The impression one may have that all this money is going to the poor is misleading. Most of this sum goes to Social Security and Medicare; the vast majority of the recipients are not poor at all. By comparison, Aid for Dependent Children (the main federal program to help single-mother families, now the largest category of poor) was $8 billion in 1984, as compared to $111 billion for Social Security, and an additional $109 billion for Medicare.[19] Actually, only about one-third of all poor families receive public assistance payments, and only 60 percent receive benefits other than cash, such as food stamps, public housing, or Medicaid. Most poor people do *not* "live off of welfare."

Nothing of what I say should be seen as a great defense of recent American social policy. In these paragraphs, I am mainly criticizing the conservative critique, because it is the one adopted by and large by the reconstructionists. Certainly liberal social policy can be severely criticized by Christians in many ways. John Perkins (no "conservative") is quick to charge the current system with fostering dependency and bringing about many other harmful effects.

But the fact is that poverty has been alleviated somewhat by government programs, especially poverty among the elderly. If it is really true that a centralized economy and welfare system is the *main* cause of poverty today, as is sometimes intimated, then we should simply be able to look back to pre-1920 days and see very little poverty. That is not the case. And because poverty—deep and miserable poverty—has been with us before there was any significant government welfare at all, it is superficial to see government bungling and excess as the main cause of poverty or as the only source of "oppression" of the poor.

4. *There is some danger of a kind of "health and wealth*

---

[18]See Gilder, *Wealth and Poverty*, 112.
[19]O'Hare, "Eight Myths," 25.

doctrine" growing out of some of the teachings about poverty-as-curse.

Gary North and David Chilton so stress the idea of wealth-as-blessing and poverty-as-curse that they have some real affinities with the prosperity doctrine of several modern charismatic teachers.

Gary North writes of the political power that will inevitably come to those believers who are faithful to God's law:

> God's law works for everyone who imposes it, as the book of Jonah should reveal. The Assyrians in Nineveh who repented, through the King's person, became Israel's conquerors. Power flowed toward them. When men honor the external laws of society that God has set forth, they will be blessed externally. . . . Today's Protestants resent such teaching. . . . There is enormous hostility to the idea that adhering to God's social laws brings external prosperity.[20]

North quotes Psalm 37:25: "I have been young, and now am old; yet I have not seen the righteous forsaken, nor his descendants begging bread," and concludes that the righteous are under a blessing that will bring economic prosperity.[21] I wish North would be more specific, so I would not have to guess about his meaning here. But apparently he is saying that, with few (or no) exceptions, obedience to God's laws brings wealth and prosperity, even to an unbeliever.

I think that is a misreading of Scripture. Psalm 37:25 is speaking of a real principle, namely, that, in general, obedience to God's law brings *both* material and spiritual blessing. The author says that *he* has never seen anyone from a righteous family begging bread. That shows that this principle often operates. Indeed, missiologists have noticed the clear tendencies of converted tribes and communities to improve economically, moving from poverty to middle-class status. (See Donald MacGavran on "redemption and lift.")[22] This very fact proves that in the Bible there is a "work ethic"

---

[20]Gary North, "Comprehensive Redemption: A Theology for Social Action," *The Journal of Christian Reconstruction* 8,1 (Summer 1981): 33.

[21]*Plenty*, "Editor's Introduction," xiii.

[22]Donald MacGavran, *Understanding Church Growth* (Grand Rapids: Eerdmans, 1970), chap. 14.

that changes a community's worldview and enables it to experience more prosperity.

But North leaves unstated (not unbelieved, I hope) the fact that righteous people are subject to all kinds of material suffering, due to calamity (Ro 8:18ff.) and oppression. "Better to be poor than to be a liar" (Pr 19:22; cf. 28:6) intimates that it may be necessary sometimes to choose between being righteous (honest) *or* being rich.[23] In any case, it means that righteous people can be poor. Commentator Derek Kidner notes that the error of Job's "miserable comforters" lay in the fact that they would allow no exception to the general observation of Psalm 37:25:

> Verse 25 attests to this provision, in its literal sense, from one man's experience; Job's comforters would grant no exceptions to that sense; but Paul, and others before him, knew of an *abundance* which might be material or spiritual as God saw fit (e.g., Ps. 73:26; Hab. 3:17f.; Mt. 4:4; II Cor. 6:10; Phil. 4:12).[24]

Those verses are just a sampling of many that teach that prosperity/comfort does not necessarily increase along with spiritual character. "You have filled my heart with greater joy than when their grain and new wine abound" (Ps 4:7).

Now I think that North and Chilton do agree that there are many, many individuals and even entire communities of persons who are poor through calamity and oppression, not through God's curse on disobedience. But even if they do know that, they give no indication of it, and without a more balanced interpretation of Psalm 37:25 and like passages, they can become "miserable comforters."

It may be a bit dangerous for me to link the charismatic "health and wealth" gospel people to this teaching of the reconstructionists. Of course, I know the "name it and claim it" cults have deep antinomian and pietist tendencies, which are the bane of the reconstructionists. And yet the charis-

---

[23]Even someone like Spurgeon, when he reads, "I have never seen the righteous . . . begging bread," has no trouble responding, "It is not *my* observation just as it stands. . ." for he had relieved many righteous paupers (*The Treasury of David*, 3 vols. [Grand Rapids: Zondervan, 1974]: 1:176.) Spurgeon recognizes it as a general order of things, not a rule without exceptions.

[24]Derek Kidner, *Psalms 1–72* (London: InterVarsity, 1973), 151.

matics share with them a very underdeveloped theology of suffering. Paul lived with a "thorn in the flesh," which must have been some sort of unhealed physical pain or material deprivation. As a result, he learned a valuable truth: "For Christ's sake, I delight in weaknesses, so that Christ's power may rest upon me . . . for when I am weak, then I am strong" (2Co 12:9–10). Somehow Paul's experience and Christ's career must be taken into account to qualify statements about political power and external blessing flowing inevitably to those who obey God's law.

My guess is that the touted confluence of charismatics and Christian reconstruction[25] is due to two factors, one good and one bad. First (the good), they are both optimistic about revival and Christ's kingly power to transform. But second (the bad), they have done little theologizing about suffering and the power of weakness. Because Paul did have this understanding of suffering, he could move from powerful appeals and even sarcasm (Gal 5:12) to being a gentle mother (1Th 2:7), present in "weakness, fear, and trembling" (1Co 2:3). Reconstructionists generally have only the former tone; a gentle, humble, and nurturant spirit is seldom seen in their writings.

THE ISSUE OF CONDITION

The reconstructionist writers stress strongly the need to place firm conditions on our charity and aid to the poor. Herbert Schlossberg is not a reconstructionist, but has, I think, put their position well:

> No theory of helping the poor may be said to be Christian if it does not discriminate among the poor. The old distinction, now despised among social workers, between the deserving and the undeserving poor is a reflection of a Biblical theme.[26]

For example, David Chilton also writes:

---

[25]Gary North, "Reconstructionist Renewal and Charismatic Renewal," *Christian Reconstruction* 8,3 (May/June 1988).

[26]Herbert Schlossberg, *Idols For Destruction* (Nashville: Thomas Nelson, 1983), 314.

Jesus declares that God's concern for the poor is discriminatory. It is not just "the poor" in some abstract, general, universal sense who are the objects of God's care. Here they are on the same level with the rich: if they reject Christ, they are themselves rejected by Him. They wanted benefits, but were ready to murder Him when they discovered He practiced discrimination in His welfare plan.[27]

Ray Sutton has written a paper, "The Theology of the Poor," in which he addresses the issue of the "conditionality" of charity.

Are churches obligated to give to every drunken and drug addicted poor person that comes to their door? No. A person who has no family or friends to turn to indicates that he has consistently violated the trust of everyone around him. He is a chronic repeater of some offense. He's unrepentant! To give to him unconditionally, sight unseen, is a waste of God's money. . . . Christ had to meet the conditions of the law. In the end, He suffered the full wrath of God the Father. He paid a price. Salvation was not unconditional. Furthermore, anyone who wants his salvation, and the offer is to everyone, must repent and believe. Are not these conditions? So, the practice of "unconditional" welfare is a denial of the gospel![28]

Let's reflect on Sutton's remarks, because they betray a theological principle at work in the reconstructionists' approach to the poor. He says that we should give only to the righteous, "deserving" poor. We should have conditions— obedience to the law and the covenant—before we give any aid. Why? Because salvation is not unconditional. Jesus had to fulfill the law (a condition), and recipients of salvation must repent and believe (a condition), and therefore, unconditional charity is a denial of the gospel.

Both theologically and pastorally, these remarks are off-center, I fear.[29] Although the procurement of our salvation

---

[27]Chilton, *Manipulators*, 107.

[28]Ray Sutton, "The Theology of the Poor," in *The Geneva Papers* no. 37 (March 1985): 4.

[29]In addition to this, it is extremely unfair and unwise to conclude that anyone without family or friends must have "consistently violated the trust of everyone around."

was conditional for Christ, Sutton as a Reformed believer should acknowledge that the *initial* reception of saving grace, regeneration, is totally unconditional—completely by grace. Man contributes nothing to it at all; God justifies the *wicked* (Ro 4:5). There are actually two phases to God's mercy—it is at first unconditional and then it proceeds conditionally. Let me explain.

There are two "classes" of Scripture texts that bear on the issue of conditions for charity. On the one hand, we are not to aid the lazy (2Th 3:10), the immoral (1Ti 5:6), and those not "widows indeed" (truly without resources). I do not need to elaborate on these passages. The reconstructionists have brought them up often and expounded them well.

On the other hand, we are told to aid even our enemies (Lk 10:25–37). *Anyone* in need is my neighbor—that is the teaching of the Good Samaritan parable. We are not to do good only to the thrifty but also to the "wicked and the ungrateful" (Lk 6:32–35). In the parallel passage (Mt 5:45), Jesus teaches that God provides physical health and agricultural prosperity even to the ungodly. Galatians 6:10 tells us to give priority to the needy of the church, but we are also to do "deed" ministry to "all people."

Following these passages, many of the Puritans believed that deed ministry, like word ministry, should be offered to all people. William Perkins, in his *Cases of Conscience*, tells us that we should even give aid to a wicked person who is in extreme need, but that we should also have him punished by the magistrate for any illegal activity that he is doing![30] And Jonathan Edwards concludes:

> We are particularly required to be kind to the unthankful and to the evil; and therein to follow the example of our heavenly Father, who causes his sun to rise on the evil and on the good, and sendeth rain on the just and on the unjust. We are obliged, not only to be kind to them that are so to us, but to them that hate, and that despitefully use us.[31]

---

[30]Thomas F. Merrill, ed., *William Perkins: His Pioneer Works on Casuistry: "A Discourse of Conscience" and "The Whole Treatise of Cases of Conscience"* (Niewkoop: B. DeGraaf, 1966), chap. 5, "Of Liberalitie," Sect. I, question II: "To whome must almes be given?" 226.

[31]Edwards, "Christian Charity," in *Works*, 2:171.

276 | Timothy J. Keller

These passages base our charity on the pattern of God's common grace. But our charity should also be based on his special grace. God's electing grace comes to the unworthy, the unexpecting, the enemies of God (Ro 3:9–18). Paul says that he was shown mercy, as the worst of sinners, to exhibit Christ's unlimited patience. When the New Testament calls ministry to physical needs "mercy" as well, are we to believe that our "mercy" (deed ministry; see Luke 10:37) is to operate on a completely different principle than the mercy of God? Are we not to offer mercy to unbelievers and enemies? We must remember that God offers his mercy to rebellious people in order to make them responsible and whole. So, we too should render our aid with that aim in view. To offer aid only to friends and relatives is not God's pattern of mercy.

How, then, can we reconcile these two sets of scriptural teaching? How can we give our mercy freely even to the wicked and the ungrateful, yet still honor the precept "He who does not work shall not eat"? The knot comes untied when we see how God's charity to us works.

When God's grace first comes to us, it comes unconditionally, regardless of our merits. His mercy is "unconditional" in that God calls us with the Gospel before we show any interest or any desire for him (Ro 3:9–18), while we are still enemies. Regeneration is "monergistic"; we do not cooperate in or merit this operation of grace. But although God's mercy *comes* without conditions, it does not *proceed* without conditions. Sanctification is "synergistic"; we cooperate with God's grace. Why? Because he loves us, and we can be happy only if we are holy. God cannot leave us in the condition in which he originally found us.[32]

So, I propose, our charity should follow the pattern of God's mercy. *At first*, we should show mercy to anyone in need, as we have opportunity and resources. We should not

---

[32]"When it is said that man takes part in the work of sanctification, this does not mean that man is an independent agent in the work, so as to make it partly the work of God and partly the work of man; but merely, that God effects the work in part through the instrumentality of man as a rational being, by requiring of him prayerful and intelligent co-operation with the Spirit. . . . [Sanctification] differs from regeneration in that man can, and is in duty bound to, strive for ever-increasing sanctification by using the means which God has placed at his disposal." Louis Berkhof, *Systematic Theology* (Grand Rapids: Eerdmans, 1972), 534.

turn them away by analyzing them as "undeserving," even if sin is part of the complex of their poverty. (Seldom is an individual case of poverty rooted in one cause; usually all three are present.) Of course we should be on the lookout for fraud, and we must not give aid naïvely in such a way that it is immediately abused. We must give as a witness to the free grace of Christ and as an effort to turn rebellious hearts to the Lord.

But the goal of mercy is not simply to provide spot relief or to stop the suffering. Our real purpose must be to *restore* the poor man. We must carefully build him up until he is self-sufficient, and that means we must, in love, demand more and more cooperation. Mercy must truly have the purpose of seeing God's lordship actually realized in the lives of those we help. We must give aid in such a way that people grow in righteousness. We must not give aid so as to support rebellion against God. Although we must be extremely patient, *eventually* aid must be withdrawn if it is abused.

We see, then, that mercy ministry operates on the same basis as evangelism and the ministry of the word. *At first*, we offer the gospel to anyone and everyone, as we have opportunity and resources to reach them. "Whosoever will. . ."! We do not wait for people to come to us. But if *eventually* a person or a group evidences a rebellious and disrespectful attitude toward the Gospel, we withdraw. We do not "cast pearls before swine." Continued pressure only hardens them and dishonors the message.

Was this approach used by Jesus? I believe it was. Jesus ministered in word and deed; he preached as well as healed and fed, and he did this to all sorts of people. Did all the five thousand Jesus fed profess faith before he fed them? See also Matthew 4:24 and Luke 6:17–18 where we read that droves of non-Israelites came to him and were healed. However, continued rejection of his claims led Jesus, in Nazareth, to "not do *many* miracles there because of their lack of faith" (Mt 13:58; cf. Lk 4:24). The discrimination mentioned by Chilton *does* come into effect, but only as time goes on.

Jesus' miracles were not merely authentications of his power, but they were ministries to the physical needs of

278 | Timothy J. Keller

people, motivated by compassion (Mt 15:32),[33] as a demonstration of the restoration of the whole creation under the all-embracing redemptive power of Christ's kingdom.[34] Jesus commissioned the apostles to go into the world as he was sent (Jn 17:18). He was mighty in word and deed (Lk 24:19). This commission is significant in that the apostles represent the ruling authority of the church, not merely individual Christians.[35]

So then, our own deeds of mercy also point forward to the promise of the new heaven and the new earth, and they also show that the promise of the kingdom is already being fulfilled in the pouring out of the love of Christ through the Spirit! When we visit the prisoner (Mt 25:36), we proclaim liberty to the captives that Christ will bring in his kingdom in the "year of the Lord's favor" Lk 4:18–19). While the final day of God's jubilee is yet to come, it is already present in the saving power of Christ, manifest in deeds of mercy through gifts of the Spirit. The church goes into the world as agents of the kingdom (Ac 8:12; 14:22; 28:23). I believe that the church cannot routinely do *miraculous* deed ministry, but we still are to demonstrate the kingdom by our deeds in the world.

I am proposing that the reconstructionist approach to biblical charity is too conditional and restrictive. Instead of demanding obedience to God's law as a *condition* of charity, I think the Bible teaches that obedience to God's law is the *goal* of charity.

This model is strongly urged by Jonathan Edwards:

> If they are come to want by a vicious idleness and prodigality; yet we are not thereby excused from all obligation to relieve them, unless they continue in those vices. If they continue not . . . and if their fault be forgiven, then it will not remain to be a bar in the way of our charitably relieving them. . . . Now Christ hath loved us, pitied us, and greatly laid out himself to relieve us

---

[33]The Bible clearly states that expressing love in word without expressing love in deed is not the expression of Christian love at all (1Jn 3:17–18).

[34]Herman Ridderbos, *The Coming of the Kingdom* (Philadelphia: Presbyterian and Reformed, 1969), 65–70.

[35]For more on the scope of individual Christian mercy ministry, see "Biblical Guidelines for Mercy Ministry in the PCA," Part V., Minutes of the Presbyterian Church in America General Assembly, 1986.

from the want and misery which we brought on ourselves. . . .[36]

Here Edwards uses the approach I have been arguing
for. The aid is extended *together with* a call to the person to
submit to Christ's ministry to the whole person. But
Edwards then asks: What if the person will not change his
course of living?

> If they continue in the same courses still, yet that doth not
> excuse us from charity to their families that are innocent.
> If we cannot relieve those of their families without their
> having something of it, yet that ought not to be a bar in
> the way of our charity.[37]

Edwards' approach is balanced! It is not full of self-
righteous suspicion and condescension toward the poor. On
the other hand, it is full of loving limits and firmness.

THE ISSUE OF STRATEGY

The reconstructionists' strategy to help the poor is a
fairly simple one. Ordinarily, it is broken into three parts:

> First, the family is the primary agency of welfare—in
> education, law enforcement (by teaching biblical law and
> self-government), care for the aged. [Second], the church,
> as the agency for collecting the tithe, also has social
> welfare obligations. [Third], the civil government has
> almost none. Even in the case of the most pitiable people
> in Israel, the lepers, the State had only a negative
> function, namely to quarantine them from other citizens.
> The State provided no medical care or other tax-supported
> aid (Lev. 13 and 14).[38]

Reconstructionists say that the state has no welfare
obligations because it has only two obligations or functions.
"The only functions allowed to the state by the Bible are
defense of its people and *punishment of criminals*."[39] Reconstructionists say, then, that the best thing the state can do for the

---

[36]Edwards, "Christian Charity," in *Works*, 2:172.
[37]Ibid.
[38]Gary North, "Free Market Capitalism," in *Wealth and Poverty*, 57.
[39]Chilton, *Productive Christians*, 188.

poor is to completely stop interfering in the free market.[40] Their argument is that government policies designed to protect the worker and the consumer (labor unions, minimum-wage laws, occupational licensing, subsidized industry) have only hurt free enterprise and decreased vocational and entrepreneurial opportunity.[41]

When it came to the first two issues, of "cause" and "condition," I disagreed fairly sharply with reconstructionists, but on this ground I am less sure of both my position *and* theirs. I absolutely agree that the family is the *primary* and the church the *secondary* institutions appointed by God for the relief of the poor. Only the church can bring the Gospel to bear on the whole life of the poor person and the poor community. The Gospel brings wholeness (holiness) in every dimension of life as each dimension is brought under the kingship and law of Christ. If the family and the church were taking their responsibilities seriously, the state would have little to do.

Yet I believe there are some "loose ends" about the reconstructionists' blueprint for the relief of the poor:
1. *The state, as well as the family and the church, may have duties of welfare and charity.*

The reconstructionists' view of the state is a large issue, one that is addressed more fully in another place in this volume. But some remarks are in order here.

Reconstructionists represent the position that the single purpose of the state is to administer justice with the sword. It does so through enforcing laws that promote justice, piety, and social order. It does so also by going to war in cases where it must defend itself from an evil nation. This view is based on Romans 13:3–4: "Rulers hold no terror for those who do right, but for those who do wrong. . . . if you do wrong, be afraid, for he does not bear the sword for nothing. He is God's servant, an agent of wrath to bring punishment on the wrongdoer."

Another view declares that the state has another purpose besides administering justice, and that is promoting the general welfare. This view is based on the interpretation of Romans 13:4, which states: "He is God's servant to do you

---

[40]Ibid., 189.
[41]Ibid., 191–201.

good." The former view sees the "good" mentioned here as nothing different from the administration of justice mentioned in the verse. But others see this as a positive role (promoting "good"), which goes along with the negative role (avenging wrath on evil). Speaking very broadly, this view has been the position of Dutch Calvinism.[42]

I believe we should exegetically grant that Romans 13:3–4 speaks of more than just the administration of justice. When Paul explains that the ruler has the power to punish evildoers, he gives as the foundation of this teaching, "for he [the ruler] is God's servant to do you good." This is a more general, positive principle, on which the administration of justice is based. Or, put another way, justice is *one* way in which "the good" is promoted. The state has the right to promote "the good" in other ways as well that do not usurp the responsibilities of the church and the family.

Charles Hodge on Romans 13:4 says:

> Government is a benevolent institution of God, designed for the benefit of men; and therefore, should be respected and feared. . . . *For good*, etc., i.e. to secure or promote your welfare. . . . The proper sphere of the civil government is the civil and social relations of men, and their temporal welfare. . . .

John Murray explains that "good" cannot be confined to a mere absence of crime, but it is defined in 1 Timothy 2:2 as "peaceful and quiet lives."[43]

Romans 13 does not provide a specific mandate for the state's aid to the poor, but it does allow the state to be involved in a wider variety of activities that positively promote temporal welfare, rather than simply involving itself in the restraint of crime and injustice. Thus Meeter said:

> The Calvinist has never hesitated to ascribe to the government such general tasks dealing with public welfare . . . the ownership and operation of public utilities,

---

[42]E.g. H. H. Meeter, *The Basic Ideas of Calvinism* (Grand Rapids: Eerdmans, 1939), 125–37.

[43]C. Hodge, *Commentary on the Epistle to the Romans* (Grand Rapids: Eerdmans, 1950), 407, 414. See also J. Murray, *The Epistle to the Romans*, (Grand Rapids: Eerdmans, 1968), 151–52: "He is a minister of God for that which is good. And we may not tone down the import of the term 'good' in this instance."

development of natural resources, social security acts, and even in certain instances, governmental ownership of factories.[44]

Meeter cites Abraham Kuyper, who attributed to the government a concern for public health, regulation of child labor, social security, and cultural development.

Meeter also appealed to Calvin, who very clearly called the civil government to make public loans to the poor, promote public hospitals, fix the price of corn and wine, and determine the proper rate of interest. Calvin even advocated the ownership by the state of the silk industry. Since the state is supposed to punish evildoers, it does not seem possible to avoid some regulation of the marketplace. Should the government legislate against homosexuality but not against landlords who gouge poor tenants with unfair rents? Both are sins condemned by the Scripture. Shall one kind of sin be punished by law but another be omitted? (See below about the issue of hermeneutics that lies behind this issue.)

Meeter explains that the Calvinist view of the state is opposed to *individualism*, but it is also against *socialism*. How? "The aim of the socialist . . . is to have society dominated by the State . . . [but] society is far broader than the State . . . the determining principle which differentiates the Calvinist from the socialist is always: *Private initiative must everywhere have the priority.*"[45] Despite this ringing affirmation, I think Meeter would consider the reconstructionists to have an "individualistic" view of the state.

A relationship of a citizen to his government is a covenantal one, and (as we have seen) the temporal welfare of the citizens is the state's covenantal responsibility. It is remarkable that God held even pagan kings responsible to see to the needs of their poor and weak citizens. For example, Nebuchadnezzar is denounced for not giving "mercy to the poor."[46] Joseph became a high-ranking civil

[44]Meeter, *Basic Ideas of Calvinism*, 133–34.

[45]Ibid., 133.

[46]On Daniel 4:27, E. J. Young observes: "with this exercise of righteousness is coupled the practice of mercy to the poor. In the OT these two virtues are frequently associated, cf. Isa. 11:4; Ps. 72:4; Isa. 41:2. . . . In Tobit 12:9; 14:11 righteousness and almsgiving are almost equated. . . ." *Prophecy of Daniel* (Grand Rapids: Eerdmans, 1949), 109.

magistrate in the pagan state of Egypt. He is the first in the line of Abraham to become "a blessing to the nations" by providing a hunger-relief program for his own nation and all the surrounding ones (Ge 41:53–57).[47]

The Bible tells us very little about the government's role in caring for the needy. It does seem fair to infer that such a lack of information *at least* means that the work of mercy is given by God more primarily to the church and the family than to the state. As we look at these three social institutions—family, church, and state—we see that the closer the covenantal connection, the greater the responsibility for mercy.

But it seems just as reasonable, in light of God's judgment on the nations and Joseph's example, that the state has a responsibility to help its poorest members. If a family neglects its God-given duties to help a poor member, is the church disobeying God if it steps in and becomes the primary care-giver (though that is not God's design)? And in

---

[47]Gary North writes: "It might be argued that Joseph's experience in Egypt serves as a biblical justification for central planning by the civil government. Such an argument, while no doubt tempting, overlooks the key fact in this incident: Pharaoh had been given a direct revelation from God, and Joseph came to him as God's prophet with the ability to interpret Pharaoh's dream perfectly. Only on this assumption, namely, that we can expect truly prophetic omniscience from salaried or elected officials of the central government, can a biblical case be made for universal central economic planning. . . . The consequence of Egyptian economic planning by Joseph must also be borne in mind. The entire nation, excepting only the priests, went into bondage to the Egyptian State (Gen. 47:13–22)."

North is right—it is quite difficult to interpret everything Joseph did to be a "blueprint" for government officials today. But is North suggesting that God was inspiring Joseph to do something expressly forbidden (sinful) for magistrates to do? And why does he call Joseph's program a "judgment on Egypt" (*Wealth and Poverty: Four Views*, 202)? I am sure everyone in Egypt would have called the program a *blessing*; the alternative was mass starvation. In fact, Edmund Clowney has suggested to me (in a personal conversation) that this was the beginning of the fulfillment of the prophecy that Abraham's descendants would be a "blessing to the nations." (Not just Egypt, but all the surrounding nations were helped by the program.)

I think the fairest conclusion is that Joseph's program was extraordinary. He was, by divine revelation, taking drastic measures for a drastic situation. But he was acting on the basis of a principle—that a good civil magistrate is concerned for the temporal welfare of his people. God did *not* briefly give Joseph permission to do something sinful. And if it was not sinful, then the principle remains that the government can do charity.

the same way, if a person is falling through the "nets" of both family and church, could not the state sometimes give aid? That would not be the case if the Scripture really forbade it, but does the word of God do so?

2. *A faith in pure, unrestricted capitalism (especially as the chief way to deal with poverty) needs to be examined critically.*

Here is another subject too broad for this chapter, but it must be addressed. Simply put, the reconstructionists do very little to analyze how human sin can corrupt the free market system to oppress people. Instead, they spend all of their time analyzing how human sin corrupts the socialistic system.

I wish they would reflect on the fact that equal opportunity does not help people who do not start out with equal resources. A great example is the poverty of black people in this country. In general, blacks were kidnapped and robbed of all their belongings when they were brought to America. As a community, they entered the free enterprise system of America far behind the white community. John Frame points out that theft in Scripture is punished by double restitution. He notes that as a result we should give voluntary support to "affirmative action" in Christian businesses and institutions.[48] That approach does not fit in with pure free enterprise, but it is in accord with biblical principles of restitution.

I wish reconstructionists would also reflect on the limitations of the "trickle down" theory, which declares that the prosperity of the middle class and the rich will naturally "trickle down" to the poor. Despite the decreasing unemployment rate of the 1980s and the rise in the stock market, the poor really are getting poorer. Between 1978 and 1984 the gap between the average income of the poor and the poverty line grew from $3,772 to $4,141. The Urban League reported that while black income was 62 percent of that of white income in 1975, it was just 56 percent in 1986. In 1986, for the first time, the Census Bureau acknowledged that "there has

---

[48]John M. Frame, *ST 323 Doctrine of the Christian Life Lecture Outline* (mimeographed syllabus, Westminster Theological Seminary in California) (February 1984), 225.

been an increase in income inequality in the United States during the last decade and a half."[49]

I wish reconstructionists would qualify their statements that say the free market rewards employers for doing the "morally correct thing,"[50] such as paying good wages or serving the needs of the consumer. The market also rewards people who do not do so. I recently heard a leading marketing expert say, "In the U.S. most of the consumer demand is generated by the companies themselves. Advertising produces it." Is that serving the consumer, or is it exploitation? I certainly agree that the Bible mandates private property and the basics of the free enterprise system, but the writers of the reconstruction school seem unwilling to admit that the wealthy can and do exploit people in a free-enterprise system just as the bureaucrats exploit people in a Marxist society.

Does the market reward the employer or the seller for doing the morally correct thing? Richard Baxter once addressed the question, "May not a landlord take as much for his land as it is worth?" Baxter answers:

> [When] landlords are of the nobility or gentry, and the tenants are poor men, who have nothing but what they get by their hard labour out of the land which they hold . . . in this case some abatement of the full worth is but *such a necessary mercy as may be called justice* . . . but, sometimes a poor man selleth a house or land to a rich man, where the scruple hath no place."[51]

We see here a much more biblically balanced approach to the free market. Baxter states unequivocally that the market often fixes a price that is actually unjust. Far more must be taken into consideration than only what the market says.

I should show my hand here and say that I am quite uncomfortable at how closely the reconstructionists tie their kingdom model to conservative ideology *and* at how closely the "radical evangelicals" tie their kingdom model to liberal ideology. Each side quotes the latest economic books from

---

[49]"Poverty Rate Dips as the Median Family Income Rises," *New York Times* 1, 12 (July 31, 1987): 1.

[50]North, *Wealth and Poverty*, 36.

[51]Baxter, *Christian Directory*, 849.

their party (usually written by non-Christian socialists or elitists) in order to refute the views of the other.

American "liberalism" tends to be hostile to the claim that the church should have public rights and public functions. Instead, the state is seen as the panacea for society's ills; the state will order society in a just, fair, rational way. The roots of liberalism are in the eighteenth-century Enlightenment, which taught that reason alone can bring man all the knowledge needed to build a just society.[52] Liberalism is also highly individualistic, defending private, individual rights against institutions such as the family (children's rights against parents) and the church (homosexuals' rights to work for a church).

But American conservatism is no real alternative, for it is just as rationalistic and individualistic as liberalism. For example, although conservatives expect the government to regulate "personal morality" (such as upholding traditional family values), they insist that "social morality" (e.g., giving to the poor) must be completely voluntary. For them, there can be no legal accountability in this area at all. Sexual morality cannot be merely voluntary, but social morality must be. This is fundamentally inconsistent, and the exact reverse of the liberals' individualism.

Conservatism tends to be blind to the systemic, corporate structures of greed and selfishness that create poverty. Instead, it sees poverty as being eliminated strictly through individual initiative. And while liberalism puts much faith in big government, the conservative has a similar blind faith in free enterprise. The ideology of the Right insists that completely free enterprise, business unhampered by any constraints or limits, will bring prosperity to the country, and this prosperity will "trickle down" to the poor. But as John Perkins writes:

> Free enterprise is handicapped by a serious flaw—man's greed. Both biblical history and American history remind us repeatedly that greedy men will use economic freedom to exploit—to profit at the expense of others. Employers pay employees as little as possible in order to maximize

[52]Peter L. Berger and Richard J. Neuhaus, *To Empower People: The Role of Mediating Structures in Public Policy* (Washington, D.C.: American Enterprise Institute for Public Policy Research, 1977), 5.

their own profits rather than treating their employee's economic interest as being as important as their own—or, to be thoroughly Christian—more important than their own. Advertisers create markets for products which no one needs, not from a motive of servanthood, but out of greed, pure and simple. Businesses measure their success primarily by their financial profits—not by how well they glorify God and serve people. What a far cry we are from a truly Christian economy![53]

I imagine that the conservative would reply, "But a truly free enterprise system would open up America as the 'Land of Opportunity.' There would be more jobs and therefore poverty would greatly decrease." But this sort of response betrays a simplistic analysis of the roots of poverty, as I mentioned previously.

A free-enterprise system, full of job and entrepreneurial opportunities will benefit the able-bodied, educated, non-elderly, adult poor. But many, many of the poor cannot simply begin their own businesses or get jobs to get them out of poverty, because of great obstacles in their lives. Many of them are illiterate; many of them are elderly, sick, and disabled; many of them are breadwinners without the skills to get a good job; many of them are children living in terrible neighborhoods, where they cannot get a decent education or learn habits of discipline. It does not help to simply have jobs available. To remove the obstacles from these millions of people will take enormous expenditures of both money and manpower.

Who will make these expenditures? I believe that the family, the church, and the state (see remarks above) have duties of charity. All three are covenantal institutions and thus have charity responsibilities to the people in covenant relationship. I do not think the state should be "savior of the poor," however. Therefore, the state needs to recognize and support through public policy the right of the church, the family, and the voluntary societies to do education and charity (as I mentioned above).

---

[53]John Perkins, *With Justice for All* (Ventura, Calif.: Regal Books, 1982), 167.

ISSUES BEHIND THE ISSUES

This chapter has been dealing with the reconstructionists' approach to poverty. Many of my criticisms of their response to the poor rest on deeper reservations I have with their interpretation of the Old Testament civil code. I realize that this is a matter that is dealt with at other places in this volume. But let me show how this problem bears on the poverty question.

Chilton writes: "In general, the laws which specifically provide for the poor are not enforced by the state. This is not to suggest that these laws are unimportant. . . . The civil government cannot punish criminals unless it is given the right to do so by Scripture."[54] This is probably the reason for his remarkable statement that the poor in Third World countries, if they obey God's law will not have to fear a tiny, wealthy elite of dictators, for these dictators will fall by God's providential judgment.[55] Chilton apparently believes that to seek to directly resist or punish oppression (with civil or legal force) is not allowed by the Scripture. We must wait for God in his providence to bring down oppressors.

This approach to interpreting the civil code of Israel is highly suspect. Chilton assumes that, if a sin has no civil stricture attached to it in the civil code of Israel, then no government ever has any right to punish for it. I think that is an unwarranted assumption. In Job 29:12–17, Job claims to have "rescued" (v. 12) the poor and to have been an "advocate" of the needy (v. 16). He "broke the fangs of the wicked and snatched the victims from their teeth" (v. 17). How is a Christian to imitate Job today? How can I "break the fangs" of an oppressor? If I do not do it through legal means, I am only a vigilante. But Chilton would, on the basis of his hermeneutic, insist that there is no biblical basis for making oppression punishable by law. (Remember, Baxter explains oppression as sometimes getting market value for your products!)

I heartily agree that Christians should seek to bring about biblical reform and transformation of our whole society. And I think the *whole* Bible should be the basis of such a cultural reformation. But the reconstructionists in

---

[54]Chilton, *Manipulators*, 74.
[55]Ibid., 119.

their mode of interpretation and application of the Old Testament do not appear to me to be sensitive to the progress of biblical theology. Reconstructionists seem to separate ceremonial from moral/civil law, saying that the ceremonial is fulfilled in Christ but the moral/civil is still binding. But in the Bible the law is spoken of as a whole, and thus the advent of Christ must have brought an *overall* change in our relation to the law. The *whole* law (moral, ceremonial, civil) is still normative but the *whole* law changed in its application to us. I like John Frame's approach here.[56] Reconstructionists are very weak on explaining the changes, the newness of our relationship to the law in Christ.

So for example, the basic requirement of ceremonial laws—approaching God in purity and under the substitutionary sacrifice—is still binding. So too, as the Westminster Confession says, the "general equity" (WCF, XIX, iv) of Israel's civil code is still binding, but many of the specific applications are not.

"Pay him his wages each day before sunset, because he is poor and is counting on it. Otherwise he may cry to the Lord against you and you will be guilty of sin" (Dt 24:15). Is this a "blueprint" for paying wages? Perhaps the reconstructionists would say, "Yes. It is a violation of God's law to pay wages weekly, bi-weekly, or monthly." But I doubt it. Then here is an example of extracting the "general equity" (WCF, XIX) but not the details. It is taking the principle (in paying wages, there should be no delay that benefits the employer unduly and creates a hardship for the worker) yet adapting the details to a different time and place. The danger of subjectivism is present, but unavoidable.[57]

Nothing that I just said is meant to deny that Israel's code is full of God's wisdom and is all applicable to our own culture.[58] No area of life is untouched by God's law.

---

[56]John Frame, "Doctrine of the Christian Life," mimeographed lecture notes, Westminster Theological Seminary (February 1979), 64.

[57]"Imitation of Old Testament Israel . . . is fraught with peril. We will often be tempted to claim for ourselves what was unique to the theocracy. On the other hand, we may dismiss as unique to the theocracy something which God wants us to observe. The job is *difficult*." Frame, "Doctrine of the Christian Life," 66.

[58]Another underlying issue is the lack of a "situational perspective" in the reconstructionists' interpretation of Israel's civil code. John Frame argues that there is a kind of "hermeneutical circularity." When we read Scripture

CONCLUSION

The good news is that reconstructionists are telling Christian people that it is a top priority for local churches to become deeply involved with the hungry, the homeless, and the poor. I am encouraged that the Christian reconstructionists are saying, "The care of the poor is *our* duty!" The bad news is that reconstructionists are supporting many common middle-class rationalizations and prejudices against the poor. These attitudes will cause patronizing approaches to the poor, with an emphasis on emergency relief, but not economic development and social justice reform.

Despite our differences, I propose that if we agree on the need to actually do this kind of ministry, Christians ought to do it together. Regardless of our views of the state or of capitalism and socialism, we can cooperate in finding jobs for the unemployed, finding homes for the homeless, beginning economic cooperatives to build up needy neighborhoods, and so on. The unhappy rifts in the evangelical church over poverty will heal only if we work together, getting to know the real poor and seeing their situation (instead of reading books about them by middle-class sociologists).

I want people to believe Christians who say the care of the poor is our duty and I want us to begin to work with those in need. I do not believe any real revival or cultural reformation will be possible until we do this (Isa 58:10).

ADDENDUM:
THE WRITING OF GEORGE GRANT

At the time of this writing, many readers of reconstructionist works consider George Grant an important author on the subject of poverty. Because his first two books, *Bringing in the Sheaves* (Atlanta: American Vision, 1985) and *In the*

(the normative perspective), we understand the world (situational) and ourselves (existential). But then, "as we understand the other areas better [the world and the self], we understand Scripture better." North lacks the situational perspective when he writes, "Missionaries should seek to impart a specifically Western way of looking at the world: future-oriented, thrift-oriented, education-oriented, and responsibility-oriented." (*Wealth and Poverty*, 49) See John M. Frame, *The Doctrine of the Knowledge of God* (Phillipsburg, N.J.: Presbyterian and Reformed, 1987), 89.

Shadow of Plenty (Ft. Worth: Dominion; Nashville: Thomas Nelson, 1986), were published by reconstructionist publishers and editors, it is commonly assumed that Grant is "in the camp." So why don't I interact with his material in this chapter?

Despite his close association through the publishing houses, Grant is *not* a reconstructionist. Certainly, there are many definitions of that term, but by virtually any criterion he does not meet the requirements. Grant does not share the reconstructionists' approach to the application of Old Testament law (which I briefly critique at the end of my chapter). He is not a thoroughgoing postmillennialist, nor does he partake of many other common reconstructionist perspectives.[59]

Fortunately, however, his publications are being read by many people in or around "the camp." And since they are, in my opinion, a clear improvement on the positions of North and Chilton, their impact has been a very salutary one.

1. In the first chapter of his book *In the Shadow of Plenty*, he lays out the thesis that deed ministry is as integral a part of evangelism as the ministry of the word.[60] This is a remarkable statement, leaving far behind the pietism that sees social concern as a mere means-to-the-end of "evangelism." Grant does not flinch from saying that if charity to the poor is omitted, "then we haven't truly evangelized. . . . Word and deed are inseparable."[61] This makes "biblical charity" a priority in the strongest terms. We can never minister in word without authenticating and actually expounding our message through deed ministry.

This is a great advance over the begrudging views of Chilton, and, as a result, Grant's books (*Bringing in the Sheaves*, and *In the Shadow of Plenty*) bristle with very specific calls and positive strategies for local churches and families to minister to the poor. Grant identifies the Great Commission (Mt 28:19–20) as being one with the "cultural mandate."[62]

---

[59]From personal correspondence between George Grant and the author.
[60]Grant, *In the Shadow of Plenty*, chap. 1: "Word and Deed Evangelism."
[61]Ibid., 10, 21.
[62]"The Commission [of Matt. 28:18–20] states that believers are to extend Christ's kingdom, making disciples in all nations by going, baptizing, and

Here he stands in the tradition of Reformed exegetes of the kingdom such as Harvie Conn [63] and Edmund Clowney, who speak of Kingdom-evangelism or "Lordship evangelism."[64] *Both* word and deed, evangelism and mercy, are means to the end of the spread of the kingdom of God. To say that social concern could be shown independently of evangelism is to cut mercy loose from kingdom endeavor, and mercy must then wither. But to say that evangelism can be done without social concern is to forget that our goal is not individual "decisions" but the bringing of all life and creation under the lordship of Christ, the kingdom of God.

    2. When it comes to the *causes* of poverty, we again meet in Grant a somewhat different approach than in North and Chilton. Unlike many other writers on poverty, Grant has personally ministered to many, many poor people.[65] He

---

teaching. This mandate is the essence of the New Covenant which is but an extension of the Old Covenant: Go and claim everything in heaven and on earth for the Kingdom, taking dominion for His Name's sake (Genesis 1:28). . . . Our call is to win *all* things for Christ. . . . We are to make disciples who will obey everything that He has commanded, not just a hazy zone of piety, but in the totality of life." Grant, *Bringing in the Sheaves*, 68.

    [63]"To be interested in things spiritual is not to be interested in things nonmaterial/supernatural/invisible/sacred as opposed to things material/natural/visible/secular. To be interested in things spiritual is to be interested in all of life, now touched by the healing hand of the Holy Spirit. . . . The heavens and the earth, what we call 'the natural half of reality,' are dignified by God as covenant witnesses (Psalm 19:1ff., Romans 1:20ff.). They are witnesses to what the earth really is designed to be, the garden of God (Ezekiel 28:13) where the Creator meets the creature in fellowship. Adam's fellowship with God is to be shown in his earthly, material activity, his subduing rule over the natural (Gen. 1:28). That is true spirituality." Harvie M. Conn, *Evangelism: Doing Justice and Preaching Grace* (Grand Rapids: Zondervan, 1982), 64. See also Conn's article, "Can I be spiritual . . . and at the same time human?" (*The Other Side* 9,5 [Sept.Oct. 1973]: 16–19, 42–47), which also identifies, as Grant does, the Great Commission with the "culture-building" mandate of Genesis 1:28.

    [64]"The renewal of Christ's salvation ultimately includes a renewed universe. . . . Christ's miracles were miracles of the kingdom, performed as signs of what the kingdom means. . . . Kingdom evangelism is therefore holistic as it transmits by word and deed the promise of Christ for body and soul as well as the demand of Christ for body and soul." E. P. Clowney, "Kingdom Evangelism" in Roger Greenway, ed., *The Pastor-Evangelist* (Phillipsburg, N.J.: Presbyterian and Reformed, 1987), 22.

    [65]In order to write *The Dispossessed: Homelessness in America* (Ft. Worth: Dominion, 1986), he spent several days on the streets of New York City, spending time in shelters for the homeless. Also he spent ten years in extensive programs of charity through his church in Houston.

discovered that "despite the popular conception that most of the homeless are these hardcore vagrants and derelicts . . . a vast majority taste only briefly the grapes of wrath. Most were . . . solidly entrenched in the work force, actively pursuing the 'American Dream.' Many were skilled industrial workers."[66]

Grant's book *The Dispossessed* recognizes the many complex causes of homelessness: mental illness, alcoholism, the "feminization of poverty," unemployment, housing shortages, the farm crisis. Chilton, in his treatment of Luke 4:18–19, will not grant that Jesus took special care to go to the oppressed poor.[67] Grant, however, is more balanced in his use of Luke 4:18–19. He quotes it to show that the oppressed poor "are the objects of God's special care."[68] This is a magnificent advance from the writings of North and Chilton; the concept of the "oppressed poor" is absent from their writings.

3. Grant is not a reconstructionist, but he is still a conservative who apparently very much supports the analyses of Murray, Sowell, Gilder, and other new conservative critics of American social policy. For example, he writes, "This extremely costly, ever-escalating 'war on poverty' has only made things worse. The very policies that were intended to help the poor have only aggravated their problems."[69]

---

[66]Grant, *The Dispossessed*, 32. Grant met Kathi Tannenbaum in New York. She had been a traditional, dedicated suburban wife and homemaker for twenty-two years. Then suddenly her only son was killed in a car accident. Soon her husband took to drink and got a divorce settlement in which Kathi did not get a dime or any alimony. At 43, Kathi was alone, without job skills. She went to work as a waitress for $900 a month, and soon she began to sink into poverty and alcoholism. Grant met Kathi in the Riverside Clinic, a rehabilitation center for indigent women. Grant's book is full of real case histories that show the complex factors that can bring a family into poverty.

[67]Chilton writes, "God does not merely relieve the oppressed or troubled in general. He graciously relieves the sufferings of those who seek Him." He stresses that God has no special concern for the poor, only for those people, rich and poor, who call upon him." Chilton, *Manipulators*, 107.

[68]Grant, *The Dispossessed*, 34.

[69]Grant, *Plenty*, 5. "Charity means getting rid of state-run affirmative action programs, subsidies, and give-away schemes . . . all state legislated impediments to labor: minimum-wage laws, occupational licensing restrictions, and 'closed shop' union regulations," 56.

Elsewhere he writes that much of homelessness stems from joblessness, and for this he blames the government-centralized economy.[70] I have already expressed my reservations about the critique of the new conservatives, who seem to be putting too much faith in the free-market system.

North and Chilton seem to think the strategy for the poor is simple: 1) the government stops helping the poor in any way, 2) the able-bodied poor are provided jobs by the free market, 3) the church and family give charity to deserving poor who are not able-bodied. In some places in his writings Grant gives the impression that he would take a similar approach. But elsewhere he shows that he is not naïve or simplistic in the least about all the many needed programs of relief, development, and social reform. These programs, he believes, must be carried out with the cooperation of the family, the church, neighborhood/regional organizations, private voluntary societies, and the government.

Grant is not a reconstructionist; he is a conservative in the tradition of G. K. Chesterton and, more recently, Herbert Schlossberg, but his works are greatly respected by the thinkers in the reconstructionist school and apparently are having a maturing effect on the whole movement's views of poverty and social problems.

---

[70]Grant, *The Dispossessed*, chap. 8, "Epitaph in Rust: Unemployment."

PART FIVE

THEONOMY AND THE REFORMED HERITAGE: HISTORICAL CONNECTIONS

One of the claims frequently made by theonomists is that theonomy represents the true Reformed heritage stemming from John Calvin through the Presbyterians and Puritans of the British Isles and the American colonies. This section demonstrates the historical flaws involved in this claim.

Robert Godfrey shows that John Calvin, with an emphasis on equity and natural law in the area of civil law, represents an entirely different line of thinking from theonomists in this regard. Sinclair Ferguson explains how the Westminster Assembly's discussions concerning the law of God manifest a Reformed inclusivism, based on generic Calvinism, that might allow some theonomic applications, but not the fundamental theonomic interpretation, of the law. Samuel Logan argues that the New England Puritans of Massachusetts Bay, although they did seek to transform their culture according to the Bible (including the Old Testament), consciously designed their civil laws in ways different from the Mosaic judicial laws.

Chapter Thirteen

Calvin and Theonomy

W. Robert Godfrey

W. Robert Godfrey

W. Robert Godfrey (Ph.D., Stanford University) is Professor of Church History at Westminster Theological Seminary in California. With other degrees from Stanford University and Gordon-Conwell Theological Seminary, he has been a minister in the Christian Reformed Church. He is the editor (with Jesse L. Boyd III) of and contributor to *Through Christ's Word,* and a contributor to *Discord, Dialogue and Concord, John Calvin: His Influence in the Western World,* and *Scripture and Truth.* He is a former editor of the *Westminster Theological Journal.*

Chapter Thirteen

Calvin and Theonomy

Theonomy or Christian reconstruction is a movement with a political agenda for America. At the heart of this agenda is a call for adopting the civil law of Moses and its penalties as current American law. Theonomists argue that the law of Moses expresses God's holy will for all nations and that any nation will be blessed in honoring God by keeping his law.

The foundational thinker in this movement is Rousas J. Rushdoony. Others such as Greg Bahnsen and Gary North have elaborated or modified Rushdoony's work. These thinkers are all Reformed in background and believe that theonomy is the most biblical and consistently Calvinistic expression of political thought in Christian circles today. They see themselves as seeking to continue to reform the church in the tradition of John Calvin. Greg Bahnsen, for example, has written positively of the influence that Calvin has had on him: "Past authors such as Calvin . . . have been of great instructional value to me. . . ."[1] He looks to Calvin particularly for his political insights: "John Calvin broke with the view that the state was autonomous, arguing for the sole rule of Christ over both church and state. . . ."[2]

---

[1]Greg L. Bahnsen, *Theonomy in Christian Ethics*, expanded edition (Phillipsburg, N.J.: Presbyterian and Reformed, 1984), xxxiii.

[2]Ibid., 2. Jack W. Sawyer, Jr., "Moses and the Magistrate: Aspects of Calvin's Political Theory in Contemporary Focus," (Th.M. thesis, Westminster Theological Seminary, Philadelphia, 1986), seeks to show the basic identity of the thought of Calvin and theonomy. But this thesis misses the fundamental hermeneutical differences between Calvin and theonomy and is subject to the criticisms of theonomy offered in this chapter.

The relationship between theonomy and Calvin is not so simple, however, as the Reformed backgrounds of theonomists might suggest. Rushdoony, the most historically minded of the theonomists, does show great appreciation for and use of Calvin's thought, but he also discusses significant discontinuities between his own thought and that of Calvin. Indeed his criticism of Calvin at times is basic and sharp. Rushdoony charges Calvin with allowing "classical humanism" to gain the ascendancy over biblical thought and relying on natural law or "the common law of nations" to direct civil government. Rushdoony labels this "heretical nonsense."[3]

The purpose of this study is, first, to examine Calvin's thought on the law of Moses and its applicability to other nations and, second, to evaluate the extent to which theonomy is indebted to or deviates from Calvin. Such an examination and evaluation cannot in itself establish whether theonomy is right or wrong. This study, however, can aid in determining whether theonomy is in accord with the original principles of Reformed thought or is basically a theological novelty.

CALVIN AND LAW: THE INSTITUTES

Calvin summarizes his understanding of civil government in the last chapter of his *Institutes of the Christian Religion*. To appreciate Calvin's discussion of civil government in the *Institutes* one must recognize that Calvin is not presenting an abstract discussion of government. Rather, he is focusing on the character of "a Christian state"[4] as he experienced it in his day. He deals with the subject of civil government in his study of Christian religion because he is convinced that civil government has a crucial role to perform in advancing the cause of true religion. Calvin's chapter on government appears at the end of Book Four of the *Institutes* that is entitled, "The External Means or Aids by Which God Invites Us Into the Society of Christ and Holds Us Therein." For Calvin civil government is one of the external aids by

---

[3]Rousas John Rushdoony, *The Institutes of Biblical Law* (Phillipsburg, N.J.: Craig, 1973), 9.

[4]John Calvin, *Institutes of the Christian Religion*, ed. J. T. McNeill (Philadelphia: Westminster, 1960), IV,xx,14.

which God preserves the society of Christ. Although civil government has "a completely different nature" from the spiritual government of the church, it complements the work of the church by promoting "civil justice and outward morality."[5]

Calvin expands his conception of the work of government as he lists some of the responsibilities of the state in a Christian society:

> Civil government has as its appointed end, so long as we live among men, to cherish and protect the outward worship of God, to defend sound doctrine of piety and the position of the church, to adjust our life to the society of men, to form our social behavior to civil righteousness, to reconcile us with one another, and to promote general peace and tranquillity.[6]

This expanded statement shows that Calvin believes the Christian state must enforce both tables of the law; i.e., it must protect the church of God as well as promote justice among people.

Calvin's belief that government has a responsibility to true religion was inherited not only from the Middle Ages, but also from the ancient world. Pagan Rome, as well as Christian society after Constantine, believed that religious uniformity was necessary for social cohesion and political stability.[7] Calvin goes so far as to argue that the state's religious responsibility is clear to all: "If Scripture did not teach that it [the duty of magistrates] extends to both Tables of the Law, we could learn this from secular writers. . . ."[8] He seems to have in mind here particularly Cicero.[9] Calvin tended to view ideas that were common to both Christians and pagan Romans and Greeks as evidence of what in some circumstances he calls natural law.

After this preliminary discussion of the responsibility of

---

[5]Ibid., IV,xx,1.

[6]Ibid., IV,xx,2.

[7]For a discussion of some of the issues in Reformed thought on church-state relations, see W. R. Godfrey, "Church and State in Dutch Calvinism," in Through Christ's Word, edited by W. R. Godrey and J. L. Boyd III (Phillipsburg, N.J.: Presbyterian and Reformed, 1985), 223–43.

[8]Calvin, Institutes, IV,xx,9.

[9]Ibid., IV,xx,9, note 23.

civil government Calvin continues to write briefly on three specific topics: the work of the magistrate,[10] the character of the civil law,[11] and the response of the governed people.[12] It is particularly in Calvin's discussion of the civil law that his differences from theonomy become clear. He begins this section by referring to the wisdom of Cicero and Plato and then notes that for the purposes of the *Institutes* he might well "have preferred to pass over this matter in utter silence if [he] were not aware that here many dangerously go astray." What is the specific concern that causes Calvin to write on the subject of civil law? He answers that "there are some who deny that a commonwealth is duly framed which neglects the political system of Moses, and is ruled by the common laws of nations." Basing a contemporary Christian state on the judicial laws of Moses, Calvin says, is "false and foolish."[13] Calvin's strong words may have been inspired in part by the radical, violent Anabaptist theocracy at Münster (1534–1535), but he comes to his conclusion from a clear line of reasoning.

Calvin begins his reasoning with the common division of the Mosaic law into moral, ceremonial, and judicial elements. The key distinction for Calvin between the moral and the ceremonial or judicial laws is that the moral law is unchangeable, whereas the ceremonial and judicial laws are changeable. Calvin summarizes the moral law as "an unchangeable rule of right living," "the perpetual law of love," and "justice, . . . humanity and gentleness."[14] For Calvin, different nations appropriately have diverse constitutions because the nations are shaped by distinctive historical circumstances. Yet all these different constitutions rest on the equity of the moral law, which is natural and common to all nations.

Calvin sees this unchanging moral law as the foundation of all particular civil laws. The moral law is the equity or the common, natural basis of all civil law. Calvin discusses equity further in these terms:

---

[10]Ibid., IV,xx,4–13.
[11]Ibid., IV,xx,14–16.
[12]Ibid., IV,xx,17–32.
[13]Ibid., IV,xx,14.
[14]Ibid., IV,xx,14–15.

> The law of God which we call the moral law is nothing
> else than a testimony of natural law and of that conscience
> which God has engraved upon the minds of men.
> Consequently, the entire scheme of this equity of which
> we are now speaking has been prescribed in it. Hence,
> this equity alone must be the goal and rule and limit of all
> laws.[15]

Calvin elaborates on this natural knowledge in his *Commentary on Romans*:

> We cannot conclude from this passage that there is in men
> a *full* knowledge of the law, but only that there are some
> seeds of justice implanted in their nature. This is evi-
> denced by such facts as these, that all the Gentiles alike
> institute religious rites, make laws to punish adultery,
> theft, and murder. . . . There is, therefore, a certain
> natural knowledge of the law. . . .[16]

Calvin seems to be saying that the basic moral law is objectively revealed in nature so as to be available to mankind and that the human conscience is so created that it responds to that law. In the fallen state man's conscience is seared, yet the conscience remains and perceives something of the equity or essence of the moral law. Such perception is not saving or even adequate by itself for a just society. Yet some elements of the moral law are perceived even in a pagan society.[17]

Calvin applies these thoughts about the moral law to the conclusion that all political constitutions properly rest on the equity of that moral law of God. Distinctive circumstances of different nations will result in different political laws from place to place and from time to time. Yet these diversities of laws are simply applications of the moral law to specific local needs.

For Calvin the judicial laws of Moses themselves are a particular constitution for the Jews. They rest on and reflect the unchanging moral law of God, but insofar as they meet

---

[15]Ibid., IV,xx,16.

[16]John Calvin, *Calvin's Commentaries, The Epistles of Paul the Apostle to the Romans*, ed. D. W. and T. F. Torrance (Grand Rapids: Eerdmans, 1976), on chap. 2:15, pp. 48–49.

[17]Calvin's belief that even unregenerate pagans have some knowledge of true justice is something like the later Reformed doctrine of common grace.

the specific historical circumstances of the Jews, they are not applicable to other nations. Not only may the specific judicial laws of the nations "differ from the Jewish law," but Calvin says sharply: "The statement of some, that the law of God given through Moses is dishonored when it is abrogated and new laws preferred to it, is utterly vain."[18]

Calvin even addresses the question whether the penalties of the civil laws of Moses are binding on Christian nations. He concludes that different nations need different penalties for the same crimes because of different circumstances in those nations. He argues that if such diversity did not exist to meet the distinctive needs of different nations, the nations would not really be observing the moral law of God.[19]

CALVIN AND LAW: A KEY COMMENTARY

Calvin offers a much more detailed look at the law of Moses in his *Commentaries on the Four Last Books of Moses*. His approach to interpreting the law of Moses is the same in the *Commentaries* as in the *Institutes*. He recognizes that the law of Moses at times simply makes explicit the moral law of God: "Let it suffice that what God here commands is dictated by nature itself."[20]

Calvin sees the law of Moses restating the moral law where it requires the state to enforce true religion. He writes, ". . . nor has any profane author ever existed who has not confessed that this is the principal part of a well-constituted state, that all with one consent should reverence and worship God."[21] From this conviction Calvin goes on to argue that the law of Moses is reflecting natural law when it requires death for those who seriously undermine true religion. "God commands the false prophets be put to death, who pluck up the foundations of religion, and are the authors and leaders of rebellion."[22] And he asks why, if

---

[18]Calvin, *Institutes*, IV,xx,16.

[19]Ibid.

[20]John Calvin, *Commentaries on the Four Last Books of Moses* (Grand Rapids: Baker, 1979), 3:18.

[21]Ibid., 2:18.

[22]Ibid., 2:76.

serious offenses against the second table of the law are punished with death, should not serious offenses against the first table be similarly punished?:

> Capital punishment shall be decreed against adulterers; but shall the despisers of God be permitted with impunity to adulterate the doctrines of salvation, and to draw away wretched souls from the faith? Pardon shall never be extended to poisoners, by whom the body alone is injured; and shall it be sport to deliver souls to eternal destruction?[23]

Calvin insists that only true religion is to be protected by the coercive action of civil government:

> We must always bear in mind what I have already said, that this severity must not be resorted to except when the religion is suffering, which is not only received by public authority and general opinion, but which is proved on solid grounds to be true; so that it may clearly appear that we are the avengers of God against the wicked.[24]

Calvin here indicates that religious persecution is justified only when religion has been proved true[25] and is legally established and popularly accepted, and when the attack on true religion is very serious. Only in these circumstances can the state punish such religious offenses as apostasy and blasphemy.

Beyond areas where the Mosaic law expresses the moral law, Calvin recognizes areas where the law given to Moses served specific purposes that were unique to Israel. For example, he sees the covenant given at Sinai as a renewal of the covenant made with Abraham augmented to accomplish additional purposes:

> Although the Law is a testimony of God's gratuitous adoption, and teaches that salvation is based upon His mercy, and invites men to call upon God with sure confidence, yet it has this peculiar property, that it covenants conditionally. Therefore it is worth while to distinguish between the general doctrine, which was

---

[23]Ibid.
[24]Ibid., 2:85.
[25]For Calvin, only Protestant Christianity could meet this criterion.

delivered by Moses, and the special command which he received.[26]

Calvin learned this distinction from Paul, who in Galatians 3:19 "opposes it [the Law] to the promise given to Abraham; because, as he is treating of the peculiar office, power, and end of the Law, he separates it from the promises of grace." Therefore what is "peculiar to the Law" of Moses is

> To fill men's minds with fear, and by setting forth its terrible curse, to cut off the hope of salvation; for, whilst it consists of three parts, each of them tends to the same end, that all should acknowledge themselves deserving of the judgment of eternal death, because in it God sustains no other character than that of a Judge. . . .[27]

The law given to Moses therefore has a unique function in redemptive history as a preparation for the coming of the Gospel. That unique function is one of the factors for Calvin that indicates that the law of Moses cannot be simply or directly applied to other nations: "Since the reason for this law [dividing the land equally among the tribes] was peculiar to the children of Abraham, its provisions can hardly be applied to other nations."[28]

Calvin sees redemptive uniqueness in some elements of the Mosaic legislation designed to separate Israel from the nations. The dietary regulations are part of that separation: "God would have His chosen people distinguished by this mark of separation from heathen nations."[29] The foods forbidden are not inherently bad but serve a distinctive role in establishing the ritual cleanness of Israel: "No animal was ever unclean in itself; but . . . this merely refers to its use."[30]

In his *Commentaries* Calvin also limits the applicability of the law of Moses by making a distinction between the permanent moral law and the temporary political laws. He observes at one point: "This was a political precept, and only given temporarily to the ancient people."[31] In his discussion

---

[26]*Commentaries*, 1:313.
[27]Ibid., 1:314–15.
[28]Ibid., 3:168–69.
[29]Ibid., 3:29.
[30]Ibid., 2:63.
[31]Ibid., 2:399.

of usury, for example, Calvin carefully distinguishes a temporary political element from a permanent moral obligation to brothers in Christ: "It is abundantly clear that the ancient people were prohibited from usury, but we must needs confess that this was a part of their political constitution. Hence it follows, that usury is not now unlawful, except in so far as it contravenes equity and brotherly union."[32] The political law of Moses against usury is now abrogated for the nations, but the underlying equity of the law does continue to bind all Christians. The equity requires Christians to love and provide for one another.

Calvin's discussion of the Mosaic laws against incest provides further insight into this distinction between political laws and the law of nature. In commending the law of Moses on incest Calvin writes, "The instruction here given is not, nor ought to be accounted, merely political."[33] Part of the basis for this conclusion is that some pagans also recognized this as proper: "The Roman laws accord with the rule prescribed by God, as if their authors had learnt from Moses what was decorous and agreeable to nature." The Romans could reach such conclusions because "whatever is prescribed here is deduced from the source of rectitude itself, and from the natural feeling implanted in us by Him."[34] Still the testimony of nature and conscience is suppressed by some. Because of that ability to suppress the truth, natural law cannot be established simply by examining the customs of the pagans. Calvin argues:

> What is natural cannot be abrogated by any consent or custom. In short, the prohibition of incests here set forth, is by no means of the number of those laws which are commonly abrogated according to the circumstances of time and place, since it flows from the fountain of nature itself, and is founded on the general principle of all laws, which is perpetual and inviolable. Certainly God declares that the custom which had prevailed amongst the heathen was displeasing to Him; and why is this, but because nature itself repudiates and abhors filthiness, although approved of by the consent (*suffragiis*) of men?[35]

---

[32]Ibid., 3:132.
[33]Ibid., 3:100.
[34]Ibid., 3:99.
[35]Ibid., 3:100.

Calvin then expands on the criteria by which he distinguishes the permanent from the temporary in the laws of Moses. Calvin writes:

> If this discipline were founded on the utility of a single people, or on the custom of a particular time, or on present necessity, or on any other circumstances, the laws deduced from it might be abrogated for new reasons, or their observance might be dispensed with in regard to particular persons, by special privilege; but since, in their enactment, the perpetual decency of nature was alone regarded, not even a dispensation of them would be permissible. It may indeed be decreed that it should be lawful and unpunished, since it is in the power of princes to remit penalties; yet no legislator can effect that a thing, which nature pronounces to be vicious, should not be vicious; and, if tyrannical arrogance dares to attempt it, the light of nature will presently shine forth and prevail.[36]

Calvin has yet another category for distinguishing the permanent from the temporary. This category is particularly intriguing and revealing because here Calvin uses the law of nature to criticize the law of Moses and declare it morally inferior. He argues that God at times made concessions to the hardness of the hearts of the people by allowing them to live below the standard of the moral law. When Calvin considers the command to exterminate the enemy in battle, he writes:

> More was conceded to the Jews on account of their hardness of heart, than was justly lawful for them. Unquestionably, by the law of charity, even armed men should be spared, if, casting away the sword, they crave for mercy. . . . This permission, therefore, to slaughter, which is extended to all the males, is far distant from perfection (and from the equity which ought to be in all God's children).[37]

Similarly when Calvin evaluates the permission given for private vengeance, he expresses his concern that such a practice tends to undermine the public, official punishment

---

[36]Ibid., 3:101.

[37]Ibid., 3:53. The parenthetical material in the quotation was added by Calvin to the French edition, which appeared the year after the original Latin edition.

of crime. He suggests that "this indulgence was conceded on account of the people's hardness of heart."[38]

Calvin takes this same approach in discussing the Mosaic legislation on divorce:

> Although what relates to divorce was granted in indulgence to the Jews, yet Christ pronounces that it was never in accordance with the Law, because it is directly repugnant to the first institution of God, from whence a perpetual and inviolable rule is to be sought. It is proverbially said that the laws of nature are indissoluble. . . . Hence it appears how great was the perverseness of that nation, which could not be restrained from dissolving a most sacred and inviolable tie. Meanwhile the Jews improperly concluded from their impunity that that was lawful, which God did not punish because of the hardness of their hearts.[39]

When Calvin speaks of those civil laws that he sees as supplemental to the eighth commandment, he writes, "Now follow the civil laws, the principle of which is not so exact and perfect; since in their enactment God has relaxed His just severity in consideration of the people's hardness of heart."[40] At another point Calvin again shows how important an interpretive tool this concession on God's part was: "From this passage, as well as other similar ones, it plainly appears how many vices were of necessity tolerated in this people."[41]

In the *Commentaries* as well as in the *Institutes* Calvin has followed a consistent interpretive approach to the biblical teaching on law and civil government. He believes that the moral law of God undergirds all specific laws and that the specific laws of Moses expressed that moral law for Israel in its unique historical circumstances. The civil laws of Moses as a whole are abrogated in the new covenant, though the equity or moral foundation of those laws remains. Even pagans know something of this moral law as natural law. A key category for Calvin in distinguishing moral from civil law in the Mosaic economy is that the moral law is permanent, whereas the civil is temporary.

---

[38]Ibid., 3:65.
[39]Ibid., 3:93.
[40]Ibid., 3:140.
[41]Ibid., 3:80.

Calvin's use of the idea of a moral law or natural law has led to an extensive debate among scholars as to how much of this natural law can be known to the unregenerate apart from the Bible.[42] The debate results in part from the fact that Calvin was not particularly interested in that question. He certainly had no interest in trying to develop an abstract natural ethics apart from scriptural revelation. His appeal to natural law was always directed to show the inescapable testimony that God had left in nature and in man to the moral order of the world. From that testimony even pagan man did some things that accorded with civic justice. Yet natural law apart from the Scriptures is not saving and cannot produce a fully just society. Calvin's conception of natural law and civil government is drawn from Scripture (especially Romans 1, 2, and 13) and is used to interpret Scripture.

CALVIN VERSUS THEONOMY

Calvin and theonomists formally agree on many points. For example, they agree that the civil government should be officially Christian. They agree that the government should enforce the first table as well as the second table of the Ten Commandments. They agree that capital punishment should be meted out for crimes such as apostasy and adultery.

These agreements, however, are purely formal. These positions are reached by entirely different lines of thinking on the part of Calvin and the theonomists. Take, for example, the matter of execution for adultery. Theonomists believe that adulterers should be executed because Moses said so. It is as simple as that. Calvin reaches his conclusion very differently. Commenting on the woman taken in adultery, Calvin defends death as a punishment for adultery, reasoning that adultery is a heinous crime that dishonors marriage and promotes illegitimacy. He does not simply

---

[42]The best discussions of this subject in English are John T. McNeill, "Natural Law in the Teaching of the Reformers," *Journal of Religion* 26 (1946): 168–82; I. John Hesselink, "Calvin's Concept and Use of the Law," doctoral dissertation, University of Basel, 1961; Arthur C. Cochrane, "Natural Law in Calvin," *Church-State Relations in Ecumenical Perspective*, ed. E. A. Smith (Pittsburgh: Duquesne University Press, 1966), 176–217.

appeal to Moses, but reasons from the equity of the moral law.[43]

Most modern Calvinists do not agree with Calvin today in those areas of formal agreement with the theonomists mentioned above. They see Calvin's conclusions as somewhat parochial and naïve, reflecting a perspective that still saw Europe both as the largest part of the world and as the Corpus Christianum. They believe that Calvin's own doctrine of depravity should make one less optimistic about the possibility or value of a Christian state. Nevertheless, most modern Calvinists share Calvin's interpretive approach to the Scriptures. They too stress the historical uniqueness of Israel and the need to examine the specifics of the civil laws of Moses in the light of the underlying moral law to find the contemporary application of those laws. This approach is not always easy, but it is the mainstream of Reformed theology.

Theonomy, by contrast, has a much simpler approach. Theonomists hold that the civil law of Moses—with some minor adjustments for modern problems—is to be followed today. Greg Bahnsen captures the spirit of this position in a chapter title: "The Abiding Validity of the Law in Exhaustive Detail."[44] In Rushdoony there are many specific cases of a contemporary, direct appeal to the law of Moses that are completely at odds with Calvin's approach to law. For example, Rushdoony's discussion of divorce is entirely different from Calvin's as presented above. Rushdoony's conclusion on divorce is that all the grounds for divorce in the law of Moses are still proper today. He writes, "The law concerning marriage and divorce remains one throughout Scripture."[45] In the unity of the Old and New Testaments the "Mosaic law is nowhere regarded as a lower or inferior legislation"[46] on divorce. In discussing the "bill of divorce" allowed in the law of Moses, Rushdoony argues, "Divorce is here certainly *not* seen as a barely tolerated evil, as some would have it."[47] Yet Calvin precisely maintains that divorce is a barely tolerated evil in the law of Moses.

---

[43]See Calvin's commentary on John 8:11 and Romans 2:15.
[44]Bahnsen, *Theonomy*, 39.
[45]Rushdoony, *Institutes*, 414.
[46]Ibid., 411.
[47]Ibid., 404.

Another example of the difference between Calvin and Rushdoony on the abiding requirement of the Mosaic law can be seen in their respective interpretations of Deuteronomy 15:1–6 as part of a general discussion of usury. Rushdoony writes:

> . . .While interest is permitted on commercial loans, all such loans are under the restriction of the sabbath law, i.e., their life is limited to six years. . . . every kind of debt by believers, whether as charity or for business reasons, must be short term debt. . . . Long-term debts are clearly a violation of the sabbath. . . .[48]

Calvin's interpretation of the passage is entirely different:

> Although we are not bound by this law at present, and it would not be even expedient that it should be in use, still the object to which it tended ought still to be maintained, i.e., that we should not be too rigid in exacting our debts, especially if we have to do with the needy. . . . The condition of the ancient people, as I have said, was different.[49]

The political agenda for theonomists—adopting the civil laws of Moses as modern civil law—is strongly supported by their optimistic eschatology. Their postmillennialism is a crucial aspect of the movement and makes their agenda not merely feasible, but inevitable. Here too they are far from Calvin's sober amillennialism.

The appeal of theonomy, like that of many contemporary Christian movements, is its simplicity and apparently biblical character. The great complexities and frustrations of the secular, modern world lead many to look for easy solutions. But in a fallen world solutions to great political problems are not always easy. The approach of theonomy is a novel one in the Reformed community and uses the Scripture in a way that is alien to Reformed Christianity.

Rushdoony called Calvin's view of the civil law "heretical nonsense." Calvin called a form of theocratic thinking remarkably like theonomy "false and foolish." When it comes to law and civil government, Calvin and theonomy do not have much in common.

---

[48]Ibid., 478–49.
[49]Calvin, *Commentaries*, 3:154.

Chapter Fourteen

An Assembly of Theonomists? The Teaching of the Westminster Divines on the Law of God

Sinclair B. Ferguson

Sinclair B. Ferguson

Sinclair B. Ferguson (Ph.D., University of Aberdeen) is Professor of Systematic Theology at Westminster Theological Seminary (Philadelphia). With other degrees from the University of Aberdeen, he has taught at Westminster since 1982. He is the author of *John Owen on the Christian Life, The Christian Life: A Doctrinal Introduction, Daniel* (Communicator's Commentary Series), *Taking the Christian Life Seriously, Discovering God's Will, A Heart for God, Grow in Grace, Kingdom Life in a Fallen World,* and several other books, and is an editor of the *New Dictionary of Theology.*

Chapter Fourteen

An Assembly of Theonomists? The Teaching of the Westminster Divines on the Law of God

Reformed theology, embracing such portions of God's word as the first psalm, has always recognized that, since the Creation, only one of two ways of life has been possible for man: either theonomy (God's law as ultimate authority, leading to true freedom for man as servant and son of God) or autonomy (man's law as ultimate standard, leading to bondage and sin). Recently, however, the term *theonomy* has come to be associated with a more narrowly defined understanding of the function of the Mosaic law. It has been customary in Reformed thought in all of its branches to recognize a threefold division in the law of God—moral, ceremonial, and civil or judicial. Theonomists, in common with other Reformed Christians, hold that the moral law expressed in the Decalogue is permanently binding. They generally hold that the ceremonial law has reached its *telos* in Christ, although they may articulate in different ways how this should be expressed theologically and what its implications are practically. Most, however, seem to be content to subscribe to the view of the Westminster Confession that the ceremonial law is "abrogated under the New Testament," whatever practical lessons might still be learned from, for example, the dietary laws.

A feature of theonomistic thinking that has come to be seen as its distinctive mark is the view that the only truly consistent (i.e., biblical) theonomy is that which regards the Judaic civil law as binding still today and therefore necessarily applicable *mutatis mutandis* to all ages and nations. A particularly emotive implication of this view is, of course, that the death penalty is as fitting in the New Testament era as it was in the Old Testament, not only for murder (Ex 21:12) but also for other deeds—such as homosexual acts (Lev 18:22), adultery (20:10), blasphemy (24:10–16), witchcraft (Ex 22:18), and incorrigible and physical rebellion in children (21:15, 17; Dt 21:20)—and that the civil authorities today remain under obligation to God to punish such acts as capital crimes under the legal code of the state.

It would not be difficult to name respected figures in Reformed theological thinking (respected, it should be said, also by theonomists) who were not theonomists in this sense. Thus, for example, Greg L. Bahnsen's study *Theonomy in Christian Ethics* finds it necessary to critique the views of the late John Murray at this point.[1]

Our interest here lies in an admittedly secondary question. The scope of this chapter will be to examine the teaching of Chapter XIX of The Confession of Faith, "Of the Law of God," to consider the appeal of theonomy to it, and to ask whether the Confession is, as has been claimed, theonomic in the contemporary sense. While of secondary importance, this question obviously carries far-reaching consequences for Presbyterians who subscribe to the system of doctrine taught in the Westminster Standards as a faithful representation of biblical teaching, and also for those Baptists and Congregationalists who subscribe respectively to the Philadelphia (or Second London) Confession or to the Savoy Declaration, both of which are minor reworkings of the Westminster Confession.

BACKGROUND AND CONTEXT

The Westminster Assembly was convened in London in 1643 by the English Parliament during a period of great social and theological unrest. It can be fairly said that in England the events of the seventeenth century involved a deeper

---

[1] Greg Bahnsen, *Theonomy in Christian Ethics* (Nutley, N.J.: Craig, 1977), 458–66.

revolution in the fabric of society than even the Reformation a century before. Interwoven with this was the integral part played in society by theological considerations. All of life, even if it is largely unrecognized as such in the twentieth century, is a theological battleground. The men and women of the seventeenth century, however, were fully conscious of this fact as is evidenced by the constant appeal to biblical teaching by all sides in their debates over issues that concerned the body politic.

Two elements in the seventeenth century context are of interest here:

1. The Reformation's doctrine of the priesthood of all believers was accompanied by a perhaps less clearly articulated but no less real appreciation of the prophethood of all believers—a fact that in some respects had even more far-reaching implications for society. One of the great fears inherent in the Roman Catholic reaction to the new evangelical theology was that asserting the freedom of individuals to read and interpret Scripture for themselves would bring with it theological and spiritual anarchy. The potential result, it was thought, could be the wholesale disintegration of society.[2]

In this context, in Scotland and England the question of the application of the Mosaic judicial laws and their penalties became a pressing one. On the one hand, the Reformation principle drove people back to the authority and relevance of the Old Testament for society; on the other hand, it led to inevitable and acute tension over the question of toleration and its limits.[3] The literature of the period of the Westminster Assembly abounds in discussions of this burning issue. The question of the limits of toleration and the magistrate's responsibility to punish heretics weighed heavily on the minds and spirits of all thinking people.

2. A second vital element in the background to the Assembly lies in the consequences of the Reformation's

---

[2]Hence, for example, Calvin's concern in his *apologia* in the Prefatory Letter to Francis I in the *Institutes* to distance the Reformed churches from the radical left wing of the Reformation. See *Institutes of the Christian Religion*, tr., F. L. Battles, ed., J. T. McNeill (Philadelphia: Westminster, 1960) 27–30.

[3]William Haller catches this mood in the title of the second volume in his study of the Puritan period, *Liberty and Reformation in the Puritan Revolution* (New York: Columbia University Press, 1955).

recovery of a biblical-theological hermeneutic, especially in Calvin's magisterial development of it. In this new covenantal understanding of both Scripture and life, one of the questions that inevitably surfaced was that of the continuity and discontinuity of God's dealings with his people. Always, in such discussions, the nature and purpose of the law of God come into sharp focus.

This issue too had important social implications for the Puritans: they found themselves faced with both theological and practical antinomianism. Theological antinomianism appeared in various guises and sects; practical antinomianism already abounded and acted as a catalyst for the short-lived Commonwealth Act of 1650 for "suppressing the detestable sins of incest, adultery and fornication." Indeed, so extensive were discussions on the theme of the law that E. F. Kevan's standard work, *The Grace of Law*, contains a twelve-page list of the books relevant to this subject that were written within a period of some sixty or seventy years.[4] This helps to explain why the Westminster Divines gave more detailed attention to the doctrine of the law than any previous assembly or council of the Christian church.

The practice of the Divines was to meet on week-day mornings for plenary sessions and to work in the afternoons in a series of three committees to which, in due time, were allotted the various chapter divisions for the Confession. Each member served on one committee but was free to attend and to participate in meetings of the others. On occasion individuals, perhaps with recognized expertise in an area of theology, would be co-opted to serve on special committees to further the Assembly's discussions.

The subject of the law of God was referred to the third of these committees on November 18, 1645. This committee reported to the Assembly on January 1, 1646, and its draft was discussed and debated on seven different days during the following weeks (on January 7, 9, 12, 13, 29 and February 2 and 9). The subject matter was later discussed again in August of that year, when (in view of depleted numbers) the Assembly met in the form of a Grand Committee, and by the Assembly as a whole on another six occasions in September, before being passed on September 25, 1646. A minor

---

[4]E. F. Kevan, *The Grace of Law* (London: Carey Kingsgate, 1964), 269–80.

(editorial) alteration was made on December 3. Parliament required the Assembly to attach Scripture proofs to the Confession, and these were debated on February 19 and 22 of 1647. The Divines were reluctant to fulfill this parliamentary demand, partly because of the limitations that proof-texting imposed and also because they believed that the document contained what were "received truths among all the churches," so that the only possible question about its teaching should be over "the manner of expression" or "the fitness to have . . . put into the Confession" some statement or another.[5] They believed they had produced a work of generic Reformed theology that would command wide acceptance.

The minutes of the Assembly provide minimal access to the issues that especially exercised the Divines in their discussion of the law. The contemporary commentators to whom we usually turn for information (Robert Baillie, George Gillespie, and John Lightfoot)[6] offer us no illumination. Here, as in many other areas, there are questions about the Confession to which we may never have answers. We do know, however, that one issue that occupied them in their discussion of the law of God was "the meaning of the description of ceremonial and judicial" and that a special committee was established on January 12, 1646, to consider this. Indication of their difficulties in doing so is evidenced by the fact that five further members were added to the committee on January 29.[7]

The subject matter itself was intricate. But this in itself does not adequately explain the difficulties the Divines encountered. They were, after all, thoroughly versed in the biblical doctrine of the law. The most probable reason for their difficulties over the ceremonial and judicial law is that

[5]A. F. Mitchell, *The Westminster Assembly* (Edinburgh, 1897), 377f.

[6]See Robert Baillie, *The Letters and Journals of Robert Baillie, A.M., Principal of the University of Glasgow*, ed. D. Laing, 3 vols. (Edinburgh, 1841); George Gillespie, *Notes of Debates and Proceedings of the Assembly of Divines*, in *The Presbyterian Armoury*, 2 vols. (Edinburgh, 1846), vol. 2; John Lightfoot, *The Whole Works of the Rev. John Lightfoot,D.D.*, ed. J. R. Pitman (London, 1824), vol. 13.

[7]A. F. Mitchell and J. Struthers, eds., *Minutes of the Sessions of the Westminster Assembly of Divines, while engaged in preparing their Directory for Church Government, Confession of Faith and Catechisms (Nov. 1644 to March 1649)* (Edinburgh, 1874), 171, 182.

they themselves were not all of one mind on some of the implications of the continuity and discontinuity of God's covenant and his law. I will argue below that the end product of their deliberations was a consensus statement, broad enough to be agreed with by Divines who held somewhat different views of the contemporary applications of the Mosaic judicial laws.

THE TEACHING OF THE CONFESSION

Following the teaching of Calvin,[8] Chapter XIX of the Confession adopts the classical threefold division of the Law (moral, ceremonial, and civil or judicial; cf. XIX,iii,iv).

Section one (i) teaches that the same law of God that was written on two tables of stone at Sinai (i.e., the Decalogue) had earlier been given to Adam as a covenant of works. The obedience required to it was "personal, entire and perpetual." The command concerning the tree of the knowledge of good and evil (Ge 2:16–17) was thus viewed as a summary text of the entire Decalogue, which in turn was seen as a transcription of Adam's God-created sense of what ought to be. At this point (as well as at others) the Confession is following Archbishop James Ussher's *Irish Articles of Religion*, which spoke of man having the "covenant of the law ingrafted in his heart, whereby God did promise unto him everlasting life upon condition that he performed entire and perfect obedience unto his Commandments."[9] This moral law is binding on all people, not only Christians (v), although it is of special value to them (vi) and the Spirit enables them to fulfill it (vii).

In addition to the moral law, God gave ceremonial laws (iii), which were "typical ordinances" whose significance lay not in themselves but in their divinely ordained function of portraying the human being's need and God's provision of grace in Christ. In one sense these laws were "external," though of course in another sense they were woven deeply into the warp and woof of the life of God's ancient people. The ceremonies included in worship elements that prefigured Christ and his work and also instructions that

---

[8]John Calvin, *Institutes of the Christian Religion*, IV,xx,14–16.
[9]*The Irish Articles of Religion*, 1615, Article XXI.

pointed to the duties of sanctification, e.g., the distinction between clean and unclean. These elements in God's law have been "abrogated." Their function has been fulfilled in Christ (cf. Heb 10:1), and the ceremonies themselves are no longer binding on Christians.

Section four (iv) deals with the judicial law. It may be useful to quote it in full, since its meaning is the *crux interpretum* of this chapter:

> To them also [i.e. the people of Israel, sect. iii], as a body politick, he gave sundry judicial laws, which expired together with the state of that people, not obliging any other now, further than the general equity thereof may require.

Here the Confession states that, in addition to the moral law, God gave laws to govern Israel as a nation. According to the proof-texts, these laws are illustrated by those in Exodus 21–22. Two things are said of these particular laws: (1) They have "expired with. . .the state of that people." They have come to the end of their appointed term, somewhat as the copyright on a book does at the end of a specified period of time. (2) They must be viewed as "not obliging any other [*sc.* people] now, further than the general equity thereof may require." The "now" here is eschatological. It points us to the work of Christ in death, resurrection, ascension, and Pentecost as marking the transition point from one epoch to another in God's redemptive purposes; "now" in the present epoch, peoples are not under obligation to the judicial law given through Moses beyond the requirement of general equity.

The logic of the Confession is clear. The moral law is central and permanent. The ceremonial law points to the provisions of grace made for transgressors of the law and ultimately fulfilled *for us* in Christ and *in us* by the obedience of faith wrought by the Spirit. In this respect, the ceremonial law that came by Moses foreshadowed the reality of grace and the fulfillment of truth, which have come to us in and through Christ (cf. sections v–vii). The ceremonial law has completed its divine task. It is now "abrogated" as law.

The statement on the judicial law appears to be less sharply but no less carefully worded. On the one hand it maintains that the judicial laws "expired" (i.e., their envi-

sioned period of validity has come to an end). These laws are
not now obligatory for other states beyond the requirements
of general equity. The critical question here is, therefore,
How are these statements in section iv to be understood?

THE THEONOMIC INTERPRETATION

Several points will help to outline the theonomistic
understanding of the Westminster Divines' teaching on the
law. In expounding the biblical basis for theonomy, the
exegesis of our Lord's teaching in Matthew 5:17 on his
fulfillment of the law of Moses is pivotal. Here, it is argued,
plērōsai ("to fulfill") has the meaning of "confirm." In his
fulfillment of the law, it is argued, Jesus did not repeal the
Mosaic judicial legislation. Rather, he confirmed it.[10] According to Bahnsen, Jesus did not repeal the death penalty for
adultery; even if one takes John 8:1–11 as part of inspired
Scripture, it does not prove the abolitionist case.[11] Further, it
is a basic hermeneutical principle underlined by theonomists
that what is valid in the Old Testament is equally so in the
New Testament, unless repealed.[12] Thus, both the Lord Jesus
Christ and the apostle Paul refer to the Old Testament case
law; rather than repealing it, they confirm it. Furthermore, it
is clear in Scripture that the Mosaic judicial laws were
applied to strangers and that prophetic judgment messages
(presented in the form of a *rib*, or lawsuit) assumed they
ought to have been applied outside of Israel also. From the
beginning, therefore, the sanctions of the Mosaic law were
not given temporarily or exclusively to the covenant people,
so that they can now safely be ignored; they were valid for all
people then, and they remain valid now.[13] They express
divine *justice*, no more, no less. To react against employing
the Mosaic penology *today* is therefore seriously to impugn
the God of Scripture. Furthermore, it is argued, the civil
magistrate cannot be artificially limited in his jurisdiction to
the final six commandments. Theonomy is, in this context, a

[10]Bahnsen, *Theonomy*, 39–86.
[11]Ibid., 231–32.
[12]See, for example, the criticism of Murray in Bahnsen, *Theonomy*, 458–66.
[13]Ibid., 339–43.

summons to take God, and his attitude to sin expressed in the law, seriously.

It is in this context that the Westminster Confession is seen as playing a real, if limited, role. It is argued that the Confession is theonomic in character. The Divines' appeal to general equity means, essentially, that everything in Mosaic judicial law that *can* be applied *must* be applied today. Moreover, Bahnsen argues that the responsibility of the magistrate to the entire moral law implies a theonomic position.[14] The text produced by the Westminster Divines themselves states in XXIII,iii that the civil magistrate

> hath authority, and it is his duty, to take order, that unity and peace be preserved in the church, that the truth of God be kept pure and entire, that all blasphemies and heresies be suppressed, all corruptions and abuses in worship and discipline prevented or reformed, and all the ordinances of God duly settled, administered and observed. For the better effecting whereof, he hath power to call synods, to be present at them, and to provide that whatsoever is transacted in them be according to the mind of God.[15]

As is well known, this particular section of the Confession has been modified in American Presbyterianism, undergoing extensive alteration in 1788. Bahnsen (controversially in my estimation) regards the revision simply as a clarification of certain elements in the original document—similar in weight, perhaps, to the qualification issued by the General Assembly of the Church of Scotland when it received the original Confession in 1647.[16] Essentially, Bahnsen accepts the doctrinal orthodoxy of the original text. Whether or not this is in conflict with the intention of the American Presbyterian emendation of the Confession, it is certainly in keeping with the traditional Scottish Reformed understand-

---

[14]Ibid., 353–63.

[15]Some Divines, such as George Gillespie, appealed to the European Confessions (Helvetic, French, Belgic) as proof that this teaching was simply generic Reformed theology, *Wholesome Severity Reconciled with Christian Liberty* (London, 1644), 4.

[16]See *Records of the Kirk of Scotland containing the Acts and Proceedings of the General Assemblies from the year 1638 Downwards*, ed. A. Peterkin (Edinburgh, 1838), 1:475.

ing of it. Indeed, at this point Bahnsen rests heavily and openly on the work of the great Scottish nineteenth-century theologian William Cunningham.[17] Further, Bahnsen's contention underlines for us a vital hermeneutical principle: the teaching of the Divines must be exegeted in terms of the document they produced, not the revision produced by another body or any standpoint believed to be more biblical that is enshrined in such a revision.

Bahnsen argues that Chapter XXIII,iii is interpretatively significant for Chapter XIX,iv. He writes:

> It should be observed also that the Westminster Confession (as evidenced in the proof texts of chapter 23. . .) considers there to be more than simply one capital crime (viz., murder); there are a number of social crimes (as indicated in the law of God) which receive this due recompense. . . . Therefore, the Westminster view of civil authority requires all magistrates to observe and carry out the whole law of God as the standard of social justice and public righteousness.
>
> The above conclusion is helpful in clarifying an often misunderstood portion of the Westminster Confession: chapter 19, section 4 . . . that the sundry judicial laws given by God to Israel as a body politic have expired with the state of that people and thus bind us today no further than the general equity of those laws may require. This statement is sometimes interpreted as saying that the penal sanctions and case laws of the Old Testament no longer bind people. . . . However, it is sufficiently clear from chapter 23, section 3 of the Confession that this was *not* the Westminster position. To attribute the abolition of the case laws and penal sanctions of God's law to chapter 19, then, would be to accuse the Westminster divines of blatant self-contradiction (even though the Confession is recognized as the most cautiously worded creed of the evangelical church). In the Westminster outlook civil magistrates have not been given autonomy in their various tasks, but are obligated to observe *all* the commandments of God (23,3), even those which elaborate and illustrate the decalogue. Therefore, whatever 19,4

---

[17]William Cunningham, *Discussions on Church Principles: Popish, Erastian, and Presbyterian* (Edinburgh, 1863), 211–34.

may mean, it cannot be understood as abrogating, say, the death penalty for blasphemers and so forth.[18]

Bahnsen's own view of Chapter XIX,iv is that it recognizes that some situations to which the Mosaic judicial law addressed itself no longer exist, but that the law is obligatory to any and every parallel situation that does exist, e.g., in terms of safety standards, and applicable to the exact crime, where that does exist.[19]

Bahnsen also finds support for his interpretation in the proof-texts added to the Confession by the Divines, particularly the references to Matthew 5:17 (the pivotal New Testament text for theonomic thinking) and 1 Corinthians 9:8–10 (seen as an illustration of the use of Mosaic case law and a substantiation of its continuing normative function). Further, in Bahnsen's view, the fact that the Divines saw the magistrate as still bound to the Mosaic judicial law, including its penology, is demonstrated by their use of Ezra 7:26; Leviticus 24:16; Deuteronomy 13:5; and 2 Chronicles 15:12–13 as proof-texts for the Confession's teaching (in XXIII,iii) that the magistrate is responsible for applying all the law of God, since these texts extend the death penalty to actions other than murder.[20]

As confirmation of this general exegesis, *Theonomy in Christian Ethics* prints as an appendix John Cotton's *Abstract of the Laws of New England* as an important aid to interpreting the Confession.[21] Although not noted in *Theonomy*, it is of interest that hopes were expressed that Cotton might be able to attend the Westminster Assembly. Is it not incontrovertible, then, that theonomy is the teaching of the Westminster Confession?

As we noted above, we have only the most superficial access to the Assembly's discussions on the doctrine of God's law. We are left, therefore, to examine the three strands of evidence that may help to reveal the Assembly's mind. We have seen already that, in Bahnsen's opinion, each of these strands confirms that the Westminster Confession's view of the law must be interpreted as a theonomic one.

---

[18]Bahnsen, *Theonomy*, 538–40.
[19]Ibid., 540.
[20]Ibid., 537.
[21]See ibid., 549–69.

These three strands are (1) the text of the Confession itself, (2) the proof-texts added to the Confession understood in their relation to the specific statements of the Confession and (3) the writings of the Divines and their contemporaries on the issue under review.

THE TEXT OF THE CONFESSION

The Confession's crucial affirmations are that (1) the judicial laws have "expired," and (2) peoples are not under obligation to them "further than the general equity thereof may require."

The Expiration of the Judicial Law

A *prima facie* reading of these words suggests that the fundamental affirmation of the Confession is that the Mosaic judicial laws have expired. This position is further qualified lest any reader draw the mistaken implication that the Mosaic judicial system is completely irrelevant to the Christian epoch. But this qualification does not negate the basic thrust of the section that these "sundry judicial laws" have now "expired." Certainly this is the interpretation the average twentieth-century reader naturally places on the wording. Just as the copyright on this book will expire after a certain period of time, and the law governing the use of its contents will no longer apply, so the Mosaic case laws have "expired." Yet they still have some value as illustrations of the way in which the principle of general equity should be applied; and to that principle of general equity the legal systems of all nations are bound.

The theonomist may respond, of course, that such a *prima facie* reading is likely to be an uninstructed one and may even contain an emotional bias against a biblical view of the judicial law and indeed of God himself.

It is true that some reactions to theonomic thinking reveal a flawed view of both God and Scripture. But this is not, in itself, an adequate justification for a theonomic reading of the Confession. For the problem with the theonomic reading is that the particular way in which the Divines have expressed their position is not the *natural* way of expressing a *theonomic* view. It is certainly not the way contemporary theonomists express their position. For the Confession, the governing principle is that the Mosaic judicial laws have *expired* (whatever else may be said to clarify their relevance), whereas for theonomists the governing principle is that the Mosaic judicials *have not expired* but are still in force; Christ has confirmed them and they are all perpetually binding.

It is essential to notice that there may be similarities in the practical outworking of these two principles (e.g., a theonomist and a nontheonomist may, on their different principles, reach the same conclusion about the appropriate response to a particular act—which almost certainly explains how it is that theonomists mistakenly assume that the response of the Puritans to specific crimes proves they were also theonomists). But whatever similarities may arise because of the Confession's qualifying clause, it would be absurd to suggest that the principles themselves are identical.

The Westminster Divines chose their emphasis and wording for Chapter XIX with great care, for by the time of the Westminster Assembly, the issue of the continuing validity of the Mosaic civil laws had been widely discussed for more than a century.

Calvin, as one would have anticipated of a legally trained theologian, carefully discusses this issue in his *Institutes*.[22] J. H. Bullinger (1504–1575) held that the judicial laws were abolished, though he maintained the appropriateness of capital punishment for a whole series of offenses.[23] In England, John Foxe (1516–1587, author of the famous *Acts and Monuments*, 1563) believed that the Mosaic judicials had been abolished, although in some cases acts such as adultery should be regarded as capital offenses.[24] Others, like William Perkins (1558–1602), while holding that capital punishment was appropriate for witchcraft, adultery, and false prophecy,

---

[22]Calvin, *Institutes*, IV,xx,16–18. See above, Chapter Thirteen, "Calvin and Theonomy," by W. Robert Godfrey.

[23]Bullinger writes, "The apostles of our Lord Jesus Christ did bind or burden no man with the laws of Moses," *The Decades of Henry Bullinger*, trans. H. I., ed. T. Harding for the Parker Society, 4 vols. (Cambridge: Cambridge University Press, 1849–52), 1:342.

[24]See *Acts and Monuments*, ed. S. R. Cattley (London, 1837–41), 8:323.

also steered a middle course.[25] The indications are that the Puritan movement developed a more rigorous view of the Mosaic law as it gained strength. Patrick Collinson records that "when the official 'Homily of the Place and Time of Prayer' threatened Sabbath breakers with the dire penalty of the Hebrew who gathered sticks on that day, it was a Puritan who protested that this was to confound 'our Sunday with the Jewes' Sabaoth . . . which doctrine is superstitious.' "[26] But some later figures, like Henry Barrow (d.1593), held that the Mosaic judicials remained in force, and John Whitgift (1530–1604), who had Barrow detained in prison, can be heard bitterly complaining, "It is now disputed at every table whether the magistrate be of necessity bound to the judicials of Moses."[27]

We will return to the view of the Puritans later. The point of the above brief excursus is a simple one: it is difficult, to the point of impossibility—in *this* context in

[25]See P. D. L. Avis, "Moses and the Magistrate," *Journal of Ecclesiastical History* 26 (1975): 168–69.

[26]Patrick Collinson, *Godly People: Essays on English Protestantism and Puritanism* (London, 1983), 431. The quotation is taken from the Morrice MS B.I. p.339 (Dr. Williams's Library, London).

[27]John Whitgift, *Works*, 3 vols. (Cambridge: Cambridge University Press, 1851–53), 3:576. For his view of the abrogation of the Mosaic judicial code, see *Works*, 1:270ff. Whitgift seeks to answer the view of Thomas Cartwright, who, while acknowledging that some elements in the Mosaic judicials were localized, and therefore temporary, adds: "To say that any magistrate can save the life of a blasphemer, contemptuous and stubborn idolaters, murderers, adulterers, incestuous persons and such like, which God by his judicial law hath commanded to be put to death, I do utterly deny." In this context Whitgift appeals to the precedents of Augustine, Cyril, Musculus, Hemingius, and Calvin.

A similar complaint may be heard running through a letter of Edwin Sandys (1516?–1588) to Bullinger, written on August 15, 1573, while Sandys was bishop of London (he became archbishop of York in 1575): "New orators are arising up from among us, foolish young men, who while they despise authority, and admit no superior, are seeking the complete overthrow and rooting up of our whole ecclesiastical polity, so piously constituted and confirmed . . . and are striving to shape out for us, I know not what new platform of a church." The final bone of contention for Sandys is their claim that "the judicial laws of Moses are binding upon Christian princes, and they ought not in the slightest degree to depart from them. . . . There are many other things of the same kind, not less absurd." *The Zurich Letters*, trans. and ed. for the Parker Society by H. Robinson, 2 vols. (Cambridge: Cambridge University Press, 1862–65), 1:296.

which the question of the continuation of the Mosaic judicial system had been long and heatedly discussed—to believe that the Westminster Divines would attempt to express a theonomic viewpoint by the wording we actually find in the Confession. At this point, the *prima facie* reading of the text not only has the virtue of common sense in its favor; it also has the weightier consideration that a theonomic interpretation is psychologically improbable, given the substantial evidence of the Puritan awareness of the issues at stake. Had they intended to state a view identical to contemporary theonomy, it would have been natural for them to stress first of all the *continuing obligation* of the judicial laws and then give ancillary recognition that, inevitably, their application must be "contextualized" appropriately to the society in which they are to be applied.

This consideration places in jeopardy the claim that the Confession is theonomic at this point as, for example, Bahnsen contends. Here theonomic reasoning is in danger of applying its principle ("if it can apply, it must apply") not only to the Mosaic law, but also to the exegesis of the Confession, by mistakenly interpreting in a theonomic grid various Puritan pronouncements of the appropriate penalty for certain specific crimes.

It is frequently assumed in this and other areas that the Confession, if it is coherent, must teach either one or other of two divergent views. But, as I will argue later, this assumption is both unhistorical and inaccurate as far as the work of the Westminster Divines is concerned. It is a hermeneutical principle that does a disservice to the wisdom of the Divines themselves and uses the Confession as an instrument of division rather than of the unity and harmony it was intended to encourage. It may be that the Confession's teaching on the Mosaic judicials extends as far as to include certain applications of the Mosaic law consistent with those sought by theonomists; but to argue that its teaching bears an exclusively theonomic interpretation is to read its intention backward and to confuse a legitimate specific application with the fundamental governing principle.

General Equity

A second important consideration here is the Divines' understanding of obligation according to the principle of "general equity." What is general equity? To the theonomist it means that where the Mosaic judicial law *can* be applied, it *must* be applied just as it was in the Old Testament. For all practical purposes this means that the second statement in Confession XIX,iv is taken to be determinative of the meaning of the first statement. The effect is that in the view of theonomists "general equity" means essentially that *the Mosaic law has actually expired minimally: it remains obligatory and must be applied maximally.*

As we have seen, there is a *prima facie* oddity about this kind of interpretation. It gives the impression that the Divines were stating their position in a decidedly Pickwickian fashion. Examination of the idea of "equity," however, confirms that the Confession's position is much more sophisticated legally and theologically.

The term *equity* is a technical one when used in relation to the law, as it is here by the Divines, and has a lengthy pedigree stretching back to the ancient Greeks. Both Plato and Aristotle discussed the idea of *epieikia*,[28] and Roman law incorporated the principle of *aequitas*. The principle of equity thus passed into the Anglo-Saxon, early Norman, and English systems of justice, and indeed in England (the relevant context for understanding its use in the Westminster Confession) it became an important element in the legal system itself. In a word, the expression "general equity" appears in the Confession as a *terminus technicus*, a well-defined concept in English jurisprudence.

Implicit in the idea of equity is the recognition that the creation of a series of laws does not in and of itself guarantee that justice will be appropriately administered. It involves the recognition that laws must be applied existentially, since the application of "the letter of the law" may in fact distort the real purpose of the law and ignore the individuality and particularity of circumstances. The legal principle of equity, therefore, meant asking and answering the question, How would the law-giver apply his law in this situation? It is this principle that lies behind what might otherwise seem to be Calvin's *apparent* indifference to the multiplicity of penal systems in his contemporary world.[29]

---

[28]In Plato's *Statesman*, 294a and in Aristotle's *Ethics*, bk.V, ch. 10.
[29]Calvin, *Institutes*, IV,xx,16.

Thomas Ashe's *Epieikia* (1609) uses an earlier definition of equity from West's *Symboleography*: Equity is

> allayed with the sweetness of mercy, and may well be compared to a shoemaker's shop, that is furnished with all manner and sorts of lasts for men's feet, where each man may be sure to find one last or other that will fit him, be he great or small.[30]

Bahnsen's understanding of equity is that it is identical with the case law, so that each crime receives the punishment it deserves, "an eye for an eye and a tooth for a tooth." Essentially, then, Old Testament penology is the perfect expression of the principle of equity.[31] Indeed, as the perfect expression, it is the *only proper* expression. Not to follow the Mosaic judicial laws *au pied de la lettre* would be to repudiate the principle of equity.

It may be appropriate to say here that theonomy commends itself to many of its adherents precisely because in seeking to take the Mosaic judicial law seriously it takes human sin seriously, as God means us to do. It therefore meets what many feel to be a profound need in Western society, which seems increasingly to have withdrawn from a *penal* philosophy, with the inevitable result that sinful actions are popularly viewed with far less seriousness than they should be. If the appropriate punishment for a crime is always seen to be less than the injury inflicted by the crime, it is almost inevitable that in society generally the crime itself will be treated less seriously. The obvious fear is that if murdering a fellow citizen is punished by nine years in prison, then the value of the victim's life is set at only one-eighth of the felon's own approximate life span. If adultery is no longer regarded as sinful theft (theologically it is the theft of a person's own self, the sundering of the one-flesh of marriage), inevitably the value and importance of marriage, not to say honesty, integrity, and self-control are correspondingly reduced in society generally. Granted that complex questions are involved here, it is understandable why some Christians resonate to the theonomists' appeal to

---

[30]See Sir Carleton Kemp Allen's discussion in *Law in the Making* (London, 1958), 392–93.

[31]Bahnsen, *Theonomy*, 437.

Romans 1:32 that those who perpetrate the sins described in Romans 1:18ff. *deserve* to die.

In view of this, it might be argued that the theonomic interpretation of the implications of general equity is the only one that would make sense to such a group of people who, like the Westminster Divines, were deeply conscious of the evil of sin in their own society. It is perhaps understandable that a theonomist who respected the Westminster Confession would simply assume that the Divines would share his understanding. But in this instance the assumption appears to be mistaken.

Bahnsen's view is that the Mosaic law *as written* (with a few culture-bound exceptions) *is* the principle of penal equity seen with respect to different sins: "None of God's penalties are excessive or lenient; hence the Older Testament does not detail *arbitrary* punishments for crimes . . . the culprit receives what his public disobedience merits."[32] Minimal contextualization is involved, in his view, in the giving of the law. The Divines' call for "equity" therefore implies that the same punishments *must* be meted out by the magistrate today.[33] Not to implement them would be sinful.

Consider, however, what evidence would be required to confirm the thesis that the Confession's view of equity is that all the Mosaic punishments are binding today for all actions designated by the Mosaic law. Not only would there need to be agreement in the Puritan mainstream tradition that, for example, blasphemy, adultery, and witchcraft should receive capital punishment, but that *all* crimes should receive the penalty prescribed in the Mosaic law. But it is precisely at this juncture that the differences of opinion we have noted among the sixteenth-century writers continued among those of the seventeenth century. Indeed, as we will see, even those Divines whose position seems to have been closest to theonomy do not seem to have drawn the same conclusions as contemporary theonomists from the principle of general equity.

One indication of the way some of the Puritans understood the principle of equity may be found in Paul Baynes, William Perkins' successor at Great St. Mary's, Cambridge.

---

[32]Ibid., 438.
[33]Ibid.

Baynes (d.1617) was one of the most influential figures in the Puritan brotherhood. Commenting on Ephesians 2:15, he acknowledges the traditional threefold division of the law into moral, ceremonial, and judicial and states that the judicial laws themselves are of three kinds. Speaking of these, he writes:

> For the first, we are free from them as ordinances political delivered; they bind us, 1, as the perpetual equity of God, agreeable to the law of nature and moral, is in them; 2, we are bound, not to the particular determination of punishment, but the general; with liberty both to intend and exchange the kind, and to mitigate or release the kind; freed from all particularities and circumstance, bound only to the substance, or somewhat proportionable.[34]

Bahnsen argues that the only way to understand the idea of equity is that *mutatis mutandis* the judicial laws should be applied in all ages and places. But the view expressed by Baynes and held by others in the seventeenth century is not quite so straightforward. In Baynes' view, the crimes of the Old Testament remain crimes, and it is "grounded on unchangeable reason" that capital punishment may be applicable. Yet not only may the punishment for such crimes be changed in kind (e.g., stoning as such is not a mandatory way to carry out the death penalty, a point with which theonomists are in agreement), but "to mitigate or release" the kind is also possible.[35] General equity, for Baynes, apparently implies that the Mosaic law be taken seriously as an expression of the law of nature, not that it be taken as the penology system binding on all generations.

In many instances the penological implications of this view might be indistinguishable from the practical implications of theonomy; but it is important to note that they do not share precisely the same theoretical basis. For Baynes (and, as we shall see, for others more intimately involved in the Westminster Assembly), *Mosaic punishments may be altered not only in mode of administration but in severity of action* (it is possible to "*mitigate* or *release* the kind"). The reason for this must be that in Baynes' view equity does not require the

---

[34]Paul Baynes, *An Entire Commentary on . . . Ephesians* [1643] (Edinburgh, 1866), 162.
[35]Ibid.

administration of Mosaic penology in all crimes. Apparently for him, some Mosaic punishments were not universalizable, but particular, contextualized expressions of general equity.

It cannot be doubted that mainstream Puritanism did believe that the death penalty was applicable to crimes other than murder. In several instances, therefore, its practical outworking and that of theonomy are one. But our investigation of Chapter XIX,iv of the Confession thus far leads us to conclude (1) that a theonomic interpretation is not the most natural reading of the syntax; (2) that a *thoroughgoing* theonomic application of the Mosaic penology was not characteristic of the Puritan tradition; and (3) that the theonomic interpretation of the principle of general equity is not identical with that adopted by the Puritan writers.

PROOF-TEXTS

Theonomy in Christian Ethics argues that the Westminster Divines' proof-texts for XIX,iv, particularly Matthew 5:17 and 1 Corinthians 9:9-10 require a theonomic interpretation of the text.[36]

The proof texts were selected, and are cited, in such a way as to provide *seriatim* confirmation from Scripture of the claims of the text itself. Thus the reference in XIX,iv to Exodus 21-22 states the *fact* that God "gave sundry judicial laws" to the Jews understood "as a body politick." Genesis 49:10 is used to establish that already in view in Jacob's prophecies was a *terminus ad quem* for the role of the lawgiver that was coterminous with the ending of the redemptive-historical role of the Jewish people.

The reference to 1 Peter 2:13-14 may perhaps be intended to suggest simply that believers have an obligation to the civil laws of their own nation. It is, however, interesting to note that Anthony Burgess, himself a West-minster Divine involved in the discussions on the wording of the chapter on the law, combines these texts (Ge 49:10 and 1 Pe 2:13) to underline that abrogation of the state of the people implies abrogation of the accessory to it, namely the particular legal system.[37] Thus 1 Peter 2:13 is understood to

---

[36]Bahnsen, *Theonomy*, 540.
[37]Anthony Burgess, *Vindiciae Legis* (London, 1646), 212.

indicate the legitimacy of the ordinances of whatever state we are placed in by the providence of God if they exhibit equity.

The critical proof-texts follow—Matthew 5:17, 38–39 and 1 Corinthians 9:8–10. The latter Bahnsen takes to show that the Old Testament case law "was still authoritative and binding after Christ's advent."[38] Certainly the text is adduced by the Divines to indicate application of the case law *to the Christian community* (in the support of Christian ministry); but it is by no means clear that this particular citation demonstrates in what sense this particular case law is to be applied *in the state*. It is doubtful if the Divines' citation here will bear the weight of Bahnsen's claim that they viewed it as "Paul's utilization of the case law of the Old Testament in a way which shows that it was still authoritative and binding after Christ's advent."[39] It is altogether more likely that the Divines understood this text as an illustration of their statement that the judicial laws are not binding now "further than the general equity thereof may require." They viewed 1 Corinthians 9:8–10 as an illustration of how general equity works; the notion that it demonstrates the binding nature of Mosaic case law on the state was not in view.

More interesting is the citation from the Sermon on the Mount: Matthew 5:17, 38–39. Bahnsen's comments here are of special interest:

> Whatever 19:4 may mean, it cannot be understood as abrogating, say, the death penalty for blasphemers, and so forth. This is evident from chapter 19 itself when one examines the Scripture proofs cited at section 4; they include not only Matthew 5:17 (Christ's statement that he did not come to abrogate the law) but also Paul's utilization of the case law of the Old Testament. . . (1 Cor. 9:9–10)[40]

We have already seen that 1 Corinthians 9:9–10 is not strong evidence for the distinctive tenets of theonomy with respect to capital punishment. Further, Bahnsen's appeal to Matthew 5:17 seems to indicate that he assumes the Westminster Divines would exegete the text in the same way he

---

[38]Bahnsen, *Theonomy*, 540.
[39]Ibid.
[40]Ibid.

does.[41] This, however, begs the question. Bahnsen does not refer to the fact that the Divines also cite Matthew 5:38–39 *alongside* verse 17: "Ye have heard that it hath been said, An eye for an eye, and a tooth for a tooth: But I say unto you, That ye resist not evil: but whosoever shall smite thee on thy right cheek, turn to him the other also" (KJV).

Bahnsen's own understanding of Matthew 5:38–39 is that here our Lord is correcting the Pharisaical abuse of the *lex talionis*. They wrongly appealed to the *civil* principle in order to justify *personal* revenge. But, argues Bahnsen:

> Christ is speaking to the situation of interpersonal relations and prohibits the exacting of wrongs suffered. In civil jurisprudence there is still to be an "eye for an eye etc." but between individuals there is to be forbearance. . . . Jesus did not repudiate this [civil] use of the *ius talionis*.[42]

In other words, the *lex talionis* remains binding. Matthew 5:38–39 does not speak to the context in which *lex talionis* is applicable.

This may well be a correct exegesis of the passage, but it clearly does nothing to explain why the Divines cited Matthew 5:38–39 as proof for their proposition that the Mosaic judicial laws have "expired" and do not bind "further than the general equity thereof may require." Although it is not always possible to be dogmatic about why the Divines combine proof-texts as they do, it seems that in this instance they viewed turning the other cheek as the *telos* of the *lex talionis*. For them, therefore, *plērōsai* does not seem to have meant "to confirm," but "to show the ultimate purpose of," and in this instance, also implies "to abrogate." In the thinking of the Divines, this combination of proof-texts indicates that the *lex talionis* is abrogated by the law of forgiveness. Here, again, is further indication that the Confession's logic cannot be squeezed into the theonomist's mold.

It is interesting to notice that Anthony Burgess adopted the view that the law was given to the people at the time of Moses because of the corrupt state in which they had left Egypt; the law was intended to restrain the kind of impiety

---

[41]Ibid.
[42]Ibid., 118.

that broke loose in the golden-calf incident. Recognizing that some of his contemporaries held that in the Sermon on the Mount Christ had abolished capital punishment, Burgess argued that in fact the *lex talionis* was given to restrain private revenge in the first place (and thus is fulfilled by turning the other cheek). In rejecting the abolitionist view of Matthew 5:38–39, Burgess holds that capital punishment may still be inflicted. But in doing so, he appeals back, beyond the Mosaic law, to the Noahic provision in Genesis 9:6 as providing the perpetual reason for capital punishment for murder. Contrary to Hugo Grotius, Burgess argues that "at least in this case there ought to be a capital punishment."[43] Here Burgess' approach (which may well form the basis for the Confession's logic) differs from that of theonomy. On the one hand, he appeals to the Noahic revelation to demonstrate what is permanent in the Mosaic provision (essentially understanding this as general equity), and, on the other hand, his words suggest that he too was conscious of a spectrum of opinion on the appropriateness of capital punishment for other crimes. It is of some interest to note that Burgess elsewhere states that "the manner of the punishment belonging to God's judicial law may be altered."[44]

An important argument to which Bahnsen alludes in *Theonomy in Christian Ethics* is that the proof-texts for Chapter XXIII,iii, outlining the duty of the magistrate, are Ezra 7:26; Leviticus 24:16; Deuteronomy 13:5; 2 Chronicles 15:12–13, and that these include references to capital punishment for breaches of the law other than murder. Here, it is argued, is confirming evidence that the Divines held to a theonomic position.[45]

It should be noted, however, that the crimes in view here do not include all those for which capital punishment was prescribed in the Mosaic code. In this context one cannot reason by synecdoche, as though holding to capital punish-

---

[43]Burgess, *Vindiciae*, 180.

[44]A. Burgess, *The Magistrate's Commission from Heaven* (London, 1644), 8. Burgess does argue, however, like many of his contemporaries, that the magistrate's duty "to preserve the Worship of God, which floweth from the Moral Law, cannot cease."

[45]Bahnsen, *Theonomy*, 523.

ment for some serious crimes implied holding to the entire Mosaic judicial system. For many writers before and during this period held that sins against the so-called first table of the law were capital offenses, yet they also believed that the Mosaic judicial law as such was no longer binding. We have already noted hints of this as far back as Bullinger. The view that the magistrate does have a role to play in relation to sins against the first table is regarded today as a distinctive of theonomy. But in the sixteenth and seventeenth centuries it was a commonplace; this fact, however, cannot be regarded as infallible evidence of an accompanying theonomic viewpoint.

In this connection it is of interest that the Westminster Divines did not appeal to Romans 1:32 to indicate that general equity demanded a wide-ranging use of the death penalty. Those Divines whose exegesis of that verse can be substantiated seem to have viewed it as a reference to the second death, and not to the death penalty as such.[46]

This consideration of the proof-texts used by the Divines leads us to a further conclusion. At important points the exegesis of the Divines and the exegesis of theonomists differ. Confidence in his own exegesis of the biblical text and admiration for the Westminster Divines has led the author of *Theonomy in Christian Ethics* to the false conclusion that the Westminster Divines could not but subscribe to both his exegesis and his conclusions.

The fact that *some* Puritans agreed with *some* of the applications of theonomic exegesis helps to explain why the theonomic argument can appeal to the seventeenth century in this way. Furthermore, given John Cotton's influential role during the first half of the seventeenth century, it is understandable why Bahnsen should place such weight on his *Abstract of the Laws of New England*. But to suggest that it is of "hermeneutical benefit when it comes to present day understanding of the Westminster Confession's declarations about God's law and the civil magistrate"[47] is misleading. It is

---

[46]See, for example, Thomas Goodwin, who consistently understands Romans 1:32 to mean that people deserve "hell and damnation," *The Aggravation of Sin* in *The Works of Thomas Goodwin*, 12 vol. (Edinburgh, 1862), 4:178. See also *Works*, 3:523; 6:313; 7:47; 10:160.

[47]Bahnsen, *Theonomy*, 557.

to use one extreme of a spectrum of views as though it were the whole. The Puritan position, as we will see, was altogether more varied.

In connection with Cotton's work Bahnsen offers a disclaimer, the potential relevance of which he does not seem to have considered:

> This is not to say that everything which we find written in Cotton's work should meet with our approval. . . . There are matters which today's Bible student may wish to dispute in Cotton's analysis (e.g. in chapter 7, article 24, Cotton appears to make all perjury punishable by death, whereas the law of God more strictly says that the false witness is to receive *whatever* punishment would have been due to the accused—and that was not always death).[48]

It is possible that Cotton's teaching here has been influenced by Proverbs 21:28, but certainly the Mosaic penalty is exactly as Bahnsen states. What he does not consider, however, is the possibility that this is not simply a matter of Homer nodding, in which Cotton has wrongly exegeted Scripture. If Cotton *knowingly* exceeded the Mosaic penalties here, the question must be raised (however extensive the parallels with theonomic thought in his writings) whether even Cotton held to theoretical theonomy. May not exceeding the Mosaic penalties, as well as mitigating them, indicate a nontheonomic theoretical foundation?

THE WESTMINSTER DIVINES AND THEIR CONTEMPORARIES

Bahnsen has appealed to the Puritan view of the law to substantiate the theonomic position. We have already noted that many seventeenth-century Puritans favored a closer approximation to the Mosaic judicial statutes and appealed to Old Testament texts to confirm their views. But we have also stressed that this position is not necessarily identical with that of theonomy. In fact, a wider study of Puritan thought reveals three salient points, the discussion of which will bring us to our conclusions.

---

[48]Ibid., 556–57.

1. To demonstrate that the Confession is theonomic in intention, it is not necessary to prove that the Divines held to precisely the same *form* of punishment as is found in the Mosaic judicial laws. It is necessary, however, to show that they appealed *consistently* to them with reference to crimes common to both the Mosaic period and the seventeenth century.

It is evident, however, that some Divines who otherwise might appear to support the theonomist position in their appeal to the Mosaic penology with respect to blasphemy, adultery, and witchcraft do not appeal to the Mosaic penology as the binding prototype for all misdemeanors, and in fact demur in particular instances. If, however, their position had been that of contemporary theonomy, there could, presumably, be no differences over particular crimes.

There is some reason to believe that in the spectrum of views held by the Divines, the Scots commissioners Samuel Rutherford and George Gillespie represented the more rigorous viewpoint. In view of their influential role at the Assembly, to secure a Confession of Faith that was acceptable to the Kirk of Scotland, all would concede that their views are of greater "hermeneutical benefit" than, for example, those of Cotton.

In his *Free Disputation Against Pretended Liberty of Conscience*, Rutherford argues that whatever rulers were commanded to do in the Old Testament, all rulers are obliged to do.[49] Using arguments at some points strikingly similar to those of Bahnsen, Rutherford employs evidence for this contention from both inside and outside of the biblical text. Further, Rutherford underlines the judicious restraint in the Scriptures: capital punishment was not lightly exercised; those who were executed were not guilty merely of an occasional failing, but were generally speaking ringleaders of evil.

Is Samuel Rutherford, then, among the theonomists? Apparently not, for he adds that although "some moral transgressions Moses punished with death, as Sabbath breaking, it followeth not therefore the godly Prince may

---

[49]S. Rutherford, *A Free Disputation Against Pretended Liberty of Conscience* (London, 1649), 177.

now punish it with death."[50] The necessity for punishment remains, but not only may the manner of it differ; the severity of the punishment, it seems, may also differ. This distinction is important, and Rutherford puts it succinctly when he writes:

> It follows not therefore, such transgressors are made free, through Christ, of all bodily punishment, as *Libertines* inferre, for though the temporarines of the punishment be only in the measure of punishment, yet not in the punishment it selfe.[51]

It is of particular importance to notice that Rutherford clearly speaks of the Sabbath commandment as "moral" in nature; it is not conceived of as "ceremonial." Further, the breach of it should be punished by the magistrate; the Sabbath law remains binding therefore on the state. The point at which Rutherford demurs from the application of the Mosaic law, therefore, lies in the nature of the punishment. It is no longer proper for the magistrate to punish Sabbath-breakers with the death penalty. Rutherford does not explain his reasoning here, but in view of his influential role in monitoring the contents of the Confession, it may not be illegitimate to conclude that this is an explicit illustration of the principle enshrined in the Confession that the Mosaic case law should be applied now only within the requirements of general equity. Apparently Rutherford recognized peculiar circumstances in the Mosaic economy that made capital punishment for Sabbath breaking appropriate then but inappropriate now. His doing so indicates the Achilles' heel of theonomy's appeal to the Westminster Divines.

Rutherford sheds more light on his position when he writes that "*Judiciall* Lawes may be *judiciall* and *Mosaicall*, and so not obligatory to us, according to the degree and quality of punishment."[52] These words, perhaps more than any others, provide the clue to the nuance of meaning intended in XIX,iv of the Confession. For Rutherford believes: (1) Some judicial laws were distinctively Mosaical in form. (2) The Mosaic punishment for breaching such judicial laws is not obligatory

[50]Ibid., 190.
[51]Ibid. 190–91.
[52]Ibid., 298.

now. (3) Nevertheless, there is a constant principle that breaches of them may properly be punished.

This, presumably, is what Rutherford understood the Confession to mean when it spoke of the judicial laws not obligating now beyond the demands of general equity. Equity required punishment; the Mosaic law prescribed fixed punishment for a temporary age. That punishment is no longer mandatory.

The remarkable George Gillespie provides equally interesting insight. The opening paragraphs of his *Aaron's Rod Blossoming*, which was specifically dedicated to the members of the Westminster Assembly, contain these words:

> I know some divines hold, that the Judiciall Law of
> *Moses*, so far as concerneth the punishments of sins
> against the moral Law, Idolatry, blasphemy, Sabbath-
> breaking, adultery, theft, &c., ought to be a rule to the
> Christian magistrate; and, for my part, I wish more
> respect were had to it, and that it were more consulted
> with.[53]

Of interest here are both Gillespie's predisposition to see the Mosaic penology more fully taken into account *and* an apparent reserve in that connection. He desires "respect" and consultation. But his tone suggests that even he may not have completely identified himself with those who held the most rigorous view. Earlier in his *Wholesome Severity Reconciled with Christian Liberty*, Gillespie had argued for the right of the magistrate to exercise coercive power "in suppressing and punishing hereticks and sectaries, according as the degree of their offence and of the Churches danger shal require."[54] He here commits himself to the position of Junias that "he who was punishable by death under that Iudiciall law, is punishable by death still,"[55] and yet he is at pains to emphasize that such judgment may be tempered with mercy *under certain circumstances*, even in the case of "those who have perverted the faith, so far as the word of God and rules of Christian moderation would have severity tempered with

---

[53]George Gillespie, *Aaron's Rod Blossoming*, in *The Works of George Gillespie*, ed. W. M. Hetherington, 2 vols. (Edinburgh, 1846), 2:2.

[54]George Gillespie, *Wholesome Severity Reconciled with Christian Liberty* (London, 1644), "To the Christian and Courteous Reader," A4.

[55]Ibid., 9.

mercy."[56] Gillespie appears to be more thoroughgoing than Rutherford; but even Gillespie does not simply adopt the viewpoint that the Mosaic penology can be applied without reference to general equity and Christian moderation and mercy.

There is, however, a further element that exercised a profound influence on the thinking of other Puritans.

2. While many Westminster Divines do appeal to the Mosaic law, their appeal is often theologically complex and sometimes stretches beyond the Mosaic law per se in illuminating ways.

It was not unusual among the Puritans to believe that the law of God was valid for the believer, not as it was given by Moses, but as it was confirmed by Christ. Samuel Bolton, chosen to serve the Assembly in March 1646/47 as a replacement for Jeremiah Burroughes, writes of this in a work published prior to his selection:

> Again, others say that we are freed from the law, as given by Moses, and are only tied to the obedience of it, as it is given in Christ: and though, they say, we are subject to those commands and that law which Moses gave, yet not as he gave it, but as Christ renews it, and as it comes out of His hand and from His authority. . . . I shall not much quarrel with this. Acknowledge the moral law as a rule of obedience and Christian walking, and there will be no falling out, whether you take it as promulgated by Moses, or as handed to you and renewed by Christ.[57]

Generally speaking, this view did not sustain support in later Reformed thought. It is a view for which theonomy would have little sympathy, since it does not harmonize with the theonomic contention that the old covenant laws stand unless specifically repealed. But that someone with Bolton's credentials could maintain relative equanimity in the face of such a view places in further jeopardy any contention that the Westminster Standards were intended to yield a theonomic interpretation. Even Rutherford expresses an element of this view when he maintains that the law binds us, not as

---

[56]Ibid., 31–32.

[57]Samuel Bolton, *The True Bounds of Christian Freedom* (London, 1645; reprint, London, 1964), 57.

it was given by Moses (for then the ceremonies also would be binding), but as Christ and his apostles press the law upon the Gentiles.[58] Here the reasoning differs from theonomic logic, which is that the Mosaic law *qua* Mosaic law stands unless repealed.

A somewhat similar view is expressed by another Westminster Divine, Thomas Goodwin. He writes that "to us Christians it is not the judicial and ceremonial, but the moral law which is obligatory."[59] Thus the laws of consanguinity are to be sustained in the New Testament era, not because of their presence in the Mosaic statutes *simpliciter*, but because they are confirmed in the New Testament.

Why, then, it may be asked, were such laws as the Commonwealth Laws passed under Puritan influence? Why are theonomists able to support with evidence from the Puritan period the view that, for example, adulterers, witches, and others should be executed? There appears to be a grave tension here between the evidence presented in this chapter and the evidence presented by *Theonomy in Christian Ethics*.

The answer is that many seventeenth-century writers did, in fact, uphold in practice many (but, as we have seen, not necessarily all) of the Mosaic judicial penalties. It is salutary to remember that in 1661, the very year in which Rutherford died, an act was passed in Scotland to the effect that children over sixteen years who "not being distracted [i.e., congenitally deranged], shall beat or curse either their father or mother, shall be put to death without mercy."[60]

The point, however, is that the Puritan writers held a spectrum of views within a common commitment to the law of God. Even those Divines who, we may suspect, held views most similar in practice to the convictions of contem-

---

[58]Samuel Rutherford, *A Survey of Antinomianisme*, being part 2 of *A Survey of the Spiritual Antichrist* (London, 1648), 6.

[59]Goodwin, *Works*, 11:26.

[60]The Scottish Parliament of Charles II also passed statutes against Sabbath breaking, swearing, and excessive drinking, and one prescribed the death penalty for "railing against God." In a celebrated case in 1697, an eighteen-year-old youth, Thomas Aitkenhead, son of an Edinburgh surgeon, was condemned to death for blasphemy. Despite recanting, he was executed on the afternoon of January 8, 1698, and his possessions forfeited.

porary theonomists did not subscribe to the view that the Mosaic judicials were to be followed *simpliciter*.

3. A concluding point must now be made. Such was the diversity of viewpoints and nuances among the Puritans that the view that the Confession is committed specifically to a theonomic understanding of the Mosaic judicial law code and penology is not viable.

It is evident that George Gillespie himself (on whose views Bahnsen places considerable interpretative authority with respect to the Confession) recognized that his own views were not shared by all members of the Assembly. The opening pages of *Wholesome Severity Reconciled with Christian Liberty* seem to reflect that, for there he comments that certain views on the magistrate and the law held by Roman Catholics, Socinians, and Arminians were also adopted in "some Bookes printed *amongst ourselves* in *this year* of confusion."[61] Since this is the case, while John Cotton's *Abstract of the Laws of New England* indicates the concern of the Puritan movement for civil holiness, it is by no means representative of a unified Puritan position. Cotton's extension of the death penalty to profanation of the Lord's Day and rebellious children (chapter 7) represents only one polarity within the range of Puritan views. The fact that there were hopes that Cotton would attend the Westminster Assembly, however, simply underscores this point.

No single position on every aspect of the doctrine of the law was held by the Divines at Westminster. They represented a variety of hues within a conservative spectrum, on many doctrines, and specifically on the doctrine of the law of God. Hence their protracted and difficult discussions. Here, as elsewhere, part of their genius lay in their ability to state doctrines clearly, yet not so narrowly as to exclude brethren among themselves who likewise were committed to generic Calvinism. Their response to Parliament's demand for proof-texts, the known theological diversity among the commissioners, and indications in the minutes that they themselves were prepared to express things in an accommodating fashion all suggest that Chapter XIX is a fine example of their Reformed inclusivism. It would have satisfied those Divines, like Gillespie, who wished that more attention would be

---

[61]Gillespie, *Wholesome Severity*, 2.

given to the Mosaic penology; it satisfied others who did not believe that the Mosaic penology as such was necessarily binding, in all of its details, though the Mosaic proscriptions generally speaking were.

It is, perhaps surprisingly, George Gillespie who gives the clearest indication of the Divines' vision for an inclusivist confession. In one of the most controversial of all the Assembly's debates, "about permission of man's fall; about 'the same decree,'" involving a veritable theological "hall of fame" including Rutherford, Whitaker, Gouge, Seaman, and Reynolds, Gillespie interjected, "When that word is left out, is it not a truth, *and so every one may enjoy his own sense.*"[62] For our immediate purposes the debate about the decrees need not concern us. What is significant is that Gillespie, one of the most acute and rigorous theologians in the Jerusalem Chamber, was suggesting wording that would be faithful to Scripture and yet provide liberty for each to read the text in the light of his own understanding of the biblical teaching. The nuances of thinking we have already observed among the Divines and their contemporaries make it quite certain that the chapter entitled "Of the Law of God" is marked by the same latitude.

Nothing could be more wrong-headed in approaching the Confession than to adopt the hermeneutical principle that it is open to one, exclusive, narrowly delimited interpretation in each of its statements. For the Confession is a self-consciously *consensus* document, containing theological accommodations expressed to encompass differing views within generic Calvinism—even on issues about which individual Divines might feel strongly.

It is this factor that leads us to our conclusion. In view of what we have already seen, we must conclude that the Westminster Confession cannot be appealed to as an expression of theonomy in its contemporary form. Further, it would be erroneous to argue that one cannot subscribe to the Confession of Faith unless one is a theonomist. Nor can it be argued that not to subscribe to theonomy is to reject the Westminster Confession's teaching on the law of God.

It should be noted that in many instances the practical implications of theonomy may not necessarily be a denial of

---

[62]Mitchell and Struthers, *Minutes*, 150–51, emphasis mine.

the teaching of the Westminster Confession. The words of Chapter XIX,iv can be understood to include the view that the Mosaic penalties may be applied by the Christian magistrate (if "general equity" so dictates). We have already noted that such views were widespread among the Divines in relation to specific crimes. But this is simply to recognize that there may be common ground *in practice* between the Confession's teaching and theonomy.

We have argued that the actual wording of the Confession suggests that the Westminster Divines regarded some elements in the Mosaic penology as "peculiar" to the Mosaic period, just as they considered (for example) elements in the seven- and fifty-year sabbath laws to be no longer applicable but bound to the old covenant *Sitz im Leben*.[63] That the most natural reading of the text is thus contra-theonomic is borne out by David Dickson, contemporary of Rutherford and Gillespie. Dickson was responsible for what is generally regarded as the earliest commentary on the Confession. He states:

> *Did the Lord by Moses give to the Jews as a Body Politick sundry judicial lawes, which expired together with their State?*
>
> Yes.
>
> *Do they oblige any other now, further than the general Equity thereof may require?*
>
> No; Exod. 21, from the first to the last Verse. Exod. 22.1 to Verse 29. Gen. 49.10. 1 Cor. 9.8,9,10. 1 Pet. 2.13,14. Matt.5.17,38,39.
>
> *Well then, do not some err, though otherwise* Orthodox, *who maintain, "That the whole Judaical Law of the Jews, is yet alive, and binding all of us who are Christian Gentile?"*
>
> Yes.
>
> *By what reasons are they confuted?*
>
> 1st, Because the Judaical Law was delivered by Moses to the Israelites to be observed, as to a Body Politick; Exod. 21. Chap.
> 2d, Because, this Law, in many Things which are of particular Right, was accommodated to the Commonwealth of the Jews, and not to other nations also; Exod. 22.3. Exod. 21.2. Lev. 25.2,3. Deut. 24.1,2,3. Deut.

---

[63]Cf. Gillespie, *Wholesome Severity*, 6.

25.5,6,7.

3d, Because, in other things which are not of particular Right, it is neither from the Law of Nature obliging by Reason; neither is it pressed upon Believers under the Gospel, to be observed.

4th, Because, Believers are appointed under the Gospel to obey the civil Law, and Commands of those under whose Government they live, providing they be just, and that for Conscience sake; Rom. 13.1. 1 Pet. 2.13,14. Tit. 3.1.[64]

Dickson's statements provide a significant example of a conviction among seventeenth-century Reformed theologians that there are elements in the Mosaic civil law that are not required by the law of nature nor commanded in the New Testament and that therefore may be regarded as no longer binding.

In the light of this, and the considerations above, I conclude that the Confession does not expound, nor does it prescribe, a theonomic viewpoint. It may be that some members of the Assembly were prepared to stretch the meaning of "general equity" as far as contemporary theonomists do. Within my limitations, however, I know of no evidence (the Scottish Statute of 1661 notwithstanding) that, for example, any individual commissioner to the Assembly believed that Sabbath-breakers and rebellious children should be put to death *on the authority of the Mosaic Law*. Rutherford specifically repudiates such a position, as we have seen. The strongest position a theonomist could adopt *on the basis of the Confession* would be that it did not *a priori* reject the application of the Mosaic judicial punishment for crimes considered *seriatim*. But *theoretical* theonomy as such is not the teaching of the Westminster Confession of Faith.

This chapter has been largely limited to a consideration of Chapter XIX of the Confession. It would be to go beyond its scope to consider further the teaching of the Divines in Chapter XXIII. But enough has been said to suggest that the teaching of the Westminster Confession needs to be handled with greater sensitivity and historical discrimination than is

---

[64]David Dickson, *Truth's Victory over Error . . . being a commentary on all the Chapters of the Confession of Faith* (Glasgow, 1749), 140–41. This work was first published in 1684 by George Sinclair, but was in fact Sinclair's translation of Dickson's dictated Latin lectures on the Confession.

evident in the belief that contemporary theonomy is the guardian of the Confession's teaching on the law of God.

One important question does, however, remain to be asked: Can present-day debaters of the theonomy issue learn anything from their forefathers, the Westminster Divines? Perhaps they can, for here were men of great learning and passionate conviction, who were generally speaking subscribers to a generic Calvinism, engaged in untold hours of discussion and debate. Uniformity was their goal. But it is evident from the way in which they achieved it that the spirit of their Calvinism was inclusive rather than exclusive. Unity in the church of God, they believed, required a sufficiently clear statement of the truth to exclude manifestly false teaching, and a sufficiently broad expression of its nuances to avoid excluding those who were in heart and head truly orthodox, whatever differences might remain. The debates among these brethren did not end when the Confession was at last sent to Parliament, proof-texts and all; but the Confession's statement is a lasting monument to the fact that they realized they were involved in a family discussion as they sought eagerly to understand and submit to the word of their common Father. We neglect that spirit to our peril.

Chapter Fifteen

New England Puritans and the State

Samuel T. Logan, Jr.

Samuel T. Logan, Jr.

Samuel T. Logan, Jr. (Ph.D., Emory University) is Professor of Church History at Westminster Theological Seminary (Philadelphia). With other degrees from Princeton University and Westminster Theological Seminary, he has taught at Barrington College, and at Westminster since 1979. He is the editor of *The Preacher and Preaching: Reviving the Art in the Twentieth Century*, and has contributed to the *Dictionary of Christianity in America*.

Chapter Fifteen

New England Puritans and the State

In a volume dealing with theonomy, a chapter analyzing the beliefs and actions of New England Puritans is most appropriate for at least two reasons. First, there is a widespread current belief that the Puritans were theonomists as that term is popularly understood. While the question of whether other Christians believed or did certain things must always and clearly be secondary to whether Scripture teaches those things, we just as surely must seek to learn from other members of the body of Christ—this is the mandate of Ephesians 5, and it is the lesson, too often ignored, of church history.

But why should we seek particularly to learn from *these* members of the body of Christ? The second reason why studying the Puritans is appropriate in the present context is that they, more than most other Christian groups in the history of the church, had both the opportunity and the inclination to structure their society as God would have them do. They were determined, to use H. Richard Niebuhr's most helpful terminology, that Christ should transform their culture.[1]

Furthermore, the New England Puritans came to their task equipped with a Reformed theological foundation. The God to whom they were committed was absolutely sovereign, in both politics and redemption. There was no false dichotomy in Puritan minds between the sacred and the secular—all came under the lordship of Christ. They and the

[1]H. Richard Niebuhr, *Christ and Culture* (New York: Harper & Row, 1951).

community they built in Massachusetts Bay thus provide an excellent case study for the kinds of concerns most often expressed in the modern theonomy movement. We would do well, then, to seek to understand what the New England Puritans thought and did with regard to the civil law.

As we move to our task, however, we must be careful to avoid the Millerian error that suggests there was a single "New England mind." In fact, a great deal of theological diversity existed in early New England as Philip Gura has powerfully demonstrated.[2] Puritans may have dominated, but they were by no means the only ones present in the various communities that grew up throughout the region. In focusing on what the Puritans said and did, therefore, we must not think that other opinions were nonexistent at the time. In fact, some of the New England minority opinions (such as those of William Aspinwall and his followers) were both strongly opposed to the Puritan consensus and quite similar to some of the positions presently identified as "theonomic."[3] So while I will seek to identify and to analyze the Puritan consensus in early New England, the presence of a dissenting voice must constantly be borne in mind.

Our task is further complicated by the fact that at least three of the separate colonies that developed in New England (Massachusetts Bay, New Haven, and Connecticut) deserve the appellation "Puritan," and, as Bradley Chapin points out, there were some differences among the three in the way in which the civil law was conceived and enacted.[4] Therefore, to be as accurate as possible, one of the colonies must be specified as the focus of our study and, for a variety of reasons, I have chosen the oldest and largest of the colonies, that of Massachusetts Bay.

But this still does not deal with all of the complexities involved because, among those generally regarded as orthodox Puritans in Massachusetts Bay in the first two decades of that colony's existence, there was significant difference of

---

[2]Philip E. Gura, *A Glimpse of Sion's Glory: Puritan Radicalism in New England, 1620–1660* (Middletown, Conn.: Wesleyan University Press, 1984).

[3]See Gura, *Glimpse of Sion's Glory*, 126–44.

[4]Bradley Chapin, *Criminal Justice in Colonial America, 1606–1660* (Athens, Ga.: University of Georgia Press, 1983), 5, 77. Some might argue that Plymouth should also be regarded as Puritan; nearly all would agree that Rhode Island surely does *not* belong in that category.

opinion on the subject of our concern, the civil law. As appears again and again both in the official documents (for example, *The Records of the Governor and Company of the Massachusetts Bay in New England*) and in the unofficial documents (for example, the *Journal* of John Winthrop) of the time, controversy regarding the civil law was not at all uncommon. Some of that controversy involved leading members of the Puritan community; so describing the opinions or the proposals of one particular Puritan may not always accurately communicate the general Puritan consensus.

The focus of my attention will be on Massachusetts Bay and, within that colony, on the official actions of those Puritans who were selected by the community to serve as magistrates. These seem to me to represent best the Puritan consensus when it comes to the matter of the political structure of the colony. Preeminently, I will deal with Governor John Winthrop. I will try to point out the issues on which Winthrop differed from others within the colony, but I will continue to argue that he is the best of the leaders to discuss because he is the most representative.

Winthrop was the first elected governor of the colony and he retained that post for most of the first twenty years of the colony's existence. With good reason Darrett Rutman entitles his study of the chief town of the colony, *Winthrop's Boston*. Indeed, as Rutman points out, it was Winthrop "whom the 'Chiefe undertakers' of the migration would not do without, 'the welfare of the Plantation' depending 'upon his goeinge' with them to the New World."[5] Also with good reason George Lee Haskins deals so thoroughly with Winthrop in his study of "law and authority in early Massachusetts"; as Haskins puts it, "Unquestionably, the leading figure among the magistrates, and the one who chiefly inspired the development of law and government, was John Winthrop."[6]

But before we deal directly with what Winthrop and the Puritans did in New England, we must consider briefly why

---

[5]Darrett B. Rutman, *Winthrop's Boston: Portrait of a Puritan Town, 1630–1649* (Chapel Hill, N.C.: University of North Carolina Press, 1965), 3.

[6]George Lee Haskins, *Law and Authority in Early Massachusetts* (New York: Macmillan, 1960), 105.

they left Old England and what they therefore were seeking to achieve in migrating from one world to another. Winthrop and many other Puritan leaders were born and reared in East Anglia, a region of southeastern England, which became known early in the sixteenth century for theological radicalism. Located as it is at the eastern elbow of England just a few nautical miles from the Continent, East Anglia provided excellent ports of entry for the subversive ideas we now call "sola fide," "sola gratia," and "sola scriptura."[7]

These ideas were explored and developed in the 1520s in such theological hothouses as the White Horse Tavern in Cambridge. Thomas Bilney, Hugh Latimer, Nicholas Ridley, and Thomas Cranmer not only shared their reflections on Luther's Ninety-five Theses; they also used as the basis of many of their discussions a new Greek text of the New Testament that had been prepared right next door to the White Horse, at Queen's College, by Erasmus, the Dutch scholar who had made the short trip from Rotterdam to Cambridge to continue his studies. Theological change was in the air before Henry VIII discovered that he had a marital problem.

Of course, Henry's divorce in 1533 and the ecclesiastical schism it produced simply intensified the discussion that had begun in Cambridge. But Henry himself was, by the 1521 words of Pope Leo X, a "Defender of the Faith," to be specific, the Roman Catholic faith; he had no interest in major theological change, and he did all that he could to limit the theological fallout of his break with Rome. During his reign, the limits largely worked and the theological revolution continued to be quietly and unobtrusively nurtured in Cambridge and in surrounding East Anglia.

But when Henry died in 1547, the regents of the nine-year-old Edward VI, first the Duke of Somerset and then the Duke of Northumberland, acted to bring the Reformation officially to England. By the end of Edward's brief reign (he died in 1553) major theological change was in the works. When Mary (Henry's eldest, female child and a devout

---

[7]See David Edwards, *Christian England*, vol. 2., *From the Reformation to the 18th Century* (Grand Rapids: Eerdmans, 1984), 31–75. See also John Adair, *Founding Fathers: The Puritans in England and America* (Grand Rapids: Baker, 1986), 57–74.

Roman Catholic) sought to reverse these changes, she only succeeded in sending many of their advocates to exile in Geneva and Zurich. Thus, when Elizabeth ascended the throne in 1558, most of those who returned from exile were unabashedly Calvinistic in theological orientation.

Elizabeth shared many of the predilections of her father Henry—she really cared only for the supremacy of her throne, and acted accordingly. But those who had been abroad knew something better, something more biblical, and they worked incessantly to bring about the full reformation of the country. Known as Puritans because, among other things, they wanted to "purify" the liturgy of the Church of England, these men found themselves attracted to Cambridge for their theological training. There, rather than at Oxford, their Reformed theological convictions broadened and deepened. Christ's College produced William Perkins and a host of other Puritan leaders, and Emmanuel College was founded with the specific purpose of training those who would work for the full reformation of England.[8]

During the years of Elizabeth's reign, even in the face of official opposition, Puritan theologians were busy developing the implications of their basic theological positions. They did not do this by creating new doctrines, as R. T. Kendall as alleged,[9] but rather by seeking to apply the Scriptures rigorously to the various situations, social and political as well as ecclesiastical, in which they found themselves. They were, by the middle part of Elizabeth's reign, self-conscious Calvinists in that they were convinced that every aspect of life comes under the control of the sovereign God and therefore must be ordered by his word. In contrast to their earthly ruler, they believed that no other priority should take precedence over glorifying God by living in complete obedience to him.

Correlatively, they understood the implications of the covenant theology they had learned from John Calvin and had accepted because they saw it in the Scriptures.[10] This

---

[8]H. C. Porter, *Reformation and Reaction in Tudor Cambridge* (Cambridge: Cambridge University Press, 1958), 180–82, 236–42, 265–69.

[9]R. T. Kendall, *Calvin and English Calvinism to 1649* (New York: Oxford University Press, 1979).

[10]Perry Miller's misinterpretation of the Puritans (and of Calvin) on this point is legendary. See Perry Miller, *The New England Mind: The Seventeenth Century* (Boston: Beacon, 1961), Book 4. One of the many scholars who seem

theology taught them that God deals *primarily* with individuals but *secondarily and really* with groups. As God dealt with all of Abraham's seed in dealing with Abraham (Ge 12) and as God deals with all of the elect in accepting Jesus' sacrifice for sin (Ro 5), so God deals *actually* with groups of people today.[11]

In the context of sixteenth-century England, this meant that God desired the nation *as a nation* to live in obedience to his word. This understanding of Scripture came to be called the National Covenant, but it never entailed the belief that God had made a unique covenant with England. The National Covenant to which England was a party was nothing more or less than the totality of Scripture, and, as such, it would have been equally applicable to any nation. To be sure, there were many statements of England's unique opportunity to obey the covenant but the covenant itself and the implied responsibility of the nation to live by God's word were by no means unique to England.

Perhaps the one document that captured this biblical truth most poignantly and brought it home to the Puritan mind most powerfully was what has popularly come to be know as Foxe's *Book of Martyrs*. John Foxe was born in Boston, England, in 1517. He went to Oxford in 1533, was later granted a fellowship at Magdalen College, and then left the university, probably under pressure because of his Protestant sentiments, in 1545. In 1554 he was protesting the readoption of the Act of Six Articles (Henry's much more Catholic doctrinal summary) and then fled to Strasbourg and from there to Frankfurt, arriving in 1555. In Frankfurt he met Edmund Grindal, a former Cambridge man also in exile, and it was Grindal who was most responsible for getting Foxe involved in producing his *Book of Martyrs*.

After Elizabeth's accession to the throne, Foxe returned

---

to adopt uncritically Miller's thesis is Leonard Trinterud, *The Forming of an American Tradition: A Re-Examination of Colonial Presbyterianism* (New York: Arno, 1970), 169–75. The best analysis of the Millerian position remains George Marsden, "Perry Miller's Rehabilitation of the Puritans: A Critique," *Church History* 39 (March 1970): 91–105.

[11]Harry Stout develops this notion superbly in his analysis of New England Puritan preaching. See his *New England Soul: Preaching and Religious Culture in Colonial New England* (New York: Oxford University Press, 1986), 86–95.

to London in October of 1559 and in November announced that he intended to publish a large work on the martyrs. The book appeared in 1563, with some twenty pages of introductory material and 1,800 pages of text. The full title was *ACTES AND MONUMENTS OF THESE LATTER AND PERILLOUS DAYES, TOUCHING MATTERS OF THE CHURCH, WHEREIN AR COMPREHENDED AND DESCRIBED THE GREAT PERSECUTIONS AND HORRIBLE TROUBLES, THAT HAVE BENE WROUGHT AND PRACTISED BY THE ROMISH PRELATES, SPECIALLYE IN THIS REALME OF ENGLAND AND SCOTLANDE, FROM THE YEARE OF OUR LORDE A THOUSAND, UNTO THE TYME NOW PRESENT. GATHERED AND COLLECTED ACCORDING TO THE TRUE COPIES & WRYTINGS CERTIFICATORIE AS WEL OF THE PARTIES THEM SELVES THAT SUFFERED, AS ALSO OUT OF THE BISHOPS REGISTERS, WHICH WER THE DOERS THEREOF, BY JOHN FOXE.* This edition was enlarged by another 600 pages and republished in 1570.

The tone of the book was most crucial. William Haller summarizes that tone well:

> The book expressed the exultancy of the returned exiles at the intervention of providence in their behalf, but also their increasing concern lest divine justice be given occasion to withdraw the favour divine grace had bestowed. There was reason for their concern. The queen [Elizabeth] appeared to be committed to their cause by the circumstances of her birth and position and to be dependent on them in some degree for support against her rivals. But they could not be certain that her dependence upon them was as absolute as theirs upon her. For them she was indispensable and irreplaceable, so that, although they naturally could not trust her woman's judgment as they did their own, or her devotion to the cause they had at heart, they dared not allow their devotion to her to flag.
>
> Yet it was a devotion more and more mixed with anxiety lest she should fail to live up to their idea of her or hold to the course they had charted for her, and lest her failure should provoke the Lord to strike at her and them with sudden death or with rebellion and invasion.[12]

---

[12]William Haller, *The Elect Nation: The Meaning and Relevance of Foxe's BOOK OF MARTYRS* (New York: Harper & Row, 1963), 119–20.

360 I Samuel T. Logan, Jr.

It would be hard to overestimate the breadth of the impact of Foxe's work. As David Edwards points out, in 1571 it was ordered that every cathedral should possess a copy and, as Haller adds, the mayor of London, prompted by the Archbishop of Canterbury and the bishops of London and Ely, ordered that the book be available to be read by all in city orphanages and the halls of city companies.[13] It was also distributed to the homes of the clergy and to the universities at Oxford and Cambridge.[14] Thus these stories were heard by Christians in churches and read by parents to children in homes as part of family devotions. The impact is nearly incalculable.

Edwards believes that Foxe's book is *the* primary answer to the question, "Why did Protestantism gradually prevail in England?"[15] Foxe gave to Protestant England a revulsion for Rome, but he accomplished much more than this. He gave to English Puritans a sense that God was doing something special among them, that they were "an elect nation." To be sure, some took the lesson further than that and began to see England as "*the* elect nation." But that was an unnecessary distortion of what Foxe was saying, and it did not predominate within the Puritan movement. Foxe was saying something similar to what Augustine had said in his City of God—that all of human history needs to be interpreted spiritually. Historical events are not religiously neutral but, rather, are part of a vast eschatological drama that *will* culminate in the full and final establishment of "the city of God." God had preserved his people through "the dreadful and bloody regiment" of Mary for a purpose, and those who read Foxe's work came away with a sense that they should be involved in the accomplishment of that purpose.[16] Not just as individual Christians, but as a nation, Englishmen felt compelled to seek the kingdom of God.

Puritans read Foxe's book and they took from the book the sense that because so many had sacrificed so much and because God had blessed England so greatly, they simply could not rest with a half-completed reformation. The *Book of*

---

[13]Edwards, *Christian England*, 2:72; Haller, *Elect Nation*, 221.
[14]Haller, *Elect Nation*, 221.
[15]Edwards, *Christian England*, 2:71.
[16]Ibid., 72–75.

Martyrs thus gave a sense of eschatological importance to the drive for further reformation in England. This is one reason why John Bunyan commented that Foxe's book was second only to the Bible in its impact on the development of Puritanism.[17]

The second reason for Bunyan's comment was the support provided by the book for the development of the idea of the national covenant as that idea is described above. England, as a nation, had been blessed with the Gospel and with the opportunity to become a genuine example of the city of God on earth. The implication was that England must not misuse such an opportunity. The drive to full reformation was a drive to seize an opportunity that could be lost. This too became an essential part of the developing Puritanism of the late sixteenth century.

The point is that the Puritans had come to see the truth of their Calvinistic heritage. God is the Almighty One; Jesus reigns. Indeed, as Colossians 1:16–17 reminds us, "By him all things were created: things in heaven and on earth, visible and invisible, whether thrones or powers or rulers or authorities; all things were created by him and for him. He is before all things and in him all things hold together." In ontology as surely as in redemption, in all spheres of life and experience, in the nation as well as in the individual, God is to rule. Thus national priorities must be focused on him and on his glory as certainly as must individual priorities. Nations exist to glorify God and all of the other (very important) things they do must be seen as means to that great end.

But Foxe's balance of exultant hope and worried concern slowly tipped in the direction of the latter in many Puritan minds during the final decades of the sixteenth century. The problem was that England clearly did not regard God's glory as her highest national priority. At least that is how Elizabeth's theological compromises appeared to the Puritans. The value priorities embodied in England's national life neither began nor ended with the glory of God. And when Elizabeth died and the Scot James Stuart became king, high hopes quickly became dashed hopes. The Word of God simply was not being obeyed in the kingdom and, worse yet,

---

[17]Adair, *Founding Fathers*, 57.

there seemed to be no desire, among those in power, even to move in that direction.

Sooner or later, anyone who takes Foxe's basic perspective seriously and who believes that God expects certain standards of national righteousness must ask himself, "What will happen if those standards are consistently and blatantly flouted?" The answer seemed clear to the Puritans from the Scriptures: God judges sin and though he may, in his gracious patience, delay his judgment to provide opportunity for repentance, he will not wait forever. By the mid-1620s this question was assuming urgency. The Separatists, those who believed that separating from society met all of their spiritual obligations, had left the country and, after a brief and unpleasant sojourn in the Netherlands, had made their way to Plymouth in Massachusetts. But now the main body of non-Separating Puritans had begun asking themselves if there was anything more that they could or should do.

One of the leaders of that larger Puritan group was John Winthrop. He owned land that had been confiscated from the monastery at Bury St. Edmunds (in the heart of East Anglia) by Henry VIII and sold to Winthrop's grandfather. Winthrop became a student at Cambridge where his appreciation for Reformed theology developed. In 1629 he was an attorney at His Majesty's Court of Wards in London; in that position, he saw first-hand the corruption that dominated the national government and the total disregard for glorifying God by obeying his word; on May 15, he penned these words in a letter to his wife Margaret:

> My good wife, I prayse the Lorde for the wished newes of thy wellfare. . . ; it is a great favour, that we may enjoye so much comfort and peace in these so evill and declininge tymes and when the increasinge of our sinnes gives us so great cause to looke for some heavy Scquorge and Judgment to be comminge upon us: the Lorde hath admonished, threatened, corrected, and astonished us, yet we grow worse and worse, so as his spirit will not allwayes strive with us, he must needs give way to his furye at last: he hath smitten all the other Churches before our eyes, and hath made them to drink of the bitter cuppe of tribulation, even unto death; we sawe this, and humbled not ourselves, to turne from our evill wayes, but

have provoked him more than all the nations rounde about us: therefore he is turning the cuppe towards us also, and because we are the last, our portion must be to drink the verye dreggs which remaine: my deare wife, I am veryly perswaded, God will bringe some heauye Affliction upon this lande, and that speedylye: but be of good Comfort, the hardest that can come shall be a meanes to mortifie this bodye of Corruption, which is a thousand tymes more dangerous to us than any outward tribulation, and to bringe us into neerer communion with our Lo: Jes: Christ, and more Assurance of his kingdome. If the Lorde seeth it wilbe good for us, he will provide a shelter and a hidinge place for us and ours.[18]

One can sense the mood here just as surely as one can sense the faith and the value priorities; all are derived directly from Scripture and indirectly from the perspective on Scripture suggested by Foxe's *Book of Martyrs*. The concern is clearly with obedience to God, and the fear is that, in temporal terms, judgment is imminent because of national disobedience. Winthrop knew where his eternal security rested, and there was no doubt about that security. But there was doubt about the continued temporal welfare of a state that ignored the Word of God. And Winthrop could not live easily with that doubt.

So Winthrop acted. He acted to bring a party of like-minded Christians to the New World. He did not come here as the Separatists did, to escape society. He came to establish a holy community that would so glorify God by its obedience to his word that the nations round about, particularly the English nation, would see and repent and be healed. Again Winthrop's own words speak most clearly. Aboard the ship bringing him and his colleagues to Massachusetts, he preached a challenge that they would make their community "a model of Christian charity":

Thus stands the cause betweene God and us, wee are entered into Covenant with him for this worke, wee haue taken out a Commission, and the Lord hath giuen us leaue to drawe our owne Articles wee haue professed to enterprise these Accions vpon these and these ends, wee

---

[18]"John Winthrop to His Wife," May 15, 1629, in *The Puritans: A Sourcebook of Their Writings*, ed. Perry Miller and Thomas H. Johnson (New York: Harper & Row, 1963), 466–67.

haue herevpon besought him of favour and blessing: Now
if the Lord shall please to heare vs, and bring vs in peace
to the place wee desire, then hath hee ratified this
Covenant and sealed our Commission, [and] will expect a
strickt performance of the Articles contained in it, but if
wee shall neglect the observacion of these Articles which
are the ends wee haue propounded, and dissembling
with our God, shall fall to embrace this present world and
prosecute our carnall intencions seekeing greate things for
our selues and our posterity, the Lord will surely breake
out in wrathe against vs, be revenged of such a periured
people and make vs knowe the price of the breache of
such a Covenant.

Now the onely way to avoyde this shipwracke and to
provide for our posterity is to followe the Counsell of
Micah, to doe Justly, to loue mercy, to walke humbly with
our God, . . . that men shall say of succeeding planta-
cions: the lord make it like that of New England: for wee
must Consider that wee shall be as a Citty vpon a Hill, the
eies of all people are uppon us.[19]

Winthrop's value priorities are clear: obedience to God
and the honoring of his name—these were to be the
foundation of the new community. Nothing is even suggested about making Massachusetts a model of liberty or
freedom; such value priorities are far too man-centered to
have had a prominent place in these early days of the colony.
Whenever such politically weighted terms do appear in, for
example, Winthrop's *Journal* or John Cotton's farewell sermon to the emigrants, they are always seen as secondary; the
means is never confused with the end.[20]
The community established by the Puritans in Massachusetts Bay reflected their value priorities, and Harry
Stout's analysis of that community is most helpful. He points
out that in building their "Holy Commonwealth," the New
England Puritans were concerned with both biblical purity
and social influence. He continues,

---

[19]John Winthrop, "A Modell of Christian Charity" in Miller and Johnson,
The Puritans, 1:198–99.

[20]See, for example, John Winthrop, *Winthrop's Journal: History of New
England, 1630–1649*, ed. James Kendall Hosmer (New York: Scribner, n.d.),
1:23–56, 2:237–39, 314–15. See also John Cotton, "God's Promise to His
Plantation," Old South Leaflet #53, 6–14.

Neither of these themes was unknown in Europe but no single church embodied both. Some churches like the "Separate" or "Brownist" churches understood the scriptural truth that for churches to be pure, they must be "gathered" out from the world and established on the basis of voluntary commitments and the "covenant of grace." But these churches separated so entirely from the world that they were in no position to influence its operations; they were so heavenly minded, Puritans argued, that they were no earthly good. Other churches like the Anglican and the Presbyterian [at least as the Presbyterian Church was structured in the seventeenth century] understood the church's obligation to the nation . . . , but they failed to keep their churches pure according to the covenant teachings of Scripture. . . . New England's "Congregational" founders dedicated themselves to the mission of fusing what had been hopelessly fragmented in England and, in so doing, pointed the way to a national renewal and divine favor.[21]

What enabled the Massachusetts Puritans to do as they believed God required them to do was the unique situation regarding their charter. While most colonial charters stipulated that annual meetings of the company would be held in England under the king's direct scrutiny and control, the Massachusetts Bay Charter contained no such restriction.[22] One's opportunity to build the society one wishes in the way one wishes increases dramatically if the primary deterrent is three thousand miles of ocean away. Such was the situation for the now Governor Winthrop and his colleagues.

But this charter situation should not be interpreted to mean that the Boston Christians were just as separatistic as

[21]Stout, New England Soul, 15. See also E. Dibgy Baltzell's very helpful analysis of the difference between Puritan and Quaker perspectives in Puritan Boston and Quaker Philadelphia (New York: Macmillan, 1979), 62, 76, 82–84, 102–3, 119–25.

[22]See, for example, "The Charter of the Colony of the Massachusetts Bay in New England" as printed in Nathaniel B. Shurtleff, ed., The Records of the Governor and Company of the Massachusetts Bay in New England, Volume I: 1628–1641, (Boston: William White, 1853), 3–10, where the charter for the colony of Plymouth is described and its meeting place in England clearly prescribed but where no place of meeting is set for the Massachusetts Bay Company. For a full analysis of the significance of this omission, see Edmund Morgan, The Puritan Dilemma: The Story of John Winthrop (Boston: Little, Brown, and Company, 1958), 45–53.

the Separatist Christians at Plymouth. Throughout all of their rhetoric and all of their reasoning, the Massachusetts Puritans reflected their conviction that they were still Englishmen, that, in fact, they were still members of the Church of England (indeed, it was this latter fact that so inflamed the super-Separatist passions of Roger Williams). They were here to build a church and a commonwealth within the larger manifestations of both; their goal was so to glorify God in both that those larger entities would see and be converted and be restored to righteousness and blessing. To use again the phraseology of H. Richard Niebuhr, the citizens of Massachusetts Bay believed that Christ was the transformer of culture, not that he was irreconcilably against culture.[23]

In the New World, with their charter's lack of provisions to aid them, the Puritans moved swiftly to their task. But since it is very much with *the way* they moved to their task that we are presently concerned, it will be necessary to deal briefly with the actual political structure of the Massachusetts Bay colony. The colony began as a chartered English trading company, quite similar to the way numerous other companies of that day began. A group of investors was granted trade and settlement rights to a tract of land in the New World. In the case of the Massachusetts Bay Company, the land was specified as that which stretched from a line three miles south of the Charles River to a line three miles north of the Merrimack River.[24] More important for our purposes, but also common in that day, it was specified that the company would be directed by a governor, a deputy governor, and eighteen assistants, all to be elected by the freemen (stockholders) of the company out of their own number.[25]

As noted above, the charter of the Massachusetts Bay Company was unique in that it contained no requirement that the company meet annually in London. Armed with this omission, the stockholders of the company *themselves* migrated to the land they had been granted. This was most unusual since normally investors would lease their rights to others or would directly hire others to utilize those rights for profit. But the stockholders in the Massachusetts Bay Company,

---

[23]Niebuhr, *Christ and Culture*, passim.
[24]Shurtleff, *Records*, 1:4.
[25]Ibid., 10.

among whom was John Winthrop, were Puritans fired by the vision of Foxe's *Book of Martyrs* and frightened by the *present* spiritual condition of England. So they (literally) packed up their charter and sailed to the land they had been granted.[26]

When they arrived, they were still the Massachusetts Bay Company, and they retained the political structure laid out in the charter—there was a governor (Winthrop had been elected on October 20, 1629), a deputy governor, and ten assistants (the full complement of eighteen had never been elected). But from their first day in the New World, they revealed that they were different from other trading companies—they "had ceased to act as an organization seeking profit from its landholdings."[27]

One of the most definitive ways in which they revealed their different orientation emerges from the records of the general court (the annual meeting of all freemen—which, of course, included all the magistrates) for October 19, 1630. Those records speak as follows:

> For the establishing of the government. It was propounded if it were not the best course that the freemen should have the power of chuseing Assistants when they are to be chosen, and the Assistants from amongst themselues to chuse a Governor and Deputy Governor, whoe with the Assistants should have the power of makeing lawes and chuseing officers to execute the same. This was fully assented vnto by the general vote of the people and ereccion of hands.[28]

To be sure, these words have been variously interpreted.[29] But certainly Edmund Morgan is correct in arguing that this action represented a dramatic extension of political power to those who, by the specific provision of the charter, had no such power.[30] Otherwise, the action simply repeats what was already stipulated by the charter. Furthermore, the phrase "general vote of the people" hardly makes sense if its

---

[26]I have simplified many hours of discussions regarding the nature of the Massachusetts Bay Company among its stockholders. See Shurtleff, *Records*, 1:42–51.

[27]Haskins, *Law and Authority*, 25.

[28]Shurtleff, *Records*, 1:79.

[29]Haskins, *Law and Authority*, 26, n.8.

[30]Morgan, *Puritan Dilemma*, 89–94.

368 | Samuel T. Logan, Jr.

referent is merely to those who were already freemen since at that time there were only eleven freemen in the entire colony, ten of whom were serving as assistants.[31] Finally, the court records indicate that immediately following the action described above, one hundred and nine individuals applied to become freemen.[32] Clearly, something dramatic was happening.

The full significance of this event becomes clear only by records of court decisions made on May 13, 1631. For that date, the court records read as follows:

> For explanation of an order made the last General Court, holden the 19th of October last, it was ordered nowe, with full consent of all the commons then present, that once in every year, att least, a General Court shalbe holden, at which court it shalbe lawfull for the commons to propounde any person or persons whome they shall desire to be chosen Assistants, and if it be doubtful whither it be the greater part of the commons or not, it shall be putt to the poll. The like course is to be holden when they, the said commons, shall see cause for any defect or misbehavior to remoue any one or more of the Assistants; and to the end the body of the commons may be preserued of honest and good men, it was likewise ordered and agreed that for time to come noe man shalbe admitted to the freedome of this body polliticke, but such as are members of some of the churches within the limits of the same.[33]

These actions effectively transformed the Massachusetts Bay Company *from* a financial organization *to* an explicitly religious one, and this change was fully in keeping with all of the theological and spiritual developments we have been tracing from John Foxe to John Winthrop. This was the fundamental way in which the Puritans would seek to build a community that genuinely honored and obeyed God. The focus of their attention was, therefore, on the people who would hold power and office more than it was on the specific legal code those people might develop. When the New England criteria for church membership were solidified,

[31]W. H. Whitmore, *The Massachusetts Civil List for the Colonial and Provincial Periods, 1630–1774* (Albany, 1870), 21. See also J. G. Palfrey, *History of New England* (Boston, 1865), 1:323n.

[32]Shurtleff, *Records*, 1:77–78.

[33]Ibid., 87.

probably by 1636, they included not only evidence of doctrinal orthodoxy and of practical piety but also a "narrative of grace," what today might be called a credible confession of personal faith in Jesus Christ as Savior and Lord.[34] They thus completed the system that constituted the New England way, the system the Puritans believed was most likely to produce a "holy commonwealth." It was challenges to this system—challenges by Roger Williams, Anne Hutchinson, and Robert Child among others—that the Puritans saw as most dangerous and therefore rejected most vigorously.[35]

Much has been written about the Puritan restriction of the franchise but only occasionally has it been noted that as large a percentage of the population could vote in New England as could vote in old England (in both cases between 11 and 15 percent of the total adult population).[36] The real difference between the two Englands was not in how many could vote but in how those who could vote were chosen. In New England the criterion was spiritual. In England the criterion was financial—those who possessed a forty-shilling freehold could vote. Which could be said to be more restrictive? Far more important, what presuppositions, what value priorities are embodied in the two sets of criteria?[37]

[34]Edmund Morgan, *Visible Saints: The History of a Puritan Idea* (Ithaca, N.Y.: Cornell University Press, 1963), 92–98.

[35]See Morgan, *Puritan Dilemma*, 144, 152, 154, 196–214. See also Cotton Mather, *Magnalia Christi Americana* (Edinburgh: Banner of Truth Trust, 1979), 2:508–9, 518.

[36]Compare the figures provided by Williston Walker, *The Creeds and Platforms of Congregationalism* (New York: Scribner, 1893), 165, with those in Perry Miller, *Orthodoxy in Massachusetts, 1630–1650* (Gloucester, Mass.: Peter Smith, 1965), 207, and with those in Edmund Morgan, *American Slavery, American Freedom: The Ordeal of Colonial Virginia* (New York: Norton, 1975), 60. Darrett Rutman's statistics are restricted to the town of Boston (rather than the entire Massachusetts Bay colony), but if those figures are used, it would appear that an even higher percentage of colonists were enfranchised. See Rutman *Winthrop's Boston*, 57–58.

[37]It seems appropriate at this point to suggest that the Puritans foreshadowed the apologetic methodology of Cornelius Van Til. Their position anticipated his in that they were convinced that collective words and deeds reveal presuppositions as clearly as do individual words and deeds. Every societal decision (about, for example, civil legislation) presupposes either "the self-contained God and his plan for the universe" or "Chaos and Old Night." Every societal action reveals whether God's interests or man's are being considered preeminent. In my opinion, when the Puritans determined

Those who would honor Christ in their societal and political life must, the Puritans would argue, answer these questions first of all.

It therefore is one thesis of this chapter that the Puritans did specifically seek to allow Christ to transform their culture. They wanted to honor and obey God as much in their public life as in their private life. They endeavored to make the adjective *holy* the preeminent one in defining their commonwealth. And they sought these things first and foremost by defining carefully and fully the qualifications of citizenship. They wanted those who exercised authority in their state to be themselves clearly under the authority of Jesus. This was, they believed, the best way to seize the kingdom opportunity that God had granted them.

But what about the matter of the civil code, the specific laws developed by the Puritans in expression of what they saw as their mandate? Were the Puritans' words and actions such that it would be appropriate to regard them as theonomists? This is a far more complex problem than has often been imagined, and the only way to do justice to its complexity is to summarize as briefly as possible what actually happened with regard to civil legislation during the first twenty years in Massachusetts Bay.

The first mention of "the law" in the sense of the civil code occurs in the charter of the colony. There it is stated that the magistrates of the company may make "lawes and ordinances for the good and welfare of the saide Company" with the stipulation that "such lawes and ordinances be not contrarie or repugnant to the lawes and statutes of this our realme of England."[38] Nothing further is said in the charter about this matter, and the exact understanding of what would be contrary or repugnant to the laws and statutes of England is left undefined.[39]

---

to make holiness and righteousness rather than liberty and freedom their highest priority, they were genuinely seeking first the kingdom of God. The way the Puritans proceeded in their new commonwealth shows clearly that they presupposed and safeguarded, again to use Van Til's terms, the "clarity," the "necessity," the "sufficiency," and the "authority" of Scripture. See Cornelius Van Til, *The Defense of the Faith* (Phillipsburg, N.J.: Presbyterian and Reformed, 1980), 216, 258.

[38]Shurtleff, *Records*, 1:12.
[39]Haskins, *Law and Authority*, 5.

The Court Records for October 19, 1630, quoted above, indicate that both magistrates and freemen understood one of the functions of the court to be that of making laws when necessary. It is important to stipulate this fact, because the actual work of the court during its early days was far more judicial than it was legislative. Indeed, in spite of the court statement on October 19, the magistrates of Massachusetts Bay seem to have been inordinately reluctant to define publicly the legislative basis for their judicial work, and this fact becomes especially important in any attempt to evaluate the Puritan consensus in terms of its possible theonomic component.

This situation was perceived as a problem as early as 1635. By this time, the political structure of the colony had been further modified; the number of freemen had grown so large that it was simply impractical to have all of them participate in meetings of the general court. Thus, beginning on May 9, 1632, each town was asked to send two representatives, called "deputies," to "confer" with the court at its stated meetings.[40] These deputies increasingly saw themselves as a popular counterweight to the authority of the magistrates, and, in 1635, this entry appears in Winthrop's *Journal*:

> The deputies having conceived great danger to our state, in regard that our magistrates, for want of positive laws, in many cases, might proceed according to their discretions, it was agreed that some men should be appointed to frame a body of grounds of laws, in resemblance to a Magna Charta, which, being allowed by some of the ministers, and the general court, should be received for fundamental laws.[41]

The court record for May 6, 1635, states, "The Governor [who was at this time John Haynes], Deputy Governor [Richard Bellingham], John Winthrop, and Thomas Dudley, Esq., are deputed by the Court to make a draught of such lawes as they shall iudge needeful for the well ordering of this plantacion, and to present the same to the Court."[42]
During the following year, the court regularly meted out

---

[40]Shurtleff, *Records*, 1:95. See also Winthrop, *Journal*, 1:79.
[41]Winthrop, *Journal*, 1:151.
[42]Shurleff, *Records*, 1:147.

justice (for example, on April 5, 1636, it was ordered "that William Barker shalbe whipt for stealing bacon, cheese, etc., from Ralf Tompkins"), but it is not until the meeting of the court on May 25, 1636, that the matter of a law code again appears in court records. Apparently, the earlier committee of four found their task difficult because at this latter meeting, the court increased the number of those on the committee (adding primarily ministers) and made their instructions even more specific:

> The Governor [now Henry Vane], Deputy Governor [Winthrop], Thomas Dudley, John Haynes, Richard Bellingham, Esq., Mr. Cotton, Mr. Peters, and Mr. Shepheard are intreated to make a draught of lawes agreeable to the word of God, which may be the ffundamentals of this commonwealth, and to present the same to the next General Court. And it is ordered, that in the meane tyme the magistrates and their assosiates shall proceede in the courts to heare and determine all causes according to the lawes nowe established, and where there is noe law, then as neere the lawe of God as they can.[43]

Although not mentioned in the court records, there apparently was one other important event at this May 25 meeting. It appears in Winthrop's *Journal* thus:

> Mr. Cotton, being requested by the general court, with some other ministers, to assist some of the magistrates in compiling a body of fundamental laws, did this court, present a model of Moses his judicials, compiled in an exact method, which were taken into further consideration till the next general court.[44]

The particular document mentioned here by Winthrop does not appear again, either in Winthrop's *Journal* or in the court records. It certainly never had any official standing in the colony. Indeed, no code was approved in 1636 or 1637, and in March 1638, noting that "the want of written lawes have put the Court into many doubts and much trouble in many perticular cases,"[45] the court selected yet another committee to deal with the issue. The committee included John Winthrop but, significantly, not John Cotton (he was

---

[43]Ibid., 174–75.
[44]Winthrop, *Journal*, 1:196.
[45]Shurtleff, *Records*, 1:222.

the only one of the three ministerial members of the 1637 committee who was omitted from the 1638 committee). Finally, on November 5, 1639, the court ordered

> that the Governor [Winthrop again], Deputy Governor [Dudley], Treasurer [Richard Bellingham], and Mr. Stoughton, or any three of them, with two or more of the deputies of Boston, Charles towne, or Roxberry shall pervse all those modells, which have bene, or shalbee further presented to this Court, or themselues, concerning a form of government, and lawes to bee established, and shall draw them up into one body, (altering, ading, or omiting what they shall thinke fit) and shall take order that the same shalbee coppied out and sent to the severall townes, that the elders of the churches and freemen may consider of them against the next General Court.[46]

According to Winthrop, two models had been presented, one by Cotton and one by Nathaniel Ward (who had been appointed as a member of the 1638 committee).[47] Cotton's model was apparently a slight revision of "Moses His Judicials" and was published in 1641 in London as "Abstract of the Laws of New England." Despite its suggestive title, this latter Cotton document had no greater official standing in the colony than did the former one.[48] It was, instead, Ward's model that seemed most to interest the court. The records for October 7, 1641, state that "the Governor [now Richard Bellingham] and Mr. Hauthorne were desired to speak to Mr. Ward for a copey of the liberties and of the capitall lawes to bee transcribed and sent to the several townes."[49]

Ward complied, and *The Body of Liberties*, as his document came to be known, was circulated among the towns. Winthrop comments that thereby the laws contained in *The Body of Liberties* were "established" for a trial period of three years.[50] But this should not be taken to mean that Massachusetts Bay now had a law code. As Haskins points out, "The

---

[46]Ibid., 279.

[47]Winthrop, *Journal*, 1:323–24.

[48]Haskins, *Law and Authority*, 124–26. See also Max Farrand, *The Laws and Liberties of Massachusetts* (Cambridge, Mass.: Harvard University Press, 1929), Introduction, vi.

[49]Shurtleff, *Records*, 1:340.

[50]Winthrop, *Journal*, 2:48–49.

Body of Liberties was less a code of existing laws than it was a compilation of constitutional provisions. . . . Viewed as a whole, it resembles a bill of rights of the type which was later to become a familiar feature of American state and federal constitutions."[51] However we view *The Body of Liberties*, the court clearly viewed it as inadequate to answer the needs of the colony and voted to commence further work on the development of a civil code at the session of June 14, 1642.[52] Since the general court of the colony did not regard Ward's work as definitive, neither should we.

Committees and discussions continued through the middle years of the decade. On May 14, 1645, the general court established three separate committees (one from each of the counties of the colony) and charged each "to draw up a body of lawes and to present them to the consideration of the next General Court."[53] In the entry for May 22, 1646, we read, "The Court thankfully accepts of the labors returned by the several committees of the several sheires, and being very unwiling such precious labors should fall to the ground without good successe," the court on that same date appointed yet another committee to examine and then to transcribe the work that had been accomplished during the past year.[54] Additional committees were appointed in November 1646 and in May 1647, with the court records now containing a note of urgency that the work be completed quickly.[55]

At its November 11, 1647, meeting, the court determined to order two each of several legal texts then in current use in England—"Two of Sir Edward Cooke upon Littleton; two of the Books of Entryes; two of Sir Edward Cooke upon Magna Charta; two of the New Tearmes of the Law, two Daltons Iustice of Peace, and two of Sir Edward Cooke's Reports."[56] Apparently the committee members wanted to make use of these materials in their final deliberations. Whether they received the volumes in time is uncertain.

---

[51]Haskins, *Law and Authority*, 129. See also Farrand, *Laws and Liberties*, vi.
[52]Shurtleff, *Records*, 2:21–22.
[53]Ibid., 109.
[54]Ibid., 157.
[55]Ibid., 168, 196.
[56]Ibid., 212.

What is clear is that a finished draft was completed and delivered to the printer in Cambridge in the Spring of 1648.[57] It is interesting that there is no record that even this code was formally adopted by the general court. However, reference is made in the court record for March, 1648, and again for May 10, 1648, with regard to the submission of the book of laws to the publisher.[58] And on October 17, 1649, the court addressed itself in the following manner to the problem of how new legislation should be handled vis-à-vis the code already passed:

> The Court, finding by experience the great benefit that doth redound to the country by putting of the law in print, doe conceive it very requisit that those lawes also that have passed the consent of the Gennerall Court since the booke of lawes were in printing or printed should be forthwith committed to the presse, and for that end appoint Richard Bellingham, Esq, Mr. Nowell, Mr. Auditor Gennerall, Capt Keayne, and Mr. Hill, or any three of them, a committee for to prepare them against the Court of Election, that, vpon approbation of the retourn of the committee, they may also be printed, as also therewith to prepare those lawes referred to in the end of the printed lawes, with a suitable table, to be printed.[59]

In addition, there is no further mention in the court records of the need to prepare a code of laws, and no further committees were established or models presented to the court. In light of (1) the frequency with which the matter before appeared in those records, (2) the information that appeared in the title page of the printed version of the 1648 code, and (3) the above statements, it is appropriate to regard this as the final and official legal code of early Massachusetts Bay.

The work was entitled *The Book of the Lauus and Libertyes Concerning the Inhabitants of the Massachusetts Collected Out of the Records of the General Court For the Several Years Wherein They Were Made and Established*, and the title page bears the notation "Cambridge; Printed according to the order of the

---

[57]Haskins, *Law and Authority*, 135. See also Farrand, *Laws and Liberties*, vii–viii.

[58]Shurtleff, *Records*, 2:230, 239.

[59]Ibid., 286.

General Court; 1648."[60] Clearly, if one is going to discuss the Puritan attitude toward the civil law, it is this document that must be the focus of attention. Earlier documents, while they may have contributed to the 1648 code, simply were not official and final, and to present them as though they were is misleading.

This is the first reason why I have taken so much time in tracing the development of a law code in Massachusetts Bay. Frequently, to be specific, material prepared by John Cotton, either "Moses His Judicials" or "An Abstract of the Lawes of New England," is cited or quoted as definitive of the Puritan mind-set. There is no question that Cotton was a theological leader in early Massachusetts Bay; one can even make the case that he was the preeminent theologian in the colony. But he was not the Calvin or the Knox of Boston. On more than one theological issue he was clearly in the minority, and his position did not prevail. This is most clearly the case in the Antinomian Controversy when the other ministers required him to answer a series of pointed questions about his teachings on justification and sanctification and where he finally was the one to bend.[61]

I would argue that the corporate reaction to the legal model(s) submitted by Cotton shows that, again, his position was a minority one. Cotton certainly had very clear ideas, at least from 1636, of what the civil code should be, but his certainty was not shared by the general court. When presented with a finished document by Cotton on at least

[60]Farrand, *Laws and Liberties*, A1.

[61]Surely Cotton's role in the affair was a complex one. David Hall's analysis may be somewhat slanted against Cotton, and Iain Murray corrects some of Hall's more obvious faults. But the import of the December, 1636, meeting, when the other ministers of the colony presented Cotton with sixteen pointed questions about his theology cannot be denied. Neither can the prior written questioning of Cotton by Thomas Shepard and Peter Bulkeley. Cotton simply was out of step with his Puritan colleagues during at least the first two years of the Antinomian Controversy and, in the end, unity was preserved because Cotton changed and joined them. See David Hall, ed., *The Antinomian Controversy, 1636–1638: A Documentary History* (Middletown, Conn.: Wesleyan University Press, 1968), esp. 3–20. See also Iain Murray, "Antinomianism: New England's First Controversy," *The Banner of Truth* nos. 179–80 (1978): 7–75; and Gura, *Glimpse of Sion's Glory*, 171–77, 245–51.

two occasions, the court chose not to adopt what he had prepared and to continue their work.

But exactly why *didn't* the court approve Cotton's proposals? No explicit statement has yet been found, either in official records or in unofficial materials like Winthrop's *Journal*. But indirect evidence can be gained by comparing what Cotton proposed to what was finally adopted, and that evidence is directly relevant to our concerns here. Making that comparison, Haskins comes to the following conclusions. First, with regard to Cotton's position:

> John Cotton, for instance, consistently took the position that most, if not all, of the "judicial" laws of Moses reflected the moral law, and hence were as eternally binding as the decalogue itself. His emphasis upon obedient acceptance of explicit divine precepts is reflected in the literalism of his proposed code of laws.[62]

Then, with regard to the consensus Puritan position:

> The provisions of the Massachusetts capital laws have been discussed in some detail because they illustrate not only the colonists' extensive reliance upon Scripture but also their unwillingness to follow its precepts when contrary to their own ethical and moral conceptions. Despite their dependence upon the word of God and the close connection they saw between sin and crime, they were demonstrably reluctant to prescribe death for every offense that the Bible ordered so punished. Had they regarded the Bible's pronouncements as dogmatic injunctions, literally to be followed under all circumstances, the criminal laws should have embraced at least as many capital offenses as John Cotton included in his draft code. In fact, the laws of Massachusetts prescribed relatively mild punishments for a number of such offenses, and the colonists' position seems to have been that no divine warrant was needed for the infliction of penalties that were *less* severe than those prescribed in the Bible (emphasis his).[63]

Haskins is suggesting that the most likely reason why the general court did not adopt Cotton's code was that the court, the official representatives of the Puritan populace,

---

[62]Haskins, *Law and Authority*, 159–60.
[63]Ibid., 151.

disagreed with Cotton about the degree to which the judicial code of the Old Testament should serve as the civil code of Massachusetts. Of course, the correctness of Haskins's judgment depends on the degree to which the 1648 code does, in fact, modify biblical judicial law. It is one of the contentions of this chapter that Haskins is correct and the brief analysis of the 1648 code offered below should demonstrate this fact.[64]

The second reason why I have given a detailed account of the development of the Massachusetts civil code is closely related to the first. The fact that it took approximately eighteen years for the Puritans to establish a law code is in itself significant. If Winthrop and the other magistrates had been absolutely sure what the laws should be, the process would certainly have been much quicker. If the general court had been in agreement in 1630 that the biblical judicial law should be the Massachusetts judicial law, what was accomplished in 1648 would have been completed in the early 1630s.

The point is that although the magistrates were sure that God's word should be the foundation of all they did and although they were sure that the colony had to be structured so as to honor and glorify God, they were not sure exactly what this meant in terms of the civil law. Specifically, they were not certain which of the particular biblical laws should be enacted and which should not. They believed that their situation in Massachusetts Bay was unique and that a wide variety of factors had to be considered in the process of building a civil code. With regard to the relationship of the Old Testament judicial situation to the present New Testament judicial situation, the New England Puritans were

---

[64]As noted earlier in this chapter, one fascinating perspective on these matters is provided by Philip Gura in the fifth chapter of his book *A Glimpse of Sion's Glory*. There Gura makes the point that the main body of Massachusetts Puritans was "unwilling to ground the colony exclusively in laws derived from Deuteronomy" (p. 127), and he goes on to present a strong case that it was the radical millenarians and the Fifth Monarchist, William Aspinwall, who followed Cotton's teachings regarding the civil code and who were regarded by the main body of Puritans in both England and New England as being outside the bounds of orthodoxy (pp. 126–52). For a discussion of the English context of the Fifth Monarchy movement, see Christopher Hill, *The World Turned Upside Down: Radical Ideas During the English Revolution* (New York: Penguin, 1975).

committed neither to absolute continuity nor to absolute discontinuity. The Mosaic judicial law was directly relevant to Massachusetts Bay, but the circumstances within which the colony found itself demanded a flexible appropriation of that Mosaic law.

Again it is John Winthrop who addressed most directly the reluctance of the magistrates to move too quickly to a civil code in Massachusetts Bay:

> Two great reasons there were, which caused most of the magistrates and some of the elders not to be very forward in this matter. One was, want of sufficient experience of the nature and disposition of the people, considered with the condition of the country and other circumstances, which made them conceive, that such laws would be fittest for us, which should arise pro re nata upon occasions, etc., and so the laws of England and other states grew, and therefore the fundamental laws of England are called customs, consuetudines. 2. For that it would professedly trangress the limits of our charter, which provide, we shall make no laws repugnant to the laws of England, and that we were assured we must do. But to raise up laws by practice and custom had been no transgression.[65]

Winthrop's words ring true to the tone of the official records of the general court, many of which have been quoted above. What one sees clearly as he reads the individual entries dealing with this subject is a group of men deeply committed to allowing *all* of Scripture, both Old and New Testaments, to structure and regulate every part of their lives—including their state. But one does not see men who were certain that this meant adopting the Mosaic judicial law as their own. For eighteen years, they struggled to develop a system that would do justice to the Old Testament but would be adapted to their own situation. And in this process, they specifically chose *not* to adopt the proposals of those who, like John Cotton, urged them in the direction of absolute continuity.

This becomes completely clear as soon as one turns to the actual 1648 code itself. First of all, there is the Preface to

---

[65]Winthrop, *Journal*, 1:323–24.

the code. Among the critical statements in that Preface is the following:

> For this end about nine years since [this would have been 1639] wee used the help of some of the Elders of our Churches [this would have been Cotton and Ward] to compose a modell of the Iudicial lawes of Moses with such other cases as might be referred to them, with intent to make use of them in composing our lawes, *but not to have them published as the Lawes of this jurisdiction: nor were they voted in Court* (emphasis added).[66]

Clearly, the work of Cotton and Ward was not seen by the Puritans themselves as expressive of the community mind. That work was surely helpful, but it was not definitive.

Then there is the fascinating statement that concludes the Preface:

> That distinction which is put between the Lawes of God and the Lawes of men, becomes a snare to many as it is misapplyed in the ordering of their obedience to civil Authoritie; for when the Authoritie is of God and that in way of an Ordinance **Rom. 13. 1.** and when the administration of it is according to deductions, and rules gathered from the word of God, and the clear light of nature in civil nations, surely there is no humane law that tendeth to common good (according to those principles) but the same is mediately a law of God, and that in way of an Ordinance which all are to submit unto and that for conscience sake. **Rom. 13. 5.**[67]

The writer of the Preface is suggesting here the method used in compiling the laws contained in the code. The word of God (I would add here, the whole word of God, both Old and New Testaments) was the source of principles ("deductions" and "rules") out of which the code was built. But the Preface does not state or imply that the laws of Scripture had automatically been made into the laws of the colony. Indeed, in light of the writer's obvious concern, in the first quotation, to distance the 1648 code from the "modell of the Iudiciall lawes of Moses," we can say that the framers of the code clearly thought they were using the sort of flexible applica-

---

[66]Farrand, *Laws and Liberties*, A2.
[67]Ibid., A3.

tion of Scripture to the colony's needs that has been described above.

This is, in fact, the case with the actual laws themselves, which were arranged alphabetically according to general category. Following a general comment about the role of law within the community, the first law, under the heading of "Abilitie," states that all persons above the age of twenty-one, whether church members or not, have the ability to make wills and testaments and to enter into real estate transactions.[68] Then follow the categories of "Actions," "Age," "Ana-Baptists," and on through the alphabet.[69]

Of special interest is the category entitled "Capital Lawes." Fifteen such laws are listed, and after all but the last specific Scriptural citations are provided, mostly from Exodus, Leviticus, Numbers, and Deuteronomy.[70] No such Scriptural citations are provided for the rest of the laws, which comprise by far the majority of the total—the entire code is approximately fifty pages in length, and the "Capital Lawes" are contained on a bit more than one full page. Clearly Haskins is right when he states that the Puritans believed they must have biblical warrant for any and all applications of the death penalty. It is further clear that the Puritans believed there to be such continuity between the Old Testament and their circumstances that what was stated in the Old Testament was of great weight and significance and relevance for them.

But *weight* and *significance* and *relevance* are terms with considerable flexibility built into them, and this is one of the crucial points that I have been making about the Puritans. Haskins is again correct when he states that, while the Puritans believed they needed biblical warrant for sentencing someone to death, they did not believe they had to make every crime capital that the Bible called capital. The evidence suggests that the Puritans considered very carefully their circumstances—their circumstances as Christians and their circumstances as Englishmen in Massachusetts Bay—and that they then sought to apply all of God's word to those circumstances in an appropriate manner. Sometimes this

---

[68]Ibid., 1.
[69]Ibid.
[70]Ibid., 5–6.

meant making something the Old Testament called a capital crime a Massachusetts capital crime; sometimes it did not.

A couple of specific examples may be helpful. Deuteronomy 17:12 states, "The man who shows contempt for the judge or for the priest who stands ministering there to the LORD your God must be put to death." *The Laws and Liberties* addresses contempt for the magistrate and the priest separately. With regard to the magistrate, the ruling was that

> whosoever shal henceforth openly or willingly defame any Court or justice, or the sentences or proceedings of the same, or any of the magistrates or other judges of any such Court in respect of any Act or Sentence therein passed, and being thereof lawfully convicted in any General Court or Court of Assistants shall be punished for the same by Fine, Imprisonment, Disfranchisement or Banishment as the qualitie and measure of the offence shall deserve.[71]

With regard to the priest or minister, the 1648 code ordered that a first offense would be met with a reproof by the magistrate and that a second offense would be punished by either a fine of five pounds or by a requirement that the guilty party stand in public on a stool four feet high on lecture day with a paper affixed to the chest on which were written in capital letters: "AN OPEN AND OBSTINATE CONTEMNER OF GODS HOLY ORDINANCES."[72]

Numerous other Old Testament capital laws were *not* enacted in Massachusetts Bay. For example, kidnapping (Ex 21:16; Dt 24:7) and Sabbath breaking (Ex 31:14) were capital crimes in Israel but not in Massachusetts Bay. But it was not just penal sanctions that the Puritans sometimes modified. Occasionally, it was the very laws themselves. Exodus 22:25 and Deuteronomy 23:19 prohibit Israelites from charging interest to their brothers. While denouncing "usurie," *The Laws and Liberties* endorses the practice of charging interest by restricting the annual amount to 8 percent.[73] On the other hand, Exodus 21:2–4 allows for and regulates the enslavement of fellow Hebrews whereas the 1648 code specifically

---

[71]Ibid., 36.

[72]Ibid., 20.

[73]Ibid., 52.

prohibits such a practice.[74] A careful reading of the 1648 code, therefore, makes it clear that the Puritans altered the Old Testament judicial law in very significant ways, ways that cannot be dismissed as arising solely from the cultural situation in Israel or from the unique status of the Israelite state.

There is no evidence to suggest that the Puritans believed the Old Testament laws that they changed were specifically revoked or repudiated in the New Testament. Their method seems to have been more general and more flexible than that. While they took the Old Testament judicial law and its penal sanctions with utmost seriousness, they sought to determine from all the evidence at hand—the New Testament, their experience with the English legal system, their specific circumstances in New England, their perceived place in the ongoing work of the kingdom of Christ—what should be adopted, what should be adapted, and what should be omitted. They spent years discussing these matters before coming to the conclusions they embodied in their 1648 code. "Studied flexibility" does seem, therefore, to be the best way to characterize the Puritan use of the Mosaic judicial law.

The Puritan commitment to the authority of Scripture was unwavering. The Puritans' belief that all of Scripture was to be used in structuring their society is unquestionable. But they did not think that basing all they did on Scripture meant simply transferring the Old Testament judicial law in its entirety into the Massachusetts context. They did not think either that the presence of a law in the Mosaic code required its presence in their code nor that the absence of a law in the Mosaic code prohibited its presence in theirs. They certainly regarded the Old Testament, including its civil legislation and its penology, as far more relevant to their cultural and political situation than most Christians seem to regard it today. But they knew that the coming of Christ has made a major difference both ceremonially and judicially, and they struggled to take account of that difference appropriately.

Frequently it seems that those who hold to theonomy claim that the Puritans support their position. They argue

---

[74]Ibid., 4.

that the Puritans (whom they see best represented by John Cotton) sought to adopt the entire Mosaic judicial law except where that law was specifically altered or repudiated in the New Testament. Just as frequently, those who oppose the theonomic position tend to dismiss the Puritans (at least in this particular area) as misguided zealots who were trying to relive the Old Testament. Both are wrong—and for the same reason. Whatever else they were, the New England Puritans as a group were not simplistic. They did not see themselves as some kind of reincarnation of the nation of Israel, and they did not want to see Israel's judicial code reincarnated in their commonwealth. Those who respond to the Puritans in either of the ways described have misunderstood what they were trying to do.

But far more important than what the Puritans were not is what they were. They were men and women passionately committed to the sovereign God of Scripture. They believed that their calling was to honor that God in all they did—as much in their state as in their church. They knew no "neutral" area, no sphere where the claims of Jesus Christ were not paramount. They believed, partially because of the work of John Foxe, that God had granted them a window of kingdom opportunity. They sought to seize that opportunity by making Massachusetts Bay all that it could and should be for the glory of God. The means used by the Puritans consisted primarily in tying political power to spiritual credentials (rather than to financial or intellectual or social credentials) and secondarily in developing a legal structure that flexibly applied all of Scripture to the particular situations of their society.

Both those who claim the Puritans and those who dismiss them would do well to study them again. In their commitment to biblical authority and in the flexible manner with which they interpreted that authority for their age, the Puritans were, in my opinion, a "model of Christian charity" and a "city on a hill." All of us who seek to have Christ transform our culture would do well to learn from them.

CONCLUSION

Although this volume is a critique of theonomy, several of the chapters have concluded on a positive note of appreciation for what the theonomists have contributed to our understanding of God's law. Even where we disagree with the theonomists—and there are many points on which we agree—we find ourselves stimulated to a deeper study of the principles God has established for human society and to a commitment to obey his revealed will.

We seek to end this volume on a similar positive note. Clair Davis offers a challenge to theonomists to join, within the broader confines of confessional commitment, in a full-orbed expression of the law and the Gospel. In this light theonomy may prove not just to be an internal issue for Reformed churches or even for the wider circle of evangelical Christians but to be a catalyst for all of us to convey to the world the message that it needs.

Chapter Sixteen

A Challenge to Theonomy

D. Clair Davis

D. Clair Davis

D. Clair Davis (Dr. theol., Georg-August Universität, Göttingen) is Professor of Church History at Westminster Theological Seminary (Philadelphia). With other degrees from Wheaton College and Westminster Theological Seminary, he has taught at the Wheaton College Graduate School of Theology, and at Westminster since 1966. He has contributed to *John Calvin: His Influence in the Western World*, *Inerrancy and Hermeneutic: A Tradition, A Challenge, A Debate*, and *Pressing Toward the Mark*.

Chapter Sixteen

A Challenge to Theonomy

If theonomy did not exist, someone would have to invent it. Christians need all the help they can get in understanding what the Bible has to say about God's pattern for society. There have been far too many generalities and platitudes; the more specific the information believers can get from the Bible, the better they can do what God expects of them. It is not easy to apply the details of the civil law of the Bible from the period of promise to our age of fulfillment, but Christians are called to act upon their conviction that "all Scripture is profitable."

That theonomy is now appearing in the life of the American church is understandable and advantageous. Earlier it could be taken for granted that Americans shared a broadly based consensus on the content of biblical ethics and its general applicability to society. Laws opposing homosexuality and abortion and regulating divorce were in broad outline based on biblical norms. Today American pluriformity is no longer limited to accommodating differences among differing Christian perspectives. Rather, it has the broader agenda of ensuring that anti-Christian values will have just as much weight in American culture as Christian ones. Christians had difficulty believing this to be true, but they have now been definitively enlightened by the appeal of the Supreme Court in *Roe vs. Wade* to "ancient religions"—what Christians have long known as paganism.

Christians have had to rethink what they mean by tolerance. Certainly it includes respect for the American commitment to freedom of worship and the rejection of an established religion. But it does not mean that biblical standards are to be rejected in favor of prevailing public opinion. While non-Christian religions and philosophies may be capable of high levels of syncretism with each other, Christians now understand that ultimately there can be no agreement between views that honor Jesus Christ as the Lord of this world and those that repudiate him. What Christians, particularly those of Calvinistic vision, have always implicitly recognized is now being explicitly explored: How should Christians exercise their responsibility to shape American society according to biblical norms?

Many have come to that question independent of theonomy. Evangelicals have given much attention to the phenomenon of "secular humanism," especially as shown by popular support for abortion. Beneath the newly clarified opposition to humanism and increasing concern for Christian values lies the old foundation of *antithesis* (the conviction that a Christian position and a humanistic one are inherently mutually exclusive) as formulated by Abraham Kuyper. While theonomy had received the thinking of Cornelius Van Til directly, other evangelicals were influenced more indirectly, either by way of Gordon Clark and Carl Henry or through Hans Rookmaaker and Francis Schaeffer. This helps account for the ready acceptance of the theonomic emphasis by many evangelicals, particularly charismatics, for the way had already been prepared.

Although that general direction appeals to evangelicals, theonomy is still unique. It is substantially more specific in its application of Scripture to the structure of society. In particular, it makes much greater use of Old Testament civil laws and punishments than do other Christian philosophies. One would anticipate that fact from its Calvinistic perspective, since that tradition has always seen much more continuity between the two Testaments than others have. But it has gone beyond that general tradition by stressing that the Old Testament is particularly useful for providing specific direction for society. The New Testament just does not offer guidelines for policies to be pursued by a Christian emperor; rather, it tells persecuted believers how to conduct themselves within a pagan state. But the Old Testament gives in detail rules for an equitable, God-honoring society. It is not surprising that in a time of manifest need for the restructuring of American society, the rich resources of the older Testament would be mined as vigorously as the theonomists have done.

Does that suggest that the theonomists are off on the wrong foot? Is it impossible to harmonize the theonomic vision of a biblical society and the New Testament picture of a persecuted church? Not necessarily. One does not need to share an "optimistic" postmillennial perspective to see the value in theonomy. Christians know they must obey God regardless of the (short-term) outcome. For example, while this age is characterized by powerful attempts to destroy the family, that has nothing to do with Christian responsibility. Statistics on divorce and abortion do not minimize the responsibilities Christians have in their homes to do what the Lord has commanded them. Similarly, if there are political responsibilities that believers have, even within an increasingly pagan America, they must exercise them, regardless of the suffering they will then experience.

That "if" is a very famous "if," especially within the heritage of Calvinism. That "if" is the heart of Calvin's argument at the end of the *Institutes*. Calvinists believe the Bible teaches that popular mass revolution is wrong (except when believers are forced by the state to sin), but a particular society may have a system of "lesser magistrates." If that is the case, these rulers have the responsibility to protect those under them from tyranny of rulers at a higher level. Whether or not that is indeed the case in a particular state is the perennial question at issue. Scottish Calvinist political writers argued that Scottish society had never been monarchist to the exclusion of the responsibilities of the lairds. Calvin argued that the French monarch was crowned only with the agreement of the people. In modern terms, if government is constitutional, not absolutist, then citizens have primary responsibility to the constitution and not to the rulers, and rulers must be held to account under the constitution.

Presbyterians note that the Westminster Catechism states that superiors have certain responsibilities for the care of inferiors. Since, because they vote, American citizens are the highest authority in the state, they are obliged to "rule" not in order to seek their own advantage, but in order that there be justice in the state. Any believer faced with that awesome responsibility is bound to consider what justice really is, and accordingly to do his best to discover it from

392 | D. Clair Davis

the law of God. Theonomy can be of great service precisely within the context of the constitution of the American republic.

If a study of biblical law is in order, then it is also worthwhile to consider biblical penal sanctions. Regardless of how they should be applied in modern America, consideration of penalties should at least give some indication of the relative importance of offenses. The lives of Christians contain trade-offs: finite beings can do only a finite number of things at a time. Studying God's priorities is bound to be helpful.

If the above considerations come close to a proper understanding of the goals of theonomy (not always easy to determine), then the American evangelical community needs theonomy. It has emerged at the right time with exactly the right questions. But not everyone perceives it that way. While many welcome it, others see its very existence as counterproductive and divisive. Even when they see nothing obviously erroneous about it, they are convinced they must resist it as a phenomenon likely to deflect the church from its proper agenda.

CREEDAL HUMILITY

Why does theonomy appear to many to be more threatening than helpful? In the first place, the Christian community always has difficulty knowing how to accommodate within it perspectives that not all its membership share. How does a community define the parameters of its fellowship? Creeds or confessions of faith are intended to express doctrinal consensus. Frequently creeds are given more specific definition. When denominations unite, they assent to "Articles of Agreement," which explain their common understanding of their creeds. Informal understandings of what constitutes the "system of doctrine," or fundamental doctrines within the creeds, frequently emerge. Denominations, especially Presbyterian ones, expect there may be substantial disagreement over pronouncements of church bodies. But since those statements do not have creedal authority, no one should consider them as excluding him from membership or office within that denomination. Instead, they constitute "pious advice": their import is to be taken seriously, but if someone decides that their conclusions are not biblical or weighty, then he may respectfully ignore them. So there is always ample room within the church for those who do not accept the pronouncements of general assemblies, since they are not constitutional. Only creeds—which within Presbyterianism can be changed only by agreement at the grass-roots level of presbyteries, and only through deliberate process—can define the priorities and direction of a denomination.

If that is correct, and if no church has adopted explicit creeds for or against theonomy, then by definition no one can regard himself threatened by those who do not concur with his evaluation of the movement. But things are never that simple. While the ordinary understanding of how the constitution of the church functions has just been described, it is also true that in the real world there are other considerations as well. It may help to remember that in the eighteenth century, virtually all American denominations were divided over the value of the Great Awakening. While there were no substantial doctrinal differences involved, priorities were perceived as so divergent that it proved next to impossible for the adherents of differing perspectives to learn from each other and to work together. In the mid-nineteenth century, almost all denominations divided over the Civil War. Theoretically, it was only pious advice when an assembly declared that obeying one's state government instead of the federal government was treason. But that declaration and others like it led to the division of the great churches of America until almost the present day. Probably the loss of the vigorous orthodoxy of the South had much to do with the capitulation of the Northern churches to liberalism.

Similar divisions have occurred and will continue to occur. What actions should evangelical groups today take regarding civil disobedience over abortion (e.g., Operation Rescue)? Should churches discipline those who encourage disobedience of the state's trespass laws? Should they discipline those who refuse to take part in significant action designed to uphold God's law? If the answer to one of those questions is yes, then the evangelical church will be just as divided as it was by abolition and the Civil War. But if the answer to both is no, what does that mean? Does it mean the churches are once again consigned to irrelevancy, or does it mean that there are areas open to different understandings by sincere believers and that the church's role is to counsel all concerning motives and attitudes? (For a parallel discussion, see Calvin and the Puritans on the question of when it is permissible for believers to make use of the civil courts. Their general conclusion was that if that is not permissible for oneself, then perhaps it may sometimes be permissible on behalf of those for whom one has responsibility.)

Theonomy is widely perceived as not being willing to permit within the church differences of interpretation concerning the application of Old Testament law to the state. Considering how many laws there are and the vast difference in cultures (deferring the question of fulfillment within the history of redemption), it is hardly surprising that there are those differences among believers (and among theonomists). If theonomists regard their own perspectives as the only correct ones within the church, they are thereby altering the understanding of the system of doctrine by which the creeds are understood and applied. That is certainly a possible option. It is easy to argue that the Westminster Confession's commitment to the general equity of Old Testament law provides ample justification for theonomic clarification of that equity. If theonomists exercise that option, however, it is probable that it will become impossible (or continue to be impossible) for those who do not accept their clarifications to work with them. That is likely to result either in denominational structures becoming less and less relevant to "movements" for and against theonomy (the classic Old Side/New Side "solution") or in realignments of pro or con people into denominations congenial to them, the latter making theonomy an obstacle to the uniting of denominations that otherwise have everything in common.

Such solutions are possible, but they hardly fit a biblical understanding of the church. I doubt that anyone wants such outcomes. Are there other possibilities (still) open? There ought to be, in an age when a theonomic approach is so desperately needed. God's people need all the light they can get from Scripture, the Old Testament law included, for the shaping of their Christian political responsibility. It should be possible for theonomists (or anyone else) to state how they believe a position to be the only reasonable understanding of the Bible, but not one that they consider a test of Christian or ecclesiastical fellowship. That is indeed difficult, but possible. Charles Hodge in nineteenth-century Princeton Theological Seminary thought it could be done. While he was personally convinced that the "Old School" understanding of the issues concerning the imputation of Adam's sin was the most consistently biblical, for him that did not mean that the "New School" views in the matter were not legitimate applications of the system of doctrine. He warned his former students in the Old School leadership about confusing questions of doctrinal consistency with conditions for ecclesiastical fellowship. Although his warnings fell largely on deaf ears, Hodge made the attempt. More successful were the Southern theologians. Although they were Old School in orientation, they considered some details of the imputation discussion as going beyond the capacity of the Bible to resolve.

Doubtless theonomists are not totally to blame for the way they are perceived, but it would help if they were to take some leadership in helping define conditions for fellowship. It goes without saying that it is not grudging accommodation that is needed, but rather the joyful fellowship characteristic of Christ's church.

Some further amplification may help. What is the purpose of a theological examination of a ministerial candidate in a presbytery? There is not one, but two: to determine the candidate's doctrinal orthodoxy and also to determine his theological competence, his ability to show that he can think theologically. Presbyteries may not always be clear about when they are serving which purpose. They may always inquire into questions that require insight into theonomic issues, as a way of testing competence. But they may not require a particular application of the general equity of Old Testament law as a criterion of doctrinal orthodoxy within the system of doctrine. This must be the case, for both pro- and antitheonomists. If that distinction proves too difficult to maintain, probably it is the path of wisdom to forego examination in these areas.

GOSPEL CLARITY AND POLITICAL AMBIGUITY

Similar to the above, but deserving of individual consideration, are the special issues created by the necessarily political character of theonomy. Theonomists appear to be committed to "conservative" politics. If that is so, is theonomy really the political position supported by the Bible? Is the Anglican church the Tory Party at prayer, and is the evangelical church the Republican Party at prayer?

For many that question hardly seems worth asking. If abortion policy is today's Christian litmus test (who could suggest a better one?), then everyone knows that liberal politics in America is for abortion and conservative politics is against it. If that is too narrow a test, then one could remember that liberalism regards man as a victim and conservatism regards him as responsible. Liberalism appeals to human goodness, and conservatism emphasizes the need for structure and restraint. The people who said, "No king," were the ones who also said, "No God"! Is it not obvious that political conservatism is more congenial to Christianity than any alternative?

But the lines can never be drawn that sharply. Adam Smith was a Deist. Political conservatives in England, Scotland, and America were opponents of the Great Awakening. The radical New Testament scholar D. F. Strauss was a political conservative. William Jennings Bryan, the Presbyterian fundamentalist leader, was a free-silver man.

Such examples encourage alertness to the complexity of these matters, but thinking about the broader context will prove more helpful. Biblical politics concerns itself with justice, and how injustice is to be overcome, ultimately finding its orientation within the context of redemptive history. That is, God has already brought deliverance (justice!) to his oppressed people, but the completion of that deliverance awaits the return of Christ. In the interim, God himself shows his patience, continuing to call men and women to repentance and faith and delaying the return of his Son in judgment. Accordingly, his people are called to join their Father in patience, waiting in faith and hope for the return of Christ and the accomplished justice that only the Lord can provide.

The biblical orientation is clear, but its application is not simple. There is always the danger of a pie-in-the-sky-by-and-by mentality leading to apathy and unconcern for injustice, particularly for the sufferings of others. Christians may find it easy to focus on accomplished salvation only in terms of forgiveness and consider deferred salvation only in terms of deliverance. It is that "Lutheran" or "fundamentalist" imbalance that theonomy seeks to correct. Theonomy's great strength is that it seeks to offer detailed, specific, biblical direction for the shape of that correction. Certainly redemptive history does not imply that only evangelism is appropriate for this age and that political and social concern is out of place.

But is theonomy concerned about stressing that this is the age of patient suffering, as the creation groans for Christ's return? Does theonomy present a comprehensive biblical response to that suffering? While theonomy cannot be held responsible for the caricatures made of it, it can be challenged to provide an even larger picture than it has yet given. Otherwise it runs the risk of being written off as just another "law-and-order" front. To be sure, one way of helping sufferers is to punish those who cause them to suffer and to restrain them from bringing further suffering. But more needs to be said. We need theonomy to show us how its concerns relate to this age of suffering victims, which is also the age of kingdom responsibility.

Imbalance can be in the other direction. One can emphasize deliverance at the expense of forgiveness. It is noteworthy that the theonomic and the charismatic communities have been building bridges for the enrichment of the entire evangelical cause. But for the same reasons that Calvinists advise charismatics not to minimize the propitiatory, justifying work of Christ as they seek to emphasize his redemptive, sanctifying, delivering work, it is likely that the theonomists could use some of the same advice. This age indeed partakes of God's judgment of sin. But it is preeminently the age of forgiveness from God and also from his people, who have themselves first been forgiven. That can be said and lived, without thereby falling into sentimental liberalism.

But it is not just a matter of balance, but of balance within the redemptive timetable. At the risk of falling into a pie-in-the-sky mentality, we must ask, Does not this age still partake more of the time of humiliation than of glory? Christ's victory is seen in his being raised up, first on the cross, and only then into glory. His people are called now especially to serve, and then to reign. The authority of the people of God is the authority of weakness.

Theonomy can be challenged to say that as well. Because of confusion within the evangelical community, even if not theonomy's fault, it must say that. It is not paradoxical to call the Lord's people to the responsibility of being victims and of ministering to those who are. It is not politically irresponsible to make sure that the reality of justification and patient forgiveness is a part of politics as well as of theology. Christian politics must vigorously and resolutely bring hope to the suffering in society as well as restrain evildoers. We look to theonomy to finish the work it has begun.

LAW AND GOSPEL

Asking theonomy to relate its concerns to the Gospel may not appear to be fair. There is only so much time and energy that any of us has, and within the kingdom of God some specialization must be legitimate. And is there not more to the Word of God than the Gospel? Some Calvinist ministers used to be opposed to the ordinary American title of "Minister of the Gospel," and asked to be called instead "Minister of the Word." Cannot theonomists ask the same thing?

If fairness were the only criterion, theonomists should be readily excused from further clarification. But within the Christian community perceptions are important too. To be sure, much concern could be alleviated through attention to the first question, that of the system of doctrine. If it could be understood that theonomists encourage other Christians to share their concerns but do not demand agreement or even interest in them, perhaps that would be enough. But that could result in a bifurcated church, with some being specialists in evangelism and others specialists in Christian social ethics. Surely we have been called to encourage each other also in our understanding of God's Word and its application. So integration of those concerns must be possible.

Naturally these issues have arisen before. Charles Finney was convinced that the great obstacle to American revival was the continued existence of black slavery. As an implication of the Awakening, Jonathan Edwards preached against land speculation. Evangelists without number have called for defeat of the political forces behind the "liquor traffic." Billy Graham presented anticommunism along with the Gospel, while others have presented the Gospel along with anticommunism. When people understand the supernatural character of salvation, before long they come to realize that God can accomplish other great things through them as well. Upon reflection one comes to see the logic of the coalition of theonomists and charismatics: both look to God in faith for a great work of transformation.

Problems have also been seen before. Agreement over the nature of the Gospel is apparently easier to accomplish than agreement over the biblical character of certain reforms. Perhaps the temperance movement accomplished a great deal, but the Anti-Saloon League succeeded in gaining the right for its lecturers to occupy evangelical pulpits without presentation of or commitment to the Gospel—as moralistic a result as anything the liberals ever accomplished. Defining beverage alcohol as inherently sinful estranged Lutherans from the mainstream of evangelical life almost to the present. As seen earlier, the overly precise definition of the Civil War as treason lost the resources of the South to the greater evangelical cause for many a year. In Germany, E. W. Hengstenberg's espousal of *Thron und Altar*, a mixture of evangelicalism and opposition to the 1848 Revolution, effectively alienated the working man from the church and drove him to atheistic socialism.

Such results warn evangelicals interested in a biblical view of society to give care to safeguard the formal principle of the Reformation. Do not mix the Gospel with an overly precise, potentially extrabiblical application of the law. That runs the risk of confusing revelation with tradition.

But the material principle, justification by faith alone, is even more critical. The passion for glorying in the flesh is always present. Jesus preached his Gospel deliberately over against the Pharisees, and Paul preached it over against the Judaizers. The Reformers defined the Gospel against the works-righteousness of Rome. Again and again, evangelical churches have been torn by the struggles of neonomians, who are convinced that being a Christian is obeying Christ, and antinomians, who are convinced that any hint of obedience in connection with salvation is bound to obscure

Christ's work. The simple Gospel seems very difficult to grasp. It seems that anyone who grows up within an evangelical church is astonished when he finally understands the Gospel, positive that he has never heard it before! At least that is the classic way an Awakening begins.

Even though theonomy may not have within its primary agenda the clarification of the Gospel, anyone who talks about the law has implicitly given himself the task of explaining the relation of law and Gospel.

There are not that many options. Does the law provide the foundation for understanding the Gospel? Or is it necessary to understand first that this is the age of the Gospel before attempting to appreciate the role of the law? Or is perhaps the first true individually and psychologically, and the second true in redemptive history? Probably the last is the most accurate and useful. It outlines the theological discussion in seventeenth-century Holland between Precisianists (with their interest in abiding ethical principles throughout the Bible) and covenant theologians (with their interest in the newness of the Gospel). The happy conclusion was the affirmation that the two sides needed each other. The Rhinelander Friedrich Adolf Lampe was able to go one step further: the abiding character of divine ethical norms can really be seen only from the perspective of the finished work of Christ. That resolution can hardly be improved upon. But it is very general. What the evangelical world still needs today are clear explications of precisely how and why particular commandments are meaningful within the context of the salvation accomplished by Jesus Christ.

Lampe's conclusion is God's continuing challenge to believers, that they be "precisely" obedient to the specific commandments of God, but within the context of the Gospel—that is, before the face of the Son of God, who has died for us and who now intercedes for us and who will return for us. It is particularly a good challenge for theonomists to think along these lines, since they continue so well the Precisianist heritage.

Concretely, the issue is the relation between change of behavior and change of heart. There is the warning of a century of New England "disinterested benevolence" leading into Calvinism's collapse into Unitarianism. That kind of emphasis on the need for a transformed heart before anything worthwhile, including faith, can be done, can only be counterproductive. All that does is to exhort people to look at the quality of their religious experience, instead of to Christ. All that came of it was a sophisticated variety of preparationism, as people sought to prepare their motives. No wonder that New England's response to that kind of Gospel was Yankee pragmatism and behaviorism. Who could ever evaluate his heart, to be able to tell whether he seeks salvation for the glory of God or because of the fear of hell? How much better it is just to do what obviously works or what can be controlled is the not-surprising conclusion of Yankee unbelief. Similar fundamentalist emphases—such as that obeying God when you do not feel like it amounts to hypocrisy—have been roundly and repeatedly lambasted by Jay Adams. Such emphases can be left in the obscurity they deserve.

Does that leave "change of behavior" as the Christian preference? If so, theonomy would be on the cutting edge of evangelistic strategy, as it can teach about the ways behavior needs to be changed, as well as how, substantially more than anyone else! Anyone who makes that much use of the great amount of Old Testament law is bound to be quantitatively ahead of everyone else.

What is certain is, even if divine ethical norms never change, that the gospel promise has been fulfilled. The time has fully come. That rock was Christ. Grace of fulfillment has far abounded over grace of promise. God's grace is lavished on us, grace unto grace. The gospel character of this age must give shape and direction to the proper understanding of biblical politics and government. The great "change" is already reality—that resurrection change that underlies and empowers personal and social changes. Whatever else should be said about God's law, the new thing about it is that he has now written it on the hearts of his people. The one who has written it is the one who applies it. Whatever the church needs to say to unbelievers about what God requires, it must say that all of this will make no sense without Christ and his Spirit. No specific change in your life is possible without change of heart attitude to Christ, which the power of the resurrected Christ will accomplish. This is the age of the Spirit, and any consideration of law must acknowledge that in faith. The Spirit points to Christ, and he will do that through all of the Word, including the civil codes.

As the age of faith, this is also the age of hope, of bold expectancy (if not necessarily postmillennial). In the midst of a world of doubt and confusion, the Bible speaks of real change to come. Specifically, the biblical emphasis on restitution, so well expounded by theonomy, points well beyond the hopelessness of prison warehousing, to restoration and renewed fellowship.

Lampe was right, but there is yet much to do. It is too much to expect theonomists alone to do it all. But they can certainly help, particularly by guarding the rest of evangelical scholarship from abstractions. Perhaps others will still conclude that theonomy has not done justice to the changes of the new day in every particular case. But since there is internal disagreement within theonomy, there hardly needs to be unqualified external approval.

The church of Christ again faces challenge. Will she hide from humanistic unbelief, or will she confront it? Will she meet it with the law alone, or with the Gospel as well?

In this time of crisis, there is also a time of increasing evangelical understanding. Not only is there astonishing rapport between theonomists and charismatics, but dispensationalists are now facing the same issues that the rest are trying to face, and the outcome of their theological conclusions is likely to bring real progress. Before the entire evangelical world is the greatest religious issue of all: law and Gospel, justification and sanctification, propitiation and deliverance, cross and resurrection, the whole Jesus Christ "in all of his offices." Remember Luther's gratitude to Erasmus, that he had finally placed on the agenda a question worth discussing, the question of free will and the Gospel. The church of Christ can unite in gratitude today, that in the face of a self-conscious attack on the name of Christ, it can again self-consciously address the most significant issue of all, that of Jesus Christ as both Savior and Lord.

Name Index

Scripture Index

Theonomy: A Reformed Critique was typeset by the Photocomposition Department of Zondervan Publishing House, Grand Rapids, Michigan on a Mergenthaler Linotron 202/N.
Compositor: Nancy J. Wilson
Editor: Gerard Terpstra

The text was set in 10 point Palatino, a face designed by Hermann Zapf in Germany in 1948. Palatino is probably one of the two most highly regarded typefaces of this century.

The display type is Bookman, a face originally designed as the boldface version of a Victorian face called Old Style.

This book was printed by Arcata Graphics / Fairfield, Fairfield, Pennsylvania.